D1744240

PARALLEL LIVES

PARALLEL LIVES

Spanish and English National Drama
1580–1680

Edited by
Louise and Peter Fothergill-Payne

Lewisburg
Bucknell University Press
London and Toronto: Associated University Presses

© 1991 by Associated University Presses, Inc.

All rights reserved. Authorization to photocopy items for internal or personal use, or the internal or personal use of specific clients, is granted by the copyright owner, provided that a base fee of $10.00, plus eight cents per page, per copy is paid directly to the Copyright Clearance Center, 27 Congress Street, Salem, Massachusetts 01970. [0-8387-5194-6/91 $10.00 + 8¢ pp, pc.]

Associated University Presses
440 Forsgate Drive
Cranbury, NJ 08512

Associated University Presses
25 Sicilian Avenue
London WC1A 2QH, England

Associated University Presses
P.O. Box 39, Clarkson Pstl. Stn.
Mississauga, Ontario,
L5J 3X9 Canada

The paper used in this publication meets the requirements
of the American National Standard for Permanence of Paper
for Printed Library Materials Z39.48-1984.

Library of Congress Cataloging-in-Publication Data

Fothergill-Payne, Louise.
Parallel lives : Spanish and English drama, 1580–1680 / edited by
Louise and Peter Fothergill-Payne.
    p. cm.
  ISBN 0-8387-5194-6 (alk. paper)
  1. English drama—17th century—History and criticism.   2. English
drama—Early modern and Elizabethan, 1500–1600—History and
criticism.   3. Spanish drama—Classical period, 1500–1700—History
and criticism.   4. National characteristics, English, in literature.
5. National characteristics, Spanish, in literature.   6. Literature,
Comparative—English and Spanish.   7. Literature, Comparative-
Spanish and English.   I. Fothergill-Payne, Peter.   II. Title.
PR675.F68   1991
822'.309—dc20   89-46404
                                                                                        CIP

PRINTED IN THE UNITED STATES OF AMERICA

Contents

6   CONTENTS

Preface

This volume of essays is a selection of the papers presented at an International Conference held in October 1987 at the University of Calgary, Canada. The aim of the Conference was to bring together a panel of distinguished specialists in the fields of English and Spanish drama in order to study the surprising parallels between the two stages at the time of their formation.

Whether similar beginnings produce similar ends is a question on which the essays in this volume attempt to throw some light. While the title might suggest to those familiar with Plutarch's *Lives* that English and Spanish drama followed the same evolutionary pattern, a closer look at how the other half lived, wrote, and acted showed that there were as many divergences as similarities. Indeed the parallel lines of development followed by both theaters neither meet in a common horizon of expectation nor represent straight and well-defined paths. Rather, the trajectory from 1580 to 1680 zigzags, changing course between common themes and variations, while in certain cases irreconcilable differences in politics and religion threaten to provoke a final parting of the ways. But then there are those plays that transcend national idiosyncracies and bring the two theaters closer in that "ritualized conspiracy of understanding that constitutes the drama" (Orrell).

It was easier to designate a starting point for the "parallel lives" of Spanish and English drama than to decide on a common end date. At first 1640 seemed appropriate for that was the year the English theaters closed their doors for eighteen years with the coming of the Commonwealth. But in 1640 the Spanish theater was in full bloom and Calderón had yet to write his best Comedias and Autos Sacramentales. So to do equal justice to the two dramas we decided on a final date of 1680.

Many people have worked to make this volume possible. In the first place we would want to thank most warmly: Professor James Black of the English Department of the University of Calgary, who helped to bring our colleagues together for the Symposium; Professors Donald Beecher of the English Department of Carleton University and José Ruano de la Haza of the Department of Modern Languages of the University of Ottawa, who offered us sage advice on conference organization and assisted us in the first stages of preparing these essays for publication. A special word of thanks is also due to Professor Susan Fischer of the Department of Modern Languages at Bucknell University for having brought us into contact with Professor Mills F. Edgerton, Director of Bucknell University Press. Their patience, encouragement, and faith in the volume have helped us immensely in our editorial task.

Professor Brian Gill, Head of the Department of French, Italian, and Spanish of the University of Calgary, deserves special mention for continuous financial support in the preparation of this volume, as does Mrs. Violette Clemente, who found the time, on top of her already onerous secretarial duties, to organize, "input," and help shape the various materials into book form.

Introduction

The years between 1580 and 1680 mark a time when England and Spain were often in each other's thoughts if not always in each other's hearts. Students of the theater of each nation have often remarked on the numerous parallels and apparent similarities in the evolution of this art form in the two countries over the same period. Both Spanish and English drama grew out of social and economic circumstances that allowed the first commercial playhouses to be built and thrive, and both freed themselves from the straitjacket of classical precedent and tradition.

Historical and social factors can explain only partly a phenomenon as complex as the theater. Just as spectators bring their own store of assumptions and experience to the playhouse, so too do critics. In this volume they observe particular plays from different angles and apply varying methodologies to their readings. Indeed, it is the editors' express intent not to espouse any one point of view but to present the reader with all these different approaches, thus offering an overview of the many potential avenues for research in this little-studied aspect of the history of dramatic literature.

As in most comparative studies, the point of departure is a researcher's own field of specialization. The destination is an exploration outside its boundaries. It takes courage to venture into new territory, as this often involves having to learn a new language and face new critics. Of the few who have gone before we should mention Walter Cohen (1985) and John Loftis (1987), who have explored this exciting field of crosscultural studies, the first from a Marxist and the second from a historical point of view. Although it had not been the initial intent of the conference organizers to invite the participants to address specific areas or employ predetermined approaches, the articles that resulted grouped themselves into four quite distinct sections that treated the performance space, common themes, divisive issues, and shared mythologies.

The Ideal Space

Unlike any other art form, drama has to be in touch with its audience—stimulating, provoking, or simply pleasing. This pleasure starts with the conditions that govern playing and viewing. The search for the ideal performance space in both countries was almost simultaneously successful and may well have been the single most important factor that led to the sudden explosion of dramatic activity in England and Spain. Therefore, in our search for similarities and differences in the concept of a public theater, our first focus is on the Spanish *corrales* and English playhouses as well as on the memory theaters of the hermetic tradition.

When dealing with similarities in design, one is tempted to fill in gaps in information on one playhouse by referring to another. John Orrell quite rightly sounds a note of caution here and, by means of concrete examples and illustrations, demonstrates that the first public playhouses developed in answer to a demand for revenue and changing audience conditions. Thus we see that in England playhouses grew by stages from the primitive inn yard into the great polygonal frame structures that set the pattern for the public theaters, while in Madrid the Corral del Príncipe developed on an empty lot between two buildings where windows, galleries, and boxes were added.

Resisting the temptation to jump to conclusions when searching for an explanation for apparent similarities, John Varey then examines the question of whether similar designs in Spanish and English theaters might not be due to a common ideological ancestry. Frances Yates's analysis of Elizabethan playhouses in the light of a hermetic tradition would of course be "an attractive theory" to apply to the *corrales,* especially as neo-Vitruvian and hermetic theories were widespread in Spain as well. But then, having tried out the theory, he finds he must reject it to come to the same conclusion as John Orrell—that the apparent similarities between the two playhouses can be explained only by a common experience of playing conditions.

Physical details such as entries and exits, ascents and descents are not often considered by critics of dramatic literature. Still, these practicalities are of crucial importance in interpreting the visual impact and emblematic significance of a performance text. To conclude this section John Allen throws light on the concrete shape and size of English and Spanish stages, thus elucidating many a puzzle of stage direction and design.

The Common Ground

Plays are meant to be performed and so, by relating performance space to dramatic text, Dawn Smith's essay links the first and second sections with a comparison of the stage adaptations of the Duchess of Malfi's story by Lope de Vega and Webster. Her analysis focuses on two parallel segments from each play—the first act and the murder scene—to show how Lope shaped his text for performance in the Corral del Príncipe while Webster wrote for a particular space and audience in the Blackfriars. In saying that Lope de Vega mixes "shades of light and dark" throughout his play, leaving his audience in suspense as to the way it will end, while Webster from the start spreads a mood of doom and gloom, leaving his audience in no doubt as to the tragic outcome, she addresses an important point that will return in our discussions.

With the examination of Webster's and Lope's dramatizations of the Bandello story, we enter the common ground of themes and concerns that the playwrights brought before their audiences. What is striking here is the common cultural heritage of two nations locked in a struggle for ultimate power in Europe. In spite of their different political aspirations or, one might venture, because of their involvement in each other's affairs, Spain and England continued to share the same humanistic tradition that goes far to explain the similarities in themes. Both stages found inspiration in Italian *fabulae* and classical world-imagery, but also in recent medical theories and contemporary perceptions of mobs, riot and revenge, love and desire. However, what matters on the stage is not so much *what* is presented but *how,* and here the various essays, as well as pointing up common ground, analyze how each playwright shaped his text to suit a different audience.

Like Dawn Smith, Cynthia Badendyck notes Lope de Vega's balancing of the comic and the tragic and wonders whether he trivialized the Romeo and Juliet story by giving it a happy ending. Lope's emphasis on love, not passion, almost dictates a happy ending, she feels, and this in turn strengthens loyalty and respect between the two houses. Thus Lope's belief in the concept of a *tragicomedia* gives his play its moral resonance and, she argues, its absence points up weaknesses in Shakespeare's *Romeo and Juliet*.

Love and revenge are the common themes in Sharon Dahlgren Voros's essay on Thomas Kyd and Calderón. Applying a completely different set of criteria, she demonstrates that plot dynamics and revenge motifs in *The Spanish Tragedy* and *De un castigo tres*

venganzas (By one punishment thrice revenged) follow the constitutional model advanced by Greimas and the *Move* grammar proposed by Thomas Pavel. But even when the decision-making
process, method of revenge, and Revenger character correspond to
identical semiotic patterns, Kyd, like Webster, moves inexorably
toward tragedy while Calderón, like Lope, moves toward "order
restored."

Sebastian Neumeister's essay compares various plays by Shakespeare and Calderón that somehow share the same *topoi* of "the
play within the play," the dream vision, and the mirror image. Here
again there are as many similarities as there are differences in the
amount of role-playing allowed by each society and the relative
reality of a world seen through a dream or the mirror as icon of
truth, deception, or self-love. Interestingly, while Neumeister points
to the rigid portrayal of kings on the Spanish stage in contrast to the
English fluidity in class distinction that allows royalty to mingle
with the crowds, Teresa Kirschner describes quite the opposite
when it comes to portraying the mob on the Spanish and English
stages. In her essay she compares Shakespeare's rigid portrayal of
the crowd as untrustworthy, fickle, and smelly with Lope's admira-
tion for the common people's solidarity and determination to fight
for their rights. She starts her examination with the well-founded
caveat that the comparatively modest output of the English bard
produced only three plays with mob scenes (*Julius Caesar, Coriolanus,* and *Henry VI,* Part 2), while Lope's "monstrous" creativ-
ity (estimated at over five hundred plays), offers us eighty-two
Comedias where crowds play a role, with *Fuenteovejuna* as the
most famous example.

When comparing the two stages, this disproportion in numbers
makes it difficult to come to a balanced view of English and Spanish drama. Still, within the same literary-philosophical tradition
there is much common ground to be covered and this Don Beecher
has done in a wide-ranging examination of the lovesick hero. Basing
himself on selected pathological theories of the time, he demonstrates that the broad exploitation of these ideas by English, Spanish, and Portuguese playwrights points to a common heritage of
medical thought. Then, applying the concept of "theatergrams" to
plot structure, he explains why on the stage a clinical diagnosis
makes it possible for an object of sexual desire to be passed from
father to son or from friend to friend without harming the honor of
either.

When it comes to deviant manifestations of love and sex, Alexander Legatt argues that incest in Shakespeare is a fundamental violation of nature, portrayed in dramatic situations and verbal innuendos. Thus, *Pericles Prince of Tyre* can be seen as a play about sexual initiation haunted by the darker side of the sexuality encountered in Antioch.

Incest is also the theme of Henry Sullivan's essay on Tirso de Molina, but treated in the light of a Lacanian perspective on mentality. Interestingly, Tirso, the mercenary monk, allows desire to be the stronger as both the comic and the tragic in his plays portray unconscious attitudes toward the universal structure of desire versus law. Then, applying the same law/desire paradox to the genres of tragedy and comedy he leads us through a historical panorama of French, Spanish, and English culture, suggesting why the genres of tragedy and comedy could flourish only in England and Spain, but not yet in France. Thus Sullivan's explanation sets English and Spanish drama apart from other European countries and firmly establishes their common ground despite certain differences of national attitude.

The Great Divide

Where the divergence of views is most prominent is of course, in the portrayal of each other's countrymen. This is as much due to each nation's unique geographic and socio-historic situation as to irreconcilable differences in religion. Thus, the third section of the volume examines character portrayal but also "the King's great matter," Henry VIII's divorce from his Spanish Queen and consequent schism from Rome. In Spain, the "great divide" was viewed with surprising tolerance by playwrights. At the same time, the parting of the ways was marked by a resurgence of religious plays that, in contrast to England's dwindling Corpus Christi plays and hagiographical drama, reached their highest potential with Calderón's philosophical speculations.

Don Cruickshank heads this section with a short sketch on how diplomatic relations between the two countries affected public opinion and how this was in turn reflected on the two stages. Basing himself on a number of historical and novelesque plays, he notes the tolerance and lack of caricature of English characters on the Spanish stage in contrast to the generally xenophobic portrayal of Spaniards as "dondegos" or worse in English plays. Don Cruickshank's article also shows how literature can elucidate the inner workings of history as much as history can explain attitudes in fiction.

King Henry's divorce from Katherine of Aragon is just such a case where the two nations expressed differing views. Consequently, Cruickshank notes Calerón's deeply human portrayal of Henry as a man whose moral weakness was exploited by Wolsey and Anne Boleyn. Kenneth Muir, however, sides with Shakespeare who, writing for a secular stage, could sympathize with Protestant and Catholic alike. Muir also points to Calderón's disadvantage in having to write for an exclusively Catholic audience, although here "faith was contaminated by the honor-code." To offset his discussion of the wife-murder plays, one should however, point out that these tragedies are few and far between in the vast corpus of Comedias. How to read these controversial plays is of course another matter. Recent scholarship has made abundantly clear that Lope and Calderón were writing an "open" text subject to multiple readings. In fact, as Muir points out, caught as he was between Church and State, Calderón was on occasion forced to be ambiguous.

Gregory Andrachuk takes up the King's great matter again, viewing the schism through the eyes of Calderón—but this time not the man who wrote Comedias but rather the deeply religious author of Autos Sacramentales. Applying metaphoric readings to *La Cisma de Inglaterra,* Andrachuk reveals the politico-religious dimension of the play and calls attention to its title: the schism of England, not the heresy. Schism, in the 1611 Spanish Thesaurus, is seen as "disobedience," hence the deeply compassionate treatment of Henry, the disobedient son of the Church.

The Protestant Reformation marked the real parting of the ways, moving Don Dietz and José Ruano de la Haza to examine what happened to the Corpus Christi plays and Saints plays in England and Spain after the schism. Dietz first dispels some myths concerning the demise of religious theater in sixteenth- and seventeenth-century England and then raises the fascinating question whether, by taking away man's freedom of choice in determining his own fate, the Protestant faith had not also robbed the English morality plays of dramatic conflict. Choice opens the door for inner conflict, he argues, and it was precisely the Catholic emphasis on Free Will that allowed the Auto Sacramental to reach its highest potential. As examples of this thesis he cites contrasting scenes of Calderón's *El gran mercado del mundo (The great marketplace of the world)* and William Wager's *Enough Is as Good as a Feast.*

José Ruano de la Haza questions why saints' plays were so rare in England and so immensely popular in Spain. Since church and state politics, he argues, cannot force people to flock to the theaters, there must be another reason. Narrowing down his inquiry to Dekker and Massinger's *The Virgin Martyr* and Calderón's *El purgatorio de San Patricio (Saint Patrick's purgatory)*, he notes certain similarities such as the element of horror, the most characteristic (and most "appealing") ingredient of saints' plays. Where the great divergence occurs is in the subject matter. While *The Virgin Martyr* is about the apotheosis of a saint, in Spanish hagiographical dramas the plot, that is, the saint's life, is only a pretext to challenge the audience to discover hidden meanings and subtext.

The same can be said of the best of classical drama in general and the Comedia in particular. To a greater extent than on the English stage, ambiguity, double meanings, and hidden truths seem to be the hallmark of language and communication in the Spanish theater, possibly because of Spain's extreme political and religious climate.

Unifying Myths

The fourth and last section in this volume transports readers to the world of romance and mythology, where Spain and England meet again on common ground. But this is a world that has no care of Church or State, a world where gods, knights, and nymphs re-enact the drama of metamorphosis and apotheosis, of mythic quests and birth-death cycles and of the symbolic creation and destruction of the universe.

With Thomas O'Connor's essay on metamorphoses we also enter the world of court theater, where adaptations of mythological stories, set to music, are the forerunners of opera and where ingenious stage machinery delights the eye. Paradoxically, these plays also introduce us to the world of tragedy as many metamorphoses imply a loss of life, identity, and future. Susan Fischer applies Northrop Frye's "key elements of romance" to Calderón's *Hado y Divisa* and notes similarities with Shakespeare's *The Winter's Tale*. As in the mythological plays, metamorphosis plays an important part in the cycle of romance, while the "play within the play" device reveals the thin line that separates reality from unreality and artifice from truth.

In the last essay of this section, Frederick de Armas combines classical astral mythology with Stoic metacosmesis (the periodical destruction of the world), as exemplified in Seneca's *Thyestes,* Shakespeare's *Titus Andronicus* and Calderón's *La Vida es sueño* (*Life Is a Dream*). But while Shakespeare follows the Senecan model in the interpretation of Astraea's fall as threat of chaos and sacrificial crisis, Calderón combines Seneca's tragic version with Vergil's portrayal in the Fourth Eclogue of Astraea's return as a sign of "order restored."

With his examination of the transmission of a classical motif, de Armas implicitly throws light on the essence of the Spanish Comedia compared to English drama. As various contributors to this volume have noted, the Spanish Comedia cannot easily be classified into "tragedies" or "comedies," but rather comes closer to tragicomedy by combining "Seneca and Virgil," that is to say, the tragic and the comic masks of theater.

Happy or tragic endings, it might be argued, do not make that much difference either, as each play is but a slice of life, an episode that ends well in some instances and badly in others, according to arbitrary convention or fashion. Plays are as episodic as mythological birth-death cycles, the periodic destruction and renewal of the world, or the temporary reassertion of order out of disorder. What matters then, is not so much how a play ends but what caused all the dramatic tension and conflict witnessed in that "mirror held up to nature."

Whether this mirror is "comic," "tragic," or even broken (Neumeister), whether shades of darkness and light are distinct or fused (Smith), whether the image is distorted or realistic (Cruickshank), clear or ambiguous (Muir) is accident. In the real world, desire never satisfied will always be pitched against inescapable law, a continuous process that, according to Lacanian genre theory (Sullivan), also explains the simultaneous flourishing of English and Spanish drama.

The varying views brought together in *Parallel Lives* open up a new perspective on that crucial period in the history of dramatic literature when the medieval theater transforms itself into modern drama. Although national boundaries and differences also crystallize at that same time, it remains essential to study the English and the Spanish stages against a common European background. A comparative study such as this, then, allows us to look across the borders and learn about the shared heritage that informed both theaters and in turn helped shape Western drama as it is known today.

Works Cited

Cohen, Walter. 1985. *Theatre of a Nation, Public Theaters in Renaissance England and Spain*. Ithaca: Cornell University Press.

Loftis, John. 1987. *Renaissance Drama in England and Spain*. Princeton: Princeton University Press.

PARALLEL LIVES

1
The Ideal Space

Spanish *Corrales* and English Theaters

John Orrell

I begin with two images. One is of the Corral del Príncipe as reconstructed by my distinguished friend, John J. Allen; the other is the Globe playhouse as I imagine it to have been and as it is currently being rebuilt on Bankside. In the first picture we see a curious kind of courtyard, open to the sky though partly covered by various rather lightweight roofs supported on very tall posts stiffened with angle braces. On the level floor of the court stands a great array of spectators uniformly facing in the same direction; opposed to them is a fairly high platform stage. To either side, left and right, there are ranges of degrees set up within the court, sheltered above by the tiled roofs on their slender supports. Behind the degrees are blank walls, but windows have been cut into these so that people seated in the rooms beyond—which belong to the houses next door—can see into the auditorium through grilles fixed across openings. Above these enclosed rooms are two levels of more open galleries. In the side of the courtyard opposite the stage there are also galleries and boxes. Beyond the stage are two tiring rooms, one above the other, and to either side of it, at the same level as the platform, are boxes of seating for those who want to be in close touch with the dramatic action.

In the second picture is the Globe playhouse, built in 1599 out of the timbers of the old Theater in Shoreditch, which had been set up in 1576. Here again there is a courtyard, with spectators standing on the level ground of the yard itself. There is a platform stage, and all around there are three levels of galleries looking in toward the center of the building. Here too there is a roof over the stage that leaves most of the yard open to the sky, although those seated in the galleries are, like their Spanish counterparts, adequately sheltered by the roof that extends over them.

It is plain that the two theaters are comparable and perhaps

Parts of this paper have appeared in my book, *The Human Stage: English Theatre Design 1567–1640*, 10–13 and 41–42. Cambridge: Cambridge University Press, 1988.

Artist's Impression of the Interior of the Corral del Príncipe.

The Bankside Globe Playhouse Project. Pentagram Design.

offered to their actors and original audiences similar opportunities for engaging in that ritualized conspiracy of understanding which constitutes the drama. In both the performer was brought close to the onlookers, in spite of the large area of the stage. Both were capable of offering a kind of medieval symbolism when required: the Heavens above, and Hell below. At the Globe as at the Príncipe there was room for action "above," and the stage boasted a trapdoor for devilry.

But I need not stress these points of similarity: they are well known. H. A. Rennert (1909) touched on them in his history of *The Spanish Stage in the Time of Lope de Vega,* and they had been expertly summarized a few years earlier by John Corbin (1906, 381). Chambers (1923) seems to have ignored them, and so did Shergold (1967), but Leslie Hotson became something of an apologist in *Shakespeare's Wooden 0* (1959, 70–78, 89–90, 105–15, 233–35), though in offering a tendentious view of the development of the English theater he seems to have dealt with the Spanish rather selectively. Glynne Wickham (1972, 98) remarked that "the resemblances, in respect of both stage and auditorium, between the Spanish 'corral' playhouses and what we know of the playhouse in the Boar's Head Inn in London at the end of the sixteenth century are so striking as to throw some light on the arrangements pertaining during the early seventeenth century at the first Fortune and the Red Bull. . . ." John Allen (1983, 111 and 114) goes further yet: ". . . the more one learns about both the Spanish and the English playhouses, the more striking these resemblances become . . . There seems to be little doubt that when we speak of the Príncipe and the Cruz in Madrid and of the Fortune and the second Blackfriars in London, we are talking about almost identical playhouses." He goes on to speculate about how the apparent cultural interchange might have taken place, positing the itinerant Italian players as a possible transmitter.

I want to sound a note of caution. The similarities do seem to be grand and broad and wonderful in respect of the great dramatic traditions the two theaters supported. But one needs to be very careful when one starts to supply gaps in the evidence about the London theaters by an appeal to those in Madrid, and vice versa. Glynne Wickham's pursuit of the analogy, for example, in his account of *Early English Stages* (1972), informs only his more speculative moments in the descriptions of two playhouses in converted inns: he supplements ideas about the tiring house at the Boar's Head and the late-recorded pit seating at the Red Bull by appeals to the Spanish model, and in his discussion of the Fortune contract he extends the argument with an unsubstantiated and unexplained observation that our understanding of it "can now be modified by reference to the contemporary playhouses in Spanish *corrales* via the Boar's Head and the Red Bull" (115).

This is all rather vague; but in one respect at least the reference to the Boar's Head does isolate what I believe to be an important distinction between the Spanish and the English playhouses. For the very fact that it was established in an existing innyard means that the Boar's Head was untypical of the usual public theaters. It belongs in a small class with the Red Bull, converted ca. 1605 "in a square court in an inn," and possibly with a group of city inns of the 1570s that may have been equipped with theatrical fittings, the extent and nature of which are unknown. All the other public playhouses, beginning with the Red Lion in 1567, were purpose built.

Nevertheless, of the one case of the Whitechapel inn we do have certain and complete notice. The Boar's Head was dedicated to use as a playhouse by a number of alterations made there in 1598, alterations that effectively prevented its continuing in the way of the victualling trade and turned it instead into a theater. The greater part of the inn consisted of a long courtyard on the northern side of the street, just beyond the city bars. An existing gallery to the northeast side of this irregular space was useful for theatrical purposes, but because there were no others already on the site new ones were built on posts across the middle part of the court, and a fourth was added against the range of buildings on the southwest side. A stage was placed out in the yard some ten feet away from the forward edge of the southwestern gallery. In this rather minimal guise the Boar's Head took its place, illegally to be sure, among the several playhouses of Elizabethan London. It seems to have thrived, for within a year its proprietors regrouped and rebuilt. The galleries of the previous year were torn down and replaced by others that extended three or four feet further out into the yard. Because these were all raised on posts, the area of the yard itself remained unchanged, save perhaps for the space occupied by a tiring house built beneath the new southwestern gallery, against which the stage was now moved to abut. At the opposite side an upper gallery was also introduced. The consequence of all this activity was that an ordinary innyard became a regular if rather small Elizabethan playhouse with a tiring house to the southwest, a stage located next to it so that its surface should be shaded in the afternoon, elevated galleries on every side so that its players performed "in the round," and a yard for groundlings, open to the sky.

Everything that is known about this conversion—and that so much is known is largely due to the insistent researches of Herbert Berry (1986)—confirms that the design was approached in an ad hoc, pragmatic way. It was intended from the start to make an upper gallery over the extended one on the northeast side, and when one of the owners, Oliver Woodliffe, found the builders measuring up for it in 1599 it occurred to him that the whole gallery structure of the theater might profitably be expanded and that there was no time like the present for doing it, before work on the upper gallery proceeded. "I would pull downe this older gallery to the ground," he said, "and buylde yt foure foote forwarder toward the stage into yᵉ yarde." He took a lath in his hand to show what he meant: "yf yt were buylt so farr forwarder then would there be roome for three or foure seats more in a gallery, and for many mo people, and yett neuₑᵣ the lesse roome in the yarde" (Berry 1986, 160). So the yard was converted and adapted for good practical reasons, measured roughly with the sweep of a lath over the ground. Another witness testified—for all this knowledge comes from the litigation so fortunately indulged in by Elizabethan theater folk—that Woodliffe had advised building the new gallery about four feet further forward, and in fact when the job was done "yt was not sett out so farr into yᵉ said yard as [he] did appoint yt by a foote at leaste" (Berry 1986, 160).

Such approximations were doubtless typical of the work of entrepreneurs like Woodliffe and his associates. Their motives were mundane and rational enough and had little to do with any intellectual program of architectural design. The *idea* of the Boar's Head was profit, whatever the quality of the works actually performed in it. Presumably the earlier innyard playhouses, the Bel Savage among them, had similarly come by whatever specific theatrical equipment they possessed. It is hard to see building work of this rough and ready type as much influencing the design of the great polygonal frames that were to arrive in Shoreditch in 1576 and set the pattern for the London public stages. James Burbage had been a joiner in his day, but not even he could imagine and plan the vast Theater with only a lath in his hand.

The Boar's Head grew into its theaterdom by degrees. It had been used by the players as long ago as 1557, though whether they then acted in its courtyard or in one of its larger rooms is not known. It became a primitive boxing-ring sort of playhouse in 1598, and then in the following year a regular Elizabethan theater almost like the newly opened Globe. In Madrid too the Corral del Príncipe developed piecemeal over the years to satisfy the demand for revenue and changing audience conditions. At first—in 1582—it was established in an empty court between the blank walls of neighboring buildings. For the opening production there was simply a stage and some seating platforms beside it, but soon lateral ranges of degrees were built along the flanking walls, together with boxes and a *cazuela* for women in the two-story block along the street frontage. By 1602, a row of boxes had been added above the *cazuela*. Some thirty years later the whole auditorium was enlarged when the owners of rooms in the next-door buildings cut viewing windows in the party walls at second-floor level, thus introducing rows of boxes above the degrees. At about the same time a new third floor of *desvanes* or attic boxes was constructed along both sides of the building and across the facade block. Much later still, in 1713, the yard was entirely roofed over (Allen 1983, 94–95).

Clearly the Corral del Príncipe was not a fully worked-out design to begin with. It grew by stages, as if by an organic process. The side boxes cut through from the neighboring houses were the result of commercial enterprise, not deliberate architectural thought. In applying to the Protector for permission to create three of them, Francisco Garro de Alegría and his partner, who had probably bought into the building next door only months earlier, cited their reasons with transparent disingenuousness:

> We state that since there is ordinarily a lack of rooms and boxes in the corrales de comedias, and gentlemen are seeking ways to see the plays, given the few rooms, and we have bought a house on Prado Street which gives on to the Corral del Príncipe, in which three boxes can very easily be opened in order to accommodate gentlemen, since they will be very good ones, we ask Your Grace's permission for them to be made and opened. (Allen 1983, 66)

The petition was granted and the boxes opened up. Almost immediately Alegría petitioned again, with equal success, to open *desvanes* above his new boxes. So the auditorium grew, its finances as fractured as the ownership of the disparate parts of its auditorium. Like the Boar's Head it gathered its theatrical form to itself, like an organic body maturing to perfection. The seeds of its full development were doubtless there from the beginning: two planks and a passion might serve for its DNA, or as Rey de Artieda put it, "diez tablas, dos tapices, y una alhombra" (ten planks, two carpets and a cushion). The playhouse grew from its roots in performance.

It did not, however, produce a great polygonal timber frame like that which distinguished Burbage's Theater in Shoreditch, the Cur-

The Swan Playhouse, ca. 1596. Reproduced by permission of the Bibliotheek der Rijksuniversiteit te Utrecht.

The Rose Playhouse, detail from John Norden, *Civitas Londini* (1600). Reproduced by permission of the Royal Library, Stockholm.

The Second Globe Playhouse, detail from Wenceslaus Hollar, "West part of Southwarke toward Westminster." Reproduced by permission of the Yale Center for British Art, Paul Mellon collection.

tain, the Rose, the Swan, the first and second Globes, and the Hope. Each of these structures was built in its fullness from the beginning, and only the Rose (reconstructed in 1592) seems to have been much altered during its lifetime (Rutter 1984, 47–49, 90–91, Orrell and Gurr 1989). It is true, of course, that there are signs of an architectural development as new playhouses were built down through the years. At the Red Lion in 1567 there was a great stage tower thirty feet high erected within the yard formed by the surrounding galleries (Loengard 1982); a similar tower appears to have been mounted on the stage at the Theater in Shoreditch nine years later, for the topmost part of such a structure is shown in the Utrecht view of London from the north rising above the top of the main frame (Foakes 1985, 8–9). At the Swan the sketch after de Witt, made in about 1596, shows such a tower erected within the yard; but attached to it in lean-to fashion is a stage roof supported by two great columns. We hear of no such cover over the stage at the Red Lion, the Theater, or the Curtain, and it appears that the Swan stage roof was an innovation.

At the Rose there was a "Heavens," which is mentioned by Henslowe in a note made in 1595. Its shape is recorded in the London panorama of John Norden, published in 1600 (Foakes 1985, 10–11). Norden shows a straightforward gabled structure with its ridge aligned radially, firmly tied in to the timberwork of the main frame. Clearly such a roof precludes the sort of tower known from the Red Lion and Swan documents: the tower, it appears, was giving way to an integral stage cover that Norden also records at the first Globe and that appears again in a larger, more elaborate form at the second Globe as recorded by the reliable Hollar (Foakes 1985, 29–30). (Claes Jan Visscher's etching of the first Globe, prepared in Amsterdam in 1616 [Foakes 1985, 18–19], has no independent authority and offers a misleading picture of the theater. It has unfortunately been very influential in modern times.) At the Fortune the tiring house was built within the yard, much as at the Swan, but it did not form the lowest storey of a tower. No tower is mentioned in the contract for the theater's construction, although the stage "shadow" or cover is specified, especially its tiled surface and the lead gutters to take the runoff. Again, the Hope had a cover all over the stage, but no tower: the tiring house, like the stage, was to be made removable so that the arena could be used for the baiting of animals. As at the Fortune, and perhaps at the Globe and Rose, the tiring house was constructed within the yard and underneath the large stage cover.

It is certain, then, that the Elizabethan public theater, considered as a building type, did change substantially between 1567 and 1614. Nevertheless in the matter of size and construction techniques it formed its pattern early, and retained it with remarkable consistency. Hollar's sketch of the second Globe and the Hope shows—as I have demonstrated (1983, 84–107)—that the two theaters were at least approximately the same size, one hundred feet across. We know that the Hope was the same size and shape as the Swan, for its builder's contract tells us so. The second Globe was built on the same foundations as the first and shared its plan, so that the first Globe was also the same size as the Hope and Swan. And the first Globe was simply the Shoreditch Theater rebuilt, so far as the main frame went, so that this too was a polygon one hundred feet across. And in this account it appears that the Theater established a design for the main timber frame of the Elizabethan playhouse as early as 1576. Unfortunately we do not know the size and shape of the galleries at the Red Lion and so cannot tell whether the pattern had already been set there. The Rose, a fourteen-sided polygon about 73 feet across, was smaller than the general run of public playhouses (Orrell and Gurr 1989); and the Fortune, eighty feet square, was both smaller and different in shape.

But the Fortune's shape leads to the next step in this enquiry. The plan of the theater is square, but no ordinary square. The playhouse yard, fifty-five feet across, is concentric with the outer wall, so that the whole is a centralized design. The forward extent of the stage is defined in the building contract as coming to the midpoint of the yard, so that the centerline of the whole scheme is emphasized by the plane of the stage front. Furthermore the proportions of the two concentric squares are such that they can be set out on the ground according to the medieval *ad quadratum* technique: a circle described around the corner posts of the central square will define the width of the outer one, measured through the centers of the posts. This practical builder's technique, of special value in an age when the tape measure was unknown, is also of course an organizing principle, as technological means of unifying a design. It now appears that it had been used earlier at the Rose, built on Bankside in 1587. The remains of this playhouse have recently been discovered, and reveal that although the stage was small and eccentrically placed, the main frame was originally laid out *ad quadratum,* with a yard three rods in diameter and the galleries planned as regular concentric polygons of fourteen sides. One small section of the Globe's foundations has also been dug up nearby, just enough to give reasons for believing that the whole plan was a regular twenty-

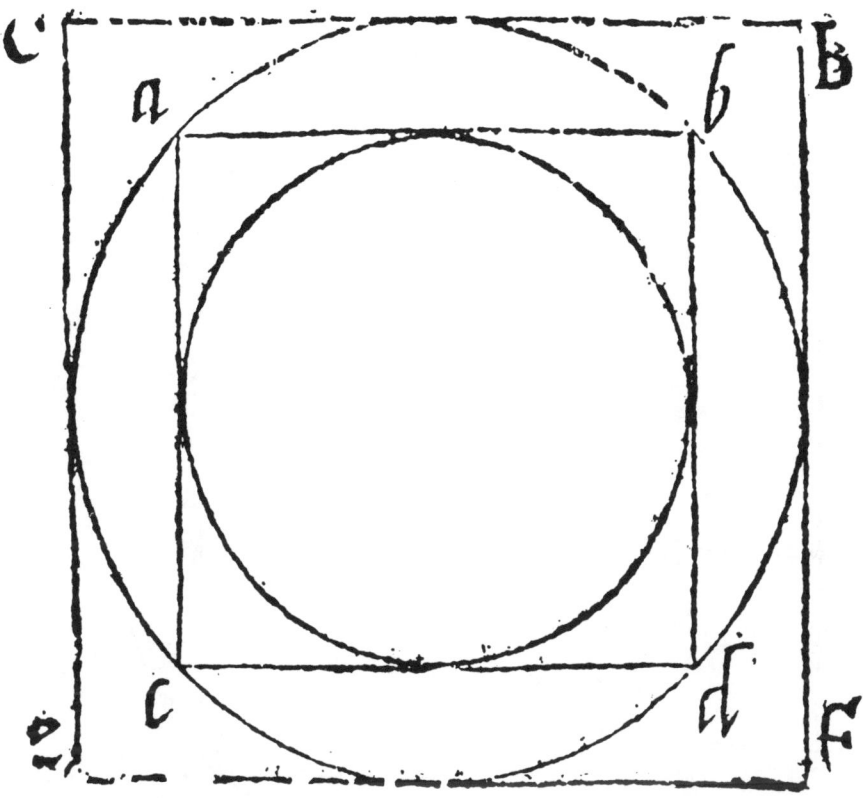

Ad quadratum diagram from Sebastiano Serlio, *The First Booke of Architecture* (London, 1611), fol. 2b.

sided polygon 100 feet across, though probably not developed by the *ad quadratum* method.

Nothing could be further from the ad hoc pragmatism of Oliver Woodliffe in the yard at the Boar's Head, lath in hand. The polygonal design is markedly central and formally integrated. It represents an idea of symmetry that could only be approximated at the Whitechapel inn and that does not seem to have entered into the deliberations of the developers of the Príncipe at all. Indeed the adoption of the great three-storied polygonal frame of galleries seems to have been an act of extraordinary faith when Burbage and Brayne set up their Theater in Shoreditch. For it is a design that is just about entirely incapable of being fiddled with: once built, the thing stands unalterable until it is cleared away and replaced by something else, as at the northern half of the Rose in 1592.

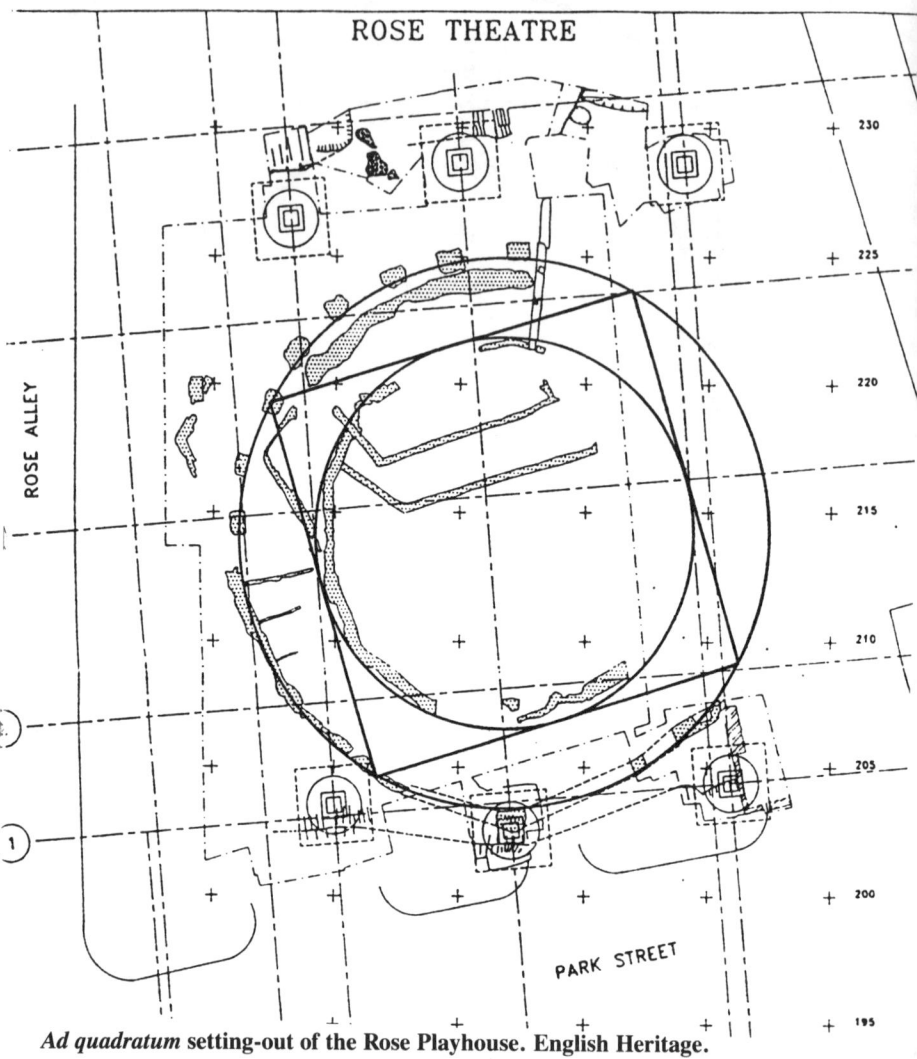

ROSE THEATRE

Ad quadratum setting-out of the Rose Playhouse. English Heritage.

Consider for a moment the problems facing a carpenter engaged in the construction of such a polygonal frame. He prepared his timbers at his own yard, remote from the site, in an area called the "framing place." Here there was good security, both for the materials and for the tools, and room for the trial framing of parts of the structure. The process was fitted to the nature of the work, for the timbers, which were dressed trunks and major branches of trees rather than milled lumber, were far from standard in their dimensions and had to be matched individually to the developing structure of the frame. Much depended on the strength and efficacy of the mortise and tenon joints, and these too had to be cut individually to match. An ordinary three-bay country house might consist of upwards of fifty principal timbers—sills, posts, bressummers, plates, principal rafters, and purlins—each to be measured, cut, and jointed to fit into its exact place in the scheme. Each was marked so that it could be recognized when transported to the site and remarried to the mortises or tenons that had been prepared to fit it. When the timbers had been delivered to the site it was necessary to sort and identify them, and then to proceed to erect them according to an exact sequence enjoined by the need to have room at every point for the tenons to be slotted into their mortises. Some easement might be gained by pegging the joints only loosely at first, so that timbers might be prised apart to admit a tenoned member between them, but there were narrow limits to such margins. In smaller structures parts of the frame could be assembled flat on the ground and then "reared" into position on the brick or stone foundation walls with the help of a tripod and pulleys. Larger buildings had to be assembled timber by timber and called for very thorough planning if the sequences were not to go wrong. First the sills had to be bedded onto the foundation walls; then principal posts were slotted into the mortises prepared for them. These heavy timbers were held in place by temporary supporting rods until they could be made firm with the lateral bressummers and tie-beams. Next came the wall plates, followed by the principal rafters together with their collars and any crown posts and purlins. As every angle of the frame was constructed the necessary braces had also to be incorporated, each in its allotted place in the whole constructional sequence. Every stage of the process had to be foreseen and allowed for (Brown 1986, 29–66).

All this was complicated enough in the matter of a small house, but at one of the great public playhouses the difficulties were much greater. The Theater, like the first and second Globes, was a timber-frame structure of three storys, one hundred feet across, polygonal in plan and with a large number of sides, evidently twenty. There must have been well over five hundred principal timbers, not counting the joists and rafters, and probably as many braces, all to be cut, jointed, and marked at the builder's framing place, then assembled in exact sequence in Shoreditch. Moreover the unusual angles of the joints all had to be allowed for, and procedures normally governed by the rectangular planning of most structures adapted to the demanding polygonal forms. The shoulders of many tenons, for example, would need to be precisely sloped, and sway braces in the roof accurately cut to intervals greater or less than the customary 90°. Plainly the business of building such a frame was not to be undertaken lightly: it must have strained the builder's skills as well as his resources to the very limit. And perhaps most of all, it must have challenged his imagination.

The building process itself was an exercise in mental integration. Whoever actually designed the Theater—and the design will almost certainly have been a cooperative enterprise between James Burbage, John Brayne, and their unknown carpenter—whoever actually designed the building possessed a vivid, concrete, and settled idea of what a modern playhouse should be. De Witt, looking around him at the Swan, reckoned to have understood the origins of that idea: "Because its form resembles that of a Roman work, I have made a sketch of it" (Gurr 1982, 122). And he labelled his sketch with Latin terms: proscaenium, mimorum aedes, and so forth. He was not alone in his perception of a Roman theme in the Elizabethan theaters: the very name of Burbage's house asserts it, and according to a tourist at the turn of the century the Bankside houses were "made out of wood, in the Roman fashion" (Chambers 1923, 2:366).

The usual history of the Elizabethan theater traces its origins in the innyard or animal baiting arena. But in fact neither of these building types was sufficiently developed to have offered a satisfactory model to Burbage in 1576, let alone to Brayne in 1567 at the Red Lion. This is not the place to speculate about the origins of the design: for the present occasion I need only note how the demands of timber-frame construction forced the builders to adopt a thoroughly worked-out, complete scheme even at the earliest theaters. Of the proportionate management of the playhouse interior nothing is known until de Witt's visit to the Swan, when he evidently recorded that the stage extended precisely to the midpoint of the yard, a feature that also distinguished the Fortune. The Hope's design was an imitation of that of the Swan, and its removable stage was doubtless similarly proportioned. Because the Fortune was generally modelled on the first Globe—despite the change of plan shape—it is probable that the Globe's stage also bisected the yard. In short, there is good evidence that the majority of the Elizabethan public playhouses were systematically proportionate in their designs. They were the product of deliberate, integral architectural thought.

The Boar's Head was not. If Herbert Berry's latest speculations on the matter are to be believed, its stage thrust forward beyond the diameter of the house; its galleries were proportioned only according to the practicalities involved, including the need not to invade too far across the yard (Berry 1986, 146). The first fitting of the playhouse in 1598 cost comparatively little and lasted less than a twelvemonth. In the refitting that then took place, the galleries were dismantled and rebuilt, the stage was lifted up and dumped down again a few feet westward. A new stage roof was installed, along with a tiring house. Only at the Rose is there evidence of such change at one of the great public playhouses of the time: in all the rest the galleries remained inviolate. The stage was often proportioned to the whole in an architectural fashion, bisecting its plan. To move it six feet would have been to dislocate the central design of the entire composition. In short, at the major public theaters of Elizabethan London the purely dramaturgical requirements of the players were expressed through a set of technical and "engineering" ideas that gave them a specifically architectural shape. The Theater, the Swan, and the Globe were the result of a fruitful contact between theatrical and architectural thought, and very likely they were enriched by their allusion—as a building type—to the wooden theaters of antiquity.

The Spanish theaters of the same period appear to have evolved slowly, developing by degrees to their completeness at some point early in the seventeenth century. It would, I think, be unwise to claim that they imitated their London contemporaries in any fashion: no observer of the time seems to have suggested such a thing, and in any case the history of the Príncipe appears to show that each step in its development was a logical exploitation of the practical opportunities offered by immediate circumstances. Nor is there any sign that the Príncipe, at least, was proportioned according to any specifically architectural scheme: its design, like that of the Boar's Head in Whitechapel, was a succession of accidents influenced by the central theatrical impulse and ultimately giving that impulse full expression. But the comparison between the public playhouses of London and the *corrales* in Madrid is not altogether a red herring: it throws into sharp relief the nature of the organic growth of the Spanish houses and the very different deliberation of design in the English ones. The design of later theaters in both countries is of course another matter.

Works Cited

Allen, John J. 1983. *The Reconstruction of a Spanish Golden Age Playhouse: El Corral del Príncipe 1583–1744*. Gainesville: University Presses of Florida.

Berry, Herbert. 1986. *The Boar's Head Playhouse*. Washington: Folger Shakespeare Library.

Brown, R. J. 1986. *Timber-Framed Buildings of England*. London: Robert Hale.

Chambers, E. K. 1923. *The Elizabethan Stage*. 4 vols. Oxford: Clarendon Press.

Corbin, John. 1906. "Shakespeare and the Plastic Stage." *The Atlantic Monthly* 97: 369–83.

Documents of the Rose Playhouse. 1984. Edited by Carol Chillington Rutter. Manchester: Manchester University Press.

Foakes, R. A. 1985. *Illustrations of the English Stage, 1580–1642*. London: Scolar Press.

Gurr, Andrew. 1982. *The Shakespearean Stage, 1574–1642*. 2d ed. Cambridge: Cambridge University Press.

Hotson, Leslie. 1959. *Shakespeare's Wooden O*. London: Rupert Hart Davis.

Loengard, Janet. 1982. "An Elizabethan Lawsuit: John Brayne, His Carpenter and the Building of the Red Lion Theatre." *Shakespeare Quarterly* 34: 298–310.

Orrell, John. 1983. *The Quest for Shakespeare's Globe*. Cambridge: Cambridge University Press.

Orrell, John and Andrew Gurr 1989. "What the Rose Can Tell Us." *Times Literary Supplement* June 9–15:636, 649.

Rennert, H. A. 1909. *The Spanish Stage at the Time of Lope de Vega*. New York: The Hispanic Society of America.

Shergold, N. D. 1967. *A History of the Spanish Stage*. Oxford: Clarendon Press.

Wickham, Glynne. 1972. *Early English Stages II (Part 2)*. London: Routledge and Kegan Paul.

Memory Theaters, Playhouses, and *Corrales de Comedias*

John E. Varey

Some historians of the Elizabethan theater have sought to account for the staging conditions in the generality of locales by a consideration of such contemporary buildings as inn-yards, or the dining halls of great palaces. In 1966 Frances A. Yates put forward another, and startling, theory. In the *Art of Memory* Yates is concerned with mnemotechnics, or the art of memory, invented by the Greeks, passed on to the Romans and inherited in the West as part of the European tradition, surviving the invention of printing and reappearing in the Renaissance systems of Giulio Camillo, Giordano Bruno, and Robert Fludd. The art of memory depended on the imprinting on the memory of a series of *loci* or places; usually the *loci* were thought of as the constituent parts of an imaginary building. The material to be remembered is then located in the different parts of the building, so that it can be recalled at will by a mental peregrination through the memorized places. A good natural memory can thus be strengthened or reinforced by training. The Greek sources of memory teaching, now lost, are preserved in a textbook of rhetoric, compiled ca. 86–82 B.C. and known as *Ad Herennium;* it was this compilation which was to be the basis of the later Western memory tradition.

One of the outstanding manifestations of the art of memory in the Renaissance is the sixteenth-century Memory Theater of Giulio Camillo, in which the artificial memory is created by placing the images to be remembered in positions located within a neoclassical auditorium, a distortion of the plan of a Vitruvian theater. In this theater the normal function is reversed: the "spectator" looks at the auditorium from the stage, and sees before him seven ranges of seats divided by seven gangways, in each of which are seven gates. Camillo's Theater is intended to represent the order of eternal truth; through it the universe can be remembered by associating each of its constituent parts with the eternal order that underlines the

universe itself. "Into the old bottles of the art of memory," writes
Yates, "there has been poured the heady wine of the currents of
Renaissance 'occult philosophy,' running fresh and strong into sixteenth-century Venice from its springs in the movement inaugu-
rated by Ficino in Florence in the late fifteenth century" (1978,
149). The classical art of memory is turned by Camillo into an
occult art.

In England, Robert Fludd was the best known of the Hermetic
philosophers. His memory system was published in 1617–19 in his
*Utriusque Cosmi, Maioris scilicet et Minoris, metaphysica, phys-
ica, atque technica Historia.* In the second volume of this work is
an engraving of a "theater" that Yates associates with the Elizabethan or Jacobean multilevel stage. "Three of the entrances are on
ground level; two are arches, but the central one can be closed by
heavy hinged doors which are shown half open. The other two
entrances are on an upper level; they open on to a battlemented
terrace. In the centre, as a very noticeable feature of this stage,
there is a kind of bay window, or an upper chamber or room" (319).
This is of course a memory theater, but Fludd himself compares it
to "a public theatre in which comedies and tragedies are acted"
(ibid.). Yates considers the problems raised for the interpretation of
this engraving by the well-known references to a canopy over the
stage of the London Globe Theatre, known as the "heavens," and
concludes that: "What we are seeing as we look straight ahead to
the back wall is the tiring house wall at the Globe, not the whole of
it but only the two lower levels; the ground level with the three
entrances; the second with the terrace and chamber. We do not see
the third level *because we are under the heavens* which are projecting invisibly above us from below the third tier of the tiring house
wall" (334. Miss Yates's italics). The side walls and the five columns
whose bases only are indicated on the stage of Fludd's theater she
interprets as distortions of the real stage introduced for mnemonic
purposes. "Once these fundamentals have been grasped," she continues, "—that the engraving shows the tiring house wall at the
Globe from below the 'heavens' and that the stage has been distorted into a memory room—we can, by combining the Fludd
engraving with the De Witt drawing, cause the stage of the Globe to
appear out of the magic memory system" (336). Her book contains
a reconstruction of the Globe "as revealed by Fludd," in which
"the mnemonic distortions are cleared away" (ibid.) The impossible
side walls are removed and two columns or "posts" rise to support
the "heavens" above. The columns are copied from those in the
"Temple of Music" in the first volume of the *Utriusque Cosmi . . .*

Historia. The 'heavens' show the zodiac and spheres of the planets, as in the diagram facing the memory theater, but the signs of the zodiac are shown by the characters only. No attempt has been made to represent their images, and this is but a skeletal outline of what the painted "heavens" at the Globe may have been like. The "gentlemen's rooms" or boxes are shown in their proper place, in the galleries on either side of the stage. Instead of being distorted into a "memory room," the stage is now clearly seen projecting from the tiring house wall into the yard, open at the sides, and with posts supporting the heavens over the inner stage. If this sketch is compared with the De Witt drawing it can be seen to be in agreement with it in the essentials of tiring house wall, projecting stage, posts, and galleries for the audience. The only difference—and it is a very big one—is that it shows us, not the stage of the Swan, but the stage of the Globe" (ibid.)

Yates returned to the question in *Theatre of the World* (1969) where she further examines the ground plan of the Globe Theater in the light of the influence of Vitruvius in England, and of the Fludd engraving. She argues that the English public theaters should be considered as Renaissance phenomena, expressive of a Renaissance, rather than a medieval, outlook on the world. The first public playing place in London was Burbage's Theater, built in 1576. The original Globe, built in 1599, was burnt down and rebuilt in 1613. Briefly reviewing the theories that the permanent commercial theaters evolved from inn-yard entertainments or from those given in great halls, she points out that a permanent theater, with its specifically designed stage and auditorium, was a completely new phenomenon. "it seems very unlikely", she writes, "that the appearance of the Theatre and its successors can be entirely explained as a prolongation of previous acting conditions by ignorant players" (102).

The key dates for Yates are 1570, the date of publication of John Dee's preface to Henry Billingsley's English translation of Euclid, which, in her view, first introduced the theories of Vitruvius into England,[1] and 1576, the year of the construction of Burbage's Theater. She argues that James Burbage, as both a joiner and a player, united in himself the possibility of a knowledge of the Vitruvian theories (through Dee's preface) and the practical knowledge of acting that together allowed him to conceive his Theater as an original adaptation of the ancient theories of Greece and Rome. She further implies that Burbage would have understood the cosmic, and therefore musical, nature of the ground plan of the ancient theater, based on triangulations within the zodiac. Burbage's Theater, she considers, "preserved the most important aspects of the ancient theatre, its cosmic and therefore religious implications, its acoustic properties and emphasis on the voice, its enhancement of poetry and the spoken words as the main theme of communication between actors and audience" (1969, 129). The Globe Theater was a hexagonal building containing a round central space into which projected the apron stage. This plan, Yates argues, enabled the square stage to be geometrically combined with the circle in a way that was practical—for players and audience—and religious, in that it provided "a statement in symbolic geometry of man's relation to the cosmos, of man the Microcosm whose harmonious constitution relates him to the harmonies of the Macrocosm" (133).

Yates then considers the Fludd engraving in more detail, and in particular the rear wall with its five entrances (three on stage level, and two on the Balcony). The rear wall she considers to be an adaptation of the classical scene, the palace façade replaced by an evocation of the grimmer castles of England, pointing to its symmetry and the use of three doors which in some way parallels the central entrance of the classical stage, flanked by two open entrances without doors.

In her consideration of Fludd's mnemonic engraving and its possible relationship to the Elizabethan and Jacobean theaters, Yates contrasts the English theaters with the court theater of Italy, but she does not take into account the virtually simultaneous growth of the Spanish commercial theaters. No precise date can be given for the establishment of the first playing house in Spain, but it may well be that Lope de Rueda established a permanent theater in Valladolid around 1558 (Alonso Cortés 1923, 15, 17–19), antedating Burbage's Theater by some twenty years and providing a direct link between the professional wandering player and the permanent playing place.

The similarity of the general layout of the theater shown in the Fludd engraving to the *corral de comedias* is evident and striking. The key questions are whether Fludd based his memory theater deliberately on the construction of theater buildings already existing in his day in England and, if so, whether both the Spanish and Elizabethan theaters have a common ancestry in the Hermetic tradition of memory theaters. If this can be proved to be true, then perhaps it can be argued that the similarity of the Spanish and the Elizabethan commercial theater is due not to direct influence of one on the other nor to a distinct and separate (although parallel) evolution from similar earlier playing conditions in both countries, but to a common ideological ancestry. This is an attractive theory in that it would satisfactorily explain the similarity of playing conditions in the two theaters.

It is necessary, of course, to provide evidence that the Hermetic ideas and, in particular, the use of theaters of memory, were known in Spain in the last decades of the sixteenth century and in the early years of the seventeenth. In effect a great deal of research has been carried out in this important area in recent years. García de la Concha (1983) has studied an anonymous Spanish *Arte memorativa* of the early fifteenth century, and Dorothy Severin (1970) has examined the way in which Fernando de Rojas combines in *La Celestina* the rhetorical and Christian traditions of memory. Múñoz Delgado (1975) has written on the *Ars memorativa* of Juan de Aguilera, of 1536, and Aurora Egido (1983) has interpreted the work of Santa Teresa in relation to mnemonics. René Taylor (1967) has pointed to various similarities in the interests of John Dee, the English mathematician, and Juan de Herrera, the assistant to Juan Bautista de Toledo, designer of the Escorial. He has also argued that Juan de Herrera was interested in mnemonics and has shown that he possessed a copy of Camillo's *L'Idea del Theatro*. Philip II also had among his books a copy of this work, dedicated to Diego Hurtado de Mendoza and with original illustrations by Titian. Taylor lists the Hermetic books of Herrera and Philip II, pointing out that "the presence of so many books of this nature in the official library of Philip II, the champion of Catholic orthodoxy, certainly gives lie to the oft-repeated contention that, thanks to the watchfulness of the Holy Office, Spain was at that time largely free of superstition and magic" (81–109). Taylor (1987) has also published a study of the *Rhetorica Christiana* published in Perusa in 1579 by Fray Diego Valadés, in which the techniques of artificial memory are adapted for the purpose of evangelizing the Indians. A recent study of the Italian Jesuit missionary Matteo Ricci, who, before leaving for Goa and China, had studied in Coimbra, has shown how in 1596 he "taught the Chinese how to build a memory palace" (Spence 1984). Fludd himself was in Spain around 1600, but this date is of course, far too late to suggest an influence on Spanish theaters constructed many years previously (Yates 1969, 63). In Spain, the interest in mnemonics continues into the seventeenth century and beyond. In 1626 Juan Velázquez de Acevedo published *El Fénix de Minerva* (Rodríguez de la Flor 1985) and Aurora Egido (1986) has related Calderón's Corpus Christi plays *El gran teatro del mundo (The great stage of the world)* and *Los encantos de la culpa (Sin's delights)* to the art of memory and studied the use of the theater of memory in Gracián's *Criticón*. It is clear, therefore, that there is a great deal of evidence to demonstrate a detailed knowledge of, and interest in, the theory of the art of memory and the use of memory theaters in Spain at the time when the first permanent public theaters were being developed in the cities and towns of Spain.

It is now necessary to consider if the design of early Spanish theaters leads one to suppose that their creators had contact with Hermetic ideas. The property that has been referred to as probably the earliest theater in Valladolid is described as a "casa y corral" (house and yard). In 1575 the *autor de comedias* Mateo de Salcedo advised the Brotherhood of San José to adapt the yard of their hospital for the performance of plays by constructing covered balconies around it for the spectators; the yard was paved and a stage and dressing-room provided. Salcedo himself leased in the same year "todas las casas questán en el corral de la longaniza e fuera de él . . . questán junto al espital de señor santo antón, que son diez y seis casas fuera del dicho corral, con el sitio y servidumbre de dentro del dicho corral y delantera dél e todo a ella anejo e pertenesciente" ("all the houses situate in the Longaniza Courtyard and adjacent thereto . . . lying hard by the Hospital of St. Anthony, to wit sixteen houses without the said Courtyard together with the site and appurtenances within and outside the said courtyard and everything attached and pertaining thereto"). The lease stipulates that the site is to be walled off from the street and that the owner, who was to be allowed to continue to live in one of the houses, should construct no more than one window opening out on to the theater (Alonso Cortés 1923, 18–24 and 23 n. 1). Valladolid thus offers examples of the two types of early public theaters in Spain: an adaptation of an existing courtyard, as in the Hospital de San José, and the purchase of a site already surrounded by houses, wherein was to be built a stage and covered galleries for spectators, windows being opened on to the theater from the surrounding houses. In both instances the site defines the shape of the theater, and in Valladolid the design of both theaters is suggested by an experienced professional actor.

In Madrid in the same period performances took place in yards adapted for the purpose. Two charitable institutions, the Cofradía de la Pasión and the Cofradía de la Soledad, hired yards belonging to private individuals where plays were given, the profits being used to support the hospitals maintained by the two Cofradías. One of these yards was known as the Corral de la Pacheca, and here the Italian *commedia dell'arte* player Ganassa appears to have intervened in the design, specifying in 1574 "un teatro y tablado cubierto todo con sus tejados" ("a stage and a platform each roofed"). The building was thus adapted to suit the requirements of the actors, and there is no evidence to suggest that Ganassa, accustomed to playing in palaces, great houses, and the public squares, had in his mind the building of a theater on Vitruvian or Hermetic lines, nor any knowledge of the art of memory. It is more likely that, like Salcedo, he had more practical considerations in mind.

When in 1579 the two Cofradías banded together to purchase a property in the Calle de la Cruz, consisting of a site surrounded by buildings containing one dwelling ("vn solar cercado y vn aposento dentro del"), they transferred thither the benches and scaffolds then in use in one of the temporary playing-places. The evidence is fragmentary, but it is clear that the shape of the theater was determined by the existing buildings which defined its space, and that the seating provision and acting area were not purpose-built or designed but transferred from another, temporary theater. As in Valladolid, windows opened up in adjoining houses were also used to accommodate spectators. Documentary evidence demonstrates that the Corral de la Cruz and the Corral del Príncipe, the site of which was purchased in 1582, were in a state of constant change, as additional accommodation was provided for the spectators and large structural alterations carried out. The ground-plans of the two Madrid theaters, as known from eighteenth-century architectural drawings, indicate the way in which their shape was predetermined by the surrounding buildings and streets; both are oblong, and the ratio of length to breadth differs according to the circumstances of the site.[2] The *corral de comedias* of Almagro, rediscovered in the 1950s, is of a similar basic layout (Allen 1983 b, 201–11; Castillejo *et al*), as is the recently discovered *corral* of Alcalá de Henares. Both are built in spaces determined by existing buildings. The Alcalá theater, constructed in 1601, was specifically designed by the carpenter Francisco Sánchez to mirror the Corral de la Cruz: "a la traza que está el patio de las comedias que dicen en la Cruz, en Madrid" ("to the same layout as that of the playhouse called the Cruz in Madrid").[3]

The shape and layout of other early Spanish theaters similarly were determined by their site. Plays were performed in the courtyard of the Hospital of Zamora from 1574 to 1606, when a theater was constructed on a site surrounded by existing buildings (Ventura Crespo 1984). In Toledo, plays were performed from 1576 in an inn, the Mesón de la Fruta. In Guadalajara a theater was constructed in the courtyard of the Hospital de la Misericordia in 1615, the stage being unusually placed in one corner of the square courtyard (Múñoz Jiménez 1984).

The earliest theaters of Seville date from ca. 1570. Jean Sentaurens (1984) notes seven, of which the best known are the Corral de don Juan (ca. 1570), the Corral de las Atarazanas (1574), the Corral de la Huerta de la Alcoba (1585) and the Corral or Huerta de doña Elvira (ca. 1578). A new generation of theaters arose in Seville in the seventeenth century. The first Coliseo, built in 1607, was designed by Juan de Oviedo, the town architect. It was rebuilt in 1614, the new building being completely roofed in. This theater was destroyed by fire in 1620, and a new theater opened on the same site in 1622, in its turn replaced in 1631 by a handsome building, circular in form, in this instance a deliberate imitation of the theaters of classical Rome. A second theater, the Montería, dated from 1626 and was constructed within an existing courtyard of the Alcázar, the Royal Palace. Sentaurens has published its ground plan, which depicts an oval theater with a thrust stage. The theater was roofed over and was designed by the *maestro de obras* of the Alcázar (Sentaurens 1984, 305–54). The history of the theaters of Valencia shows much the same pattern, the early theaters being replaced in the early part of the seventeenth century. The newly rebuilt Corral de la Olivera, a roofed theater with seating accommodation in the pit and a semicircular tier of sixteen boxes facing a thrust stage, opened its doors in 1619 (Juliá Martínez 1950).

It has been argued that the theaters of Spain can be divided into two distinct types that correspond to geographical divisions: rectangular theaters open to the skies in Castile and the north of Spain, and oval or circular theaters in the south, covered by roofs. It is evident from what has been said above that this theory is by no means watertight, and research at present in progress will conclusively prove it to be an oversimplification. The presence of roofs in theaters of the south and the Levant is not surprising; a roofed theater permits performances earlier in the day than is otherwise possible in the heat of a southern Spanish late spring, summer, or autumn.

This theory is, in any event, not relevant to the particular question here addressed, for such theaters are obviously second generation. If we are to test the validity of Frances Yates's theory by a comparison of the theaters of Spain and England, we must confine ourselves to the first generation of Spanish theaters, those constructed in the last decades of the sixteenth century. From what we know of their designers, the theaters are the product of practical men of the theater and working architects, and, more importantly, their design is almost without exception constrained by external factors: they are constructed in the main either within the courtyard of an existing building, or on a parcel of land surrounded by existing properties. There is no evidence, therefore, to support the view that the design of any sixteenth-century public theater in Spain reflected the memory theaters of Camillo, Fludd, and their like.

Nevertheless, the fact remains that the sixteenth-century Spanish public theater and the contemporary English theater present close similarities of playing conditions. The typical stage of a Spanish commercial theater is a thrust apron, surrounded on three sides by the audience, many of whom would be standing in the pit. The pit was normally open to the heavens, and performances took place in daylight. The rear of the stage was decorated by simple hangings, the *paños* of so many stage directions. Gaps in the hangings at stage right and left formed the principal exits and entrances; in the center, the curtains could be drawn back to reveal a discovery space, used to depict a cave or prison, to reveal the results of violence, to display tableaux and large properties, or as a separate entrance, particularly useful for bringing on to the stage properties such as tables and chairs. Above the stage, at first-floor level, ran a balcony, and there could be access to the balcony from the open stage as well as from within the theater building. A second balcony at second-floor level appears to have been used as the access to the simple stage machinery, notably a cloud machine, useful for plays on the lives of saints—to take a saint's soul up to heaven or to bring down angels or the Virgin. The counterpart to this use of the upper levels is the trap doors, from which emerged devils, or which postulated the grave. Such a description—albeit generalized, and in which documentary evidence is supplemented by the staging requirements of plays—does not differ in significant ways from the generally accepted picture of an Elizabethan stage. How, then, are we to account for this similarity?

The solution is obviously not to be found in any direct influence of one theater on the other. It is, however, relevant to note that the theater as the chief entertainment of the general public in the London of Elizabeth I and the Madrid of Philip II and Philip III comes into being almost simultaneously in the two centers of population. An economist might point to the importance of the growth of the metropolis, sucking in population and wealth from the surrounding countryside; a historian of social structures might perhaps indicate the importance of the emerging bourgeoisie, the role of standing armies in the creation of an underemployed, even if often unpaid, mass of men who sought entertainment, and the similar growth of large noble and royal households with their many servants. When seeking to account for the physical shape of the public theaters of the sixteenth century, theatrical historians have long pointed to the performances of plays in the various locales that preceded the creation of the commercial theater. The height of the stage may well derive from the need, when playing in a public street or square, to allow adequate sight lines for a standing audience, as John Allen (1983, 29–37) has convincingly argued. English theatrical historians have looked to the performance of plays in innyards and also to the representations that took place in great halls, both of the nobility and of the Crown and of the colleges of Oxford and Cambridge and, in London, of the Inns of Court. The latter theory, elaborated by Richard Southern (1962, 127–30), has obvious attractions for the historian of the Spanish stage, who might seek to trace a similar connection between the performance of plays at royal and ducal courts—Encina and Fernández at the court of the Duke of Alba, Gil Vicente at the Portuguese court, Lope de Rueda in many cities and noble households—and the later rise of the commercial theaters. Southern notes that the typical dining hall was oblong in shape, and at one extremity were doors leading to a covered passage—still known in Cambridge as a "screen"—beyond which were the kitchens. The screen had two doors, through which the food was brought in and the dirty dishes cleared away. Over the screen was a balcony. Dinner ended, a play could be performed before the screen, using the empty space between the high table and the lateral tables at which sat the guests of lower rank, and the players could use the two doors for their exits and entrances and, if they so desired, the balcony. Certainly this type of actor/audience relationship continued into the seventeenth century. It can be seen in a drawing of a performance in the Palais Cardinal[4] and in the *Ballet comique de la Reine,* and I have argued elsewhere (1968; 1984) that it is the basic structure of the play/audience relationship in the performances that took place in the *Salón dorado* of the *Alcázar* of Madrid from 1640 to the end of the seventeenth century. Furthermore, the use of three levels, representing Heaven, the terrestrial sphere, and Hell or the grave, has an evident origin in the vertical multiple staging of theatrical performances in the late Middle Ages in the cathedrals and great churches of Spain, in the streets of towns and cities, and in the great halls of palaces. The use of three levels is apparent enough in the Spanish *comedia de santos* where, as in the medieval church spectacles, they represent

Heaven, Earth, and Hell. While the balcony of the *corral de come-dias* has at times a representational purpose—when used, for instance, to represent the walls of a town,—we should not discount the large number of plays in which the spatial relationship between a character at a higher level and one at a lower level is indicative of their moral relationship. The reconstruction of the staging of secular plays in the *corrales de comedias* permits us to glimpse through the secular *comedia,* as in a double negative, the basic spatial relationships of the multilevel religious performance (Varey 1986). While the play itself, then, puts on the stage Renaissance themes and makes use of Renaissance imagery—is based, indeed, on a Renaissance world-picture—the basic structure of the stage remains medieval, and the continuity between the religious theater of the later Middle Ages and the commercial theaters of the sixteenth and seventeenth centuries cannot, in my view, be denied.

The similarity between the Elizabethan and Jacobean stage and that of sixteenth- and seventeenth-century Spain is therefore to be accounted for not by means of a reference to neo-Vitruvian or Hermetic theories, but by the way in which men who had learned their craft within the playing conditions of an earlier age chose to apply their knowledge to the new demands of an enclosed permanent theater. The stages of the Elizabethan theater and the Spanish *corral* derive from or replicate the playing conditions of the itinerant companies that preceded the permanent theaters, the performances in the great halls of palaces, and the world-picture of the late medieval religious theater.[5]

Notes

1. Professor J. B. Bury, in a letter published in the *Times Literary Supplement* on 6 February 1981, drew attention to Shute's *First and chief groundes,* first published in 1563, which comprehensively sets out the Vitruvian role of the architect as *uomo universale.*

2. For the Madrid theaters, see N. D. Shergold (1967, 177–88) and J. E. Varey and N. D. Shergold (1987, 11–12; 1951, 319–20); Allen (1983); Castillejo *et al* (1984).

3. The quotation is from Sánchez's contract. See Mercedes Higuera Sánchez Pardo (1986, 95).

4. Reproduced in *Le Lieu théâtral à la Renaissance,* edited by Jean Jacquot, plate 3, fig. 5, between pp. 404–5 (Paris: *Centre National de Recherche Scientifique,* 1964).

5. I acknowledge with gratitude my indebtedness to Aurora Egido and to Francisco Rico for bibliographical information relating to the art of memory in Spain.

Works Cited

Allen, John J. 1983 a. *The Reconstruction of a Spanish Golden Age Playhouse. El Corral del Príncipe, 1583–1744*. Gainesville: University Presses of Florida.

―――. 1983 b. "Hacia una revalorización del Corral de comedias de Almagro." *Journal of Hispanic Philology* 7:201–11.

Alonso Cortés, Narciso. 1923. *El teatro en Valladolid*. Madrid: Tipografía de la Revista de Archivos.

Castillejo, David et al. 1984. *El corral de comedias. Escenarios, Sociedad, Actores*. Madrid: Ayuntamiento.

Egido, Aurora. 1982. *La fábrica de un auto sacramental: "Los encantos de la culpa."* Salamanca: Ediciones Universidad.

―――. 1983. "La configuración alegórica de *El castillo interior.*" *Boletín del Museo e Instituto "Camón Aznar"* 10:69–93.

―――. 1986. "El arte de la memoria y *El criticón.*" In *Gracián y su época,* Actas de la I Reunión de Filólogos Aragoneses, 25–66. Zaragoza: Institución Fernando el Católico.

―――. 1987. "El nuevo mundo y la memoria artificial." *Insula,* nos. 488–89 (July–August).

García de la Concha, Víctor. 1983. "Un *Arte memorativa* castellana." In *Serta philológica F. Lázaro Carreter* 2:187–97. Madrid: Cátedra.

Higuera Sánchez-Pardo, Mercedes, Juan Sanz Ballesteros, and Miguel Angel Coso Marín. 1986. "Alcalá de Henares: un nuevo corral de comedias." In *Edad de Oro, V,* edited by Pablo Jauralde Pou, 73–106. Madrid: Universidad Autónoma.

Juliá Martínez, Eduardo. 1959. "Nuevos datos sobre la Casa de la Olivera de Valencia." *Boletín de la Real Academia Española* 30:47–85.

Le Lieu théâtral à la Renaissance. 1964. Edited by Jean Jacquot. Paris: Centre National de Recherche Scientifique.

Múñoz Delgado, V. 1975. "Juan de Aguilera y su *Ars memorativa* (1536)." *Cuadernos de Historia de la Medicina Española* 14:175–90.

Múñoz Jiménez, José Miguel. 1984. "El patio de las comedias del Hospital de la Misericordia de Guadalajara (1615–1639," *Wad-Al-Hayara. Revista de Estudios de la Institución Provincial de Cultura "Marqués de Santillana" de Guadalajara* 11:239–55.

Rodríguez de la Flor, Fernando. 1985. "Mnemotecnia y barroco: *el Fénix de Minerva,* de Juan Velázquez de Acevo." *Cuadernos Salmantinos de Filosofía* 12:183–203.

Sentaurens, Jean. 1984. *Séville et le théâtre de la fin du Moyen Age à la fin du XVIIe siècle*. Lille: Atelier National de Reproduction des Thèses.

Severin, Dorothy Sherman. 1970. *Memory in "La Celestina."* London: Tamesis.

Shergold, N.D. 1967. *A History of the Spanish Stage from Medieval Times until the End of the Seventeenth Century*. Oxford: Clarendon.

Southern, Richard. 1962. *The Seven Ages of the Theatre*. London: Faber and Faber.

Spence, Jonathan D. 1984. *The Memory Palace of Matteo Ricci*. London: Faber and Faber.

Taylor, René. 1967. "Architecture and Magic: Considerations on the *Idea* of the Escorial." In *Essays on the History of Architecture Presented to Rudolf Wittkower,* edited by Douglas Fraser et al., 81–109. London: Phaidon.

———. 1987. *El arte de la memoria en el Nuevo Mundo.* San Lorenzo de El Escorial: Swan.

Varey, J. E. and N. D. Shergold. 1987. *Fuentes para la historia del teatro en España* XIII. *Los arriendos de los corrales de comedias de Madrid: 1587–1719. Estudios y documentos.* London: Tamesis.

———. 1951. "Tres dibujos inéditos de los antiguos corrales de comedias de Madrid." *Revista de la Biblioteca, Archivo y Museo de Madrid* 20:319–20.

Varey J. E. 1968. "L'Auditoire du *Salón dorado* de l'*Alcázar* de Madrid au XVIIe siècle." In *Dramaturgie et Société* 1, edited by Jean Jacquot, 77–91. Paris: Centre National de Recherche Scientifique.

———. 1984. "The Audience and the Play at Court Spectacles: the role of the King." *Bulletin of Hispanic Studies* 41:399–406.

———. 1986. "Cosmovisión y niveles de acción." In *Teatro y prácticas escénicas* 2, edited by José Luis Canet Vallés, 50–65. London: Tamesis.

Ventura Crespo, Concha María. 1984. "Creación del patio de comedias de Zamora en 1606: estudio y documentos." *Studia Zamorensis* 5:18–37.

Yates, Frances. 1969. *Theatre of the World.* London: Routledge and Kegan Paul.

———. [1966] 1978. *The Art of Memory.* Harmondsworth: Penguin Books Ltd. (repr.).

The Memory Theater depicted in Robert Fludd, *Utriusque Cosmi, Maioris scilicet et Minoris, metaphysica, physica, atque technica Historia* (1617–19). Reproduced by permission of the Warburg Institute, London.

The second Memory Theater from Fludd's *Historia*. **Reproduced by permission of the Warburg Institute, London.**

The Disposition of the Stage in the English and Spanish Theaters

John J. Allen

I cannot help being struck by the elegance and precision that characterize the work of the historians of the English theater in their pursuit of a task which, for me at least, has been a kind of stumbling in the dark. Most of the features of my model of the Corral del Príncipe are not as they are because I concluded that they ought to be that way, but rather because, through a process of elimination, it didn't seem possible for them to be any other way.

Not having had the benefit of Professor Orrell's book on the Globe, which came out in the same year as mine on the Príncipe, I did not think of the London theaters as a group exemplifying a "specifically architectural scheme." I would have agreed with Michael Hattaway, who in 1982 could say that "it is impossible . . . to produce one monolithic theory about the nature of the Elizabethan public playhouses" (14). Professor Orrell's note of caution is well sounded. When I said in my book that "when we speak of the Príncipe and the Cruz in Madrid and of the Fortune and the second Blackfriars in London, we are talking about almost identical playhouses," I meant only the acting and seating space and the audience orientation toward the stage in those two London theaters as depicted by Wickham and Hosley, much as I assume that, when Professor Orrell (1983) says that Burbage's Theater "set the pattern for the London public stages," he means that it set the pattern for the relationship between stage and auditorium, since, as he says in his book, the evidence "hardly points to the existence of a standard-sized stage" (166). Another way to put my point would be to say that the Corral del Príncipe is more like the Fortune theater than it is like most of the other five Spanish *corrales* that I will talk about today. Wherever Italian *commedia dell'arte* people like Ganassa got the ideas that helped shape the first *corrales,* I do not suppose that they arrived in Madrid and said to the officers of the *cofradías:* "Let us tell you how to build buildings." It is, I believe,

54

clear that they said: "Let us tell you the kind of playing space we need" (Shergold 1967, 183).

Having said this, and wishing also not to lose sight of nonstandard London theatres such as the Red Lion and the Boar's Head, I stress that it is on *stages* rather than on playhouses that I wish to concentrate my attention today.

I will begin with an image to complement the two just conjured up for us by Professor Orrell. We are in the central box in the third story (American style) of an open-air playhouse, facing the stage that rises some five or six feet off a yard or pit. The paved yard slopes gently downward toward the stage from ground level beneath our box. Some sixty or seventy feet from us at the back of the stage is the tiring-house wall, and a curtain or arras hung from the forward edge of the floor of an upper gallery masks double doors in the center, flanked by another door at each side. Spectators are seated on benches or stools on either side of the central stage, and standees fill the yard below, between us and the stage, which is roofed by a shadow or cover supported by two posts or pillars. It is three o'clock in the afternoon, the play has just begun, and we see a character rising from beneath the stage through a trapdoor; he parts the central pair of curtains, revealing that the double doors are open to a sort of tableau. Are we in London or Madrid? I think it is impossible to say.

Before the permanent arrangements just described were provided in the two capitals, the players performed in innyards such as the Boar's Head or the *mesón/corral* of Almagro or in rented yards with removable stages on trestles or barrels. Even some of the early permanent theaters were multipurpose structures: the Curtain was used for fencing and later for prizefighting (Hattaway 1982, 12) and the *corrales* for puppet shows and acrobatics; the Hope, built in 1613, apparently on the plan of the Globe and the Theatre, had a removable stage to convert the arena for bearbaiting (Hattaway 1982, 13). Professor Orrell notes that this polygonal design "is just about entirely incapable of being fiddled with; once built, the thing stands unalterable until it is cleared away, and replaced by something else." For that very reason one might wish to say, with Peter Thomson (1983, 37), that "we should be cautious about assuming that Burbage had the nerve to erect a building suitable for the staging of plays and for nothing else." Thomson concludes that "the likelihood is that, when he built the Theatre [in 1576], Burbage gave it a stage that could be removed." Platforms from the Corral de la Puente were brought over to the Corral de la Cruz soon after it opened in 1579 (Shergold 1967, 183).

One aspect of the Spanish theaters about which a good deal is known is stage dimensions and proportions. The present state of knowledge about them suggests to me that one can usefully group them in three categories. 1) First of all, there are the two Madrid municipal playhouses, El Corral de la Cruz (1579) and El Corral del Príncipe (1583). They are the earliest ones that there is any information about, and those with the most extensive staging capabilities. It seems clear, based upon knowledge of their physical characteristics as well as the requirements of a significant number of plays, that in these theaters a central acting stage was flanked by two lateral platforms, which were occupied by benches for spectators during performances of the so-called *capa y espada (Cape and Sword)* plays and were available for scenery and scenic effects for more elaborate spectacles. The Corral de la Cruz had a central stage sixteen feet deep and twenty-seven feet wide between the posts, with a dressing room/discovery space thirteen feet deep behind it (fig. 1). Something more than seven feet are available to each side for the lateral platforms. The Príncipe stage is about fifteen feet deep and twenty-eight feet wide, with a shallow dressing room a bit more than eight feet deep (fig. 2). Some ten feet are available to each side (even more at stage left) for the lateral platforms (Varey and Shergold 1951, plates). Each of these theaters has two balconies or galleries above the stage, and plays require them at least by 1604 and probably much earlier (Shergold 1967, 204).

2) A second category of stage is represented by the Corral de la Montería, built in Seville in 1626 (figs. 3 and 4). The plans, drawn up in 1691, were published in 1984 (Sentaurens 1984, 325; 331). Astonishingly small for this huge oval auditorium, the stage was eleven feet deep and twenty-four feet wide, with dressing rooms backstage to each side and a large sixteen-by-twenty-four-foot space behind the stage available for discoveries. There were two balconies above the stage, as can be seen in the section drawing of the roofed *corral.* As the ground plan shows, there were no lateral platforms flanking the Montería stage, but other extracts provided by Sentaurens from the archival documents make it clear that some sort of portable arrangements were available for lateral scenery or scenic effects. When a man rented the third lower box on the left in 1640, he did so on condition that "whenever there are machines [*tramoyas*] in the plays put on in the *corral* that block the view and occupy the aforesaid box, he must be given another lower box" (Sentaurens 1984, 404–5; 453).

3) The third type of *corral* had the most limited capabilities for staging. Outside the large cities, I know of no indication that these

lateral platforms were available at all, and there is some textual evidence that suggests that they were not. The platform stage in the Corral de Toro, purpose built in 1605, was twelve feet deep and twenty-four feet wide (fig. 5); the contract stipulated that four feet at the rear of the stage were to constitute the tiring room, with a single gallery above (Nieto González 1979, 232). The section drawing shows two levels of spectators' galleries above, facing the stage, with a belvedere roof covering the entire yard (fig. 6). Although the auditorium was scarcely half the size of the Montería, the stage was almost exactly the same size (Nieto González, 1979, 226; 228).

The *corral* in Almagro, discovered, or "uncovered," in 1953, is of unknown date but seems clearly to belong among the rest discussed here (Allen 1983). As in Toro, there is a single balcony above a three- to four-foot tiring-room area and no apparent provision for lateral staging (fig. 7). The stage is fifteen feet deep and twenty-seven and one-half feet wide, with a full cover or shadow.

Finally, there exists a plan for a peculiar corner stage in Guadalajara, where the use of existing balconies in a hospital yard for spectators seems to have dictated the atypical arrangement (fig. 8) (Múñoz Jiménez 1984, 253). No provision is known to have been made for a curtained tiring room or a balcony above the stage, but it does not seem improbable that one is missing the details of an arrangement similar to that in Toro, where the tiring-room space stipulated in the contract does not appear on the plan of the stage. The Guadalajara platform as shown is eighteen feet deep and thirty-three feet wide.

Among these six playhouses, then, the width of the stage is fairly consistently roughly twice the depth, in ratios ranging from that of the Cruz (1.7:1) through Guadalajara (1.8:1), the Príncipe (1.9:1), and Toro at exactly 2:1, to the Corral de la Montería at 2.2:1 and the Corral de Almagro at 2.3:1. The widths of the five of which scholars are sure of the tiring-house arrangements range from twenty-four feet to twenty-eight feet, and the depths from eleven feet to sixteen feet (fig. 9). It is clear that although the typical London stage described by Professor Orrell may have been completely unrelated to the actors' needs—the product of the marriage of the *ad quadratum* layout technique and the length of a standard measuring rod—the Spanish stages share general proportions and sizes unrelated either to the auditorium or to standard measures, and thus seem to be actor/director generated.

How do these figures compare with the dimensions and proportions of the London stages? This turned out to be a rather more difficult question than I had imagined. The Theater Globe/Swan/

Hope architectural scheme has been thought to contain a stage forty-one (Cranford Adams, Smith) or forty-three (Hodges, Hosley) or thirty-five (the Hodges Harvard model) or now, as more plausibly proposed by Professor Orrell (1983), forty-nine and one-half feet wide. He puts the depth at "no more than half its three-rod width" (167) or about twenty-five feet. The stage at the Red Lion, the earliest London stage we know about, was thirty feet by forty feet, at the Boar's Head thirty-nine feet, seven inches by twenty-five feet, and at the Fortune twenty-six or twenty-seven and one-half feet by forty-three feet. Among these, the specific recorded dimensions are those of the Red Lion and those of the Fortune, where the depth of the stage is expressed as extending to the middle of the fifty-five-foot wide yard. The ratios of the above dimensions vary widely, from 1.3:1 at the Red Lion, through 1.6:1 at the Boar's Head, 1.65:1 at the Fortune, and perhaps 2:1 at the Globe and others of its type. Private playhouses of the time represent even greater variation. Where the proportions just reviewed are similar to those of the *corrales,* notably in Professor Orrell's Globe, the dimensions are much greater, more like those of the Madrid *corrales* including the lateral platforms and the tiring rooms; if Orrell's Globe is forty-nine feet, six inches by twenty-five feet, the total Príncipe space is perhaps something like forty-eight feet by twenty-two and one-half feet.

And in fact there was seating at the sides of the stage in the public theaters of London. As Glynne Wickham (1972, 180) has put it:

> I think we must accept the fact that the dimensions of the stage in Jacobean public playhouses reflected the need to allow some ten feet of its width at either end to accommodate spectators rather than dramatic action.
> If this is taken into account, then the actual acting area provided for in the first Fortune (and thus, presumably, at the first Globe) measured twenty-five feet square.

David George remarked in his presentation on "Shakespearean Stages" to the "Not the Globe" seminar at the Shakespeare Association of America meeting two years ago that "these stages had to be so large surely not because actors needed all that room to perform, but because the wealthiest clientele sat on them to watch the show."

But if the estimate of the width of the acting stage must be curtailed, it seems that one must adjust one's idea of the depth as well. Remember Professor Orrell's remarks about the tiring houses in these theaters:

At the Red Lion in 1567 there was a great stage tower 30 feet high erected *within the yard* formed by the surrounding galleries; a similar tower appears to have been *mounted on the stage* at the Theatre in Shoreditch. . . . At the Swan the sketch . . . shows such a tower erected *within the yard*. . . . At the Fortune the tiring house was built *within the yard,* but it did not form the lowest storey of a tower. . . . As at the Fortune, and perhaps at the Globe and Rose, the tiring house [at the Hope] was constructed *within the yard*. (italics mine)

Peter Thomson (1983) also assumes a tiring house in the Theatre "that stood against the frame but separate from it" (38).

I know of no indication of the depth of any of these tiring-houses "mounted on the stage," but it seems clear that, just as the lateral seating must reduce the width of the stage to a dimension approaching the width of the *corral* stages, so the intrusion of the tiring-house on the stage will reduce its depth to something in the range of the Madrid theaters. I should think that the *corral* dimensions and proportions can legitimately be adduced in corroboration of this hypothesis of the tiring-house placement, which in turn contributes somewhat to the amelioration of the "severe problem," as William Empson (1986) called it, of the stage cover blocking half the circular opening above the yard, with the "inner stage at the far end of the resulting dark hole" (202). Lessening the depth in this way might provide more light and be less implausible than either Hotson's mirrors or Empson's reflector screens. Perhaps by controlling the tiring-house depth and the lateral seating, the London actor/managers were able after all to get the size and shape of stage they wanted.

Having compared as well as I can the size and shape of the English and Spanish stages, I should like next to give some examples of the possible utility of the comparative study of the two theatrical traditions in resolving doubts about other aspects of design and staging.

1) As Empson (1986) notes: "Adams makes the brick floor of the yard [of the Globe], trodden by the groundlings, sink one and one-half feet in a stretch of almost thirty feet, from the main entrance to the front of the stage; he is very convincing about the need for this" (188). It is relevant that the 1605 contract for the Corral de Toro specifies that the floor of the yard is to slope down three feet from the back of the yard to the stage, a distance of fifty feet (Nieto González 1979, 230). The lay of the land on which the Corral del Príncipe was built would also have produced a drop of about three feet in the yard unless it were otherwise compensated for.

2) In discussing the Swan drawing designation of the yard as *"planitie sive arena,"* Peter Thomson (1983) says that "we do not know that the yard was ever used during the performances, but the possibility that it was is strong" (40). There is abundant evidence of the use of the yard in Madrid, and of the use of a special ramp *(palenque)* for going up to the stage on horseback, at least as early as 1600 (Lope de Vega, *La hermosa Ester*).

3) R. B. Graves (1980) notes that "only one indication of a regular starting time [for the London plays] survives," the specification of 3:00 in April, 1614 (235). Starting times in Madrid are known to have ranged between 2:00 and 4:00 according to the season of the year.

4) The problem of lighting in the London theaters, which continues to generate a good deal of critical interest, might benefit by taking into account the fact that the Corral de la Cruz had its stage on the south and the Príncipe on the east, and by considering the effect on the lighting of the canvas sun shade that was regularly drawn over the yards of the Cruz and the Príncipe.

5) Although stage heights have been set at between five and six feet in both the Spanish and the English playhouses, I believe that the first definite specification for either is the five-foot height of the Red Lion stage. This is useful corroboration for calculations for the *corrales.* Knowledge that the Madrid *corrales* had ten feet of understage height and that Almagro and Alcalá certainly had excavation beneath the stage may be useful in thinking about the London stages, tempered, of course, by the limitations imposed by the marshy Bankside sites of many of them.

6) The question of the number and arrangement of doors in the tiring-house facade, with the attendant problem of the famous—or infamous—"inner stage," might be illuminated by the clear analogies with the contemporaneous *corral* arrangements. In reconstructing the Fortune playhouse, Hosley (1980) has "postulated three doors in the tiring-house facade. These are double hung, outward-opening doors essentially similar to those shown in the De Witt drawing of the Swan playhouse" (20). But of course the Swan drawing shows only two doors and none in the center. The ground plans of the Príncipe and the Montería and the disposition of the Corral de Almagro as well as numerous early play texts make clear the tripartite division of the facade wall in the *corrales,* with lateral openings or doors for entry and exit and a central discovery space. John Varey has published a comprehensive discussion of the varied uses of the discovery space in the *corral* plays that might be of help

in interpreting stage directions in works written for the London stages (Varey 1986).

As Shergold (1967) has observed, trapdoors, the scaling of walls, and discoveries by means of a rear curtain are all used in Cervantes's early plays of the 1580s and by Juan de la Cueva (192). Lope de Vega has a discovery at the gallery level in *Lo fingido verdadero* (1608) ("with music doors open above on which are painted the image of Our Lady and a Christ"). The tripartite division of the tiring-house facade is repeated on each of the gallery levels above in the Madrid *corrales,* and at one point Tirso deploys seven "discoveries" in succession in seven different sections of these nine *(Doña Beatriz de Silva).* In Calderón's *Tres justicias en una,* reference is made in sequence to the two lateral doors, followed by this stage direction specifying double doors in the center: "He opens the doors, which will be the ones in the middle of the stage, and D. Lope, the son, is seen in a chair." ("Abre las puertas, que serán las del medio del teatro, y vese a Don Lope, hijo, en una silla.")

The reluctance of Thomson and others to accept any discovery space in the center is more difficult to share in view of the frequent and explicit use of this standard device in the Spanish *corrales.*

7) As Hattaway (1982) has written: "[A]bove the entrances there certainly ran a gallery. . . . It may have overhung the entrances below so that the arras could be hung from . . . its forward edge" (29). This is exactly the situation in Almagro and is clearly the arrangement intended by the Toro contract stipulations.

8) The Spanish repair records allude to winches, machines, and counterweights; the English have property lists, and the two can sometimes be looked at together to advantage. In a recent article on "Counterweights in Elizabethan Stage Machinery," John Astington (1987) finds evidence for their possible use in Furttenbach's *Mannhaffter Kunstspiegel,* from 1663. Another important support for his hypothesis is the order that was given in 1664 to lay three beams in the Corral de la Cruz "in the galleries above the tiring room . . . leaving unobstructed the traps for lowering the counterweights of the discoveries *(apariencias)*" (Shergold 1959, 246).

Finally, there is a distinctive feature of Spanish *corral* staging that appears only rarely in the plays written for the London theaters and that was perhaps excised from the Spanish texts that were used in the provinces: the hill or mountain scene.

Some sort of "hill" does seem necessary for the staging of certain scenes played in the Elizabethan theaters. Peter Thomson notes that Thomas Heywood has Hercules "enter from a rock above tearing down trees" in *The Brazen Age,* probably played, he says, at the Red Bull in 1613. "It would be surprising," he adds, "if the King's Men could not by then, have matched the effect at the Globe, and presumptuous to claim to know just how they would have done it" (Thomson 1983, 50). In Middleton's *Family of Love,* probably played at the Fortune in 1602 (publ. 1608), according to Empson, Lipsalve recounts having seen "Samson bear the town-gates on his neck from the lower to the upper stage" (1.3). Empson (1986) suggests that "Henslowe might well have a ladder brought on, concealed in an imitation of a rocky bit of hillside"; he further suggests that "the gates appear in the aperture of one of the big side doors, leaving the centre for the mountain" (163; 164).

The *corral* plays contain a great number of very explicit references to these kinds of ascents and descents; Shergold (1967) notes "the requirement, in a number of early plays by Lope de Vega that characters should walk down from above, usually from the top of a 'hill,' in full view of the audience" (203). He says that "the hill must either have been represented by a large and solid piece of scenery, or, more likely, by staircases leading down from the upper gallery to the stage" (220). John Varey (1986), in referring to the most famous descent in all of the Comedia—the opening scene of *La vida es sueño*—has said that: "It is clear that [Rosaura and Clarín] descend a staircase [from the balcony] as they deliver their respective speeches, and that when Rosaura appears 'en lo alto de un monte,' the stage directions describe what the audience has to imagine, rather than what it really sees" (279). David Castillejo has opted for a simulated mountain, rather than a staircase, in his visualization of one of these scenes, and I think the awkwardness of the result argues well for a simple staircase in his theater, which is Enrique Nuere's modification of my own (fig. 10). Empson's suggested staging of the hill scene described by Lipsalve seems equally awkward. Even more difficult to imagine in these circumstances is the two-mountain scene that one finds in more than one *corral* play. Shergold (1967) cites an autograph manuscript of Lope's *El cardenal de Belén* (1610): "from one mountainside shepherds descend, from another, three kings" ("por un lado de monte bajen pastores, por otro tres reyes"). José Ruano (1987) has recently cited another text that is quite explicit about the location of the "montes": "Two armies come marching out on the crests of two hills which there must be at the sides of the stage" (51). The lateral stages I postulated in my reconstruction of the Corral del Príncipe are essential for this staging, and Castillejo's staging problem described above was created when the Nuere modifications removed these plat-forms. To close this brief consideration of hill scenes, let me point out a correspondence in this regard between *corral* staging and that of the Auto Sacramental that I believe is probably not accidental. Jean Sentaurens (1984, 849) has published a graphic recreation of the three-cart auto arrangement as it became standard after 1609, here reproduced as figure 11. Note that the tiring-room arrange-ments on these carts actually necessitate the construction of build-ings, mountains, or some sort of elevation at each side to conceal them. Before the advent of the three-cart pattern, something similar must have been necessary, if on a smaller scale, in the days when only a single cart was used. Another citation picked up by Sen-taurens is very suggestive. In 1560, Juan de Figueroa decorated the cart for *El triunfo de la iglesia* with "buildings" and a "monte" made of sixteen yards of sewn cloth ("16 varas de angeo, hilo y agujas, para el monte") (Sentaurens 1984, 165–66). Perhaps it is here that the distant antecedents of Rosaura's famous entry in *La vida es sueño* are to be found. It is less likely that the lateral platforms in the *corrales* relate to any feature of the London play-houses, but I do hope that some of the points I have raised may be relevant to these two traditions that do in fact seem to share a great many common features.

Works Cited

Allen, John. 1983. "Hacia una revalorización del corral de comedias de Almagro." *Journal of Hispanic Philology* 7: 201–11.

———. 1986. "Los aposentos laterales del Corral de Comedias del Príncipe." *Anales del Instituto de Estudios Madrileños* 23: 39–44.

Astington, John. 1987. "Counterweights in Elizabethan Stage Machinery." *Theatre Notebook* 41: 18–24.

Castillejo, David. 1984. *El corral de comedias.* Madrid: Ayuntamiento de Madrid.

Empson, William. 1986. *Essays on Shakespeare.* Edited by David B. Pirie. Cam-bridge: Cambridge University Press.

Graves, R. B. 1980. "Shakespeare's Outdoor Stage Lighting." *Shakespeare Stud-ies* 13: 235–250.

Hattaway, Michael. 1982. *Elizabethan Popular Theatre.* London: Routledge and Kegan Paul.

Hosley, Richard. 1980. "A Reconstruction of the Fortune Playhouse: Part II." *The Elizabethan Theatre* 7: 20.

Múñoz Jiménez, José Miguel. 1984. "El patio de las comedias del Hospital de la Misericordia de Guadalajara (1615–1639)." *Wad-Al-Hayara* 11: 239–55.

Nieto González, J. R. 1979. "Trazas para una casa de comedias: 1605." *Acta Philologica Salmanticensia* 4: 221–32.

Orrell, John. 1983. *The Quest for Shakespeare's Globe*. Cambridge: Cambridge University Press.

Ruano de la Haza, José. 1987. "The Staging of Calderón's *La vida es sueño* and *La dama duende.*" *Bulletin of Hispanic Studies* 64: 51–63.

Sentaurens, Jean. 1984. *Séville et le théâtre*. Bordeaux: Presses Universitaires de Bordeaux.

Shergold, N. D. 1959. "Nuevos documentos sobre los corrales de comedias de Madrid, 1652–1700." *Boletín de la Biblioteca de Menéndez Pelayo* 35: 209–346.

Shergold, N. D. 1967. *A History of the Spanish Stage*. Oxford: Clarendon Press.

Thomson, Peter. 1983. *Shakespeare's Theatre*. London: Routledge and Kegan Paul.

Varey, John E. 1986. "Valores visuales de la comedia española en la época de Calderón." *Edad de Oro* 5: 271–97.

Varey, John E. and N. D. Shergold. 1951. "Tres dibujos inéditos de los antiguos corrales de comedias de Madrid." *Revista de la Biblioteca, Archivo y Museo del Ayuntamiento de Madrid* 20: 319–20 and plates.

Wickham, Glynn. 1972. *Early English Stages, 1300–1660*. Vol. 2, part 2. New York: Columbia University Press.

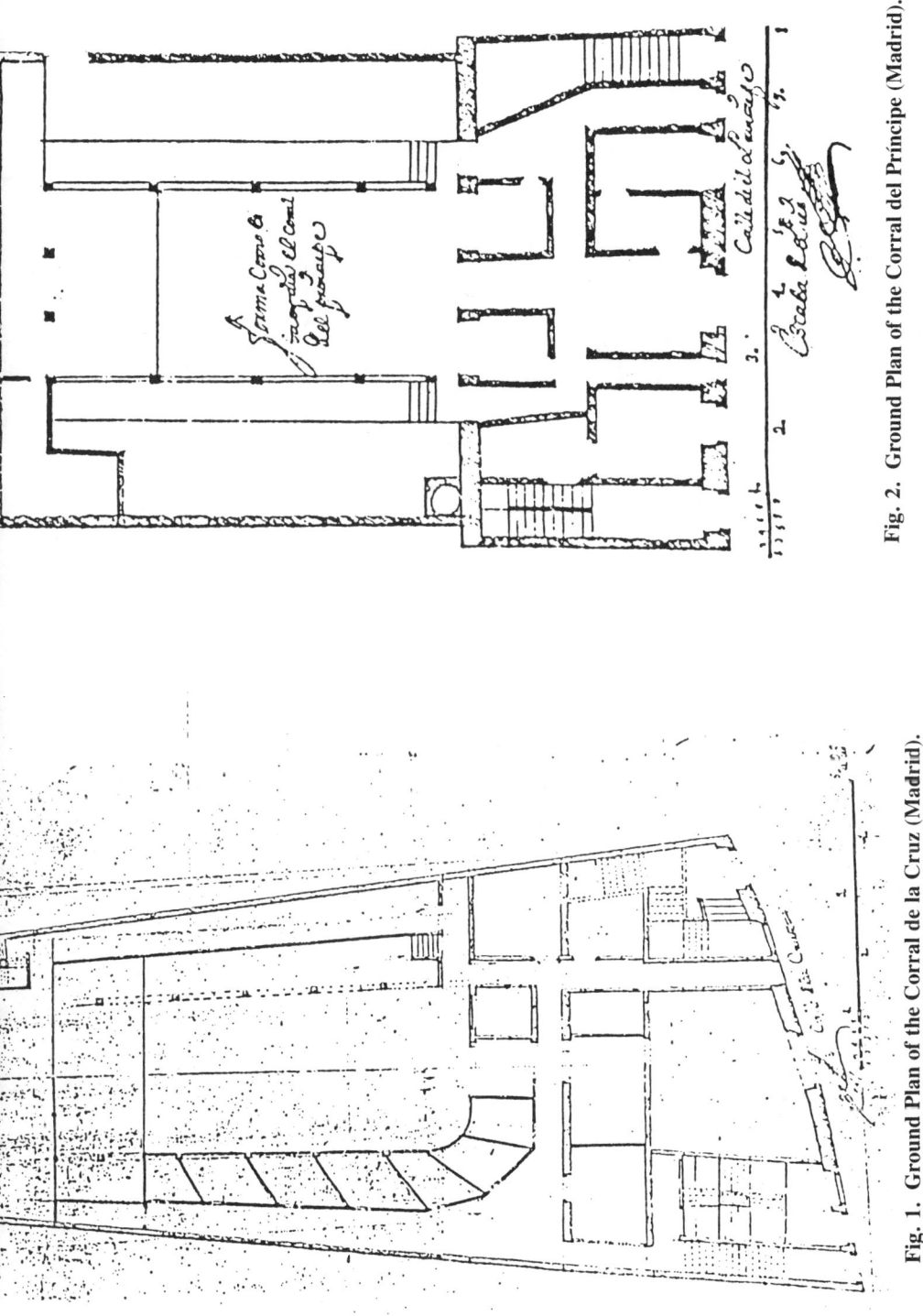

Fig. 2. Ground Plan of the Corral del Príncipe (Madrid).

Fig. 1. Ground Plan of the Corral de la Cruz (Madrid).

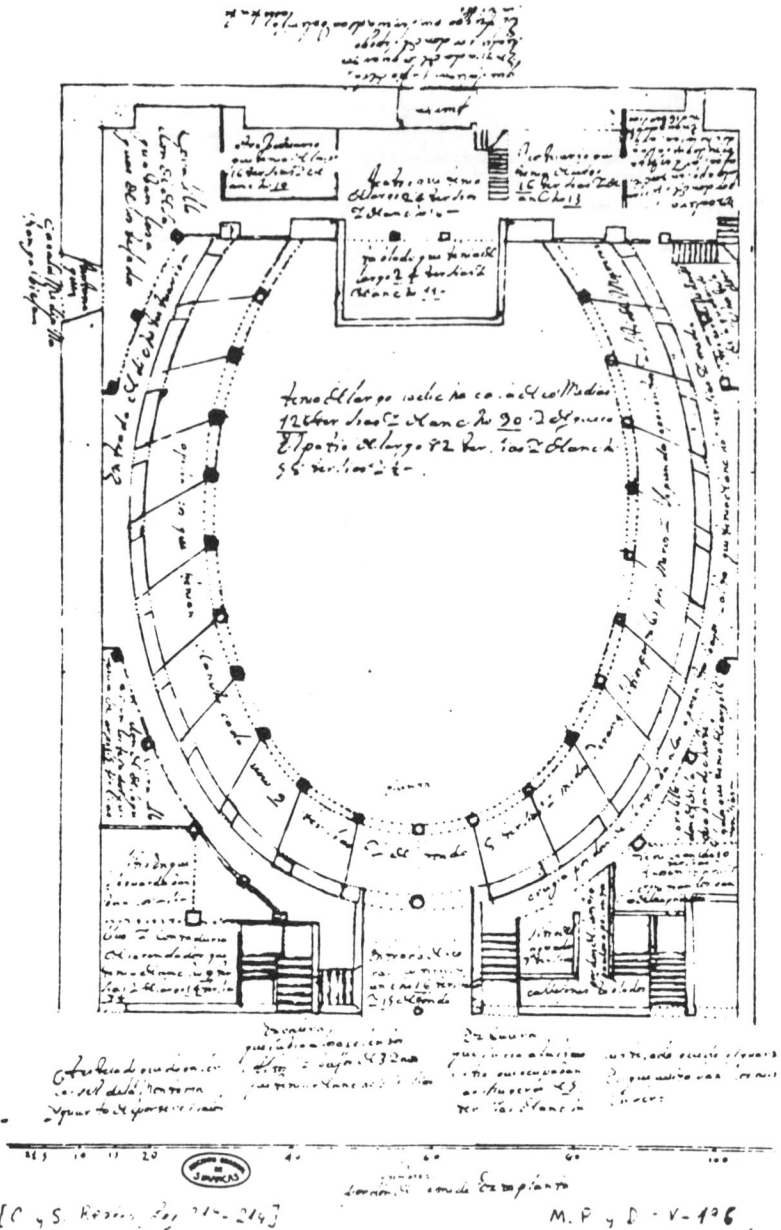

Fig. 3. Ground Plan of the Corral de la Montería (Seville).

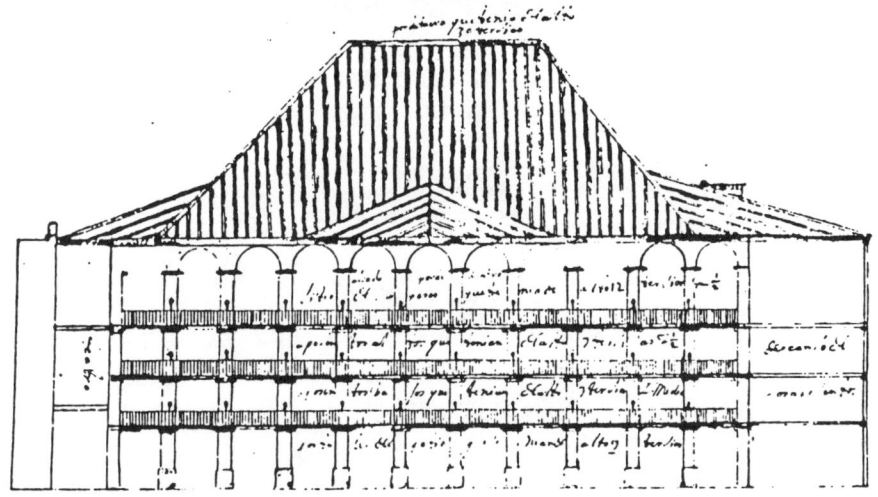

Fig. 4. Section Drawing of the Corral de la Montería.

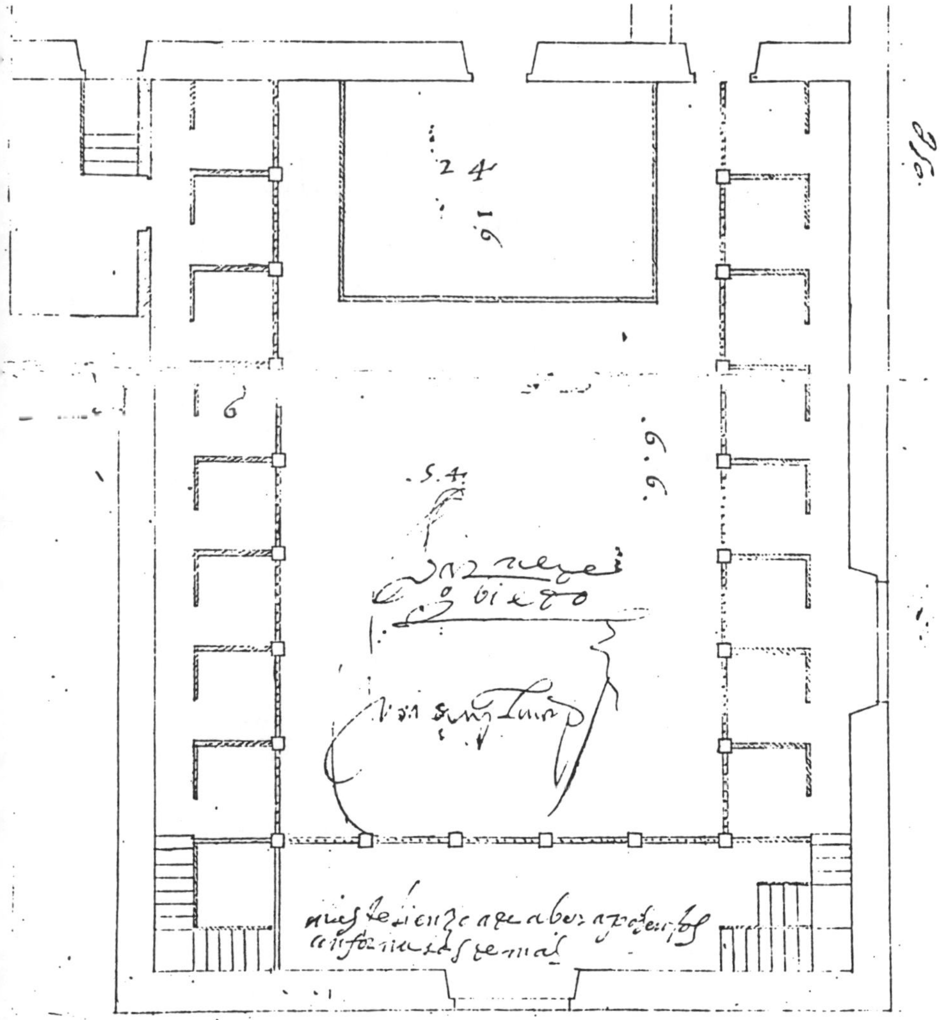

Fig. 5. Ground Plan of the Corral de Toro.

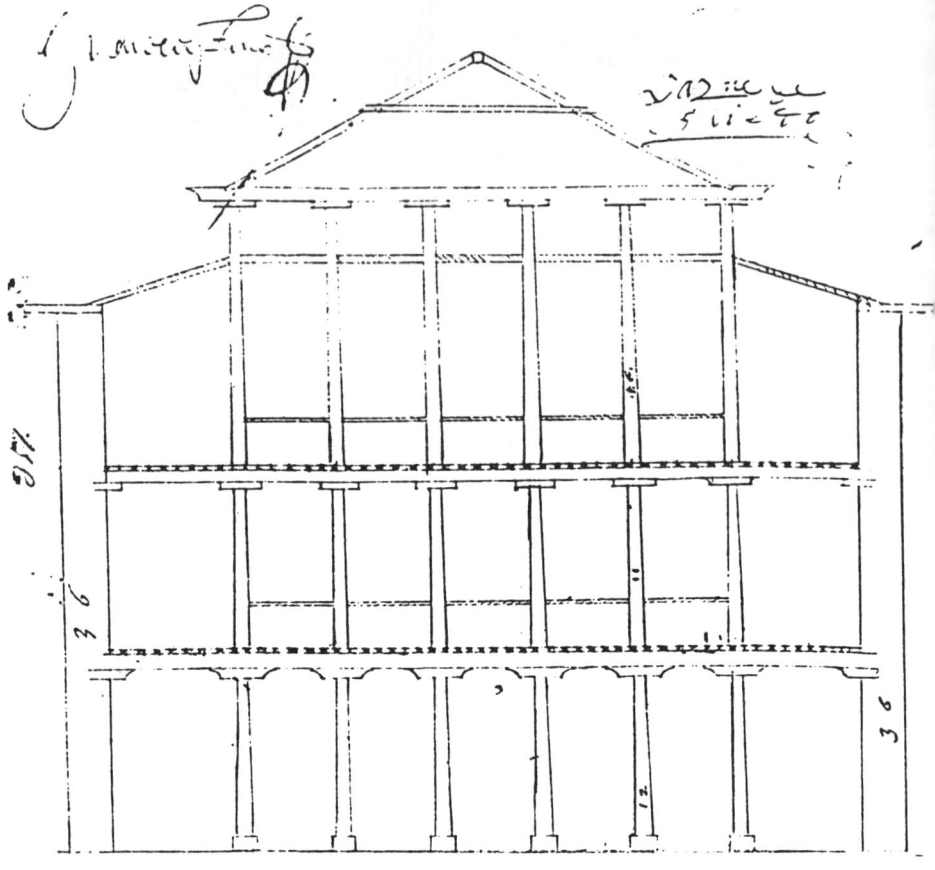

Fig. 6. Section Drawing of the Corral de Toro.

Fig. 7. Reconstructed Stage of the Corral de Almagro.

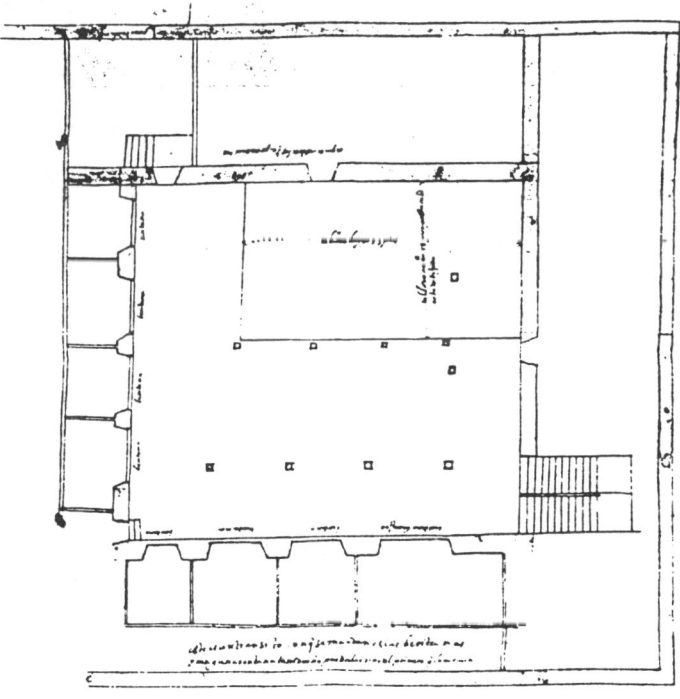

Fig. 8. Ground Plan of the Patio de las Comedias (Guadalajara).

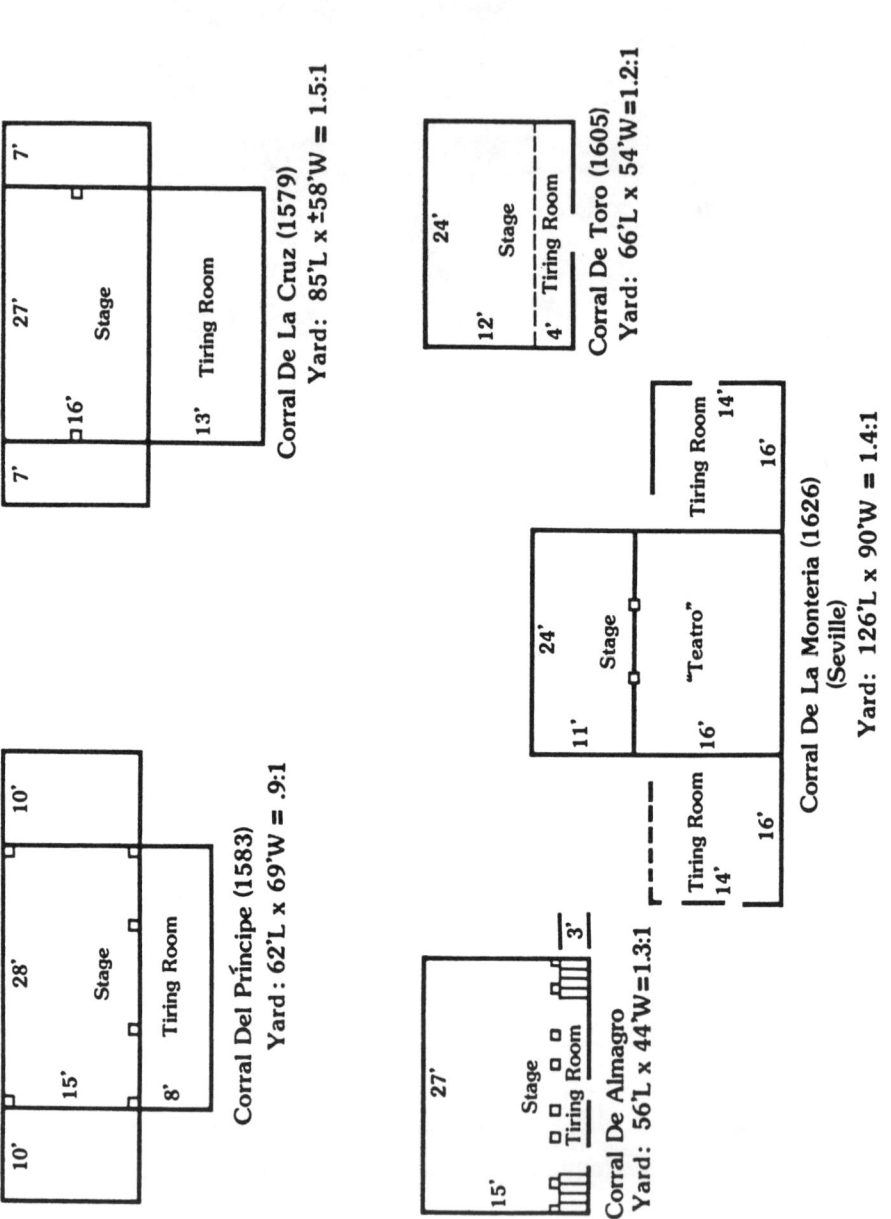

Corral Del Príncipe (1583)
Yard: 62'L x 69'W = .9:1

Corral De La Cruz (1579)
Yard: 85'L x ±58'W = 1.5:1

Corral De Almagro
Yard: 56'L x 44'W=1.3:1

Corral De Toro (1605)
Yard: 66'L x 54'W=1.2:1

Corral De La Monteria (1626)
(Seville)
Yard: 126'L x 90'W = 1.4:1

Fig. 9. Five Stages of Golden Age Corrales.

Fig. 10. Mountain Scene as Conceived by David Castillejo in *El Corral de Comedias*.

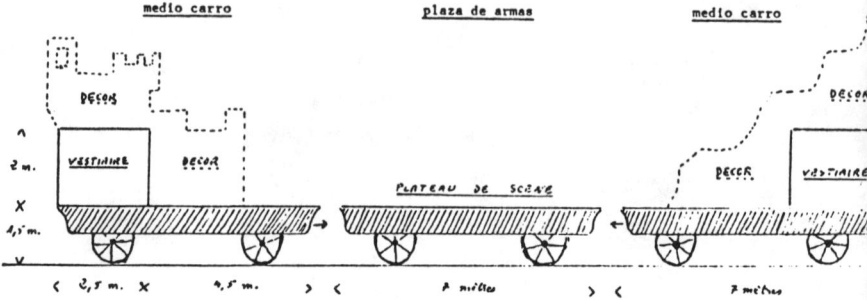

Fig. 11. Staging for an Auto Sacramental as represented by Jean Sentaurens.

2
The Common Ground

Text, Stage, and Public in Webster's *The Duchess of Malfi* and Lope's *El mayordomo de la Duquesa de Amalfi*

Dawn L. Smith

> The study of the drama is the study of how the stage compels its audience to be involved in its actual processes. The spectator interprets and so contributes to and finally becomes the play, whose image is all and only in his mind. (Styan 1975, 4)

The valuable insights that semioticians have brought to the elusive subject of theatrical communication have focussed attention in particular on important areas of study often ignored in the past or, at best, only vaguely defined. One such area is what has been called "the awareness of the audience," a term itself ambiguous because of its possible application to all the participants in the theatrical experience. On the part of the playwright it involves a careful deployment of material and techniques calculated to appeal to a particular audience and to influence its reaction. The spectators, for their part, react as a group made up of individuals whose disparate perceptions reflect the complex pattern of familiarity, convention, and belief that forms the background of their own experience—what H. R. Jauss has called "the horizon of expectations." While the present study does not take a theoretical approach, it is concerned with the question of theatrical communication and audience reception and acknowledges, in particular, the seminal work of Elam (1980), Pavis (1982), and Jauss (1982).[1]

At the beginning of the seventeenth century the English dramatist John Webster and the Spaniard Lope de Vega both wrote plays that were based on a *novella* by Matteo Bandello. The object of this study is to compare these plays as theater, to consider some of the characteristics of the stages and the audiences in seventeenth-century Madrid and London, and to suggest how these may have influenced the two texts and, at the same time, combined with them to create the respective performances.

*   *   *

Matteo Bandello's twenty-sixth *novella* is based on the true story of Antonio Bologna, who was murdered in Milan in 1513 by order of his brothers-in-law. His death was an act of family revenge for what was regarded as his effrontery in marrying the widowed Duchess of Amalfi, whom he served as majordomo, or steward. The story appeared in the first part of Bandello's collected *novelle,* published in Lucca in 1554, which subsequently enjoyed great popularity throughout Europe.[2]

According to Morley and Bruerton (1960, 356), Lope de Vega wrote his tragedy, *El mayordomo de la Duquesa de Amalfi (The Duchess of Amalfi's Steward),* between 1599 and 1606 (more probably after 1604) and it was published in 1618 in the *Parte XI* of Lope's plays. In his early forties at the turn of the century, Lope was already a legend in Spain, although most of what are today considered his best plays were still to be written. Nevertheless, he was admired not only as the man who had introduced a new kind of drama to the Spanish theater, but also as a brilliant and prolific poet. Although nothing is known about the first performance of *El mayordomo,* it is likely that it took place in Madrid at a public theatre, that is to say, at the Corral del Príncipe or the Corral de la Cruz, sometime after 1604, and perhaps not until after the Court returned from Valladolid in 1606.

John Webster's play, *The Duchess of Malfi,* was first performed in 1614, or possibly late in 1613 (Brown 1964, xvii–xviii). However, the play was not published until 1623. If, as is generally supposed, Webster was born in 1579 or 1580, he would have been in his mid-thirties in 1614 (Bradbrook 1980, 1).[3] At this time his reputation as a dramatist rested on several plays written in collaboration with Thomas Dekker and John Marston, and on *The White Devil,* which failed to please when it was first performed at the Red Bull in 1612, although it later proved a success in the private theatre (Bradbrook 1980, 4–5).

The title page of the published version of *The Duchess* (1623) states that the play was "Presented privately at the Blackfriars, and publicly at the Globe, by the King's Majesty's Servants." Formerly known as The Lord Chamberlain's Men, the company associated with Shakespeare took the name of The King's Men when it gained the patronage of James I, subsequently becoming the most successful and prosperous acting company in London. After 1609, it played at the Globe during the summer and at the Blackfriars Playhouse during the rest of the year.

Although *The Duchess* is known to have been performed also in the larger public theater (that is, the rebuilt Globe after 1613), this study will focus on performance conditions at the Blackfriars for three reasons: because, as J. J. Allen has pointed out, there were striking physical similarities between the Corral del Príncipe and the Blackfriars; because the ambiance of the indoor theater seems especially suited to the staging of *The Duchess;* and because Webster himself blamed the initial failure of *The White Devil* specifically on the conditions of the public theater, which, he complained, was "so open and black a theatre," lacking "that which is the only grace and setting-out of a tragedy, a full and understanding auditory."[4]

From J. J. Allen's research on the Príncipe (1983, 113–15) and Richard Hosley's study of the second Blackfriars (1970, 74–88) it seems that the acting space provided by both theaters was very similar in size: that is, approximately twenty-eight or twenty-nine feet across, while the stage at the Blackfriars had a depth of some eighteen and one-half feet in front of the tiring house, compared with fourteen and one-half feet at the Príncipe. Both theaters probably accommodated several rows of seated spectators on either side of the stage. The facade of the Spanish playhouse had three levels, which made for flexibility in staging entrances and discoveries. Hosley (1970, 79) suggests that at the Blackfriars the facade resembled the screen of a great hall and provided a number of bays and entrances on two levels.

The capacity of the Príncipe in the early seventeenth century was about one thousand, as compared to six to seven hundred at the Blackfriars. At the Príncipe the audience represented every level of Madrid society and included a large proportion of poorer patrons. Although the Blackfriars was designated "private," its audience was by no means as exclusive as the term implies. In fact, admission was restricted only by the ability of patrons to pay a minimum of 6d, instead of the 1d charged by the public playhouses. The main difference between the two audiences was not so much in their composition as in their disposition. Whereas in the Spanish *corral* (as at the Globe and the other public playhouses in both countries) the *mosqueteros,* or groundlings, stood immediately in front of the stage, at the Blackfriars the opposite was true: the more prosperous and discriminating spectators sat closest to the stage while those who paid less were seated in the gallery (Gurr 1985, 53–54; 203–5).

Another major difference between the two playhouses was the

fact that the public theater in Spain (as in England at this period) was for the most part unroofed, whereas the Blackfriars was housed in what had previously been the great hall of a Dominican Priory (Hosley 1970).[5] The lighting in the indoor setting was therefore dependent for the most part on candles and sconces, a feature that doubtless affected staging conditions as well as the ambiance of performance.

Acting companies in Spain in the early 1600s consisted of thirteen or fourteen players, including women, and a director, or *autor de comedias* (Rennert 1909, 145). Since *El mayordomo* has twenty-two named characters, plus an unspecified number of soldiers, obviously some parts had to be doubled. The cast list also calls for two children, aged eight and six respectively, to play the young son and daughter of the Duchess and Antonio.

A good deal is known about the actors who took part in the first performance of *The Duchess*. According to Brown (1964, xviii–xxiv) this was the first English play to be published with a cast list. Richard Burbage of "inchaunting toung," the most noted tragedian of his time, played the part of the Duchess's villainous brother Ferdinand. Burbage was also famous for his portrayals of Richard III, Hamlet, Lear, and Othello, as well as of Jeronimo in *The Spanish Tragedy*. The female roles were, of course, played by boys.[6] Since the English companies were no larger than their Spanish counterparts, some doubling of parts was also necessary in *The Duchess,* for the list of characters has fifteen named parts, plus two pilgrims, eight madmen, three young children, and various attendants.

*   *   *

When we compare the two texts from the standpoint of theater (that is, performance) rather than of drama or literary text (Elam 1980, 2), it becomes clear that each writer was influenced by different considerations in his selection and presentation of the source material. The playwright's perception of the conditions imposed by performance and his assessment of the audience's horizon of expectations determined how he would structure the play. It also affected the way in which he dealt with emphasis, mood, and suspense—elements that help to orchestrate the dramatic action.

Two parallel segments drawn from each of the plays under consideration will serve as examples of how Lope and Webster shaped their texts for performance. The first segment corresponds to the first act in each play (that is, 1148 lines or one third of Lope's play, compared with 506 lines, or approximately one fifth of Webster's play.)[7] The second segment concerns the murder of the Duchess, Antonio and their children: in Lope's play this event takes place in the last act, in Webster's play it is spread over two acts.

In her excellent translation of Lope's play, Cynthia Rodríguez-Badendyck (1985) addresses the question of the different emphasis that Lope and Webster have placed on the Duchess and Antonio, a difference reflected in the titles of the plays. She demonstrates convincingly that the implication of this choice is fundamental to their interpretation (31–37).

In *El mayordomo* Antonio's opening monologue, addressed to the audience, immediately establishes a central theme of the play. It also points to the primacy of Antonio's perspective as he speaks of his presumptuous love for the Duchess, which urges him to fly, like Icarus, too close to the sun. The theme of love and its powerful attraction is then taken up by Otavio de Medicis, a suitor for the Duchess's hand, who seeks to enlist Antonio's assistance as go-between. The scene is both tense and ironic, since the audience is aware of Antonio's own feelings for the Duchess, whereas Otavio misunderstands his concern and resents his boldness. The following scene is touched with comedy, as the Duchess teasingly questions a pompous old servant about her young son's progress in his lessons. When left alone with her maid, Livia, she resumes a conversation that has obviously been interrupted: a discussion indicating her love for Antonio and her intention of marrying him. It blends a sense of foreboding, as expressed in Livia's fears and warnings, with a touching impression of the Duchess's feelings for her steward. The long sequence in which the Duchess woos Antonio is full of poetry, witty dialogue, and *double entendre;* it also has a coquettish quality that demonstrates how well Lope understood the passion and playfulness of two people in love. The love theme takes a new turn when the secretary, Urbino, misunderstands what he sees and believes that Antonio is courting Livia, whom he himself loves. The scene between Antonio and the secretary in which Urbino demands to see the letter from the Duchess that Livia has just given to Antonio is full of wit and teasing suspense. Of course, such a scene can only realize its full theatrical potential on stage in front of a responsive audience. The love theme reappears in a pastoral subplot involving two old peasants and a youth who is in a hurry to marry his sweetheart. This subplot is stock Lopean comic relief and makes for good theater. At the same time it serves two other purposes: as parody of the main plot and as ingenious solution to a moral dilemma, inasmuch as the peasants' wedding enables the Duchess and Antonio to be married anonymously by the same priest, thus validating their union in the eyes of the Church. Lope plays with different moods and shades of darkness and light that leave the audience in doubt as to whether the outcome of the plot will be happy or tragic. The brisk, lively dialogue, interspersed with a series of asides that draw the audience into the play, suggests a strong counterpoint of nonverbal discourse: gesture, facial expression, and other stage business.

In Webster's *Duchess,* Antonio also delivers the opening lines, although he directs them to his friend Delio, rather than to the audience. Unlike Lope's steward, Antonio's comments are not concerned with love but rather with the disorder of the court. He has just returned from France, and his praise for the French king's judicious rule is clearly intended to convey Webster's own criticism of the court of James I. The whole of the first act (and, indeed, the greater part of the play) is set in the Duchess's palace, which represents a microcosm of the larger world beyond its gates—a microcosm transposed, moreover, to the prudently remote setting of sixteenth-century Italy. Webster also hints at the disorder latent or existent in the Duchess's own household (at least as perceived in her brother Ferdinand's fevered imagination) and creates an appropriately claustrophobic setting for the violent events that follow.[8] The note of foreboding sounded in Antonio's first speech is relentlessly developed throughout the first act. Whereas Lope does not bring on the villanous brother Julio until the last act of his play, Webster presents his main characters in rapid succession. Only when the brothers have left their sister's palace—after sternly forbidding her to remarry—does the hectic action slacken. The scene in which the Duchess proposes to Antonio and marries him forthwith in a clandestine ceremony is shorter and less complex than its counterpart in Lope's play. However, like its counterpart in *El mayordomo,* it is also marked with touching expressions of love and tenderness. Such, for example, is the Duchess's playful stratagem in pretending to use her wedding ring to cure Antonio's bloodshot eye in order to slip it on his finger. The poignancy of this scene is heightened by the threat of the brothers' revenge that hovers over the Duchess's court in the form of the spy Bosola.

Throughout the act it is the Duchess who dominates the action. Even when she is not actually on stage, her presence is felt since the attention of the other characters is constantly fixed on her. Indeed, she will continue to dominate the action even after her death in act 4. The characters who oppose her—her brothers and Bosola—are drawn so forcefully that the figure of Antonio is relegated to the periphery. Webster's Duchess is strongwilled and even

wilful, but these apparent flaws will become strengths when she
faces her death alone. The audience senses that the clash between
the Duchess and her brothers is inevitable from the outset and that
her marriage with Antonio merely hastens the outcome. Antonio,
by contrast, is a more passive partner than his Spanish counterpart
and little more than a bystander who is drawn into the tragedy,
albeit as a compliant victim. By the end of the first act the audience
may well have been in two minds as to whether to condemn the
Duchess for her imprudence or to sympathize with her. Webster
appears to share this ambivalence by having the waiting-woman
Cariola end the act with a significant aside to the audience:

> Whether the spirit of greatness or of woman
> Reign most in her, I know not, but it shows
> A fearful madness; I owe her much of pity.

$$(1.1.504-6)$$

As in Lope's play the staging of this act depends for the most part
on a rapid succession of exits and entrances. Action, however, is
secondary to the drawing of character and to the creation of mood
and tension. Most notable is the web of deceit into which all the
characters enter, whether knowingly or otherwise. Webster fills out
the dimensions of the characters by having each of them comment
on the other in his absence: Bosola and Antonio report on the
brothers; Delio and Antonio comment on Bosola; Ferdinand
praises Antonio and Antonio praises the Duchess.[9] As in *El mayordomo,* the text provides ample scope for stage business and nonverbal discourse, particularly in the scenes with Ferdinand and in the
wooing scene. By the end of the act the rhythm of the play is firmly
established and the audience drawn into the center of the intrigue.
Like Cariola, they will await the consequences of the Duchess's
wilful defiance of her brothers' wishes with trepidation.

The second set of segments chosen for comparison are the murders of the protagonists. In *El mayordomo,* both the Duchess and
Antonio die with their children in the final act of the play. In
Webster's play, however, the Duchess dies at the end of act 4,
whereas Antonio is killed in act 5, as part of a final orgy of revenge
and intrigue. Since act 4 represents the true climax of Webster's
play, the treatment of the last act of *The Duchess* falls outside the
scope of the present study, although for Webster it was essential to
the working out of the revenge motif.

The third and last act of *El mayordomo* follows the eventful
narrative of the Italian source closely at the outset: the lovers are

finally reunited and announce their marriage to the Duchess's followers, most of whom abandon her. The Duchess resolves to live
privately with her husband and children for the rest of her life. The
audience sees the fury of the jilted suitor, Otavio de Medicis, and of
the Duchess's brother Julio de Aragón, who appears on stage for
the first time. Here Lope departs from his source to show the
Duchess's son (who features only in name both in Bandello and in
Webster's play) stepping forward to play a decisive role in shaping
the dénouement: he forgives his mother because of her love for
Antonio and because she is legitimately married. At this point the
audience is entitled to expect a happy ending and the outcome is
left in suspense until the final moments. First Antonio flees from the
unrelenting Julio while the Duchess and the children are taken into
custody by her brother. Then Antonio learns of the son's forgiveness and comes to the young Amalfi's court for the expected
reconciliation. However, Julio de Aragón has his revenge, despite
the magnanimity of the young Duke and in defiance of the written
command of his own brother Ferdinand the Cardinal. He secretly
poisons the Duchess and then, before she dies, shows her the
severed heads of Antonio and their two children. Otavio goes mad[10]
and young Amalfi vows vengeance on his treacherous uncle.

The staging of this act is again based on movement and action. In
fact, there is only one purely theatrical effect in the entire play: the
"discovery" in the closing moments when the curtain is drawn back
to reveal a Senecan tableau: "Abranse dos puertas y véase una
mesa con tres platos: en el de en medio la cabeza de Antonio, y a
los dos lados las de los niños" ("Two doors are opened and a table
is seen with three platters; the middle one bears the head of Antonio and on either side lie those of the children"). Once again the
drama is conveyed by the words, the alternating moods, and the
increasing sense of tension as the conflicting forces of the drama
turn toward tragedy.

The Duchess's death scene in act 4 of Webster's play takes place
in a chamber in her own palace, which now serves as her prison.
When Bosola prepares the Duchess to receive her brother, he tells
her that Ferdinand refuses to look at her:

> . . . he comes 'i the night;
> And prays you, gently, neither torch nor taper
> Shine in your chamber
>
> (4.1.24–26)

The Duchess then bids Bosola remove the lights. Ferdinand
enters and gives her a dead man's hand to kiss. When she realizes

what it is, she takes it for Antonio's hand and calls out, "Hah! lights—O, horrible" (4.1.53). The scene would have been theatrically compelling in the Blackfriars, where performances took place in candlelight with a correspondingly more claustrophobic effect.[11] By contrast, Lope's play, performed in daylight, would have relied entirely on the power of words to evoke the various scenes that call for darkness and shadow, as indeed would have been the case in productions of the Webster play in the public theater in London.

There are other aspects of act 4 that seem particularly suited to the indoor setting. One is the staging of the direction that directly follows the incident with the hand: "Here is discovered, behind a traverse the artificial figures of Antonio and his children, appearing as if they were dead" (4.1.55). At this point the audience, like the Duchess herself, would not have known that Antonio was still alive; the mistaken belief that he and their children had already been murdered would, therefore, have increased the dramatic pathos of the scene and provided a moment of surprise, consternation, and ambivalent relief when Antonio reappears on stage at the beginning of act 5.[12]

The second scene in act 4 is also well suited to the indoor setting at the Blackfriars. In it, a chorus of madmen sing and dance "to a dismal kind of music" (4.2.61).[13] Critics suggest that the audience would have recognized this cruel mockery of the Duchess's wretched plight as an antimasque, in the tradition of Jacobean court entertainments. The masque itself follows when Bosola, disguised as an old man, leads on the Duchess's executioners "with coffin, cords and a bell" (4.2.166). Bosola's funereal dirge is also seen as a parody of a bridal epithalamium, a reminder to the audience watching the murders of the Duchess, her waiting maid, and her children, of the grim juxtaposition of life and death.[14]

*   *   *

While both Lope and Webster relied heavily on the Bandello source, their treatment of the original diverges in a number of ways—particularly in emphasis and mood.

Among the differences of emphasis is that placed on the Duchess's brothers. Although both playwrights follow Bandello in making them the instruments of revenge, in Lope's play their actual presence is not important until the last act when Julio finally comes on stage. For Webster, on the other hand, the characterization of both brothers is a major feature of the play, and, if Ferdinand dominates, the portrayal of the Cardinal is no less commanding. One reason for Lope's different emphasis was undoubtedly his unwillingness to portray a man of the Church (especially a cardinal) in an unfavorable light. Moreover, it is significant that Julio actually carries out his murderous scheme against the express wishes of his absent brother. Another significant change in *El mayordomo* is the young Duke's forgiveness of his mother and Antonio. This generous act increases the pathos of the ending, but also denies Julio his triumph. Although Julio is motivated by outrage at the dishonor to the House of Aragón and claims that he has acted in the interest of his nephew's own honor (3.1012), the audience knows that Amalfi had already put aside the baser thoughts of revenge when he chose to honor Antonio as his mother's husband. The Spanish understanding of the honor code is thus satisfied by young Amalfi's magnanimity while his vow of revenge against his uncle adjusts the balance of justice and makes it clear where Lope's own sympathies lie.[15]

Webster's play is not about honor in the Spanish sense; it is about revenge and the horror of lawless personal vendetta—which Francis Bacon called "a kind of wild justice" in the opening words of his essay "Of Revenge." In a recent study Wendy Griswold (1986) has suggested that Jacobean revenge tragedy represented a nightmarish inversion of contemporary concerns about order, justice, and the establishment of English Protestantism.

In this context, Antonio's opening allusions to the "corruption of the times" would have left the audience in no doubt that he was referring to contemporary England. Part of this concern took the form of an intense xenophobia toward Catholic countries, particularly Spain. Obviously the political events of the previous century had prepared the ground for this distrust. Despite the formal end of hostilities between the two countries in 1604, Protestant suspicions of Spain ran especially high during the first three decades of the new century, and James I's pro-Spanish attitude was widely resisted.

What John Loftis (1987, 217) refers to as "the systemic and long-continued denigration of Spain and the accomplishments of Spaniards known as the Black Legend" undoubtedly affected the Jacobean theater, where Spaniards and Italians were stereotyped as cunning, jealous, bloodthirsty, and untrustworthy. Webster's play with its Italian setting and villainous Spanish brothers is thus in tune with contemporary chauvinism and xenophobia. In seventeenth-century England the name of Aragón carried a special significance, not only because of its association with Henry VIII's unfortunate first wife Katharine, but also because of the widespread belief that another Ferdinand of Aragon was the model for Machiavelli's Prince.

It is not known how the Jacobean audience reacted to the Duchess's unquestionably imprudent conduct. William Painter, the translator and adaptor of Bandello's novella, made it clear in 1567 that he disapproved. Forty-three years later, in 1614, Webster leaves the question open. We know from contemporary accounts that the play moved the audience, and it is difficult to believe that by act 4 they were not sympathetic with the Duchess, even if they may not have approved entirely of her behavior in act 1. Moreover, the closing lines of the play—"Integrity of life is fame's best friend, / Which nobly, beyond death, shall crown the end"—serve as an epitaph for the unhappy lovers that surely reflects Webster's own sentiments as well as those of the greater part of his audience.[16]

It is even more difficult to speculate about the possible political concerns expressed in *El mayordomo*. Although social preferment and misalliance are common themes in seventeenth-century Spanish theater, critics disagree as to their significance as a reflection of real life. J. W. Sage (1973) points out that popular interest in these topics was also rooted in a longstanding fascination with love as a subversive and all-conquering force. At the same time, the events of Lope's own life are inextricably enmeshed in his plays. For many years he had served a series of noble masters including the Duque de Alba and the Marqués de Sarria as secretary and *gentilhombre*. At about the time that *El mayordomo* was first performed, he began his long and devoted attachment to the young Duque de Sessa. He also wrote a cluster of plays in which secretaries or gentlemen of the houschold feature prominently—most notably *El perro del hortelano (The Dog in the Manger)*, written in 1613(?) and published in 1618. It may be noted that his own love life included the painful experience of being supplanted by a rival of nobler birth. On the subject of love Lope was almost invariably a romantic and a subversive. For this reason and from the evidence of his other plays it seems likely that he wanted his audience to sympathize with the lovers. Indeed, in this play he even tips his hand when he has young Amalfi approve of his mother's marriage.

*   *   *

The points of comparison made between the two plays lead to three general conclusions:

1. The playhouses shared a number of common characteristics, even when comparison is made between a Spanish *corral* and a private theater, the Blackfriars. There were resemblances in the design and size of the stage, as well as in the size and, to some extent, the composition of the audience. However, the different disposition of the audience and the ambiance of the indoor theater

may have significantly affected the reception of *The Duchess* (and perhaps some of the features of its composition as well).

2. From the perspective of performance the plays diverge widely—not so much in what they borrow from Bandello as in how they present the material. In both cases the action moves with speed and suspense, but the mood created is very different: Lope's play balances the contrasting elements of tragedy and comedy, while Webster creates a tragedy that is almost obsessive in its doom-laden intensity.[17] This divergence may also owe a great deal to the influence of contemporary literary fashion: by choosing the tragicomic mode, Lope was deliberately flouting the neoclassical conventions of tragedy and establishing the pattern of his own distinctive approach to drama.[18] Likewise, Webster, in writing a revenge tragedy, follows the rules imposed by the genre while, at the same time, shaping the convention for his own moral and artistic purposes.[19]

As regards staging, neither play requires any particularly elaborate effects, except in the two death scenes that call for a tableau in the discovery space.[20] Although, for the reasons suggested earlier, Webster's play may have benefited incidentally from being played indoors, both plays use language as the principal means of conveying mood and emotion. While they differ in the type of language used, Webster's fluid use of blank verse and prose and Lope's supple polymetry admirably serve their respective theatrical purposes. It is an interesting comment on the inherent nature of the two languages that Cynthia Rodríguez-Badendyck's translation of *El mayordomo* is rendered in an English that resembles Webster's prosody. Perhaps a Spanish translation of *The Duchess* might best be attempted in Lopean octosyllables.

3. The largest and most elusive dimension of all was provided by the audience and the way in which their expectations influenced the reception of the performances and, to some degree, shaped each play in order to accommodate those expectations. I have suggested some of the concerns that may have influenced the public for whom Webster and Lope wrote their plays, but obviously there are many more that could be mentioned.

In the end, of course, we cannot expect to recapture all the factors that contribute to the creation of a given performance. As J. L. Styan (1975, 4) reminds us: "The spectator interprets and so contributes to and finally becomes the play, whose image is all and only in his mind." Such is the nature of theater that each performance is a unique experience for all concerned in the act of its creation. Nevertheless, the principal value of attempting to reconstruct the circumstances of the original performance lies in the appreciation it gives of the complexity of the dramatist's achievement. What is more, it makes us stand back from the text on the printed page and consider all the aspects of the theatrical event. A clearer understanding of how plays succeeded in their own time, help us to interpret them better, first as readers and then, by extension, as directors, performers, and spectators, in the collaborative exercise of recreating classical drama on the modern stage.

Notes

1. Less theoretical approaches include Ralph Berry (1985), Anne Righter (1962) and J. L. Styan (1975). Previous comparisons of the plays include two articles by John Loftis (1969; 1982). However, neither of these studies focuses on the perspective of performance.

2. Belleforest translated the *novella* into French in an expanded version that appeared in the second volume of his *Histoires Tragiques* (1565). It was this version that William Painter used for his translation into English, published in 1567 in *The Palace of Pleasure;* this, in turn, was the source for Webster's play (Brown 1964, xxvi). As for Lope, it is thought that he read the story either in the original Italian version, or the Spanish translation of 1589 (Kohler n.d.). For the titles of other plays by Lope that are based on stories by Bandello, see Kohler, 134–35.

3. *The Oxford Companion to English Literature* (1985, 1053) suggests 1578 as a possible birth date.

4. Webster also notes in his introduction "To the Reader" of *The White Devil* that "it was acted in so dull a time of winter" and goes on to comment that "since that time I have noted, most of the people who come to that playhouse [i.e., The Red Bull] resemble those ignorant asses who visiting stationers' shops, their use is not to inquire for good books, but new books."

5. Although, as a general rule, the *corral de comedias* was unroofed, in Seville there is evidence that *corrales* were built that were covered (Sentaurens 1984, 308;327).

6. Webster's contemporary, Thomas Middleton, attested to the ability of the boy playing the part of the Duchess to move the audience. In the commendatory verses that prefaced the first published edition of the play, he wrote:

> Thy epitaph only the title be—
> Write "Duchess," that will fetch a tear for thee,
> For who e'er saw this duchess live, and die,
> That could get off under a bleeding eye?

For a cogent description of acting styles on the Elizabethan and Jacobean stages, see Bertram Joseph (1973).

7. *El mayordomo* has a total of 3292 lines, divided into three acts. *The Duchess* totals 2821 lines, divided into five acts.

8. See, for example, Ferdinand's warning to his sister in act 1: "You live in a rank pasture here, i'th' court—" (1.1.306). All references to Webster's play are to *The Duchess of Malfi,* edited by John Russell Brown (London: Methuen, 1964).

9. One may note the recurrent allusions to hypocrisy, cunning, and dissem-

bling in act 1. For example, the Cardinal and Ferdinand are both characterized as dissemblers (1.1.156–72); Antonio comments on Bosola's "foul melancholy [which] Will poison all his goodness" (1.1.76–77), and Ferdinand warns his sister against cunning and hypocrisy (1.1.305–16).

10. The direction in Spanish reads "Váyase furioso Otavio", an echo, perhaps, of Ariosto's influential epic, *Orlando Furioso,* which is about a man who is driven mad by love. All references to Lope's play are to *Obras de Lope de Vega,* 32 (Madrid: Biblioteca de Autores Españoles, 1972).

11. At the same time, critics have noted that it would not have been practicable to act out the episode in a light that was too subdued, since the audience would not have been able to see what was going on. See, for example, Lois Potter (1975). The question also arises as to how the staging of these scenes differed from the rest of the play, which calls for daylight. This may have been effected by a corresponding increase or decrease in the number of candles used on stage, although Gurr (1980, 170) doubts that any actual distinction in lighting was made. R. B. Graves believes that darkness was simply indicated by the carrying of tapers (to denote indoor scenes) and lanterns or torches (to denote outdoor settings), but that these were symbolic props and not necessarily illuminated (quoted in Dessen [1984, 75–76).

12. The question arises as to why the directions call for "artificial figures" when the actors portraying the figures in life could also have been used to portray them in death (this is presumably the case in Lope's play, which calls for the heads of the murdered steward and his children to be displayed). Did Webster's audience take the wax figures for the actors themselves, feigning death? It is more likely that the choice of wax figures was intended as a variation on the Elizabethan theatrical tradition of the dumb show, which Webster uses elsewhere in this play and also in *The White Devil.* It may also be seen as a parody of the court masque and, as such, part of the overall design of the act. See M.C. Bradbrook (1980, 142–48) and Ralph Berry (1985, 108).

13. Gurr (1980, 170) notes that the Blackfriars was well known for its consort of musicians, who were probably seated in the gallery.

14. Ralph Berry (1985, 108) suggests that the audience would also have seen it as an implicit challenge to the system of values associated with the Court masque.

15. Diego Muxet de Solis later wrote a sequel with the title *La venganza de la Duquesa de Amalfi,* in which the Duke's threat is carried out. The play was published in Brussels in 1624.

16. Modern critics are divided in their opinions on this point, see J. R. Brown (1964, xlvii–1).

17. Nevertheless, it is arguable that Webster does indulge in black humor, particularly in act 5: see Lois Potter (1975) and Jacqueline Pearson (1980, 53–70).

18. The *Arte nuevo de hacer comedias,* in which he specifically advocates mixing the two styles, would be published several years later in 1609.

19. For an assessment of Webster's place among the writers of revenge tragedy, see Bowers (1940, 177–80). A wide range of critical assessments of Webster's artistic achievement is found in Webster *"The White Devil" and "The Duchess of Malfi"* (1975).

20. The similarity of this requirement has led some critics to speculate that Webster knew Lope's play; a more likely explanation is that both were influenced by Seneca. It is also thought that Lope may have been influenced by another Italian tragedy, Giovanni Battista Giraldi's *Orbecche.* See Antonio Gasparetti (1930).

Works Cited

Allen, J. J. 1983. *The Reconstruction of a Spanish Golden Age Playhouse: El Corral del Príncipe, 1583–1744.* Gainesville: University Presses of Florida.

Berry, Ralph. 1985. *Shakespeare and the Awareness of the Audience.* New York: St. Martin's Press.

Bowers, Fredson. 1940. *Elizabethan Revenge Tragedy.* Princeton: Princeton University Press.

Bradbrook, M. C. 1980. *John Webster: Citizen and Dramatist.* London: Weidenfeld and Nicolson.

Dessen, Alan C. 1985. *Elizabethan Stage Conventions and Modern Interpreters.* Cambridge: Cambridge University Press.

Díez Borque, J. M. 1976. *Sociología de la comedia española del siglo XVII.* Madrid: Cátedra.

Elam, Keir. 1980. *The Semiotics of Theatre and Drama.* London and New York: Methuen.

Gasparetti, Antonio. 1930. "Giovanni Battista Giraldi e Lope de Vega." *Bulletin Hispanique* 32:392–403.

Griswold, Wendy. 1986. *Renaissance Revivals: City Comedy and Revenge Tragedy in the London Theatre, 1576–1980.* Chicago and London: Chicago University Press.

Gurr, Andrew. 1985. *The Shakespearean Stage, 1574–1642.* 2nd ed. Cambridge: Cambridge University Press.

Hosley, Richards. 1970. "A Reconstruction of the Second Blackfriars." In *The Elizabethan Theatre,* edited by David Galloway, 74–88. Oshawa, Ontario: Archon Books.

Jauss, Hans Robert. 1982. *Towards an Aesthetics of Reception.* Minneapolis: University of Minnesota Press.

Joseph, Bertram. 1973. "The Elizabethan Stage and Acting." In *The Age of Shakespeare,* edited by Boris Ford, 147–61. Harmondsworth, England: Penguin.

Kohler, Eugene. N.d. "Lope et Bandello." In *Hommage à Ernest Martinenche.* Paris: Editions d'Artrey.

Loftis, John. 1969. "The Duchess of Malfi on the Spanish and English Stages." In *Research Opportunities in Renaissance Drama XII* (1969), edited by S. Schoenbaum, 25–31. Evanston: Northwestern University Press.

———. 1982. "Lope de Vega's and Webster's Amalfi Plays." *Comparative Drama* 16:64–78.

———. 1987. *Renaissance Drama in England and Spain.* Princeton: Princeton University Press.

Morley, S. G. and C. Bruerton. 1960. *The Chronology of Lope de Vega's Comedias.* New York: The Modern Language Association of America.

Pavis, Patrice. 1982. *Languages of the Stage: Essays in the Semiology of the Theatre.* New York: Performing Arts Journal Publications.

Pearson, Jacqueline. 1980. *Tragedy and Tragicomedy in the Plays of John Webster.* Totowa N.Y.: Barnes and Noble.

Potter, Lois. 1975. "Realism versus nightmare: Problems of Staging *The Duchess of Malfi.*" In *The Triple Bond,* edited by Joseph Price, 186–87. University Park: Penn State University Press.

The Oxford Companion to English Literature. 1985. Edited by Margaret Drabble. Oxford: Oxford University Press.

Righter, Anne. 1962. *Shakespeare and the Idea of the Play.* London: Chatto & Windus.

Rennert, Hugo A. 1909. *The Spanish Stage in the Time of Lope de Vega.* New York: The Hispanic Society of America.

Sage, J. W. 1973. "The Context of Comedy: Lope de Vega's *El perro del hortelano* and Related Plays." In *Studies in Spanish Literature of the Golden Age Presented to Edward M. Wilson,* edited by R. O. Jones, 63–72. London: Tamesis Books.

Sentaurens, Jean. 1984. *Séville et le théâtre.* 2 vols. Bordeaux: Presses Universitaires de Bordeaux.

Styan, J. L. 1975. *Drama, Stage and Audience.* Cambridge: Cambridge University Press.

Vega Carpio, Lope F. de. 1972. *Obras.* Madrid: Biblioteca de Autores *Españoles* 240.

———. 1985. *The Duchess of Amalfi's Steward.* Translated by C. Rodríguez-Badendyck. Ottawa: Dovehouse Editions.

Webster, John. 1964. *The Duchess of Malfi.* Edited by John Russell Brown. London: Methuen.

———. 1975. *The White Devil and The Duchess of Malfi.* Edited by R. V. Holdsworth. London: Macmillan.

The Neglected Alternative:
Shakespeare's *Romeo and Juliet* and
Lope de Vega's *Castelvines y Monteses*

Cynthia Rodriguez-Badendyck

When we approach Lope de Vega's *Castelvines y Monteses* for the first time, knowing that it shares sources with *Romeo and Juliet,* we are likely to anticipate little more than another opportunity to point up Shakespeare's genius.[1] It is a truth universally acknowledged, furthermore, that, when the Restoration gave Shakespeare's play a happy ending, the action was trivialized; and, of course, the most striking change Lope made in the story was just that—to give it a happy ending. We assume Lope's play will be trivial. It is difficult not to assume that.

But if one peruses the Spanish play carefully, something unexpected begins to happen. *Castelvines y Monteses* reveals itself as rather a good play, in fact as an exceedingly good play. Now, contemporary approaches to text do not talk about good plays and bad plays, of course. But questions of hegemony aside for the moment—and they are formidable questions—the extremely disparate reputations of these two plays are based upon just such assumptions. And what is interesting about *Castelvines y Monteses* is not that an entirely new approach will reveal what was invisible before, but that traditional approaches could have rescued it from its undeserved neglect any time these three hundred and some odd years, and that Lope's play points up not the strengths, but the weaknesses in *Romeo and Juliet,* those familiar, oft-rehearsed weaknesses that up until recently have been conceded early in the introductions to most standard editions: The story is pathetic rather than tragic. The causes of the catastrophe are uncertain or unconvincing. The character of Romeo is less than admirable. Much of the dialogue can seem artificial and inappropriate.[2] That is to say, *Castelvines y Monteses* reveals itself over and over again to be deliberate, resonant, and masterly in just those areas where *Romeo and Juliet* has been perceived to be unsatisfactory.

What about the question of genre, for example? That is, what about that ending? Does a happy ending really violate some inevitable logic in the story? When we come to consider it, it is not only the play's early revisers who have quibbled with the tragic ending of *Romeo and Juliet*.[3] Perfectly reputable scholars of the twentieth century have questioned whether that ending is really justified. The most notable is H. B. Charlton, who explains the central weakness of the play by calling it "an experimental tragedy." In writing it, says Professor Charlton, Shakespeare is attempting for the first time to follow the innovative theories of the Italian Cinthio, using a tale from modern fiction to address a modern audience. The great theme of "modern" fiction, of course, is love. And so Shakespeare chooses a simple tale of young love thwarted and attempts to give it pith and moment by emphasizing the portentous operations of fate and an implacable feud, which together bring about the destruction of these "ravishingly attractive young folk" through no significant fault of their own.

What the playwright discovers is that the new formula does not work, or at least that he cannot make it work. The forces that destroy the lovers—fate and the feud—are not convincing. And even if they were, the destruction of innocents would still not qualify as an edifying spectacle. *Romeo and Juliet,* concludes Professor Charlton, "is indeed rich in spells of its own. But as a pattern of the idea of tragedy, it is a failure. Even Shakespeare seems to have felt that, as an experiment, it had disappointed him" (*Twentieth Century Interpretations* 1970, 59).

Other critics have gone even further, developing Professor Charlton's perception that the play is not only inadequately tragic, but in some respects is actually comic. Young lovers of the minor aristocracy and irascible old parents who forbid their marriage are the traditional stuff of comedy from classical times well past the Renaissance. And indeed no harm is done in the first confrontation of the play, which features buffoonery from the servants and impotent spluttering from the overheated old men. That young love will heal this foolish enmity is a reasonable expectation. The world, furthermore, is at first a world of choice and accommodation, not tragic inevitability. Romeo changes his undying love for Rosaline to undying love for Juliet with the agility of Proteus, Demetrius, Phoebe, and Olivia, the pliant lovers of comedy. Tybalt is overruled by the laws of feasting, and neither vengeance nor anything but love seems at first very urgent. The characters of the Nurse and Friar Laurence, those pragmatic and indulgent facilitators, are characters from a comic vision of the world in which there is always a way out of a scrape.[4]

"*Romeo and Juliet* is in essence a comedy that turns out tragically," writes John Wain succinctly. And again: "Its gaiety and good fortune are drained away by the fact—also a donnée—that the lovers are 'star-crossed.' It is, to that extent, arbitrarily shaped" (*Twentieth Century Interpretations* 1970, 104).

When we turn to *Castelvines y Monteses,* we realize with some interest that Lope's radical decision to change the outcome of the story is not the result of a mere lightweight preference for the upbeat. By choosing a comedic ending, Lope avoids many of the inconsistencies that plague Shakespeare's "experiment" and is in the long run able to achieve much greater coherence and plausibility in his play.

Moreover, if we have assumed that Lope's choice of a comedic ending must inevitably entail the sacrifice of seriousness, we must check ourselves again and remember that some of our most important theorists of genre—Northrop Frye (1976, 1986), for example, and more recently Harry Levin (1987)—have argued for the dignity and importance of the comedic vision and for its particular relevance to a Christian culture.[5] Indeed, one may argue further that Christian comedy appropriates to itself the authority of pagan tragedy, because the redemptive ending is part of a central philosophic metaphor, a paradigm of Christ's promise that human history itself has been made comedic. The ending that ends all endings shall be a wedding feast, and the final season shall be springtime. For Lope as the most viscerally Catholic of all playwrights, the comedy of divine forgiveness embraces tragedy, which is merely the agon, and not the epiphany, hence the distinctive Lopean form of his play: *tragicomedia*. Lope did not need nor, I believe, intend to make his play in any specific way a religious allegory, but there is a recurring allegorical dimension to it. And the moral vision that makes sense of his story is inevitably both deeply Catholic and deeply Spanish. More importantly, it is a whole, integrated vision in which all the parts serve a central purpose. That this vision does make sense of the story in a way that Shakespeare's divided, quasi-pagan vision could not, it will be the intention of this paper to make plain.

To begin with, Shakespeare's play seems to have difficulty in deciding what is the real cause of the lovers' doom. Is it the feud? Is it fate? Is it rashness? But why is the feud such an obstacle to

Romeo's romance with Juliet? It has been no obstacle at all to his romance with her cousin Rosaline. Moreover, Capulet himself so downplays the enmity that he refuses to allow Romeo to be frowned at in his house: "All ill-beseeming semblance for a feast" (1.5.67).

"A feud like this," as Professor Charlton puts it, "will not serve as the bribe it was meant to be; it is no atonement for the death of the lovers" (*Twentieth Century Interpretations* 1970, 58).

Is the problem fate, then? Or defects in the characters of the lovers? "The doctrines of individual responsibility and of fate as a social Nemesis offer divergent motivations," points out Professor Stauffer; "this play may fail as serious tragedy because Shakespeare blurs the focus and never makes up his mind as to who is being punished, and for what reason" (ibid. 55–56).

As Frank Kermode sums it up in the very first paragraph of his introduction to *The Riverside Shakespeare* (1974, 1055), "A certain unease about the dramatist's intention, some suspicion that, in the early moments of the play at any rate, he lacks the rhetorical control which marks his great period, and—above all—a conviction that he offends against his own criteria for tragedy by allowing mere chance to determine the destiny of the hero and heroine—all these have conspired to limit the critical prestige of *Romeo and Juliet*."

Lope's neglected little cape-and-sword, on the other hand, presents no such confusion. The playwright guides us with a steady hand. Explicitly and consistently, the central conflict is between young love and the family feud. Young love wins and heals the enmity. Were this all, of course, the play might be a bit of pleasant fluff, better success at a much smaller endeavor. But Lope does in fact go for something deeper. He examines *why* this love is the unique vehicle for this redemption, how it is that this love and this feud come to be locked together in a life-and-death struggle for the loyalties of these characters. He sets forth the pernicious way in which the feud falsely defines the nature of family for the Castelvines and Monteses, and with a concentrated, careful progression of illustration shows us how this false definition devours the young, becoming progressively more incestuous until in the end it almost destroys the family identity it purported to assert. Behind the sure and steady unmasking of this false idea of family is always implicit the family as a deeply held Spanish value and the silent presence of the Church, with all its family images and terminology—the Holy Family, Holy Mother Church, the Blessed Mother, and Father and the Son, Madonna and Child, bride of Christ, father (a priest), brother (a monk), sister (a nun)—all declaring an ideal of the family as a sacramental bond defined not by formalized antagonism that seals off the center, but by love and commitment that radiate from the center outward, ultimately embracing all who are willing to enter.

It is not necessary to share Lope's theology—any more than it is necessary to share that of Homer, Sophocles, or Dante—to appreciate the aesthetic strength that such a highly refined, culturally grounded system can provide for a work of art. It is, however, necessary—as with Homer, Sophocles, or Dante—to be able to respond positively to something essential in the human values of the system. As a deeply held commitment to feminism may hopelessly disgust one's palate for *Paradise Lost* or a fierce moral objection to *Liebestod* may raise one's gorge against *Tristan und Isolde* (or *Romeo and Juliet,* for that matter), so an extreme position on individualism must hopelessly alienate a reader or playgoer from Lope, for whom individualism is only half a human identity— and love the other half. To this ideal, moral awareness and free will are essential.

But in Shakespeare's play, free will is scarcely an issue. Passion, not reason, governs conduct. One tends to think of *Romeo and Juliet* as an "immature" work. It is often referred to as such, although Shakespeare was over thirty when he wrote it. And what gives this impression is in part the failure of promising parts to cohere into an integral and convincing whole. But it is also in part the extreme immaturity of the protagonists, who, even for young teenagers, are extraordinarily lacking in awareness or self-governance. The lovers struggle *against* various obstacles, real or perceived, but not *with* moral choices. Indeed, although young lovers in Renaissance drama are commonly two-dimensional, critical introspection rarely being their strong suit, Shakespeare's Romeo is almost bizarre in his failure to consider either the causes or the consequences of his actions.

When Romeo first acquiesces to Benvolio's suggestion that he attend the Capulet ball, and then later when they join Mercutio and the other merrymakers, the possibility that Romeo might be attacked by anything more hostile than fair eyes is simply not brought up. Mercutio says, "Oh then, I see Queen Mab hath been with you," and Romeo fears "some consequence, yet hanging in the stars," but no one so much as alludes to a nasty concrete contingency. However one may deplore that none of Lope's young gallants says, "Oh then, I see Queen Mab hath been with you," one must find it still enormously refreshing that they do say alert and appropriate things like:

Pero el peligro es notable,
Porque del bando Montés
Tu padre cabeza es.
Y aún no sufre que se hable
Deste gente en su presencia
Cuanto más verla en su casa.[6]

(1.1.1)

[But the danger is considerable. Your father is head of the Montés faction. And Castelvín will not even suffer these people to be mentioned in his presence, much less countenance them in his house.]

The difference is not simply that Romeo and his fellows live in a world more surcharged with tragic significance, but rather that the obsession with tragic significance often causes them—all of them, but especially Romeo—to be particularly and maddeningly not-at-home on the literal level.

When at the sight of Juliet Romeo instantly forgets Rosaline, the woman for whom he has been risking "some consequence" (what the less poetic might call death), he never gives Rosaline another thought nor examines his own change of heart. "I have forgot that name and that name's woe," is all he has to say (2.2.46).

When he is informed of his banishment from Verona, he throws himself upon the ground and flails about hysterically, offering to remove surgically that part of his anatomy in which his name resides (3.3.105–8). Although this is a fairly safe offer—since the part cannot be ascertained—his infantile performance in a crisis disgusts not only Friar Laurence and the Nurse, but numerous critics as well.[7] And if one accepts the stage direction in which the Nurse disarms him, Romeo becomes even more clearly a baby in a tantrum, and the comic potential of the story surfaces irresistibly once more, as if Shakespeare himself could not resist sending up this material, however determined he was to bring it off as a tragedy in the end.

Hearing that Juliet is dead, Romeo bribes a starving apothecary to sell him poison (he never does bring himself to draw his own blood)—an illegal sale for which, since Romeo makes no attempt to protect him by secrecy, the wretched man may well be executed. At Juliet's grave he desperately slaughters County Paris, surely an innocent man. For none of this does Romeo take any real responsibility. He scarcely commits an action in the entire play that is not suggested by passion or someone else. Indeed, he is so singularly without cognitive initiative that his being directed by passion *rather* than by someone else (the conventional love poets, Benvolio,

Juliet, Friar Laurence) strikes some critics as an important symp-tom of maturation. Relatively, perhaps, it is, but Romeo never adds up to a man.

In striking contrast, the characters in *Castelvines y Monteses* are held fully accountable for their actions. The extravagant body count that Shakespeare felt he needed to sell a serious play at this stage in his career is not apparent in Lope's play, but not *because* Lope's play will be a comedy, quite the contrary—it is the value Lope's characters place on human life which makes his comedy possible. More than once—but not invariably—a character will stop himself on the brink of violence, when we least expect him to. In this way the thickness of real experience is assimilated into a Christian vision. When people in a crisis make choices, they seem suddenly to leap out of flatness into recognizable humanity. They are no longer walking humors or embodied passions, they are conscious people.

Unlike Shakespeare's Romeo, Lope's Roselo Montés grows stronger in our regard with every difficulty he encounters. Viewers watch him grow in the course of the play from a likable scapegrace into a man that others may turn to and respect, a man worthy to be the head of a house. He earns his family, as it were, because his passionate feeling for Julia is not *merely* passion: it is love. Passion isolates; love binds. Thus the sexual dimension of his feeling is life-giving on the spiritual as well as the physical level, and the arousal and consummation of physical love seem to liberate courage, gener-osity, strength, speed, and clarity of mind in him. Indeed, the pure, joyous, physical exhilaration of his liberated energy floods the play, brings hope to the weary old men, and touches hands with an audience.

Roselo's first foray with his friends into enemy territory is an act of youthful daring, the kind of escapade that is causing his father to want to see him married off and restrained. And at the ball, sur-rounded by Castelvines, he drops his mask in awe at Julia's beauty, to the horror of his comrade Anselmo. The error having been made, however, he conducts himself with what that noted Hispanophile Ernest Hemingway has called "grace under pressure," never losing his nerve under hostile scrutiny. His courage is as exciting to watch as his courtship, because he is aware he is in danger in a way that Shakespeare's Romeo never seems to be. Yet at this stage his courage is still something very close to boyish cheek, or at least to a simple physical courage.

However, when the feud breaks out into open aggression in the second act and the two families square off in the street, Roselo faces a much more complex challenge, requiring courage of a much more complex sort. On one side are his father, his best friend Anselmo, and all the men of his house. On the other are all the men of his bride's family. Lope has made Roselo's bond to Julia's family much clearer to us than Shakespeare has made Romeo's relationship to Tybalt. Tybalt is, after all, only a cousin by marriage, related to Juliet's mother, and not a true Capulet at all, and we have never seen him treated with much respect or affection by anyone in the family he is so warm to defend. In contrast, Lope has actually shown us Antonio, Teobaldo, and Otavio Castelvín in situations of familial intimacy and trust, their strengths and their weaknesses exposed to one another and accepted. We can understand how one might feel loyalty to these people. At the same time, from what we know of Roselo, we can readily imagine how he could be assimilated into a family of this sort. Yet there they are, swords drawn, blood hot, arrayed against him and the people he has loved all his life.

But again, Roselo keeps his nerve and his wits. He places himself physically between the warring factions and pleads for peace, so shrewdly and with such good will, that he actually wins over both the old Castelvines—everyone, in fact, except the jealous Otavio, who indignantly rejects Roselo's suggestion that marriages should heal the old enmity between their houses. One of the marriages, of course, would be between Roselo and Julia, and Otavio will have none of it. When Otavio offers to kill him whether he defends himself or not, Roselo turns to both sides to witness that he has been provoked beyond endurance, and then, in self defense, kills Otavio. In the uproar that follows, Roselo's first thought is to get his father away. This is the madcap boy that Arnaldo Montés worried over in act 1. The moment is quick, uncloying, and deft: a moment for every old man in the audience to say to himself that he would not be ashamed to have a son like that.

At the same time, it is Roselo's secret bond to the hostile family, his seeming betrayal of loyalty, that has brought out the best in him. Not only has it prompted him to act decisively and courageously, to the credit of his family, but it has also pointed him toward a reconciliation that is in the best interest of his family. It has made him not a worse Montés, but a better one. Thus clearly, cleanly, Lope makes his case, without a tedious word preached, without an elbow of palpable design obtruding upon our pleasure. And yet there is not a moment in the play that does not serve the wholeness of its moral vision.

That Lope's Julia is more resourceful and strong-willed than

Shakespeare's Juliet, for example, does more than recapitulate the clever wench of comedy. It shows us something about the family that raises such a daughter. Here is Juliet with her father:

> CAPULET. How, how, how, how, chopp'd logic! What is this?
> "Proud," and "I thank you," and "I thank you not."
> And "not proud," mistress minion you?
> Thank me no thankings, nor proud me no prouds,
> But fettle your fine joints 'gainst Thursday next
> To go with Paris to Saint Peter's Church
> Or I will drag you on a hurdle thither.
> Out, you green-sickness carrion! Out, you baggage!
> You tallow-face!
>
> . . . .
>
> JULIET. Good father, I beseech you on my knees,
> Hear me with patience but to speak a word.[8]
>
> (3.5.149–57; 158–59)

Here is Lope's Julia with *her* father.

> ANTONIO. Quitaréte yo la vida.
> JULIA. ¡Ojalá que la quitases!
>
> (3.1.p5)

One trembles to imagine the response had young Juliet Capulet dared to reply to her father's offer to kill her with this terse, "I wish you would." Lope's Julia proceeds in this scene to give her father a perfectly plausible—albeit equivocal—reason that she cannot marry Paris: because he has failed to avenge the murder of her cousin and kill Roselo. Antonio is momentarily discomfited, not only, it appears, by her argument, but also by the strength of her feeling. In other words, he is actually listening to his daughter. Say what we will about the relative restrictions of women in English and Spanish societies, the Spanish heroine here is not only less restricted than her English counterpart, but considerably less despised. What is missing from Shakespeare's view of the sequestered Mediterranean daughter is the complexity and seductiveness of the governing idea to which both parent and child consent. The daughter is not chattel in this view; she is treasure. She is not condescended to, she is doted on; not imprisoned, but lovingly guarded. Simple-minded Old Capulet, snapping back and forth between sentimental indulgence and brute oppression, is incapable of the tensions that Antonio Castelvín's exchanges with his daughter express. When Antonio finally overcomes her resistance, it is not because he has simply bullied down an adversary, as Capulet characteristically does. "Que es fuerte la palabra," he pleads, and to this she can return no argument. It never occurs to her to suggest that her father break his word. But, as she well knows, his brief anger is more thunder than lightning; she respects him, but she never cringes before him. And he now expresses real regret that he is forced by the circumstances into making her unhappy. "Si tu voluntad supiera / Jamás al Conde llamara" ("If I had known how you felt, I would never have summoned the Count").

When he finally requires her assent, he does not require it in the form of submission, but in the form of reconciliation:

> Hija, no estés de esta suerte,
> Ni seas cruel conmigo:
> Que no soy tu enemigo,
> Ni el que a Otavio he dado muerte.
> Mira que salir no puedo
> De mi promesa, y que soy
> Hombre principal.
>
> (Ibid.)

[Daughter, do not be this way, nor be cruel with me. I am not your enemy, nor he who slew Otavio. Only see, I cannot go back on my promise, and I am a prominent man.]

The poignancy of Antonio Castelvín's recognition that he is himself constrained, by his word and by his position as "hombre principal," makes us realize yet again that more than one generation is vulnerable to tragedy in this story. Moreover, his recognition that Roselo is morally innocent of the death of Otavio gives his character a dimension of justice that makes us wish him to be spared—as in the end Lope does spare him.

If *Romeo and Juliet* seems "immature" in its inconsistency, in the questionable sentimentality of its vision, and likewise in the extreme immaturity of its protagonists, *Castelvines y Monteses* must appear by comparison extremely mature. The vision is unified and sustained, the sequence dynamic and purposeful, the protagonists aware and responsible. At the center of the play are not just the young and frisky, but the old men, too, particularly the brothers Castelvín. In comedy we expect the old to be scapegoats. But that is not what happens in this *tragicomedia*, because the life/ love force of the young is not ultimately an anarchic principle or a principle of overthrow. On the contrary, love is meant to be the primary instrument of the moral order. And a man's love for the child his sexuality has produced—even for the man whom his child's sexuality has selected, the man whose virility is an extension of rather than challenge to his own—is the linchpin of this order. The old men are saved from tragedy, not in spite of themselves, but *because* of some essential goodness in them, some willingness to admit error, some deep inclination to be loving, that only sometimes fails them. The brothers Castelvín are as essential to the meaning of the story as the ostensible hero and heroine; the love between parent and child, between brother and brother, is as essential as the love between man and woman. If *any* of these love bonds fails, a tragic action will occur.

When Roselo and his friends first crash the Castelvín ball, Roselo is recognized by Antonio Castelvín himself. No spluttering pantaloon, Antonio is the powerful leader of his clan, and there is no one to overrule him in his own house as Tybalt is overruled in Shakespeare's play. The moment is a dangerous one. But, by the most ingenious of ironies, the man who intervenes now is the man who will become the tragic center of the play, Antonio's brother Teobaldo. Simply and reasonably he chides his brother for his passion and reverses all the incendiary terms. Roselo's coming is not an insult to the house, but an honor. Antonio's murderous intent is not honorable, but cowardly.

> Pues yo no os pienso ayudar
> A hacer tan cobarde muerte.
> Este, como simple azor,
> Se ha entrado en el palomar
> A ver si puede cazar
> Algunas aves de amor.
>
> (1.4.p2)

[I have no mind to help you commit so cowardly a murder. This boy, like a simple sparrowhawk, has come into the dovecote to see if he can catch some lovebirds.]

The noble Teobaldo succeeds in calming his brother—his brother consents to be calmed—and Roselo is spared. Thus Teobaldo sets forth at the outset of the play the redemptive vision that must, if anything will, save them all from their own folly.

Lope has tightly knit together the idea of the feud and the idea of the family, so that the feud is not merely an excuse for the personal belligerence of certain servants and hotheads as it is in Shakespeare, but a device three old men have mistakenly used to circumscribe their loyalties and those of their children. That the

Castelvines are also loyal to one another in the best sense, and the Monteses to one another likewise, Lope makes clear. Parents and children treat one another with a respect that is the formal surface of profound love. When Teobaldo stands up for his old enemy's son, therefore, he is not stepping out of character, but only extending what he has hitherto reserved for his own. And it is this single act of Christian charity that will in the end prove to be the salvation of his house. The climax of his argument is his refusal to aid his brother in a dishonorable act. To be loyal to his brother's folly is to be disloyal to his brother in deepest consequence. "Si tenéis hija aquí," he adds in postscript, "yo también" ("If you have a daughter here, so do I"). That is, both old men know exactly what they are risking when they let young Monteses into their dovecote.

In the central act of the play, then, the tragedy is the more painful and monitory because it is Teobaldo himself who, forgetting his own counsel, calls up the feud again. And behind the enactment of the central moral choices stands—physically—the Church. The action takes place in the street outside a church, and the characters go in and out as the scene proceeds. Now a church was certainly no unusual element in a Spanish play. Scenes were often set in and before churches. Religious plays might even be performed in and before churches. What is noteworthy here is how seamless and delicate Lope's artistry is in complecting the literal and the symbolic levels of the action—the visual, verbal, and dramatic levels of the argument—while maintaining the simplest level perfect and undistorted. Yet, performed, as it were, on the doorstep of the church like an old Morality, the action begins almost magically to extend into an allegorical dimension. Either consciously or subliminally, Lope's audience would have understood that a higher definition of family was present, witnessing each human choice; that figuratively if not literally the image of Christ with arms outstretched stood silently in judgement of the scene enacted on the human stage; that each action of the mortal houses of Castelvín and Montés was spread against and measured by the eternal values of the House of God. Thus, each natural consequence seems not merely poetic justice, but part of a wordless divine dialogue between the Almighty Father and the protagonists.

Teobaldo becomes embroiled in a silly squabble that his daughter brings him over places in church. A servant of the house of Montés has placed *their* dais where *our* dais should be. A typical and perfectly ordinary sort of squabble on the literal level, it smacks of the irrational fury that can be aroused when someone steals your parking space or cuts ahead of you in line. But on the allegorical level it is a perfect symbol of the folly of the feud. It is not the petty vanities of the houses of Castelvín and Montés that will govern place and precedence in the House of God, nor have the mortal fathers of these earthly families the authority to divide the children whom a greater Father claims, all, as his own. But the squabble escalates. Teobaldo upbraids his son Otavio for mooning over his cousin Julia and not being there to defend his sister. Teobaldo and Otavio stride into the church, and by the time they burst out again into the street, they are in the midst of a verbal brawl, both families collected, swords drawn.

It is at this point that Roselo, married to his enemy's daughter, struggles to make peace and almost succeeds. But Otavio's pride is smarting from his father's rebuke. Over and above his jealousy over Julia, he has been pushed to prove himself and will not be appeased. He provokes Roselo and is killed by him. In an agony of grief and remorse, Teobaldo realizes what he has done: "¡Que yo soy la causa desto!" ("I am the cause of this") (2.8.p10). Lest we think of *Castelvines y Monteses* as light, or easy in its solutions, we must remember that this moment is at the center of the play, the father causing the death of his only son by prompting the boy's own weakness.

And it is this tragedy at the center that ennobles and makes sense of the ending's redemptive character. It shows us what it is that the houses of Castelvín and Montés are being saved *from*. By the time the Capulets and the Montagues are reconciled at the end of *Romeo and Juliet,* after all, the two families are effectively extinct; nothing lives on but two graven images and a pathetic story. But, in Lope's vision, if salvation is to have any meaning a house must be saved, not merely from physical extinction, but from extinction as a moral entity; that is, not merely the "body" of the family is at stake, but its "soul" as well.

Therefore, Lope has placed the death of Otavio at the center of a play sparkling with beautiful, irreverent, much-loved and much-loving young people. He has folded the tragic within the comedic as mortality is folded within the eternal. For it is not merely the *mixing* of comic and tragic elements, but the *relationship* of those elements that can give the *tragicomedia* its singular tenderness and moral resonance.

After the killing of Otavio, Roselo, like Romeo, is banished. And Julia must agree to marry Paris. But when she takes the sleeping potion sent to her by the friar, neither she nor the audience knows what it is. She leaves the stage crying out aloud. Now Teobaldo has lost his son and Antonio his daughter. The brothers face the annihilation of their house and the passing of the family estate into the hands of an outsider. To preserve the estate and the family name, the brothers grimly request a papal dispensation so that Antonio, as the elder brother, may marry his young niece Dorotea, Teobaldo's daughter, and beget an heir. There is no suggestion that pantaloon-ian lust plays any part in this. It is an arrangement distasteful to everyone.

Soon the terrified Julia, buried alive in the tomb of her ancestors, awakes, not knowing if she is living or dead. The metaphor is clear. The house of Castelvín has become a tomb for its children—Otavio, Dorotea, Julia, all buried in it, their grieving fathers reduced to an obscene, incestuous pact for the breeding of another heir to hold their estate within the ever-constricting boundaries of the family.

Into the blackness of the tomb comes the light of Roselo's lan-tern. Roselo and his nervous manservant Marín boldly enter the house of their enemy, the house of death, to rescue Julia, with the faithful Anselmo covering their escape. Again Lope opens out the allegorical dimension noiselessly, for this scene is a perfect parallel to the ball scene, and both are symbolic of Roselo's role in the salvation of the house of Castelvín. He comes, it seems, as an interloper, to steal away their daughter, but his real function is to rescue her from the sterility of the closed house, which, beginning as shelter for a feast, has become a charnel. And in rescuing her he rescues the house itself. Love comes with a lamp and leads the soul out of its earthy tomb. In the courtly love tradition of the Middle Ages, religious imagery was transferred to sexual passion, which in turn became a pseudo-religion, the religion of the lovers in *Romeo and Juliet*. But Lope inherits another medieval vision that is the reverse. In this vision human love—the love of parents and children as well as the love of men and women—is not a religion in itself, but is an earthly paradigm of divine love.

In the last act, we and Roselo learn from Anselmo a perfect Christian sort of paradox: that Julia is dead and that she lives; both items of news are told at the same time. Then, fittingly, the first place that Lope makes us laugh aloud—the setting of the first scene played for pure, broad comic effect—is the tomb. Because Roselo is a Christian Orpheus, he will succeed in leading his bride out of an underworld reduced to a funhouse for slapstick terrors and for lovers to grope in to find one another in the dark. O Death, where is thy sting, you old fathead?

The last scenes of the play take place in the Castelvín country house, where the nuptials are being prepared for unhappy Dorotea and her grieving, aged uncle. But by a comic ruse Julia forestalls them and reconciles her father to her marriage. When Roselo is captured by Teobaldo, then, it is the chastened Antonio this time who pleads for him and Teobaldo who agrees to abjure vengeance. For intimately patterned into the story of Julia's relationship to Roselo are the stories of her father's relationship to him and her uncle's relationship to him. Lope has placed the three moral choices of Teobaldo symmetrically: at the beginning, at the middle, and at the end, to shape the moral structure of the play; and each of these choices has to do with Roselo. At the beginning, Teobaldo's spontaneous act of charity, the saving of Roselo's life at the ball, becomes the cause that both the lives and happiness of others are saved. The dark center of the play, in which that very Roselo becomes the unwilling murderer of Teobaldo's son, is shown to be not Roselo's fault, but Teobaldo's. And at the end, with Roselo's life again in his hands, Teobaldo allows himself to be persuaded by his brother Antonio, as once Antonio had been persuaded by him, to spare another man's son. For his advocacy of hatred he has lost his own son, but for his championing of love he has won the fruitful continuance of his line. The two old men see their house resurrected in the joyful marriages of their daughters to the two scions of the house of Montés.

This is a happy ending for which no individual character is alone responsible, neither hero nor magician. And yet each character was required to act individually and consciously to achieve it. The weddings are not simply bonds between two individuals, but complex and various new relationships among many individuals, each of whom must consent distinctly to the singularity of each commitment. This, Lope tells us, is the true definition of family.

Romeo and Juliet is an experiment by a brilliant journeyman. But *Castelvines y Monteses* is not an experiment, and it is certainly not by a journeyman. Lope's play is the coherent product of a belief system still intact, with taproots deep in Spanish Christianity, but with trunk, branches, and vivid foliage rich with the sap of the playwright's own mature and life-affirming genius. Far from trivializing the Romeo and Juliet story, Lope's *tragicomedia* rendering has made sense of it.

Notes

1. This seems to be true even for those approaching the comparison from the Spanish side, as recent articles by Ronald Wadley and Pedro Juan Duque Díaz de Cerio evidence. Although neither of these articles is primarily an aesthetic analysis, both take time for some brief, derivative, and superficial aesthetic comparison with the foregone conclusion in Shakespeare's favor.

2. See, for example, G. B. Harrison's introduction to the *Complete Works* (1948,

473): "*Romeo and Juliet* lacks the depth of the later tragedies, partly because Shakespeare's skill had not yet matured, partly because the theme itself is pathetic rather than tragic"; Frank Kermode's introduction to *The Riverside Shakespeare* (1974): "*Romeo and Juliet,* though it has always enjoyed popular esteem, has not often been ranked by professional critics with the tragic masterpieces which followed it." The introductions to most standard editions, while emphasizing appreciation, will usually catalogue the same list of generally accepted weaknesses. I wish to emphasize that I break no new ground here in my analysis of *Romeo and Juliet;* indeed, I owe my analysis almost entirely to others of much greater authority than myself.

3. Hazelton Spencer's *Shakespeare Improved* (1963) is extremely interesting in regard to this and other revisions of *Romeo and Juliet.* George Curtis Branam's *Eighteenth-Century Adaptations of Shakespeare* (1956) gives the actual texts. These revisions may have been poorly executed, but they do point to certain elements in the play that have rather persistently caused dissatisfaction. The most enduring revision, for example, introduced originally by Thomas Otway, is the reviving of Juliet before Romeo's death. One need not praise Otway's dialogue to acknowledge that there is something odd about the fact that the lovers in Shakespeare's version do not die together, but each achieves individual oblivion in a transport of emotion over the inert body of the other.

4. See particularly Franklin Dickey (1957) quoted in *Twentieth Century Interpretations* (1970, 98–100) and Susan Snyder (1970 and 1979).

5. Professor Frye (1976) makes a careful distinction between comedy and romance, calling comedy social, romance individualistic, and markedly favoring the latter. For him Christianity is strongly comedic.

6. All my quotes from *Castelvines y Monteses* are taken from the Biblioteca de Autores Españoles edition, using their act and scene divisions, followed by page numbers.

7. See, for example, J. Dover Wilson's introduction (1971, xxix). "He behaves contemptibly. His conduct is infantile. And it must be noted, too, with however much regret, that Juliet is capable of behaving in a similar manner, though this is not shown on stage."

8. All my quotes from *Romeo and Juliet* are taken from *The Riverside Shakespeare* (1974), edited by Blakemore Evans (Boston: Houghton Mifflin, 1974).

Works Cited

Branam, George Curtis. 1956. *Eighteenth-Century Adaptations of Shakespearean Tragedy.* Berkeley: University of California Press.

Charleton, H. B. 1948. *Shakespearean Tragedy.* Cambridge: Cambridge University Press.

Dickey, Franklin. 1957. *Not Wisely But Too Well: Shakespeare's Love Tragedies.* San Marino, Calif.: The Huntington Library.

Duque Díaz de Cerio, Pedro Juan. 1979. "La presencia de España en *Romeo y Julieta." Letras de Deusto,* 9: 63–94.

Frye, Northrop. 1976. *The Secular Scripture: A Study of the Structure of Romance.* Cambridge, Mass: Harvard University Press.

———. 1986. *Northrop Frye on Shakespeare.* Edited by Robert Sandler. New Haven: Yale University Press.

Garcí-Prada, Carlos. 1927. "*Castelvines y Monteses* de Lope de Vega." *Hispania,* 10:67–87.

Levin, Harry. 1987. *Playboys and Killjoys: An Essay on the Theory and Practice of Comedy.* New York: Oxford University Press.

Shakespeare, William. 1974. *The Riverside Shakespeare.* Edited by G. Blakemore Evans. Boston: Houghton Mifflin.

———. 1971. *Romeo and Juliet.* Edited by J. Dover Wilson. London: Cambridge University Press.

———. 1952. *Shakespeare: The Complete Works.* Edited by G. B. Harrison. New York: Harcourt, Brace and World.

Snyder, Susan. 1970. "*Romeo and Juliet:* Comedy into Tragedy." *Essays in Criticism* 15, 4:391–402.

———. 1979. *The Comic Matrix of Shakespeare's Tragedies: "Romeo and Juliet," "Hamlet," "Othello," and "King Lear."* Princeton: Princeton University Press.

Spencer, Hazelton. 1963. *Shakespeare Improved: The Restoration Versions in Quarto and on the Stage.* New York: Ungar.

Stauffer, Donald. 1949. *Shakespeare's World of Images: The Development of His Moral Ideas.* New York: Norton.

Twentieth Century Interpretations of "Romeo and Juliet": A Collection of Critical Essays. 1970. Edited by Douglas Cole. Englewood Cliffs, N.J.: Prentice-Hall.

Vega, Lope de. 1860. Reprint 1952. *Comedias Escogidas de Frey Lope de Vega Carpio.* Edited by Juan Eugenio Hartzenbush, 4:1–23. Biblioteca de Autores Españoles, vol. 52. Madrid: Ediciones Atlas.

Wadley, Ronald R. 1979. "Lope and Shakespeare." *The American Hispanist* 4:13–19.

Wain, John. 1964. *The Living World of Shakespeare.* New York: St. Martin's Press.

Thomas Kyd and Pedro Calderón: Toward a Semiotics of Revenge Drama

Sharon Dahlgren Voros

While Thomas Kyd's *The Spanish Tragedy* and Pedro Calderón's *De un castigo, tres venganzas (By one punishment thrice revenged)* take place beyond their borders of origin, Kyd's play in Spain and Calderón's in Burgundy, they display a close bond in the treatment of political intrigue.[1] My study centers on a comparison of dramatic sign systems within revenge drama and the Senecan tradition common to both works. I will examine three main dramatic situations, in conjunction with Thomas Pavel's *Move* grammars (1985) and A. J. Greimas's constitutional model (1970) with its analysis of the main axes of conflict. The first dramatic situation involves the dual function of the traitor as both adjuvant and opposant, both Greimasian terms (Ubersfeld 1982). I will then examine the play within a play and the hunt as dramatic analogues, since it is through these two staged events that traitors are brought to justice. The hunt in *De un castigo,* like Hieronimo's playlet, is carefully orchestrated to expose and eliminate wrongdoers, as divergent plot lines are brought together in the concept of Just Revenge (Bigelow 1981). I conclude with the comparison of sign systems suggested by the similar plot structures in an application of *Move* grammars. While Calderón's play is not a tragedy, it employs dynamics comparable to revenge motifs in *The Spanish Tragedy.* Thematically and structurally, these two plays show parallel concerns for an advice to princes on the importance of judging the loyalty of one's subjects wisely.

Semiotic Models and Their Use

Both semiotic models used in this study, the Greimasian square and the Pavelian *Move* grammar derive from the linguistic principle of binary opposition, already found in natural language (Pavel 1985,

16). In analyzing parallel structures of revenge drama, I have constructed three semiotic models, two from Greimas and one from Pavel. The plot dynamics established in both works is such that one iteration of the semiotic square is not sufficient to account for dramatic development. While Greimas uses this model to account for characterization in the narrative, Pavel has devised his *Move* grammar specifically for tracking the decision-making processes responsible for plot dynamics. The purpose of applying both models is to establish comparable structural elements in revenge plots in two very different works, the tragedy and the *comedia*.

Greimas's model is particularly useful in analyzing the functions of characters within the plot structure. Keir Elam's discussion (126–31) of Greimas's modifications of models, from Vladimir Propps *Morphology of the Folk-Tale* (Hawkes 1977, 91) and Etienne Souriau's *Les deux cent mille situations dramatiques*, does not include the constitutional model (Greimas 1970, 137), which incorporates the notions of adjuvancy or assistance and opposition from his actantial model (Greimas 1966, 185). The constitutional model is a four-point configuration, the left-hand side of which is the positive or prescriptive axis, the Good, and the right-hand side of which is the negative or interdictive axis, the Evil. If we contrast love and hate in the model, as an illustration, love appears in the upper left-hand corner as S1 and hate the upper right-hand corner as S2. S1 to S2 constitutes the main oppositional contrast of a given plot scheme. The model also includes a subordinate set, with not-S2, not hate, and not-S1, not love; the square intends to account for an oppositional scheme in all its complexity. Thus we have the first figure with LOVE and HATE as principle actantial or functional opposites within the narrative trajectory (Greimas 170, 137). The adjuvant or assistant to S1 is located at the not-S2 node, while the opposant or opponent to S1 appears at the not-S1 node. These four positions indicate actantial roles within plot structure, those roles that define the progress of plot dynamics (Greimas and Courtés, 1982, 5–6).

The *Move* grammar developed by Thomas Pavel (1985, 17) focuses on the decision-making process responsible for dramatic action. The purpose of the model, based on a combination of the game theory of moves and transformational grammars, is to trace the dynamics of plot advance and the hierarchical system of dependencies, already found in natural language sentence structure (16). The *Move*, italicized to indicate its sign-producing function, quite simply emphasizes the choice of action taken from among a set of alternatives that in turn establishes a chain of causality, as one

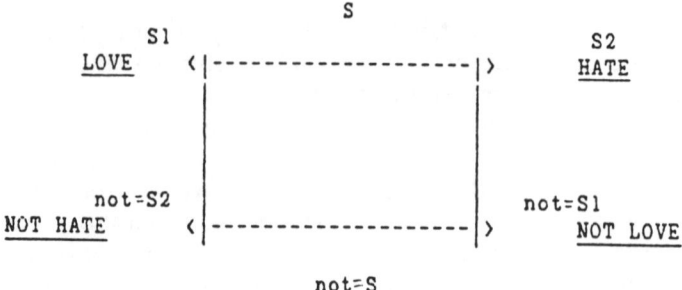

The Greimasian Semiotic Square

Move embeds itself into another. Thus, the main dramatic problem carries with it a series of problems and solutions. Further, the *Move,* with its binary structure of *Problem* versus *Solution,* can be complicated by an intermediary stage, an *Auxiliary* (19), to facilitate the transition from one structural component to another. Pavel then restates this modified basic *Move* structure as: *Move: Problem + (Auxiliary) + Solution.* Characters or actants, faced with the *Problem,* make a series of choices to solve it and, in doing so, formulate the series of *Moves.* In essence, Pavel is telling us that all theater can be viewed as solution(s) to problem(s), since this binary system is at the base of all action on the stage, at least for that action responsible for plot development.

Actantial Parallels: The Greimasian Model

In comparing *The Spanish Tragedy* and *De un castigo,* I begin with Greimas's semiotic square, with its attendant emphasis on principal axes of conflict among actants, set in terms of a hierarchy of relationships. Two iterations of the model become apparent in the course of analysis of actantial parallels, those actant or character functions that contribute to plot development. If I project these functions onto the semiotic square, the two configurations emerge. The first set of parallels clarifies the structure of political power within each work, while the second brings into perspective the avenger himself, a situation that sets the dramatic structure into motion. The principal axis of conflict, to begin *The Spanish Tragedy,* is the war between Spain and Portugal.[2] Andrea's death at the hands of Balthazar initiates the revenge theme, while the Prince of Portugal, captured by Horatio and brought to Spain, becomes a means for negotiating a truce.

Paralleling Kyd's war is Calderon's letter from the Duke of Saxony warning Charles of Burgundy of deception in his own ranks, which prompts him to banish his nephew Enrique, his advisor Manfredo, his knight Federico, and embrace the traitor Clotaldo. In both revenge plays under consideration here, *Moves,* or pivotal decisions in Pavel's transformational model, often lead to multilevel results in dramatic plot structure.

In Calderón, Clotaldo reveals his true devious nature early on, as he articulates the dual objectives of his dramatic function: the quest for the love of Flor and the usurping of political power, the further ramifications of which I shall discuss with Pavel's *Move* grammar and game theories:

> Bien me ha sucedido todo,
> pues seguro el Duque, tengo
> aqueste enemigo menos;
> que he de ser dueño de Flor
> y de estos Estados dueño.
>
> (1.40)

[All's well; the Duke's won over—that's one enemy less; and Flor's going to be mine and I the ruler of all their wide dominions.]

Clotaldo parallels Kyd's Balthazar in that he wishes to possess Flor, who in turn loves Federico, the Duke's faithful knight. Calderón complicates this situation, as the *Move* grammar will show, in that Clotaldo murders Enrique, the Duke's nephew, who has come to Flor's house surreptitiously to meet her scheming friend Flérida. Only the servants, Laura and Floro, know the identity of the *embozado,* who conveniently leaves the dagger in Flor's hand as she faints.

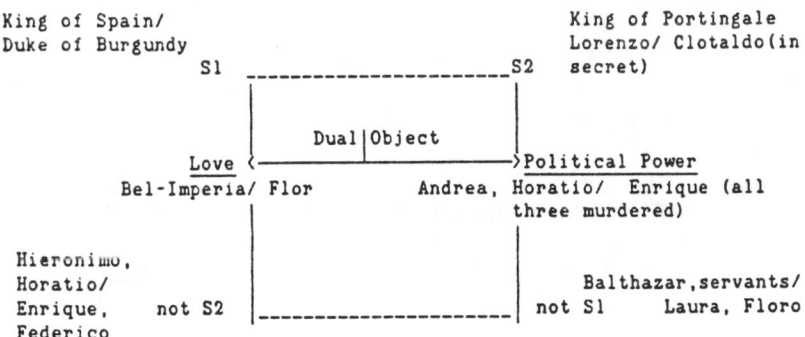

The Greimasian Model of Political Power

In Kyd's tragedy and its companion piece *The Spanish Comedy,* Lorenzo holds the actantial position of conspirator (S2), enlisting the assistance of the servant Pedringano, from whom he extracts that Horatio, Hieronimo's son, is his sister Bel-imperia's new love.[3] The love-struck Balthazar is little more than an instrument for Lorenzo's revenge on the warrior Horatio, a duplication for Andrea.[4] Balthazar's role (not S1), is reduced in the semiotic model, since his love for Bel-imperia serves Lorenzo's ambitions, rather than his own. Meanwhile, the marriage between Balthazar and Bel-imperia has already been arranged as a means of securing peace between two warring nations. Thus, the love relationship moves between the two spheres of personal commitment and power politics (2.3.89). The Greimasian model of political power remains in force up until Horatio's murder, in which Lorenzo and Balthazar, surprising the lovers during their tryst, hang and then stab Horatio in Bel-imperia's presence. Hieronimo's inability to take action immediately, even though he knows the identity of the murderers through Bel-imperia's letter, indicates his actantial role remains within the semiotic model of political power (Ardolino 1985, 43; Freeman 1967, 92). Hieronimo seeks to gather the facts (3.2.104), using all the tools that the power structure and his high political position afford him. Operating within the law, he appeals to the King for justice. Like Federico, who brandishes his weapon in the presence of the Duke, not to kill him but to save him from Clotaldo (2.52), the Lord Marshal lashes out at Lorenzo, who attempts to keep him from addressing the King directly (3.12.133)—an action which places Hieronimo in an indefensible position. With the "Vindicata mihi" soliloquy (3.13), Hieronimo decides to act, but his vengeance depends on his ability to play a dramatic role and to act at the proper time. Hieronimo's desire for knowledge and appropriate action require that he move with caution, lest he lose all ability and opportunity for success. Act 3 concludes with what could be construed as a step backward in plot progression, in that Hieronimo, at the behest of Lorenzo's father the Duke of Castile, reconciles with his enemy.

Clotaldo, in Calderón, combines the roles of Lorenzo and Balthazar into one S2 function, with only bribed servants as assistants. Having murdered Enrique, he now attempts to assassinate the Duke, with all Germany his enemy (2.51–52). The banished Federico, however, awakens the Duke just in time to have Clotaldo turn the tables and accuse him of the attack, as he boasts, "Ya no habrá acción que pueda / intentar yo, que bien no me suceda" (2.52)

("No longer will there be any undertaking of mine in which I do not succeed").

Hieronimo's role as avenger becomes two actantial roles in Calderón. Manfredo, Flor's father, believes his daughter has killed Enrique, and he attempts to cover up the deed by placing the body in a chest and removing it to an obscure place for burial. On the road, he meets Federico, the second actant in the S1 position in the revenge model, who assists, disguised as a laborer. Chance intervenes once more as Federico with the chest meets the Duke and Clotaldo, who arrest him. Each revenge play has double interpretations for events, as we see in the actantial role of Lorenzo, who plays the adjuvant or assistant, convincing his own sister and father that he is really acting in the best interests of all concerned, while the audience witnesses his devious plotting with servants (125 and 150). With Calderón's Clotaldo, viewers get the information about bribing of servants second hand from the servants themselves, although the audience witnesses Enrique's murder. Clotaldo's scenes of evil plotting are reduced to spontaneous reactions to situations, rather than any passion for revenge or rivalry, as in Kyd's Lorenzo, whose hatred for Horatio stems from competition on the battlefield, in *The Spanish Comedy* (7–8). As with the murder of Horatio, Enrique's death appears as an on-stage event, in the presence of a lady. Manfredo finds the dagger in his daughter's hand and then, in the opposite direction of Hieronimo, who attempts to reveal the identity of the murderers, endeavors to conceal the identity of the murderess: "Pues, Flor, mira y calla; / que vida y honor nos va" (1.48). ("Well, Flor, observe and Be silent; for life and honor are at stake.") Since Manfredo has been exiled by the Duke, and now, with the Duke's nephew murdered by Flor, he must use all of his capacities to hide the fact. It is not until his role in the cover-up is shared by Federico that Manfredo moves into S1 in the second iteration of the actantial model (fig. 3). Manfredo, like Hieronimo, is constrained by the power structure, and he works around it by means of two staged events: the transportation of Enrique's body in the chest and the potion to feign death that he gives Federico, now accused of the killing. Like Hieronimo, he cannot confront the power structure head on. Never using weapons, he has recourse to disguises and, instead of blaming Flor, he realizes the danger for the entire family: "¿Quién no ha de creer que ha sido / esta traición y venganza?" (2.48). ("Who would not believe this to be treason and revenge?") The murder could be interpreted as his family's attempt to avenge itself against the Duke.

Therefore, as with Hieronimo, means must be found to survive this crisis and eventually to succeed in resolving conflict.

While Balthazar's love for Bel-imperia directly influences the balance of political power in the play, Clotaldo's love for Flor appears somewhat gratuitous. While she is the daughter of the Duke's trusted advisor and mentor, Manfredo, she does not have the political status of Bel-imperia (Ardolino, 119 and 136). The exiling of her father and the unexpected presence of Enrique in her house to seduce her untrustworthy friend Flérida are two dramatic events that become confused in Flor's mind, as she worries her father suspects her of concealing a lover: "¡Oh, qué cosas, fortuna, / se eslabonan y se enlazan, todas posibles, y todas / en mi agravio conjuradas" (1.46). Thus, in Calderón, relationships between political power struggles and love may not appear so closely enmeshed as in Kyd, although Fortune has had a hand in bringing these two divergent spheres into the same dramatic framework.

As both plays move to another kind of actantial model, decisions to find new dramatic solutions emerge. Hieronimo's parting words from act 3 show his determination to take command of the situation himself, in light of his increasing mistrust of the power elite (3.15.53): "Your Lordship's to command. / Pha! Keep your way." The move is now made to transition from the first Greimasian model of political power to its second iteration, the Actantial Model for Revenge or Justice. In Calderón, Manfredo's role shifts in favor of Federico, Flor's *galán*, who, awaiting execution, is granted a personal audience with the Duke. It is significant, however, that the Duke himself requests to see the imprisoned Federico (3.63)—a situation that does not appear in Kydian tragedy. In his soliloquy, the Duke reports the necessity for judicious reasoning in the face of Federico's past heroic events and unswerving loyalty (3.62). Hieronimo, however, fails in his attempt to find justice from the King and is compelled to take the matter into his own hands. In Calderón, Charles the Just listens to his inner feelings for Federico and addresses him directly, while in Kyd, the King and his entourage do not understand Hieronimo even after his revenge playlet eliminates all heirs to the crowns of Portugal and Spain.

The Actantial Model for Revenge or Justice

The second iteration of the Greimasian model shows that Hieronimo's role, in transition in that famous soliloquy in act 3, parallels Calderón's plot structure after the death of Enrique. The actantial father figure expands and replaces the role of the ranking aristocrats, whose previous decisions or *Moves* determined dramatic action. While Manfredo defers to Federico in displaying weapons or confronting the Duke, he continues to work behind the scenes. His insisting that Federico receive food and drink is a means of causing a deathlike trance, more persuasive than Federico's accusatory rhetoric toward the treacherous Clotaldo. The Duke has no recourse other than to put to the test the last words of his "dying" knight. Thus, Charles of Burgundy, in the position of S2, as main enemy, is restored to the position of principal actant, S1.

As a solution to the traitorous actions in Kyd and Calderón, two staged events occur, each controlled as a means of exposing wrongdoers and eliminating them. In *The Spanish Tragedy,* Hieronimo's playlet parallels the hunt scene in act 3 of *De un castigo.* While his tragedy is the subject of the entire act 4, the hunt scene occupies only the final scenes of act 3. Yet these two staged events acquire the status of dramatic analogues, since they are vehicles for bringing the traitor(s) to justice. Hieronimo cautiously remains within the structure of political power and runs counter to it only at the end of the work to bring about the tragic dénouement. In Calderón, a great part of stage time is spent outside the power structure, either in banishment, cover-ups, secret trysts, disguises, concocting trance-producing potions, or imprisonment. Revenge is brought about, however, not by a departure from the acceptable pattern of political relationships, but by a return to those relationships that were initially severed by the Duke of Burgundy himself. The Duke then becomes both disrupter and restorer of political alliances. In Calderón, a circular pattern of action emerges in that the Duke, S1 of the first semiotic model, causes his own betrayal, resulting in the forced secret actions of his faithful adjuvants. He then restores the system by moving from S2 in the second model back to S1, a move that allows Clotaldo to ascend hierarchically to S2 from not-S1 (65). The traitor stages the hunt scene as well, for, as the Duke searches for him, Clotaldo urges his cohorts to withdraw so that he alone

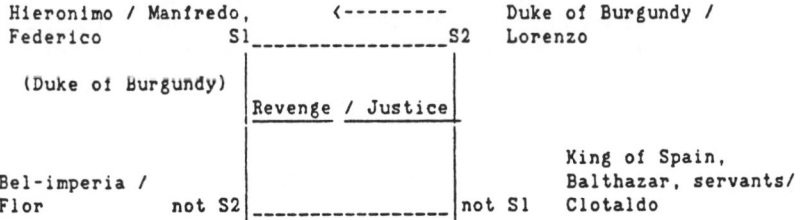

The Actantial Model for Revenge or Justice

may prepare the ambush. With prior knowledge of duplicity, Charles of Burgundy defeats the enemy and forces his confession, adding new information: Clotaldo was the instigator of the mysterious letter from the Duke of Saxony, warning of treason: "Yo al de Sajonia escribí" (3.67) ("I have written to the Duke of Saxony"). Clotaldo manifests his true actantial role as S2, in the two attempted assassinations. Thus, the first *Move* occurs with the principal adversary, Clotaldo, not with the Duke's faulty judgment of his adjuvants. Thus, to conclude Calderonian as well as Kydian revenge drama, a change in the actantial relationships is necessary and can be shown in diagram form in the second version of the semiotic model.

In Kyd's *The Spanish Tragedy* as well, Hieronimo manages to manipulate the ranking aristocrats into a false sense of security, personal victory, and overconfidence. Until the end, he accomplishes his revenge plan by skillfully allowing his victims to participate in the playlet, *Soliman and Perseda*. Justice is meted out by placing the murderer, Lorenzo, in the same position as his victim, Horatio. Hieronimo definitely holds the advantage over his adversaries, since they are ignorant of the revenge scheme. The playlet is as follows: Erastus (Lorenzo) is married to Perseda (Bel-imperia), whose beauty enthralls their guest, Soliman (Balthazar). The Bashaw (Hieronimo), also in love with Perseda, kills Erastus. Perseda slays Soliman, thinking he is the murderer, and herself. The Bashaw, suffering from remorse, hangs himself. Thus, all four actantial positions are eliminated in four moves. While Lorenzo is not his sister's husband but her brother, he is made to suffer the same fate as his real murder victim, Horatio. In playing the traitor's role, Hieronimo must eliminate himself from the paradigm. Although Murray (1969, 150) contends that Hieronimo misunderstands his own piece in casting himself in the role of his son's killer, the placing of the murderer in the victim's position conveys a sense of Poetic Justice. In essence, two potential dynasties are obliterated: the Knight Marshal Hieronimo, his son Horatio, and his wife Isabella; as well as the Duke of Castile, Don Cyprian, brother to the hierless King of Spain, Lorenzo, the Duke's son, and Bel-imperia, the Duke's daughter (Ardolino 151). This kind of dramatic cancelling out of two warring families is not only a Senecan trait, but a device for ending further revenge plot dynamics (Freeman 65 and 101). The King of Spain, ill-prepared to comprehend the mechanisms of action performed outside his system of political influence, remains alone and heirless.

In examining the concluding structures to revenge plot dynamics

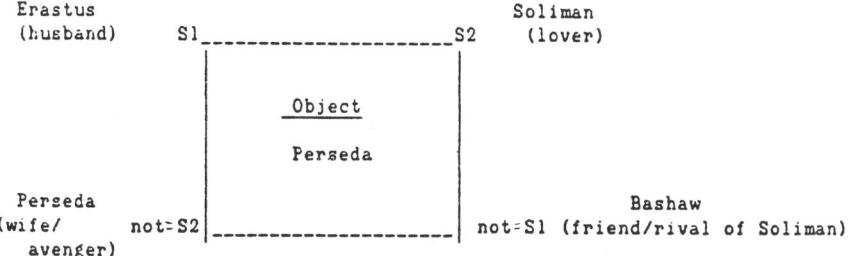

```
Erastus                                    Soliman
(husband)      S1_____S2   (lover)
                |                    |
                |       Object       |
                |                    |
                |      Perseda       |
                |                    |
Perseda                             |              Bashaw
(wife/       not=S2|_____|   not=S1 (friend/rival of Soliman)
 avenger)
```

The Actantial Model of Revenge in Hieronimo's Playlet

through the prism of semiotic actantial relationships, we see that Hieronimo's play follows a carefully orchestrated plan of total annihilation, except for the two ranking aristocrats, the King of Spain and the Viceroy of Portugal. Hieronimo stops just short of regicide. Had he not, we could then contend that his blood lust had simply carried personal vengeance too far. Further, vengeance is not merely a question of personal feelings, but extends into the sociopolitical realm. Hence, to characterize Hieronimo's actions as a "killing frenzy," as does Thomas Pavel (89), is inaccurate. Hieronimo's revenge reinforces the sense of Poetic Justice with the irony of his suicide. After biting out his tongue, he "makes signs for a knife to mend his pen" (173), with which he kills Castile and then himself. Had he written down his thoughts, one would have understood his motives for the murder of Lorenzo's father, the Duke of Castile. Instead, audiences have as a substitute for the written text—a performance text of Hieronimo's final statement on revenge in the murder/suicide and the annihilation of both families.

The Revenge Plot Dynamics of *Move* Grammars

While Thomas Pavel (1985) sees Kyd's plot structure as deliberately perplexing the audience with its Byzantine dynamics (85), he nonetheless provides a succinct *Move* grammar for *The Spanish Tragedy*. The play evolves as the *Solution* to the *Problem* of Andrea's death in ten *Moves*, in the reproduced narrative tree (87). While I agree that the revenge plot determines the dynamics of the play, I cannot accept Pavel's view that Hieronimo's personal tragedy does not interact with the politics of war between Spain and Portugal. Pavel's *Move* grammar may skew the conclusions of the analyst in favor of plot dynamics at the expense of other factors, such as the system of actantial roles operative within dramatic

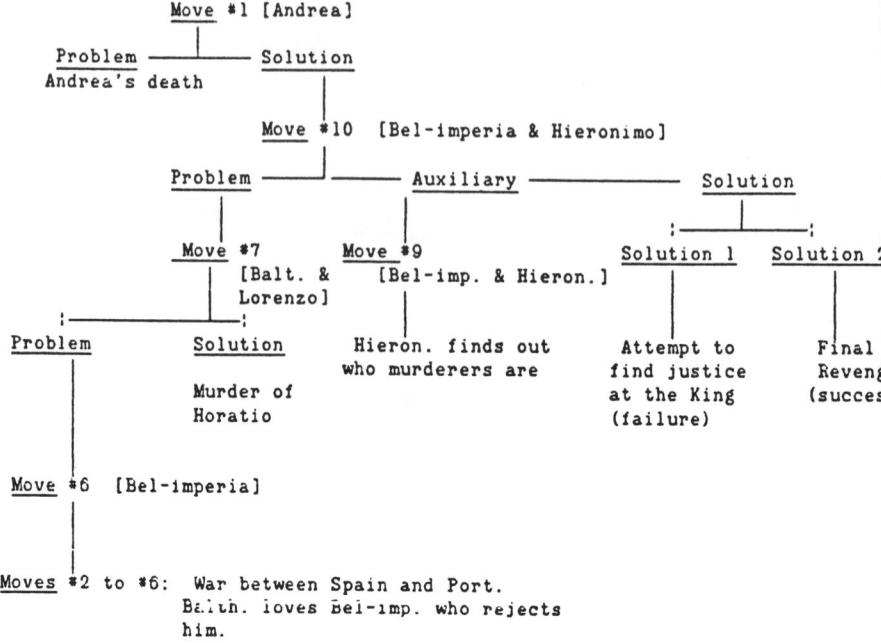

Pavel's *Move* Grammar for *The Spanish Tragedy*

structure. Pavel almost completely disregards Lorenzo's role in instigating the murder of Horatio and using Balthazar to consolidate his own political power base as nephew of the hierless King of Spain. Pavel details Hieronimo's revenge plans in his ten-part *Move* diagram, while he lumps *Moves* 2 to 6 under the same rubric, with Bel-imperia as the prime mover for the war between Spain and Portugal and for Balthazar's falling in love with her. Had Pavel placed this war in *Move* 1, a more accurate description of plot dynamics could be achieved. The war is not merely a pretext to introduce Balthazar to Bel-imperia, as Pavel contends (86). It sets in motion the bitter rivalry between Lorenzo and Horatio, who has managed to show up the ambitious nephew to the King on the battlefield. Lorenzo's reasoning for murdering Horatio serves not just as a way to facilitate the Portuguese Prince's love quest, but also as a clear-cut example of the ways in which Kyd, like Calderón, projects a political problem into the sphere of the love relationship.

Since Pavel's narrative tree skirts around Lorenzo's actantial role, the *Move* grammar does not link Andrea's death with Horatio's murder. Bel-imperia herself performs this function of associating the two unavenged deaths. What with Lorenzo's obvious influence at the Spanish court, he could have found ways of removing Horatio from royal favor, especially since his friendship with the Portuguese Prince appears secure and the King of Spain had already decreed that Bel-imperia marry him for reasons of state. While Pavel reduces the importance of some plot events to benefit a main plot—often necessary in analysis—he does not see that Villuppo's treachery in the Portuguese court, when he wrongly accuses Alexandro for Balthazar's death, fits neatly into his *Move* grammar (1.3.72). Treason and murder occur or are about to occur on both sides, since they form part of the *Move* structure dealing with the war between Spain and Portugal. Villuppo's actantial role parallels Lorenzo's villainous actions (Ardolino 169, Murray 32). Perhaps if we need to derive maxims from Kyd's work (Pavel 91–92), we could say that peace is more complex than war, that heroism on the battlefield can lead to personal vendettas and envy, especially when a King's nephew is upstaged by a Knight Marshal's son in front of his own troops. I would view Kyd's title *Spanish Tragedy* as indicative of a series of interconnections between personal grief and power politics, much as occurs in Calderón, whose Duke of Burgundy displays his emotions on the stage in his difficult decision to execute Federico. Ultimately, this war between Spain and Portugal has resulted, as many wars do, in the extermination of the new generation, leaving the Viceroy and the King of Spain hierless. Thus, Pavel needs to take his *Move* grammar another step back, to the war and to Andrea's death, which brings about Horatio's death and finally the solution in terms of Hieronimo's revenge. This would also allow for inclusion of diverse plot components that enrich the work and make it a more subtle piece of dramatic artistry.

As seen in Pavel's analysis of Kydian tragedy, *Move* grammars can be as simple or as complicated as the analysis requires. If we proceed on the basis that only certain *Moves* are essential to plot dynamics, then we may and indeed must exclude the less important elements. The *Move* grammar in itself does not evaluate the significance or hierarchical structure of plot elements, although this particular model can and does show which elements are derived from, or embedded in, previous *Moves* in the Chain of Causality. For this reason, the *Move* must be a dramatic juncture at which the character is confronted with a set of alternatives. The alternative chosen then leads to a particular event in the solution of a problem. Just as Pavel chooses the revenge plot structure as predominant in Kydian drama, so I select treason as predominant in Calderón's *De un castigo, tres venganzas,* for even the title suggests a kind of economy of dramatic action. Clotaldo, operating alone, is responsible for three violations of trust against (1) the Duke of Burgundy, (2) Manfredo and Flor, and (3) the Duke's nephew, Enrique.

Seven major decisions account for plot dynamics in Calderón's revenge drama. In almost all instances, an *Auxiliary* is operative to move toward a solution. I have included Clotaldo's confession as the last *Move*, since it has bearing on the first *Move* and justifies the Duke's revenge. Clotaldo himself, in communicating with the Duke of Saxony, was responsible for the initial letter in *Move* 1. Plot dynamics then moves full circle in that the final confession of guilt throws new light on previous events. The traitor himself is responsible for the Duke's apprehension and erroneous judgment of his faithful subjects (Bigelow 21).

Thus, the Duke's Solution to the *Problem* in *Move* 5 is the face-to-face encounter with the accused, which then prompts his need to seek the identity of the traitor in *Move* 6, facilitated by the *Auxiliary* of the staged hunt scene. Embedded within this *Auxiliary* is Clotaldo's decision to confess all in order to save his soul, since he is quite aware of his imminent death (67). *Move* 7, embedded within the hunt scene, allows the traitor to expiate his crimes—a function not performed in Kydian plot dynamics. Hieronimo the Avenger retells the series of events after the playlet, since all wrongdoers are silenced during the dramatic action. The Duke, then, clearly understands that there is only one traitor, not many, as he had assumed in *Move* 1. The second "death," Federico's sleep, allows for a resurrection scene, in contrast to Kyd's Horatio, whose body is returned to the stage to justify Hieronimo's revenge. While Calderón restores social and political order, Kyd opens the way for a new regime in eliminating the heirs of Spain and Portugal, as political readings of the text would have it (Ardolino 1983, 37–49). Thus, the Evil and the Good have cancelled one another out in the series of Kydian *Moves*, while in Calderonian counterparts the Good, or more accurately the Just, have annihilated the one Evil by eliminating Clotaldo.

Conclusion

In examining parallel structures in *The Spanish Tragedy* and *De un castigo, tres venganzas*, I have constructed three semiotic models, two from Greimas's semiotic square and one from Pavel's *Move* grammar. Actantial parallels in dramatic contexts are perhaps the closest between these two dramatists as regards revenge themes

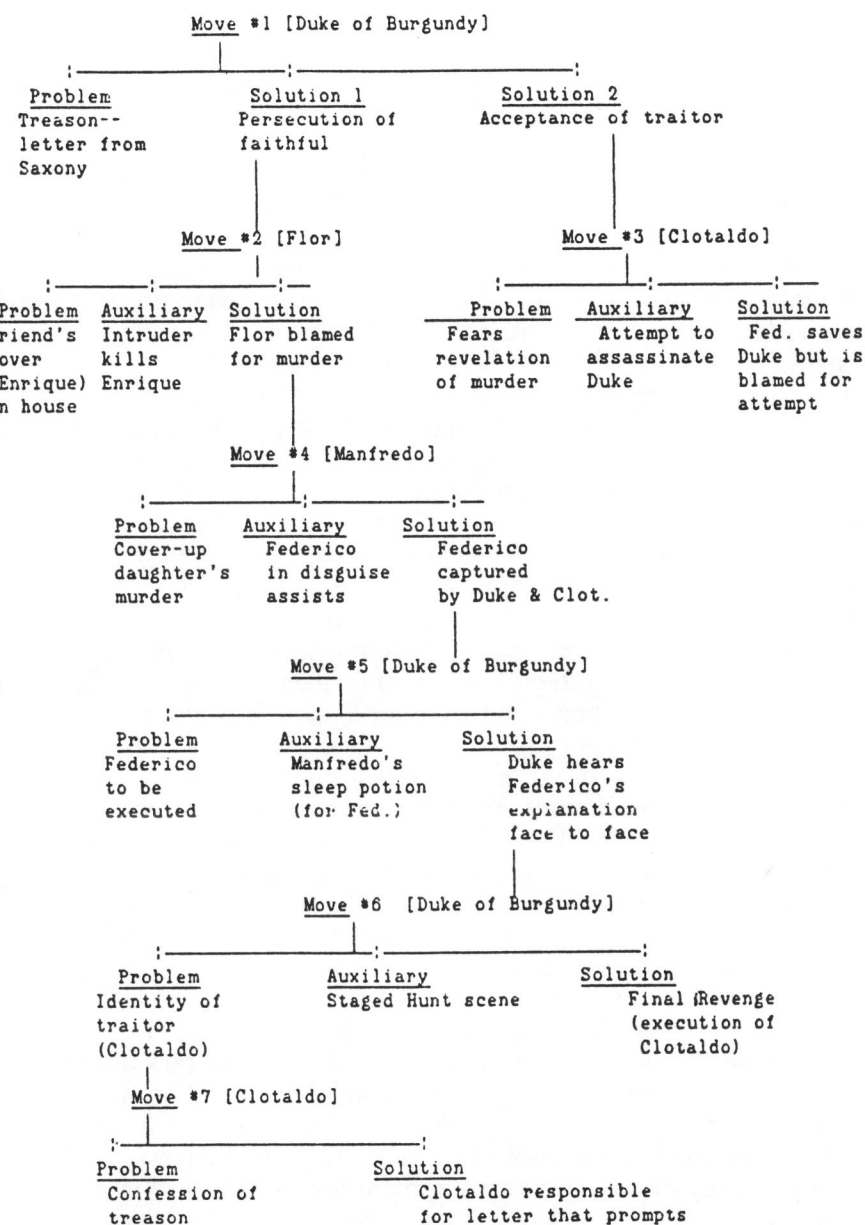

Move #1 [Duke of Burgundy]

Problem	Solution 1	Solution 2
Treason--	Persecution of	Acceptance of traitor
letter from	faithful	
Saxony		

Move #2 [Flor]

Problem	Auxiliary	Solution
Friend's	Intruder	Flor blamed
lover	kills	for murder
(Enrique)	Enrique	
in house		

Move #3 [Clotaldo]

Problem	Auxiliary	Solution
Fears	Attempt to	Fed. saves
revelation	assassinate	Duke but is
of murder	Duke	blamed for
		attempt

Move #4 [Manfredo]

Problem	Auxiliary	Solution
Cover-up	Federico	Federico
daughter's	in disguise	captured
murder	assists	by Duke & Clot.

Move #5 [Duke of Burgundy]

Problem	Auxiliary	Solution
Federico	Manfredo's	Duke hears
to be	sleep potion	Federico's
executed	(for Fed.)	explanation
		face to face

Move #6 [Duke of Burgundy]

Problem	Auxiliary	Solution
Identity of	Staged Hunt scene	Final Revenge
traitor		(execution of
(Clotaldo)		Clotaldo)

Move #7 [Clotaldo]

Problem	Solution
Confession of	Clotaldo responsible
treason	for letter that prompts
	Duke's Move #1

The *Move* Grammar for *De un castigo, tres venganzas*

and recourse to warrior heroes, father figures, traitors, and ranking aristocrats. In the figure of the traitor, common to revenge-plot dynamics, Calderón uses the same actantial role (S2) for Clotaldo, both principal enemy (S2) and opposant (not-S1). Kyd, however, employs two separate actants, Lorenzo (S2) and Balthazar (not-S1), to accomplish this function. A certain dynamic is set up in both works, as seen by the semiotic square, in that one iteration of the model is not sufficient to account for dramatic development. Both the *galán* Federico and the mentor Manfredo qualify for the key position S1, while Hieronimo is the sole avenger in S1. Calderón then further complicates this S1 actantial role by allowing the Duke of Burgundy to perform the final dramatic action of vengeance.

Both dramatists use analogous staged events—the play within the play and the precalculated hunt scene—as part of the revenge plan. With Kyd, revenge takes on a political cast that meshes well with notions of conflict between Catholic Spain and Protestant England. While his plot stops short of regicide, the King of Spain remains heirless. Both works assume a kind of ritualistic elimination of wrongdoers and show the complexities of personal relationships and their integration or entanglement in the political sphere. Both Bel-imperia and Flor serve as linking characters between these two fields of love and politics. Bel-imperia, associated with Astrea and the motif of justice restored (Ardolino 21), allows one to evaluate Hieronimo's methods as Just Revenge. Flor's actantial role parallels Bel-imperia's in that she also swoons into a deathlike trance upon hearing the news of Federico's demise (66)— her last scene upon the stage. While she does not die or commit suicide, her performance code stands as an analogue to Bel-imperia's final dramatic moments.

With Pavel's *Move* grammar, additional flexibility is possible in tracing the decision-making process within each work. Both plays involve the reactions of subordinates faced with arbitrary decisions foisted upon them by ranking aristocrats. Neither Hieronimo nor Manfredo initiates dramatic action but must respond by moving outside acceptable sociopolitical frameworks to avenge murder or protect family honor. Hieronimo remains essentially within acceptable dramatic frameworks, while his asides and soliloquies indicate that larger revenge plans are in the making. Manfredo employs disguise and stealth to protect his daughter and maintain family honor during his exile from the court of the Duke of Burgundy. Federico, performing in disguise, in keeping with the dramatic tenets of the *comedia,* pursues his ladylove and saves the Duke from assassination. Both this action and his transporting of Enrique's body are misconstrued as treasonous acts. Unlike Federico and Manfredo, Hieronimo is not accused of treason until after his revenge plan has been carried out, since his plotting, including a feigned reconciliation with archenemies, has been skillfully conducted within acceptable courtly frameworks.

Semiotic models, however, cannot eliminate the scholarly prejudices of those who apply them. Neither can *Move* grammars. Pavel, for instance, could not integrate the scenes of the Portuguese court into his systematic approach. Yet, had he considered his own observation that in *Move* 2 Bel-imperia had some influence on the war with Portugal, he could have placed this conflict in *Move* 1 and broadened the base of his grammar to include this overplot.

Scholars such as Murray (1969) and Ardolino (1985) have noted as well parallel actantial roles in Kyd between Villuppo and Lorenzo and between Andrea and Horatio. Such parallel role-structuring is more apparent in Kyd than in Calderón. Perhaps the most significant parallel structure between these two dramatists is the overplot, as Pavel calls it (86), in which political powerplays involve personal relationships. In this regard, the female characters Flor and Bel-imperia hold pivotal roles in linking these two spheres. Flor associates Enrique's surreptitious entrance into her house with her father's exile from the court of the Duke of Burgundy. Her "murder" of Enrique, although in appearance only, parallel's Bel-imperia's desire to avenge the deaths of Andrea and Horatio through the assassination of a political enemy, Balthazar. The Pavelian *Move* grammars permit an evaluation of the ways in which stage events are embedded within previous or subsequent stage events, so that analysts of dramatic style can sort out the transformational processes involved in the Chain of Causality of plot dynamics. Both revenge plays employ ritual slaying as a dramatic means of bringing together diverse plot structures for a Just Revenge in Calderón, marking the restoration of the authority of the Duke of Burgundy, or a revenge tragedy in Kyd, signalling the annihilation of two opposing political houses. With both revenge plays, the semiotic approach assists in comprehending the complexity of actantial roles and decision-making in plot dynamics. Actantial roles, even binary oppositions, often obscured in a dramatic context as mistaken identities and alliances, eventually give way to recognition scenes. Revenge drama as a genre is particularly well suited to Pavel's *Move* grammar, since the plot develops according to decisions and choices made by both transgressor and avenger. Comparing two such diverse works as *The Spanish Tragedy* and *De un castigo, tres venganzas* in their capacity as revenge plays can only enhance understanding of this period of flourishing national theater in Spain and England.

Notes

1. All references are to Thomas Kyd, *The First Part of Hieronimo* and *The Spanish Tragedy,* edited by Andrew S. Cairncross (Lincoln: University of Nebraska Press, 1967) and to Pedro Calderón de la Barca, *Obras completas,* edited by Angel Valbuena Briones, 5th ed. (Madrid: Aguilar, 1966).

2. This war begins in Kyd's *The Spanish Comedy,* also titled *The First part of Hieronimo.* As Cairncross (1967) observes, *The Spanish Tragedy* "suffers to some extent from being a sequel" (xxiv) in that the Induction must summarize the events leading up to Andrea's death. Certain actantial roles, such as Lorenzo's villainy and evil scheming, are established early on in *The Spanish Comedy* (3.11–15).

3. Arthur Freeman (1967, 75–79) discusses the historical content of the play.

4. Peter Murray (1969, 29) quite accurately observes that Andrea and Horatio become fused into one role.

Works Cited

Ardolino, Frank R. 1985. *Thomas Kyd's Mystery Play: Myth and Ritual in "The Spanish Tragedy."* New York: Peter Lang.

———. 1983. "Corrida of Blood in *The Spanish Tragedy:* Kyd's Use of Revenge as National Destiny." *Medieval and Renaissance Drama in England* 1:37–49.

Bigelow, Gary. 1981. "Analysis of Calderón's *De un castigo, tres venganzas:* Structure, Theme, Language." In *Critical Perspectives on Calderón de la Barca,* edited by Frederick A. De Armas, David M. Gitlitz, and José A. Madrigal, 13–37. Lincoln: University of Nebraska Press.

Elam, Keir. 1980. The Semiotics of Theatre and Drama. London and New York: Methuen.

Freeman, Arthur. 1967. *Thomas Kyd: Facts and Problems.* Oxford: Oxford University Press.

Greimas, Algirdas J. 1970. "Les jeux des contraintes sémiotiques." In *Du Sens,* 135–55. Paris: Editions du Seuil.

———. 1966. *Sémantique structurale.* Paris: Larousse.

Greimas, Algirdas J. and Joseph Courtés. 1970. *Semiotics and Language: An Analytical Dictionary.* Translated by Larry Crist, et al. Bloomington: Indiana University Press.

Hawkes, Terence. 1977. *Structuralism and Semiotics.* Berkeley and Los Angeles, California. University of California Press.

Kyd, Thomas. 1967. *The First Part of Hieronimo* and *The Spanish Tragedy.* Edited by Andrew S. Cairncross. Lincoln: University of Nebraska Press.

Murray, Peter B. 1969. *Thomas Kyd.* New York: Twayne.

Pavel, Thomas G. 1985. *The Poetics of Plot: The Case of English Renaissance Drama.* Minneapolis: University of Minnesota Press.

Propp, Vladimir. 1968. *Morphology of the Folk-Tale.* Translated by L. Scott. Austin and London: University of Texas Press.

Ubersfeld, Anne. 1982. *Lire le théâtre.* Paris: Editions sociales.

World Picture and Picture World in Shakespeare and Calderón

Sebastian Neumeister

1. The Play Within the Play

Through *The First Part of Henry IV,* Falstaff enters into the world of Shakespeare. In this play Falstaff assumes the role of the *gracioso,* that integral part of the Spanish Comedia. Both of them represent a social class opposed to the upper-class world of the noble protagonists; both of them are made to reflect that class by their dishonorable and spontaneous way of acting.[1] Falstaff—as is evident in his speeches—is averse to everything noble and especially to honor:

> Can honor set-to a leg? No. Or an arm? No. Or take away the grief of a wound? No. Honor hath no skill in surgery then? No. What is honor? A word. What is that word honor? Air—a trim reckoning! Who hath it? He that died Wednesday.
>
> (5.1.131–35)[2]

The *gracioso* of the Spanish Comedia could talk in the same way, but there is an important difference. Whereas, in the Comedia, the two opposite social layers remain strictly separated—the *caballero* never acts like a *gracioso,* the *gracioso* never acts like a *caballero*—*The First Part of King Henry IV* shows a sort of transition. Falstaff is allowed by Prince Henry to act as Prince Henry and as Prince Henry's father, a dialogue full of comical effects because of the role-changing halfway, making the histrionic element visible. Prince Henry changes position as well. As a member of the royal family, to be sure, but without being recognized as such and without any privilege, he is able to talk to everyone: "I can drink with any tinker in his own language during my life" (2.4.17–19). Even so, he does not give up the inner substance of his being by that kind of mimicry. He always respects his mission as the King's son, for, as he tells us in *The Second Part of Henry IV,* "in every thing the purpose must weigh with the folly" (2.2.164–65). Falstaff, on the other hand, is always playing roles, always changing roles; his inner substance *is* playing roles.

The play-within-the-play scene of the second act of *Henry IV, First Part,* brings two social worlds into very close contact, but it does not mingle them. By introducing the figure of Falstaff, however, Shakespeare is going beyond the limits of the historical and political subjects of his drama. Falstaff acting as the Prince, Prince Henry acting as the "good fellow" King, open the way for a much more human view of class distinction and social difference. Shakespeare, by the invention of Falstaff, stands halfway between the upside-down world of medieval carnival plays and the rigid hierarchy of the Spanish Comedia, hermetically closed to any mixing or changing of social roles.

We must admit that Prince Henry, too, while playing his role of good fellow in the London underworld learns to be a good King for both sides of the social cosmos: he never forgets his mission. He may say in *The First Part of Henry IV:* "I have sounded the very basse-string of humility" (2.4.5–6), but in *The Second Part,* when Falstaff is trying personally to profit from him, he adds: "But being awaked I do despise my dream" (5.5.32). The temptation to compare this sentence with Calderón's *La Vida es sueño (Life Is a Dream)* is great. But one has to notice some slight differences. The distinction between life and dream is no longer so easily established as in *Henry IV* or in *A Midsummer Night's Dream:* changing places in society or playing a play like a dream develop philosophical dimensions. The accent Calderón puts upon moral teaching is stronger than in Shakespeare. King Basilio, in *La vida es sueño,* stages the life of his son Segismundo as a dream in order to test his qualifications for real life. So far one may compare Segismundo with Prince Henry testing himself. But the dream test of *La vida es sueño* is useless unless its crucial character is respected: life is a dream, dream is life. Having learned through bitter experience, Segismundo deserves to be the King:

> A reinar, fortuna, vamos;
> no me despiertes, si duermo,
> y si es verdad, no me duermas.
> Mas, sea verdad o sueño,
> obrar bien es lo que importa:
> si fuere verdad, por serlo;
> si no, por ganar amigos
> para cuando despertemos.
>
> (525)[3]

[Oh, Fate! We go to reign! Do not awaken me if I'm asleep; And if all this is real, please do not put me back to sleep. But be it true or just a dream, to do right is what matters most. If this be true, then for those very ends; if not, that when we wake we may win friends.] (75)

In writing these lines Calderón obviously takes the same point of view as Catholic metaphysicians who relate earthly existence to eternal life. Wordly decisions concern individual and public affairs, but the crucial point is how they affect the chances of damnation or salvation of people's souls.

Shakespeare keeps the problem of salvation completely in the background. His picture of the world does not break down into antithetic positions but remains a whole, as "the great chain of being" relating microcosm to macrocosm (Lovejoy 1936; Rico 1970). Shakespeare's world is still full of tension but in its substance is not undermined by it. Turning back from *La vida es sueño* to Shakespeare, one must look at *Hamlet*. Metaphysical problems are of course discussed in *Hamlet*—Hamlet's own existence and his love for Ophelia are renowned for their philosophical implications. But the play within the play, which Hamlet, like that other King, Basilio, stages, is a stratagem and nothing more: disguise and dissimulation reign on both sides—in the dialogue between Ophelia and Hamlet at the end of act 3, for instance, when Ophelia on the one hand is acting under the control of the King and Polonius while Hamlet on the other is playing the fool. Basing himself on Thomas Kyd's *Spanish Tragedy,* Shakespeare performs a strategic game in order to reveal the double standard of morals in human relations. To show the other worldly background of the world, Shakespeare introduces the famous ghost of Hamlet's father—a special effect far more impressive than any philosophical comment by Hamlet himself. Shakespeare introduces the ghost not as a simple stage effect but in order to complete the picture of the Elizabethan world (Frye 1984; Wilson 1935). Putting the transcendental dimension onto the stage as a real figure, Shakespeare at the same time preserves and expands this completeness: he preserves it by making visible the other world within this world; he expands it by making the stage the scene for things invisible to normal people. "Whereon do you look?", the Queen asks and Hamlet answers:

On him, on him! Look you, how pale he glares!
His form and cause conjoined, preaching to stones,
Would make them capable.

(3.4.125–28)

Like other dramatists of the Spanish Golden Age, Calderón invents miraculous effects: the *demonio* and the beautiful girl changed into a skeleton in *El mágico prodigioso (The prodigious magician)*, for instance. The dream construction of *La vida es sueño*, however, enables him to dispense with the miraculous precisely in a drama the main issue of which is the subordination of man's actions to metaphysical values. Shakespeare's dreams are recounted, like Lady MacBeth's, for example, or they are acted out, as in *A Midsummer Night's Dream;* but they are not identified with real life. It is only in *La vida es sueño* that one is faced with a dream that is real life.

Unlike Shakespeare, Calderón has a special genre at his disposal for showing the other side of the world: the Auto Sacramental.[4] The Corpus Christi play of the Spanish Golden Age takes up medieval techniques for representing transcendental subjects through allegory. Calderón, in particular, develops the genre and its capacity for animating conceits of a higher, metaphysical degree. Perhaps the best-known example of Calderón's mastery in this field is his *El gran teatro del mundo (The Great Stage of the World)* based on the well-known classical motif of the play within the play (Mehl 1965; Schmeling 1977; Orozco Díaz 1969, 171–216). The play that God orders from his own company echoes the play to which Segimundo is exposed. God, author of the play in the old Spanish sense of *autor* (stage manager) and at the same time in the modern sense of the word, like King Basilio in *La vida es sueño,* is watching a play of his own making executed by *el Mundo:*

> Pues soy tu Autor, y tú mi hechura eres,
> hoy de un concepto mío
> la ejecución a tus aplausos fío:
> una fiesta hacer quiero
> a mi mismo poder, si considero
> que sólo a ostentación de mi grandeza
> fiestas hará la gran naturaleza;
> y como siempre ha sido
> lo que más me ha alegrado, y divertido,
> la representación bien aplaudida,
> y es la representación la humana vida,
> una comedia sea
> la que hoy el cielo en tu teatro vea;
> si soy Autor, y si la fiesta es mía,
> por fuerza la ha de hacer mi compañía.
>
> (36–50)[5]

[I being your Maker, you the thing I made, I now wish to employ you in a thing invented for my joy. I mean to celebrate my power infinitely great: for does not mighty Nature find her sole delight in showing forth my might? Now as we know that the most pleasing entertainment is a show, and since we can interpret thus the entire Life of Man, I choose that Heaven shall today upon your stage witness a play. I, being audience and manager together, can make the company perform this, whether they would or not.] (2)

The subject matter of *El gran teatro del mundo* and of *La vida es sueño* is the same: putting man's free will to the test in the ordeals of everybody's individual life. The fortune of the two authors on the other hand is different: King Basilio's testing play becomes a test for himself, whereas God remains the one and unchallenged master of the play. By means of a very simple action staged by a handful of archetypes of a more medieval than baroque society, Calderón succeeds in evoking the working of the world and the rule of God.

In order to achieve the same result within the limits of his dramatic system Shakespeare has to proceed differently. He too speaks of universal order, especially in Ulysses' speech on "degree" and its possible ruin in *Troilus and Cressida* (Colahan 1978). Like Segismundo in his famous first monologue in *La vida es sueño,* Ulysses views the world order from his own unique perspective. But while Segismundo, contemplating his tower prison, compares the world order to his own unfortunate situation, Ulysses uses the Trojan War to reflect on the world as a whole, connecting "the heavens" and "communities" into "a picture of immense and varied activity, constantly threatened with dissolution and yet preserved from it by a superior unifying power" (Tillyard 1943, 10).

> The heavens themselves, the planets, and this centre
> Observe degree, priority, and place,
> Insisture, course, proportion, season, form,
> Office, and custom, in all line of order.
>
> (1.3.85–88)

And, on the opposite side, with an allusion to the conceit of world harmony:

> Take but degree away, untune that string,
> And hark what discord follows.
>
> (1.3.109–10)

The Elizabethan individual in Shakespeare's world does not complain, he states. Shakespeare's protagonists suffer from the effects of discord and appetite, "an universal wolf . . . seconded with will and power" (1.3.121–22), but at moments of testing or failure, they do not sacrifice their moral dignity. In Shakespeare, human dignity derives from divine sovereignty; Segismundo's triumph is perfect when, under this aspect, he realizes the human condition.

In speaking of universal order, Shakespeare assumes the point of view of individual experience. By contrast, Calderón not only presents this order through the learning process of Segismundo; he shows us God's realm itself, in the allegorical Auto Sacramental. Shakespeare has the advantage of painting social interplay in all its movements and facets, without the strict rules of Spanish social etiquette. Both confront questions of morality presented as either responsible or irresponsible acts. The soul-searching of Hamlet and King Basilio, the disruption and re-establishment of order, the failure or success of free will are but examples of Shakespeare's and Calderón's plays within the play.

2. The Mirror Image

Common ground and differences in painting and judging human behavior in the Renaissance and Baroque periods are illustrated by another metaphor, the mirror image as used by Shakespeare (Grabes 1973) and Calderón. The mirror is a twin brother of the theater—both are serving truth:

> . . . the purpose of playing . . . was and is, to hold, as 'twere, the mirror up to nature, to show virtue her own feature, scorn her own image, and the very age and body of the time his form and pressure.
>
> (*Hamlet* 3.2.19–23)

When, after staging the play within the play for the King and his mother, Hamlet is summoned by the latter, he sets out to complete the work of cognition:

> Come, come, and sit you down. You shall not budge,
> You go not till I set you up a glass
> Where you may see the inmost part of you.
>
> (3.4.19–21)

The dramatic dialogue is meant to complete the image that the play within the play had started. The theater as image of life is to be continued by the interpretation of that image in the mirror of speech. Both theater and mirror are the means for helping the Queen find a way out—the fact that she does not accept the proffered opportunity leads to her ruin.

Persons like the King and Hamlet's mother who avoid looking into the mirror have to be confronted with others who are longing for the truth. As Thomas Randolph puts it in *The Muses Looking glasse,* theater and mirror are made especially for them:

> So comedies, as poets do intend them,
> Serve first to show our faults, and then to mend them.
> Upon our stage two glasses oft there be;
> The comic mirror and the tragedy.
>
> (186)

Richard II, for instance, in Shakepeare's tragedy of the same name, is a person who uses the mirror correctly. He knows that the mirror tells the truth, but he also knows that mirrors may lie. The wise king is very up to date: some fifteen years before, an Italian scientist, Raffaele Mirami from Ferrara, had written in his *Compendiosa introduttione alla prima parte della specularia:* "For some people mirrors were a hieroglyph of truth because they can reveal all things presented to them—as is the habit of truth which cannot be hidden. Others, on the contrary, take mirrors to be symbols of falsehood because they often show things to be different from what they are" (Baltrusaitis 1978).

Coming to the end of his rule and in the presence of his triumphant rival Bolingbroke, Richard asks for a mirror:

> An if my word be sterling yet in England,
> Let it command a mirror hither straight,
> That it may show me what a face I have
> Since it is bankrout of his majesty.
>
> (4.1.264–67)

King Richard expects the mirror to answer truly his questions about his state. But the mirror shows him the same face as before; it lies like a flattering courtier:

> No deeper wrinkles yet? Hath sorrow struck
> So many blows upon this face of mine
> And made no deeper wounds? O flattering glass,
> Like to my followers in prosperity,
> Thou dost beguile me!
>
> (4.1.277–81)

There is only one way, then, to reestablish the correspondence between origin and effigy; between the real state of King Richard and his portrait in the mirror; namely to destroy it:

A brittle glory shineth in this face.
As brittle as the glory is the face,
                    (Dashes the glass to the floor)
For there it is, cracked in a hundred shivers.
Mark, silent King, the moral of this sport—
How soon my sorrow hath destroyed my face.

                                        (4.1.287–91)

The individual of the Renaissance remains, so one may conclude
from this scene, superior even in failure. Reality has priority; inner
state and appearance must coincide. Richard refuses to accept his
opponent's theory that there are only shadows on both sides:

> BOLINGBROKE. The shadow of your sorrow hath destroyed
>   The shadow of your face.
> RICHARD.   Say that again.
>   The shadow of my sorrow? Ha! let's see!
>   'Tis very true: my grief lies all within;
>   And these external manners of laments
>   Are merely shadows to the unseen grief
>   That swells with silence in the tortured soul.
>   There lies the substance.

                                        (4.1.292–99)

Looking forward from here to the late Spanish Golden Age, one
notices that self-assurance is no longer to be found. People in
decadent Spain either are fond of mirrors because they flatter them
or they fear mirrors because they tell them the truth. *Engaño*
(deceit) and *desengaño* (desillusion), *philautía* (self-love) and vanity
are the two sides of the mirror or, more exactly, the two ways of
using it (Grabes 1973, 176–82). In satire or in sermon the mirror
may be an admonition to self-reflection and self-complacency or
even self-deception. In aphorism 110 of his *Oráculo manual* (1647),
for instance, Baltasar Gracián recommends the beauty advanced in
years to smash the mirror like Shakespeare's Richard II: "Rompa el
espejo con tiempo, y con astucia / la belleza, y no con impaciencia
después, / al ver su desengaño" (398) ("Let beauty wisely break the
glass in time and not impatiently, when the time is passed and she
sees her disenchantment"). Diego Saavedra Fajardo on the other
hand, in his *Idea de un Príncipe político christiano* (1640) goes so
far as to use the broken mirror as an ideal transcending reality. The
emblematic figure of a lion reflected twice in a broken mirror
(*empresa* 33) has these words in the *subscriptio:*

Divida la inconstancia y envidia del tiempo en diversas partes el espejo de los Estados. Pero en cualquiera dellas, por pequeña que sea, hállese siempre entera la majestad. El que nació príncipe no se ha de mudar por accidentes extrínsecos. (327)

[Let the fickleness and envy of the times split the mirror of state in diverse parts. But in each, no matter how small, let majesty remain entire. He who was born to rule will not be changed by accidents foreign to his condition.]

Calderón is no exception to this double use of the mirror. Theater for him is not any longer, as in Lope de Vega's *Arte nuevo,* a simple mirror held up to the world, "espejo de las costumbres y una viva imagen de la verdad" (123–25). Rather, for Calderón theater is an instrument for judging the world and for improving it. Calderón's Comedias remind us of Thomas Randolph's "comic mirror" made "to show our faults and then to mend them," recalling the "grave tragedy," "the sad glass of cities and of courts" (186).

Leaving the orbit of *desengaño,* one is confronted with the opposite genre typical of Calderón: the court plays, especially the mythological ones where the ruling monarch is glorified in the shape of pagan gods (Neumeister 1978; Díez Borque 1986). In two instances one finds here the mirror as a motif of great importance: in the mythological play *Eco y Narciso (Echo and Narcissus)* and in the *Loa* of Calderón's last comedy, *Hado y divisa de Leonido y Marfisa (Fate and [heraldic] device of Leonido and Marfisa).* In both cases the mirror stands for *philautía,* self-love leading the protagonists to their own ruin (Fuchs 1977).

Narciso, in *Eco y Narciso,* does not succeed in severing the link with the mother in order to bestow his love on Eco. Persevering in a kind of ignorant puberty, he overrates the dead perfection of his own mirror portrait and disregards Eco, who could open the way to real life for him. Eco tries in vain to tell Narciso about the physical nature of the mirror's reflection:

> ¿A quién ves en esa fuente,
> Con quién a esa fuente hablas,
> Si cuanto está dentro della
> Sólo es una sombra falsa
> Que a nuestros ojos ofrece
> La reflexión en el agua?
>
> (2691–96)

[Whom do you see in the fountain and to whom do you speak, for all that is inside it is but a false shadow that the reflection in the water puts before our eyes.]

Narciso, under the fascination of the beautiful face seen in the fountain, despises the music of love:

> Como tú, hermoso prodigio,
> Sólo me miras y callas,
> Yo no hago más que mirarte
> Y callar. Pero esto basta,
> Porque, como yo te vea,
> ¿Qué más dicha?

(2619–24)[6]

[Just as you, o prodigy of beauty, only gaze on me and are silent, so do I not more than gaze silently on you. But that suffices for what greater bliss can there be but to look on you.]

Narciso fails in the initiation rite; he does not grow up and is therefore placed back in the order of creation from the level of a human being to that of a plant. It is only Achilles in *El monstruo de los jardines (The monster of the gardens)*, the mythological play intimately connected with *Eco y Narciso*, who gets out of this impasse by deciding in favor of his destiny and of (Christian) love *(amor divino)* (Neumeister 1978, chap. 5).

Narcissism, as Sigmund Freud would have called the behavior of Narciso, the charging *(cathexis)* of the mirror image with the whole *libido* of the *ego*, is normally a transitional stage, "le stade du miroir comme formateur de la fonction du Je," as Lacan designated this attitude in one of his early lectures (1966, 93–100). In *Eco y Narciso* Calderón demonstrates how dangerous it is to remain and to lose oneself in this narcissism meant by nature as a transition stage.

How dangerous narcissism can prove to be, even for society as a whole, can be seen, despite the best intentions of Calderón himself, in the second text, the *Loa* of *Hado y divisa de Leonido y Marfisa*. Here too, the mirror is of great importance (Neumeister 1978, 277–83; Varey 1984). Like *Eco y Narciso*, Calderón wrote the play for a court performance, to be held in the Coliseo theater of the Buen Retiro palace of Madrid. It is known that, during performances at the Coliseo, the king was seated not in the royal box but in the middle of the pit, right in front of the stage (Hartzenbusch 1850, 356; Brown and Elliott 1980).

José Caudi, stage designer of Carlos II, intensifies the eminent role the king is playing in such an arrangement by an optical effect of great symbolical significance: he confronts the king with his own portrait on the stage as if it were a mirror placed in perspective (Stoichita 1986). This device is described in the *Loa* to the play *Hado y divisa* as:

> En la frente del salón, ocupando el medio de la perspectiva, se hizo un trono cubierto de un suntuoso dosel, debajo del cual había dos retratos de nuestros felicísimos monarcas, imitados tan al vivo, que como estaban frente de sus originales pareció ser su espejo en que trasladaban sus peregrinas perfecciones. (358)[7]

> [On the front wall of the hall, occupying the middle of the perspective, was a throne covered with a sumptuous canopy, beneath which were two portraits of our most happy monarchs, so lifelike that, as they were placed opposite their originals, they seemed to be a mirror into which their rare perfections were transferred.] (39)[8]

Narciso gazing at his image in the water is echoed here by the king gazing at not his realm, not his subjects, but himself. The fourteen ancestors of the king placed on both sides of his painted mirror portrait as witnesses to his noble origins cannot conceal the fact that one is offered a case of public narcissism in its most pernicious form. The decadence of the Spanish Habsburgs comes to light precisely in the place intended to conceal it, the court theatre.[9] Calderón's mythological plays—the peak of perfection of the Spanish court theater of the seventeenth century—glorify the reigning dynasty in the figures of Greek mythology. In Calderón's last Comedia, however, the symbolic and allegorical dimensions of the mythological action are replaced by a dumb mirror followed by a simple Comedia *novetesca: el Rey se divierte*, the king is enjoying himself—and nothing more.

Calderón brings a long century of courtly *divertissements* to an end. The courts of London, Paris, Dresden, Vienna, Torino, and Madrid show how strong was the fascination of court pageantry. Princes and sovereigns are not only present as spectators; they also join in. Jacobean theater, above all in the masques of Ben Jonson designed by Inigo Jones, offers the royal family the best opportunities for taking part in the dramatic action: Prince Henry acts

Oberon without uttering a word; Queen Anne, her face painted black, plays a negress in Ben Jonson's *Masque of Blackness*.[10]

Theater turns into a royal toy: flattery and narcissism make the mirror dim; the theatre becomes idle motion. In 1637 Giovanni Lorenzo Bernini, better known as an artist than as a dramatic author, stages a *Commedia dei due teatri* in Rome. It is a piece of art worthy to be taken as a symbol of the Baroque age. Bernini, like Calderón, shows on the stage that which is in front of it. Dramatic action mirrors what is happening in the audience:

> si vide dalla parte di dentro, cioè di la della scena un popolo parte vero, è parte finto, che tutto insieme era così ben concertato, che rappresentava quasi il medesimo, che veramente era dalla parte di quà in molto numero per vedere detta Comedia.[11]

> [There can be seen partly backstage and partly onstage, a crowd partly acted and partly real which represented almost half of that great number that had come to see the play.]

Bernini fuses into one the conceit of the play within the play and the conceit of the mirror. And even more: according to John Evelyn, who visited Rome in 1644, Bernini "gave a Publique Opera (for so they call those Shews of that kind) where in he painted the seanes, cut the Statues, invented the Engines, composed the Musique, writ the Comedy and built the Theatre all himselfe" (Evelyn 1955, 1:261 and Orozco Díaz 1969, 202–4).[12] The personal union of artist, composer, and author enables Bernini to avoid the quarrels between dramatic author and scenographic engineer reported of Ben Jonson and Inigo Jones (Gordon 1975; Strong 1973), Calderón and Cosme Lotti (Neumeister 1978, 58–62).

Actually it does not matter who triumphs over whom in the quarrel: both parties are in the king's service, both are working in the golden cage of courtly culture and art.[13] Theater is losing contact with social reality outside the palace, a contact that still existed in Shakespeare and Lope de Vega, in Ben Jonson and Calderón, insofar as they were writing for a greater audience. But the paradox is that precisely through this isolation the court theater succeeds in bringing about one of the highest achievements of art: a *Gesamtkunstwerk* (in the word later coined by Richard Wagner), a synthesis of all literary and artistic possibilities in the same performance. And a further paradox: this work of art, reflecting itself in its own mirror, playing its own play, turns out to be the authentic representation of the Baroque. The picture world of the seventeenth-century theater corresponds perfectly with a world for which all outward appearance is mere illusion. It was the task of the following century to find the way back to reality.

Notes

1. On Falstaff, see J. Dover Wilson (1979); on the Calderonian *gracioso*, see Alberto Navarro González (1984).
2. Quotations are from the *Complete Pelican Shakespeare* (Harmondsworth: Pelican, 1981). On Falstaff and honor see Wilson (1979, 70–73).
3. References to this play are to *Obras completas*, vol. 1, edited by Angel Valbuena Briones (Madrid: Aguilar, 1966) and *Life Is a Dream*, translated by William E. Colford (Woodbury, New York: Barron's, 1958).
4. On the Corpus Christi plays in England and Spain see the contribution of Donald Dietz in this volume.
5. References to this play are to *El gran teatro del mundo*, edited by Domingo Yndurain (Madrid: Retorno, 1973) and to *The Great Stage of the World*, translated by George W. Brandt (Manchester: Manchester University Press, 1976).
6. Both quotations are from Calderón de la Barca, *Eco y Narciso*, edited by Charles V. Aubrun (Paris: Institut d'Etudes Hispaniques, 1963).
7. References to this play are to Pedro Calderón de la Barca: *Obras Completas* vol. 2, edited by Angel Valbuena Briones (Madrid: Aguilar, 1966).
8. Translated by Wardropper 1982.
9. Emilio Orozco Díaz (1983, 1062–63), quoting from the *Avisos* collected by Jerónimo de Barrionuevo between 1654 and 1658, concludes that even then in the "comedia del Retiro" "la gente era consciente de la triste realidad española; pero también de que todos olvidaban o *dormían*, entregados al sueño de esas comedias en que seguía ofreciéndose España en ideal plenitud de poder" ("The people were aware of the sad condition of Spain; but also of the fact that all were forgetting or *asleep* given over to the dreams of their Comedias in which Spain kept indulging at the height of her power").
10. Nevertheless, like Prince Henry in Shakespeare's *Henry IV*, the royal family appearing in a masque do not turn into actors: "Masquers are not actors; a lady or gentleman participating in a masque remains a lady or gentleman, and is not relieved from observing all the niceties of behavior at court. Queen Anne and her ladies danced in the masque because dancing is the perquisite of every lady and gentleman. It was, however, unthinkable for the Queen to become an actress and play in a play. For speaking roles, therefore, professional actors had to be used, and this meant that the form was by nature divided between players and masquers, actors and dancers. In the hands of Jonson and Jones, this practical consideration became a metaphysical conceit, and the form as they developed it rapidly separated into two sections. The first, called the anti-masque, was performed by professionals, and regularly presented a world of disorder or vice, everything that the ideal world of the courtly masquers was to overcome and supersede" (Harris, Orgel and Strong 1973, 35–36).
11. Massimiliano Montecucoli, letter to the Duke of Modena, 20 February 1637 (Fraschetti 1900, 263–64). The only surviving text upon which to base a judgement about Bernini as writer of as many as twenty plays is his untitled prose comedy *Fontana di Trevi*, edited under this title by Cesare d'Onofrio in 1963 and translated into English by Donald Beecher and Massimo Ciavolella (1985) under the title *The Impresario*.

12. Bernini thus reminds us of Inigo Jones in England and Filippo Aglié at the court of Savoy (McGowan 1970).

13. As Torquato Tasso puts it in a poem on an aviary erected by Federico II, Duke of Mantua: "La prigione è sí bella, / ove il nostro signor n'involve e tiene, / che 'l perder libertate onor diviene" (*Opere*, no. 1319). See Neumeister (1983).

Works Cited

Baltrusaitis, Jurgis. 1978. *Le Miroir*. Paris.

Bernini, Gian Lorenzo. 1985. *Fontana di Trevi (The Impresario)*. Edited and translated by Donald Beecher and Massimo Ciavolella. Ottawa: Dovehouse Editions.

Brown, Jonathan and J. H. Elliott. 1980. *A Palace for a King. The Buen Retiro and the Court of Philip IV*. Yale: Yale University Press.

Calderón de la Barca, Pedro. 1966. *Obras completas*. Vols. 1–2. Edited by Angel Valbuena Briones. Madrid: Aguilar.

———. 1973. *El gran teatro del mundo*. Edited by Diego Yndurain. Madrid: Retorno.

———. *Eco y Narciso*. 1963. Edited by Charles V. Aubrun. Paris: Institut d'Etudes hispaniques.

———. 1976. *The Great Stage of the World*. Translated by George W. Brandt. Manchester: Manchester University Press.

———. 1958. *Life Is a Dream*. Translated by William E. Colford. Woodbury, N.Y.: Barron's.

Colahan, Clark. 1978. "Calderón and Shakespeare on Universal Order: Two Passages Compared." *English Studies* 8:127–55.

The Complete Pelican Shakespeare. 1981. Hammondsworth: Pelican.

Díez Borque, José María. 1986. *Teatro y fiesta en el Barroco*. Barcelona: Serbal.

Evelyn, John. 1955. *The Diary of John Evelyn*. Edited by E. S. de Beer. Vol. 1. Oxford: Clarendon Press.

Fraschetti, Stanislao. 1900. *Il Bernini*. Milano: Hoepli.

Frye, Roland Mushat. 1984. *The Renaissance Hamlet*. Princeton: Princeton University Press.

Fuchs, Hans-Jürgen. 1977. *Entfremdung und Narzissmus*. Stuttgart: Metzler.

Gordon, D. G. 1975. "Poet and Architect: The Intellectual Setting of the Quarrel between Ben Jonson and Inigo Jones." In *The Renaissance Imagination*, edited by Stephen Orgel, 77–101. University of California Press.

Grabes, Herbert. 1973. *Speculum, mirror und looking-glass*. Tübingen: Niemeyer.

Gracián, Baltasar. 1969. *Obras Completas*. Vol. 1. Edited by Miguel Batllori and Ceferino Peralta. Madrid: Atlas.

Harris, John, Stephen Orgel, and Roy Strong. 1983. *The King's Arcadia: Inigo Jones and the Stuart Court*. Catalogue. London: Art Council of Great Britain.

Hartzenbusch, Juan Eugenio. 1850. "Descripción de la comedia . . ." In *Obras de Calderón de la Barca* 4. Biblioteca de Autores Españoles no. 14. Madrid.

Lacan, Jacques. 1966. *Ecrits*. Paris: Seuil.

Lovejoy, Arthur. 1936. *The Great Chain of Being*. Cambridge, Mass.: Harvard University Press.

McGowan, M. M. 1970. "Les fêtes de cour en Savoie; l'œuvre de Philippe d'Aglié." In *Revue d'histoire du théâtre* 3:183–241.

Mehl, Dieter. 1965. *The Elizabethan Dumb Show.* London.

Navarro González, Alberto. 1984. *Calderón de la Barca: De lo trágico a lo cómico.* Kassel: Reichenberger.

Neumeister, Sebastian. 1983. "*La Servil catena.* Von der freiwilligen Gefangenschaft des Dichters Tasso." In *Italien und die Romania in Humanismus und Renaissance,* edited by Klaus V. Hempfer and Enrico Straub. Wiesbaden: Steiner.

———. 1978. *Mythos und Repräsentation.* München: Fink.

Orozco Díaz, Emilio. 1969. *El Teatro y la teatralidad del Barroco.* Barcelona: Planeta.

———. 1983. "Sobre el barroco, expresión de una estructura histórica. Los determinantes socio-políticos y religiosos." In *Homenaje a Antonio Domínguez Ortiz,* 1057–76. Madrid: Ministerio de Educación y Ciencia.

Randolph, Thomas. 1875. *Poetical and Dramatic Works.* Edited by W. C. Hazlitt. London.

Rico, Francisco. 1970. *El pequeño mundo del hombre.* Madrid: Castalia.

Saavedra Fajardo, Diego. 1976. *Idea de un príncipe político-cristiano,* 1. Edited by Quintin Aldea Vaquero. Madrid: Editora Nacional.

Schmeling, Manfred. 1977. *Das Spiel im Spiel.* Rheinfelden: Schäuble.

Stoichita, Victor I. 1986. "Imago Regis: Kunsttheorie und königliches Porträt in den Meninas von Velázquez." *Zeitschrift für Kunstgeschichte* 49: 165–89.

Strong, Roy. 1984. *Art and Power. Renaissance festivals 1450–1650.* Woodbridge, Suff.: Boydell Press. First ed. under the title: *Splendour at Court,* 1973.

Tillyard, E. M. W. 1943. *The Elizabethan World Picture.* New York: Vintage.

Tasso, Torquato. 1964. *Opere.* Edited by Bruno Maier. Vol. 2. Milano: Rizzoli.

Varey, John E. 1984. "The Audience and the Play at Court Spectacles: The Role of the King." *Bulletin of Hispanic Studies* 61:399–406.

Vega, Lope de. 1971. *El arte nuevo de hacer comedias en este tiempo.* Edited by Juana de José Prades. Madrid: C.S.I.C.

Wardropper, B. 1982. "Calderon de la Barca and Late Seventeenth-Century Theatre." *Record of the Art Museum,* Princeton University 41, 2:35–41.

Wilson, J. Dover. 1979. *The Fortunes of Falstaff.* Cambridge: Cambridge University Press.

———. 1935. *What Happens in "Hamlet."* Cambridge: Cambridge University Press.

The Mob in Shakespeare and Lope de Vega

Teresa J. Kirschner

Introduction

The purpose of this paper is to trace the similarities and differences in the staging and treatment of mobs in Lope de Vega and Shakespeare. As will become clear, both playwrights use parallel techniques in the staging of the mob but have radically different attitudes toward it. Shakespeare brings out its contemptible characteristics; Lope, by contrast, emphasizes its willpower.

Within the general framework of the collective character that includes all the representational aspects of a group in a play, I have narrowed down the topic to the study of the "pueblo airado" or mob, variously designated as the criminal or baiting crowd in studies on mass psychology (LeBon 1969, 150–55; Canetti 1962, 49–52). This will enable me to discuss the dramatic devices used to evoke the presence of the multitude at a greater length. Examples of these are the visual presence of the mob as mass-actor on stage and the forceful sound effects of a group speaking in unison.

A quick perusal of the literature on mobs reveals an unevenness in the quantity of critical material available on each of the two authors. Even though both dramatists have made extensive use of crowds in their plays, only in the case of Shakespeare has the subject been studied in a comprehensive manner. There is no equivalent in Lope's bibliography to the studies by Brents Stirling (1965) and Lucy de Bruyn (1981), to name but two.

One reason for this lack of scholarship on the Spanish dramatist is the sheer volume of his plays, which makes it very difficult to master the totality of the *corpus* (Lope's output exceeds four hundred authenticated plays). Drawing on the published literature in the field, one can speak confidently of the representation of mobs in Shakespeare, as only three plays are involved: *Julius Caesar* and *Coriolanus*, with Cade's revolt scenes (4.2–10) in *The Second Part of Henry VI.* By contrast I can speak only of instances of mob occurrences in Lope. My research on Lope de Vega for this paper has covered eighty-two plays, a small dent in the playwright's total production. Therefore, when speaking about Lope de Vega, I will only generalize about the role of mobs in his national history plays. The baiting crowd appears in thirteen of these plays, *Fuenteovejuna (The Sheep Well,* in some English translations) being by far the most famous.[1]

The Multitude's Numeric Presence

One of the main problems facing any playwright who wants to portray a crowd is that of having enough bodies on stage to create a feeling of density, that being one of the main attributes required for the very formation of a crowd (Canetti 1962, 29). Lope, being a man of the theater, knew, however, that actors cost money and that the "autores" or company directors had limited budgets. Therefore, one usually senses in his various stage directions a wish to render the crowd as numerous as possible within the size limitations of a regular company.

For example, in *La tragedia del rey DonSebastián y bautismo del Príncipe de Marruecos (The tragedy of King Don Sebastian and the christening of the Prince of Morocco),* the people of Andújar are ready to rise in arms ("Andújar se alborota"—3, fol. 288ʳ) in order to prevent the Prince of Fez from converting to Christianity. The text reads as follows: "Enter Albacarín, Almanzor, Zayde, Dau, Axa, and Fátima, moors, carrying halberds and guns, and all those who are able to"[2] ("y otros que puedan," fol. 228ʳ). In other words: one sees on stage six of the Moorish characters already known to the audience, plus all other actors available at that time for the part.

In *El Nuevo Mundo descubierto por Cristóbal Colón (The new world discovered by Cristopher Colombus)* one witnesses the rebellion of the native Indians against the Spanish invaders, with Dulcanquellín, the Indian leader, pitted against the conquistador Terrazas and "los demás indios sobre los otros" (42a) ("the remaining Indians against the others"), "others" referring here to the Spaniards. Therefore, with proper costuming most of the company could participate in this uprising.

The same concern seems to be present in Shakespeare. In *Coriolanus* the play begins with the entrance of "a company of mutinous Citizens" (1.1.3). In *The Second Part of King Henry VI,* John Cade, Dick the Butcher, Smith the Weaver, and a Sawyer enter with those intriguing "infinite numbers" (4.2.82) of supposed mutineers; in *Julius Caesar*, Brutus and Cassius enter "with the Plebeians" (3.2.174), their number unspecified, but at one point Cassius exits with "some of the Plebeians" (3.2.175), and there are still enough plebeians left on stage for five different individuals to speak up. It is interesting to notice that, in the scene showing the lynching of Cinna the Poet, only four plebeians speak, thus giving Shakespeare or another director the chance of having the role of Cinna and the Fifth Plebeian played by the same actor, if needed.

However, if one is to believe the reviews that survive since the turn of the century, the success of these mob plays has been in direct proportion to their ability to convey a feeling for the electrifying force of a dense crowd (Humphreys 1984, 61–63; Kirschner 1977, 258 n. 24). When these scenes are portrayed with scant personnel, the plays founder, no matter how good the lead actors may be.

The Character "All"

Besides density, another main attribute of the crowd is equality. Equality "is absolute and indisputable and never questioned by the crowd itself. It is of fundamental importance and one might even define a crowd as a state of absolute equality" (Canetti 1962, 29).

Both Lope de Vega and Shakespeare have dramatically portrayed this idea of equality with the use of an all-encompassing character, usually called "All," which incorporates in itself the leveling of the individual within the nameless crowd. The main characteristic of this persona is that it speaks anonimously and/or in unison, its voice being the reflection of many voices.

Rather than the sound of sweet voices, however, what the audience hears is a loud scream or shout, the augmented sound being representative at the same time of the might of the crowd and of the contagious rhythmic throbbing attached to the criminal multitude. Thus a double crowd is created in the theater, the one formed by the actors on the stage and the other by the audience, who also become vicariously involved in the emotional discharge of the primordial hunting pack.

However, this multitudinous voice, which inherently carries in itself such emotional power, has the technical disadvantage of losing clarity of enunciation through its volume. Thus, as shall be seen, its speeches tend to be very short and often monosyllabic or repetitive. In this way the playwright avoids the choruslike, monotonous, long recitative that would break the frantic inner rhythm of the riot scenes. At the same time, he properly depicts the crystalization of the mob's intentions or desires in a more direct manner.

The extraordinary opening of *Coriolanus, in medias res* during a mutiny consists of four consecutive answers by the character "All" to four questions by a Citizen: 1. "Speak, speak." (1.1.3); 2. "Resolved, resolved." (1.1.6); 3. "We know't, we know't." (1.1.9); 4. "No more talking on't; let it be done. Away, away!" (1.1.12–13). In the well-known scene 8 of act 4 of *The Second Part of King Henry VI* a similar character "All" speaks also in syncopated short lines: 1. "God save the king! God save the king! (4.8.19); 2. "We'll follow Cade, we'll follow Cade!" (4.8.33); 3. "A Clifford! a Clifford! we'll follow the King and Clifford." (4.8.53–54).

In *Julius Caesar,* a crowd of Romans ransack the city after Caesar's assassination. The mob speaks for the first time through the generic character called "Plebeians" (3.2.174). Thereafter, throughout scenes 2 and 3 of act 3, during which the uprising takes place, the multitude speaks under the character renamed "All the Plebeians." The list of repartees by the crowd is too long to be examined in detail; however, I have chosen one example that is representative of all the exchanges in these two scenes: "The will! The will! We will hear Caesar's will!" (3.2.139). Again, as in Shakespeare's other instances and in those of Lope de Vega still to be examined, one finds many short words and sentences often repeated, a lot of exclamations and verbs of action, and no connectives to show cause and effect.

Lope is particularly fond of the character "All" ("Todos"). I have found it in thirty-four of the eighty-two plays examined. Many of these "Todos" portray homogeneous crowds of either soldiers honoring their leaders or peasants peacefully celebrating some sort of festivity, thus falling outside the parameters of this paper. There are, however, numerous instances in which the character "Todos" appears in the representation of uprisings. I have chosen some examples, diverse enough to give an idea of the range of variants of the topic in Lope's hands.

In *El galán de la Membrilla (The gallant gentleman of Membrilla),* a group of peasants (about thirty lads serving in the household of Tello), attack with halberds and slings another group that is singing a slanderous song against the patriarch of the household. In answer to Tello's directive: "¡Muera el ynfame mal naçido!"

("Death to the foul bastard!"), the character "All" answers "¡Muera!" (3.2264–65) ("Kill him!"), causing the persecution and eventual flight of the adversaries.

The play *El conde Fernán González (Count Ferdinand González)* shows the growing rebellion of the Castillian people who want to liberate their imprisoned Count. This play, even though dramatically very poor, is relevant to this analysis because it shows the transformation of a potentially murderous mob into a vindictive military force. One witnesses the mutiny of the noblemen with the character "All" shouting: "¡Sí juramos!" (2.1722) ("Yes, we swear it!"), "Sí prometemos" ("Yes, we promise") (2.1727); and the mutiny of the countrymen (2.1728–65) is seen in two separate but juxtaposed scenes. It is worth noting that, as the different towns and villages join the insurgents, and as their numbers grow, one of the noblemen says, "Cosa es de ver qué obedientes / vienen tantas varias gentes" (3.3137–38) ("Look how meekly all these people are coming"). He thus comments on the channeling of the multitude's raw impetus.

However, the most famous and dramatically successful embodiment of the character "All" in the whole of Lope de Vega's theater is to be found in *Fuenteovejuna*. There the totality of the rebellious town, after having killed their lord and master, Don Fernán Gómez de Guzmán, Grand Commander of the Military Order of Calatrava, utter only one monosyllabic word: "Sí" (3.2097) ("Yes"). Thus they succinctly summarize the collective resolve that has so far moved them.

To this point, I have discussed the techniques of representation connected with the presence of the mass-actor on stage and have been able to show that, as far as the mechanism is concerned, both Shakespeare and Lope de Vega, dramatized their crowds with the same devices. I shall now proceed to examine the role of the multitude in their plays in order to determine whether the crowd's actions and motivations are also depicted in the same manner.

The Depiction of the Multitude

As I mentioned in my introduction, the role of mobs has long attracted the attention of Shakespearean scholars. The clear consensus is that the populace is always portrayed with negative undertones. A long and never resolved debate has thus evolved as to the meaning of the playwright's rendition.

To give just a few examples, some critics, such as Upton Sinclair

(1925, 98–104), consider Shakespeare to have personally hated the masses. Others explain the role of the mob in dramatic structural terms: for example, the mob's portrayal reflects only the view of the aristocratic characters in the plays and not Shakespeare's own; or what Shakespeare is saying is "that the people are a power to be reckoned with in public life," and nothing more (McCloskey 1942). Still others look for historical reasons in Shakespeare's times to explain the poet's depiction of mutinous people: the playwright is writing for a public that has an endemic fear of rebellion (Boas 1969, 96–101) or is concerned at the rise in popularity of the Anabaptists (Stirling 1965, 190–91).

What has surprised me is how differently Shakespeare and Lope de Vega treat their mutineers. In Lope, as I shall show later, the irate people are determined and righteous; in Shakespeare they are represented as having two negative characteristics: fickleness and stench.

In the opening scene of *Julius Caesar,* for instance, the crowd, still tranquil at this point, has gathered in the streets to celebrate Caesar and "rejoice in his triumph" (1.1.31). But, upon hearing the harsh and scornful words of the Tribunes, Flavius and Marullus, for having already forgotten Pompey, they leave "tongue-tied in their guiltiness" (1.1.62), their devotion to Caesar forgotten.

Likewise, after Caesar'a assassination, the crowd shows its love for the fallen leader. The audience is told that "Men, wives, and children stare, cry out and run, / as it were doomsday" (3.1.97–98). The first words uttered by the plebeians during the famous funeral scene, "We will be satisfied!" (3.2.1), still show their concern for Julius Caesar by demanding a public explanation for his murder. But as soon as Brutus speaks, one can see them swayed away from their previous allegiance. Not only are they ready to forgive the Republican conspirator Brutus for his deed, but ironically they are willing to embody Julius in Brutus by naming the latter Caesar and offering to crown him (3.2.51).

The last and most notable transformation is that triggered by Mark Antony's "mischief" (3.2.253), which once again reverses the crowd's feelings toward the rehabilitation of Julius Caesar's memory. More important, he changes the very nature of the peaceful crowd by turning it into a criminal mob in pursuit of the men once called honorable, but now renamed traitors.

The same fickleness of the multitude is shown in *Coriolanus* and in *The Second Part of Henry VI.* Without going into the same detailed discussion as for *Julius Caesar,* let me just mention that in *Coriolanus* one sees the people in the Forum totally accepting

Coriolanus as Consul and considering him a "good friend to the people" (2.3.134) and then, upon their manipulation by the Tribunes, "repent in their election" (2.3.254) and march in mutiny towards the Capitol. In *The Second Part of Henry VI*, in the verbal duel between Lord Clifford and Jack Cade to win over the multitude to their cause, one witnesses the mob's will swayed from one to the other. Cade's ultimate loss prompts him to exclaim in the famous lines that summarize Shakespeare's mob representation: "Was ever feather so lightly blown to and fro as this multitude?" (4.8.55–56).

As for the so-called "stench motif" in Shakespeare's populace (Sterling 1965, 73), the examples are plentiful. To name just one taken from each of the three featured plays: in *Julius Caesar,* Casca describes the refusal of the crown by Caesar with the following words: "the rabblement hooted, and clapped their chopped hands, and threw up their sweaty nightcaps, and uttered such a deal of stinking breath because Caesar refused the crown that it had almost choked Caesar, for he swooned and fell down at it. And for mine own part, I durst not laugh, for fear of opening my lips and receiving the bad air" (1.2.242–48). In *The Second Part of King Henry VI*, one is reminded that Cade's "breath stinks with eating toasted cheese" (4.7.10). In *Coriolanus,* Menenius tells a "troop of Citizens" that they make the air unwholesome when they cast their stinking greasy caps (4.6.131–32). It is very difficult to defend such adjectives as dramatically necessary to the development of these plays.

In Lope's works there is no mention of either the crowd's foul smell or its unreliability. Such motives would be contradictory to his dramatic intent, since his crowds are always consistent in their purpose and are presented as a political force to be reckoned with, a force that goes, depending on the play, sometimes for and sometimes against the national interest as perceived by the dramatist.

Las famosas asturianas (The famous Asturian women) opens with a very brief scene in which a group of mutinous people is persecuting King Alphonse until he finds sanctuary in a monastery and is liberated from his pursuers by the noblemen who defend his cause. In the exchange of words that occurs during the flight scene the only negative epithets used to describe the rebels are those of "traidores" and "villanos" (1.4–5) ("traitors" and "villains"), which are very much standard for any of these plays.

Arauco domado (Arauco tamed) shows the rebellion of the Chilean Indian nation against their Spanish invaders. Even though Lope's play is obviously written from the Spanish imperial point of view, it shows to the very end the bravery and determination of the "bárbaro" ("barbarian") and "fieros" ("fierce") natives. He depicts their plight and shows their feelings in an evenhanded and sympathetic manner. Addressing the Spaniards, they say, "Ladrones, que a hurtar venís / el oro de nuestra tierra / y disfrazando la guerra / decís que a Carlo servís, / ¿qué sujeción nos pedís?" (1.133) ("Thieves, who have come to steal our gold and who hide your warlike intentions by feigning that you serve Charles, what servitude do you require of us?").

Furthermore, in act 2 viewers watch the Araucan people debate whether to attack the Spaniards. Their rebellion is consequently the result of deliberation among themselves and the expression of their desire to defend their freedom, not the response to a wild hate impulse or to a charismatic leader.

El hijo de Reduán (The son of Reduan), one of Lope's earlier plays, presents an example of a very abstract dramatization of the devastatingly fierce power of a mob. The Moors of Granada are up in arms because Gomel has killed their King. The crowd is never seen on stage in its totality: only four mutineers are shown although one is told that another "one thousand are by the door" ("Y mil que a la puerta están" 3, fol. 176ʳ). Since Lope does not use the mass-actor in this play, he conveys the fright that the enraged people arouse around them by having a lion enter on stage, thus creating instant horror among the courtiers and the audience.

Only Gomel is not frightened. The taming of the wild beast, icon of the unruly horde, is equated to the turning of the people's wills, who, upon seeing Gomel's courage, instead of killing him, recognize him as their legitimate new King. The emblematic significance of the taming of the lionlike mob is further emphasized by having Gomel fall asleep with the tame lion at his feet, thus adding to the scene the supernatural magic of the dream.

However, in this dramatization no nasty attributes are given to the mutineers. On the contrary, even though the play is written around Gomel's life exploits from childhood until he becomes king, the motivation of the rebellious forces is well explained: he has broken the law by slaying the king; the kingdom has living princes who are the legitimate heirs; they are offended by Gomel's deeds: "y dicen que en matarle allí / rompiste la misma ley; / y de dos hijos que son / legítimos de la Reina, / el mayor dicen que reina" (3, fol. 177ᵛ) ("and they say that in killing him you broke the selfsame law and that the eldest of the children the Queen had by him should reign in his stead").

The mob is thus represented as a natural force whose inpetus is uncontrollable but whose motivation is not contemptible, as it so often is in Shakespeare. In fact the rebellion is in defense of the *status quo* because the people of Granada want to continue living within the boundaries of the established monarchy and not under the rule of a usurper. Lope's solution is to make Gomel the lost eldest crown prince who unknowingly had already shown his noble nature through his courage; and thus the people are vindicated by accepting him as their new king.

Fuenteovejuna is the ultimate example of sublimation of a crowd's might in pursuing a predetermined goal. The group of peasants who, after long suffering and deliberations, rise against their lord by killing him are not only not foul, smelly, and unruly, but are full of a sense of dignity and honor. After the killing, they rally round to the cry "Fuenteovejuna," which is the expression of their collective will and which cannot be broken even under the harsh "questioning" of the King's prosecutor (3.2203–58).

Thus if *Julius Caesar* is the prototype of the mob's fickleness, *Fuenteovejuna* is a model for the mob's willpower. However, both plays describe the destructive powers of the multitude with nearly the same wording: "¡Rompe, derriba, hunde, quema, abrasa!" (3, 1858) ("Smash, break, destroy, demolish, burn, set alight!")[3] says Lope; "Revenge! About! Seek! Burn! Fire! Kill! Slay!" (3.2.199), says Shakespeare.

In *Julius Caesar* one sees the crowd from the outside, through the eyes of their leaders and manipulators. In *Fuenteovejuna* one sees the crowd from within and learns about their long path to self-determination. Both playwrights were right in choosing different perspectives, given their different dramatic objectives.

It is quite puzzling to see such divergent treatment of the same subject by two authors who were writing at approximately the same time and for very similar popular, mixed audiences.

At the beginning of this century, under the influence of the Romantics and Menéndez Pelayo, Lope was viewed as the democratic writer par excellence while Calderón was seen as a conservative. Subsequently, since the fifties, in the revisionist mood of a much needed reevaluation of Calderón's theater, Lope has been put down as a traditionalist writer. Since such simplistic labels are quite meaningless in terms of the seventeenth-century mentality, one might more appropriately say simply that Lope and his public had a great affinity for the low and honorable man. The message is that people will rebel for a cause close to their heart: their personal honor, their religion, and their king. In Shakespeare one senses that there is no cause worth a rebel, let alone a base rebel.

Conclusion

I have tried to demonstrate the importance of the multitude in both Shakespeare's and Lope's plays. Similar in their representational techniques, yet different in their meaning, the mob plays of each author include some of their best works. *Coriolanus, Julius Caesar,* and *Fuenteovejuna* are rightly considered masterpieces.

To conclude on a disheartening note, a review of the secondary material on the literary use of mob scenes corroborates Francisco Ruiz Ramón's theory (1978, 125–29) of the perennial invisibility of Spanish literature in the Western literary world in general, and the lack of impact the Spanish theater has had in the English-speaking world in particular.

Indeed, despite the extraordinary international fame of *Fuenteovejuna* and despite the preeminence of the collectivity in this work, I have not found one single reference to this play or to its author in the general discussion of the literary and/or psychological studies of the crowd.

Such seminal works as Paul Reiwald's (1948) and George Boas's (1969), as well as the article by Aureliu Weiss (1967–68) on mob scenes, totally omit Lope's contribution to the subject while remembering Shakespeare's.[4] I hope that in the future a more balanced overview of this subject will be given and such an unjust omission corrected.

Notes

1. Comedias in which the baiting crowd appears:

> *Las almenas de Toro*
> *Arauco domado*
> *Las Batuecas del Duque de Alba*
> *El conde Fernán González*
> *Fuenteovejuna*
> *Las famosas asturianas*
> *El galán de la Membrilla*
> *El hijo de Reduán*
> *La montañesa (La amistad pagada)*
> *El Nuevo Mundo descubierto por Cristóbal Colón*
> *La tragedia del rey D. Sebastián y bautismo del Príncipe de Marruecos*
> *El valiente Céspedes*
> *La vida y muerte del rey Bamba*

2. My thanks to Professor Dawn Smith for her help with the English translation of all quotations from Lope's texts.

3. It is interesting to note that William E. Colford's translation of *Fuenteovejuna* (1969, 129) fails to recognize the need for a series of verbs of action: "Now smash and burn the place, and kill them all!"

4. Even more extraordinary is the book on crowds by Rémy Martel (1974), which omits both Lope's and Shakespeare's contributions to the topic.

Works Cited

Boas, George. 1969. "Shakespeare." In *Vox Populi: Essays in the History of an Idea,* 96–101. Baltimore: The Johns Hopkins Press.

Bruyn, Lucy de. 1981. *Mob-Rule and Riots: The Present Mirrored in the Past.* London & New York: Regency Press.

Canetti, Elias. 1962. *Crowds and Power.* London: Victor Gollancz.

Kirschner, Teresa J. 1977. "Sobrevivencia de una comedia: historia de la difusión de *Fuenteovejuna.*" *Revista Canadiense de Estudios Hispánicos* 1, no. 3:255–71.

Lebon, Gustave. 1969. *The Crowd.* New York: Ballantine.

Martel, Rémy. 1974. *La foule.* Paris: Librairie Larousse.

McCloskey, John C. 1942. "Fear of the People as a Minor Motive in Shakespeare." *The Shakespeare Association Bulletin* 17:67–72.

Reiwald, Paul. 1948. "Der Führer als Redner. Die Leichenreden in *"Julius Cäsar."* In *Vom Geist der Massen. Handbuch der Massenpsychologie,* 598–603. Zürich: Pan-Verlag.

Ruiz Ramón, Francisco. 1978. *Estudios de teatro clásico y contemporáneo.* Madrid: Fundación Juan March & Ediciones Cátedra.

Shakespeare, William. 1960. *The Tragedy of Coriolanus.* Edited by John Dover Wilson. Cambridge: Cambridge University Press.

———. 1968. *The Second Part of King Henry VI.* Edited by John Dover Wilson. Cambridge: Cambridge University Press.

———. 1984. *Julius Caesar.* Edited by Arthur Humphreys. Oxford: Clarendon Press.

Sinclair, Upton. 1925. *Mammonart.* Pasadena, Calif.: Published by the author.

Stirling, Brents. 1965. *The Populace in Shakespeare.* New York: AMS.

———. 1945. "Shakespeare's Mob Scenes: A Reinterpretation." *The Huntington Library Quarterly* 3:213–40.

Vega Carpio, Lope de. *Parte XI de las comedias de Lope de Vega Carpio* (R-13862), *La tragedia del rey Don Sebastián y bautismo del Príncipe de Marruecos.*

———. 1980. *El Nuevo Mundo descubierto por Cristóbal Colón.* Edited by J. Lemartin and Charles Minguet. Lille: Presses Universitaires de Lille.

———. 1962. *El galán de la Membrilla.* Edited by Diego Marín and Evelyn Rugg. Madrid: Anejos del Boletín de la Real Academia Española.

———. 1963. *El conde Fernán González.* Edited by Raymond Marcus. Paris: Centre de Recherches de l'Institut d' Etudes Hispaniques.

———. 1981. *Fuenteovejuna.* Edited by Maria Grazia Profeti. Barcelona: Planeta.

———. 1969. *Fuenteovejuna.* Translated by William E. Colford. Woodbury, N.Y.: Barron's.

———. 1982. *Las famosas asturianas.* Edited by Alonso Zamora Vicente. Salinas, Asturias: Ayala.

———. 1954. *Arauco domado.* Edited by Antonio de Lezama. Santiago de Chile: Zig-Zag.

———. *Parte I de las comedias de Lope de Vega Carpio* (R-13852), *El hijo de Reduán.*

Weiss, Aureliu. 1967–68. "Les foules sur la scène." *Chronika Aisthetikes. Annales d'Esthétique* 6–7:50–63.

Lovesickness, Diagnosis, and Destiny in the Renaissance Theaters of England and Spain: The Parallel Development of a Medico-Literary Motif

Donald A. Beecher

The great Catalan physician Arnald of Villanova, late in the thirteenth century, wrote a *Tractatus de amore heroico,* a medical treatise on erotic love in which he defined the condition as a disease ensuing from a "violent and obsessive cogitation upon the object of desire accompanied by the confidence of being able to obtain the pleasure perceived from it" (46).[1] If this confidence is well placed and the erotic appetites can be satisfied, the psyche will be released from its fixations, the body purged of excessive semen, which was reckoned to be among the material causes of erotic melancholy, and the person will return to a state of health. If the confidence is misplaced—either due to a deranged reason that dotes upon an impossible object, or because it is itself simply "fantastical" and corrupt—the lover will fall prey to a series of pathological crises that will lead to despondency and death. The challenge for the medical philosopher was to find those counterbalancing agents in diet, induced evacuation, exercise, and psychological distraction that could break the cycle of psychopathological events that must otherwise lead to a state of chronic disease—therapy that, I might add, included coitus with other women as a means for diverting the attention of the patient from the chosen object and for evacuating the redundant seed.[2]

One would seem to be still quite far from the theaters of Renaissance Spain and England. Yet in a chronological sense one is never far, since these medical ideas remained essentially unchanged down to the seventeenth century; the Renaissance medical specialists on the *topos* cited Gordon and Arnald as well as Galen and Rhazes as their contemporaries, and as having equal authority. Hence the generic portrait of the pathologically eroticized lover created by the physicians was likewise a contemporary portrait.[3] The point is that in such a portrait there is much of potential interest to the dramatist. Arnald had identified the half-demented fixation of the melancholy *amoroso* whose attention to an object of desire must produce union or conduct the victim to a funest end, since death by disease or suicide was believed to be inevitable. It was simply a matter of superimposing the melancholy lover upon an action in which the medical vocabulary could legitimate the eccentric behavior of the protagonist, while the physiological necessity of the condition could become both motivation and destiny within that action. In short, the discovery to be made was the potential for theatrical novelty in bringing together the medical perspective and the patterns of intrigue leading either to the happy union characteristic of romance comedy or to the doleful demise of the unrequited protagonists in romance tragedy. The point remaining to be established is that precisely such a commingling of elements took place in the theaters of Renaissance Spain and England.

Although the Elizabethan and Spanish Golden Age theaters were largely, if not totally, isolated from one another in a way that precluded an immediate cross-fertilization or sharing of theatrical components and elements, there were, nevertheless, ideas and disciplines, such as the Galenic philosophy concerning the passions, that crossed religious and political barriers and allowed for the parallel development of *topoi* in these two theaters. What one must attribute to the accidents of parallelism is that the dramatists of both countries actually did recognize, more or less simultaneously, the theatrical potential in the portrait of the lover possessed of a "violent and obsessive cogitation," that is to say, the lover driven by his physiological constitution, the lover characterized by compulsive grief, madness, and a withdrawal from society and in due course from life itself. Yet through a set of common literary sources, even that simultaneous development becomes less accidental. Once the literary tradition concerned with pathological eroticism had recommended itself to playwrights in both countries, experimentation in the theater would teach them the means for joining the generic portrait of the melancholy lover to a paradigmatic plot through which the erotic desire could be discovered and made the motivation for action or the precondition for the tragic dénouement.

These two elements in the theater belong, on the one hand, to the study of characterological prototypes and, on the other, to the study of plot units that function as "theatergrams" held, as it were, in a common repository of integral miniature scenarios that could be assembled and reassembled into new and compound fables.[4] As was so often the case, the theatergrams that will concern us began as adaptations of fables drawn from prose fiction, from romance tales, and, in particular, from the novelle of the Italian writers from Boccaccio to Bandello. Moreover, just as the novelists themselves could interpret their fables according to commonplace medical ideas, so the dramatists could seek to join idea and action in a single theatrical unit revolving around certain medical commonplaces.

The nucleus of narrative and idea involving amorous melancholy was so entirely ubiquitous as virtually to thrust itself upon the attention of the dramatists in both countries. It was a nucleus that lent itself to a variety of dramatic exploitations from the comic to the sentimental. One is reminded by Pilarte in António Ferreira's *Comédia do Fanchono ou de Bristo* (1562) that "melancholy is à la mode among today's youth, and that is why you see so many heartsick young women" (3.2.279).[5] That was precisely Rosalind's message to Orlando in act 3, scene 2 of *As You Like It* where she accuses him of being a fraud since he had none of the marks of pathological love about him: lean cheeks, sunken eyes, taciturnity, a neglected appearance, "everything about you demonstrating a careless desolation." Even Pilarte was aware of the scientific origins of the mode and could not deny that the individual constitution or complexion was a true differentiator of persons, just as Rosalind clearly knew the medical language of love. By contrast, Tirso de Molina offers in *El melancólico* a portrait of a young man undone by amorous grief. Rogerio is educated, creative, generous, a man of moderation until his love for a woman, separated from him by class differences, attacks his vital spirits, corrupts his judgment, and drives him to despair. The English drama provides a similar range of developments from fashionable melancholy poseurs and characters in their humors to suicidal lovers and abject erotic psychopaths. The challenge in both theaters was to accommodate this characterological potential to a suitable structure of action, which, in fact, meant to appropriate narrative sequences from romance and ballad literature that featured crises resulting not only from amorous fixations on the part of the protagonists, but also from extreme passions threatening mania or death.

At this juncture my argument must take a specific turn. I have held that the theaters of England and Spain possessed a certain potential in common with regard to their representation of deep erotic passions, given the universalization of the medical ideas describing the pathology of erotic love. I have held, too, that the investigation of the medical tradition can, to a degree, elucidate the behaviors of such characters, based as they are upon popularized commonplaces involving the humors and the corruption of the imagination. I have held that there was an abundance of prototypes in the ballad, romance, and novella traditions that became popular in both countries. But the transition from received ideas and units of fable to drama cannot be made without some attention to the demands of the theatrical medium itself. Theater is an art form of action and requires that the inner life of each character somehow manifest itself as motivation leading to encounters, conflicts, and resolutions that can be demonstrated through action. More specifically, though the playwright may well have appreciated the pathological lover as a type, the antisocial, taciturn, and passive behavior of the character is antithetical to dramatic portrayal. The psychological portrait must somehow be incorporated into an intrigue wherein others are concerned first with the nature of the malady and then with finding a cure for love. One resolution to the problem is the introduction of a physician, who serves first to discover the cause of the secret grief, and who then offers his services on the social level as an *alcahuete* or go-between in order to cure his patient through joining him with the object of his desire. That solution was discovered in the theaters of both England and Spain and is of particular interest since the generic theatergram created by the presence of the physician is identical to the clinical scenario recommended by the physicians of the age—a parallel derived ultimately from a common source.

For the origins of that narrative unit one must look to a single source in the story of Erasistratus and his cunning analysis of the lovesick Antiochus, son of King Seleucus of Babylon, smitten by his beautiful young stepmother Stratonice. If the story has a basis in history, it must be traced to the fourth-century B.C. physician Erasistratus, who was allegedly called by an anxious king to the bedside of his languishing son. The historical evidence is slight, but there can be little doubt that by the early years of our era the story was already a staple of Greek romance. It was popularized by Valerius Maximus in the first century B.C. in his *Factorum et dictorum memorabilium* (261–63), and by Plutarch in his *Life of Demetrius*.[6] It was the version by Plutarch that caught Galen's attention, for Plutarch not only elaborated upon the way in which the young man sought to avoid wounding his father by fighting down his desires and how he sought to escape from his despair by resorting to sickness and starvation, but Plutarch also remarked upon the curious leaping of the pulse when Stratonice entered the room—a fact noticed by the doctor—and he enlarged upon other symptoms as well: "stammering speech, fiery flushes, darkened vision, sudden sweating, irregular palpitations of the heart, and finally, as his soul was taken by storm, helplessness, stupor and pallor" (92,94).[7] In short Plutarch joined to his romance narrative a medical component that was to become the subject of debate among physicians during the following sixteen centuries.

Through the pulse, Erasistratus diagnosed the cause of the disease, but he knew no cure except to join the lovers together, a cure as suited to the advancement of a romance narrative as to the practices of medicine, provided the physician could find a way to circumvent the problems of honor, previous marriage, and the conflict of interests between father and son over an ostensibly nonnegotiable object of desire. In that early tale, Erasistratus forces the king to choose, with the result that Seleucus is prevailed upon to transfer to his son not only his wife but his kingdom. That story is passed down to the Renaissance, on the one hand, in the treatises of nearly all the physicians who wrote of *amor hereos* and the *pulsus amatorius,* and on the other, in dozens of literary sequels that include versions by Appian, Suidas, the authors of *The Thousand and One Nights,* of the *Gesta Romanorum,* and of the *Mesnewi,* as well as by Boccaccio, Ascanio dei Mori, Leon Battista Alberti, Petrarch, and Bandello, to name but a few. It was largely through Petrarch and Bandello that the story became popular in both England and the Iberian peninsula, but its classical forms were widely known, and its counterpart versions in the medical literature were likewise seldom far from sight.[8]

The motif enters the Spanish theater directly from a reading of the classical sources, whether Plutarch, Appian, or Valerius Maximus, in the *Aquilana* of Torres Naharro (Kennedy 1940). The play is faithful to the romance tradition in which a foreign prince in disguise wins favor at the Spanish court, falls secretly in love with the king's daughter, wins, then loses her love, and is finally betrayed to the king by the doctors of the court called in to treat him during an illness. That illness turns out to be lovesickness caused by Feliciana's momentary rejection of his love. His condition is discovered by the physician Esculapius through holding the young man's pulse as the women of the court are brought into the room. There is hope for a comic solution because Feliciana has a change of heart, because she is not the king's wife but his daughter, and because the young man is a crown prince in disguise, a fact related at the right moment to serve a happy dénouement. But the central dramatic structure is built upon his melancholy despair, and the medical technique through which the fortunes of the lovers are ultimately reversed is the identifying gesture. That Feliciana threatens suicide by leaping from a tower when her father meditates a harsh punishment for the presumptuous intruder is a certain indication that Naharro had also read the *Celestina,* since Melibea, in her melancholy, leaps from a tower. That he read the *Celestina* also reminds us that he could have remembered the words of Calisto: "Let darkness encompass my woe, solitude be the companion of my despair. My misery flies from the light of day. O death, how welcome art thou to wretches that summon thee in anguish! Oh, even if those learned doctors Hippocrates and Galen were here now, they could not abate the pain I feel! O Seleucian pity, soften the heart of Pleberio's daughter, and abandon me not to the fate of Pyramus and most unhappy Thisbe!" (2).[9]

The *El-Rei Seleuco* of Luis de Camões, written around 1545 when he was perhaps twenty or twenty-one years old, also antedates the appearance of Bandello's short story on the theme. Nevertheless, Ruth Lee Kennedy (1940) argues, on the basis of the story's appearance in 1540 in Pedro Mexía's *Silva de varia lección,* that "the theme was common knowledge." One need not pause long over Camões's play, for it is a curious mixture of dramatized narrative and interludelike diversions including song and dance brought in as therapy for the suffering prince. The play takes the narrative at face value and simply concentrates upon the dramatization of doleful grief. There is a new dimension, however, in the fact that Stratonice herself joins in the lamentations in a way suggesting a hidden sympathy for the prince. Few before Camões had consulted her feelings, though the Stratonice figure will have a central role to play in subsequent renditions of the story. In the same fashion, Camões is sensitive to the plight of a father bereft, by his own declaration, of both wife and kingdom. The king's pathos was no doubt inspired by Petrarch's *Trionfo d'amore,* in which Seleucus appears in the train of the torturing Cupid as the result of his sacrifice.[10]

After Camões, the story was kept alive in the ballads of the age, as in part 3, canto 7 of Alonso de Fuentes's *Libro de los quarenta cantos pelegrinos* (1564) and in the *Coro febeo* of Juan de la Cueva, and re-emerges in the mid-seventeenth century in the *Antíoco y Seleuco* of Agustín Moreto.

Tirso de Molina was perhaps too fundamentally theatrical in his instincts to be tempted into dramatizing the story because of the conflicting ethos between the narrative of long suffering and melancholy and the comic solution that is not brought about by the lover's own industry. Dramatic inclinations suggest either a degree of collusion between the young lovers, a feigned illness, a tool-character doctor, and a trick to dupe the old one, or else tragic suffering and death. The story was predestined to evolve in the theater toward either total intrigue or total tragedy. Yet Tirso realized the dramatic force inherent both in the lovesick protagonist and in the discovery scene employing medical means. His *La venganza de Tamar (Tamar's revenge)*, with its reference to the lover's pulse, is a dramatization of the biblical story of Amnon's tyrannical love for his half-sister and of a feigned sickness, though motivated by true distress, by which he lures her to his chamber in order to rape her. It is worth adding that this story had also entered the medical literature as an example of compulsive love in which the lover could be known by the signs of erotic depression.

An even more striking embodiment of these patterns of action and characterization, however, is to be found in Lope de Vega's *El castigo sin venganza (Punishment without revenge)*, in which the Duke of Ferrara's illegitimate son Federico falls in love with Casandra, a girl soon to be married to the Duke. The relationships to the story of Antiochus are readily apparent. A gesture of munificence on the part of the Duke toward his son, however, is the course not taken in this play, revealing how easy it is to turn the action to a tragedy of revenge. The marriage to the Duke takes place, while the young man's burning love makes him forget all honor. Moreover, variations on the prototype produce an unfaithful husband and a discontented young bride who is drawn by degrees to the son. Federico nevertheless falls into a stage of deep lovesickness. Their love is given a moment to bloom during the Duke's absence, but once they are betrayed to him, his vengence is swift and sure, for he arranges first Casandra's death, killed in error by Federico, and then the execution of his own son. The revenge of a father upon a bastard son for daring to take his wife from him is the inverse of the solution granted by Seleucus, but the story continues to turn around compulsive eroticism, disease, and desperation. The variation reminds one of the archetypal contest between father and son for the mother as sex object that underlies the generic story. The questions of taboos and of incest are just under the surface, whether the solution is paternal generosity or paternal hostility. Sickness and imminent death as the results of love are also the rhetoric whereby the son can beg grace from the rival character who is also his own progenitor. In Lope's variation, as in the others, the medical definition of *amor hereos* provides the repertory of received ideas upon which the action is based.

Passing to the English theater, I have been unable to discover a single play before the eighteenth century dealing by name with Antiochus and Stratonice, though major playwrights in the Jacobean and Caroline periods rang a series of changes on the theatergram containing the essence of the narrative.[11] That idea-action cluster calls for a secretive lover slowly perishing from unsatisfied love, a physician figure who employs a stratagem of discovery, and an ensuing action in which the physician or his counterpart seeks to unite the lover with the object of his desire. The success of that intrigue, of course, depends upon the cooperation of the patient, the beloved, and those who may have prior claim to her. Antiochus wins favor through his persistent display of consideration for his father's honor, but the formula is subject to a significant number of recombinant possibilities. One such is to intensify the misery of the lovesick protagonist by confronting him with insuperable obstacles to the realization of his erotic desires; they include the barrier of consanguinity and incest, total rejection by the beloved, and the refusal of the party with prior claim to relinquish custody. The compulsive motivations of the pathological lover, likewise, serve the mannerist ends of the Jacobeans interested in examining the human psyche in states of extreme torment, pushed to the limits of sanity on the stage. They found in the mechanisms of love as a chronic disease the means for carrying the protagonist from a state of desire to a state of psychic stress, paralysis, or frenzy. In short, it is a theatergram that allows for a gamut of exploitations from the familiar intrigue-generated union of lovers to an examination of erotic insanity.

No doubt, too, the search for theatrical novelty among these dramatists was part of the incentive behind their kaleidoscopic manipulation of such narrative motifs. It is often difficult to say whether variations were the fruits of their own invention or the product of a refitting of pre-established motifs. It is easy enough to substitute a friend and his fiancée for the Seleucus father figure, and easy to replace the physician with a shrewd and observant bystander. Moreover, most of these readings have their literary antecedents. Pandarus, in a sense, plays the doctor in Chaucer's *Troilus and Criseyde* by diagnosing the pining Troilus and by serving as matchmaker. The generosity of Seleucus has its counterpart in tale 171 of the *Gesta Romanorum,* in which a knight bestows his fiancée and her private fortune upon a friend in order to spare his life. The girl was very beautiful, and when his friend saw her during a visit, "he fell sick and pined away" (322).[12] The story has features in common with Chaucer's "Knight's Tale of Palamon and Arcite" and with the story of Antiochus and Stratonice, though it derives, in fact, from the *Clericalis Disciplina* of Petrus Alphonsus and afterwards produces a heritage of its own that includes Boccaccio's *Tito and Gisippo* and Lydgate's *Tale of Two Merchants of Egypt and of Baldad*. Many of its elements become apparent in the play *Monsieur Thomas*.

Perhaps the first major exploration of the motif in the English theater appears in *The Two Noble Kinsmen*, a play assigned jointly to Shakespeare and Fletcher and based on Chaucer's tale of Palamon and Arcite. In the subplot, the jailer's daughter falls in love with Palamon, but cannot reveal her love since she is far below him in station. Moveover, Palamon has his attentions frantically fixed upon another and is, in any case, a ward of the girl's father and an enemy to her country. Since any one of these obstacles would have been sufficient to dash her hopes, her only recourse is to madness and death—an end averted only through the therapeutic trickery imposed upon her by a cunning physician. Diversionary tactics and ruses of this nature, in fact, had long been recommended for the treatment of distracted and melancholy persons, and the great Avicenna himself boasts of having effected several cures in this way. The jailer's daughter is a charming melancholiac. She treats the audience to the "nonny" songs of bedlam they seemed to appreciate. "She is continually in a harmless distemper, sleeps little; altogether without appetite, save often drinking; dreaming of another world and a better" (4.3.3–5).[13] These are the conventional symptoms of the disease; the thirst is caused by the intense heat and dryness of atrabilious melancholy, for, as the doctor states, " 'tis not an engraffed madness but a most thick and profound melancholy." A willing wooer, upon the doctor's advice, disguises himself as the longed-for object and meets her in a dimly lit room, where he speaks to her of love and where he is instructed even to lie with her if she asks it "in the way of cure," for, as the doctor declares, "it cures . . . *ipso facto,* / The melancholy humor that infects her" (5.2.36–37). Hippocrates himself said as much in *The Diseases of Young Women*, where he prescribes the benefits of marriage as being the only cure for erotic hysteria.

As we pass to Fletcher's *Monsieur Thomas,* a play written in the same period as *The Two Noble Kinsmen,* that is, sometime between 1610 and 1616, one discovers the familiar triangle of lovers and a case of lovesickness that creates the conflict, but in circumstances transformed through the influence of new sources. The play contains both the act of generosity of a man toward his afflicted friend in sacrificing his interests in a cherished fiancée and the medical detection scene of the Antiochus and Stratonice story. The substitution of a friend for the father is in keeping with the model set out in the *Gesta Romanorum* already described. When the young lady, Cellide, is sent to the patient's bedside, she is called "a virtuous fair Physician," and the lovesick protagonist is half detected when it is remarked that his pulse "beats like a drum" (4:108).[14] Valentine, when he learns of the true cause of his friend's plight, determines to abandon his interests in Cellide in order to save his friend's life. The most significant departure from the story in prototype is the consideration of the feelings of the lady. Unlike Stratonice, Cellide becomes utterly confused, for she sees herself as being prostituted to another for whom she has no special affection, while at the same time, when she consents to visit the patient, she finds herself scorned and rejected as an inconstant and perfidious woman by the man she would comfort. The discovery of the Stratonice figure is a new and adaptable dimension implicit in the theatergram that will attract subsequent dramatists. Fletcher resolves his story in the conventional way after several complex detours that include Cellide's flight to a nunnery. But after time and testing, Valentine's magnanimous offer stands firm and Cellide transfers her affections to the friend according to formula. That consultation of the lady's feelings, in light of the *Gesta Romanorum* and the Antiochus and Stratonice models, would seem to be a spontaneous variation arising with an interest in character motivation. In fact, in Fletcher's case, Cellide's behavior points, rather, to a new source in which the two previously named traditions had already been fully integrated, namely the tale of Celidée in Honoré d'Urfey's *L'Astrée*. Petrarch had, to a degree, discovered the feelings of the bereaved father, tormented by Cupid for his losses. Now the drama of the psyches extends to the third character in the triangle. In D'Urfey, the Stratonice parallel, Celidée, loathes her destiny, is caught between a demanding lover and a hostile patient. Hence, to escape her fortune, which, like Emelia in the *Two Noble Kinsmen,* she blames upon her own beauty, she disfigures her face with a diamond and presents the hideous spectacle to the court. Her beauty lost forever, she is spurned by the man whose disease she alone could cure and is returned to her original fiancé who, it is proved, loves her for inward beauty.

Massinger, in his own way, takes up the cause of the lady forced in the name of medicine to cure this disease of melancholy with her

honor in *The Virgin Martyr*. Dorothea, as the fated object of pathological desire, is beyond reach, not by dint of a previous marriage or
of incest taboos, but on account of her Christian religion and her
resolute virginity—an obstacle to union that is made all the more
absolute by the fact that the young man who sought her was an
aristocratic Roman war hero and clearly not of her world order. His
pathological appetites become the pretext for her bid for sainthood
by martyrdom following a contest between Christian continence
and the Roman power to command. The lovesickness afflicting
Antoninus occasions the arrival of the doctors and leads to a
discovery scene. Little of their skills is needed, however, since he
cries out for Dorothea in his sleep. Though the foolish doctors are
driven out in anger, they nevertheless manage to predict that he will
"lose life, if by a woman / He is not brought to bed" (4.1).[15] Again
coitus with the desired person is invoked as the only cure in
keeping with the medical tradition, and Dorothea is sent for to pay
the debt to medicine with her virginity under dire threats from the
young man's father. But the patient himself intervenes and refuses
the treatment, preferring her honor to his own life. In effect, an
Antiochus refuses the gift of the father in deference to the feelings
of the mother, though in ways now largely modified both in terms of
character and circumstance. The play then pursues its own course
toward a conversion and a spiritual union of the lovers in a Christian afterlife. Nevertheless, the pathological dimensions of eros
serve as the psychological force behind the action, and the vestiges
of the clinical sequence remain visible.

There are perhaps one or two last turns of the plot before the
principal elements of the theatergram exhaust themselves or are
altered beyond recognition through conflation with other theatrical
motifs. There is a hint of the January-April theme in some of the
earliest romance versions of the Antiochus-Stratonice narrative,
suggesting that the two young people had already discovered their
love before the onset of the illness and that, in fact, the sickness was
a ruse they had discovered together whereby Stratonice could get
out of an unequal marriage with the old king and into a more
vigorous one with the prince without offending the king's honor, in
essense by having the king initiate the match as the sole remedy for
his son's desperate condition. In such a construction of affairs, the
doctor, with his cunning diagnosis, merely serves as the unwitting
tool-character of the two lovers. None of the dramatists, to my
knowledge, has exploited this variation, though James Shirley, in
The Witty Fair One, understands that a similar collusion between
doctor and patient could be worked out in order to move a lady to

love and compassion through this sure sign of sincere and unfeign-ing passion. In anticipation of the social climate of the Restoration, it becomes the trick, not to deceive the old one, but to deceive a lady of considerable wealth who had to protect her interests from dandies and estate hunters. Two young gallants seeking their for-tunes light upon two heiresses whom they quite cynically set about to win through social machinations and disguises. Fowler sets up his ploy by feigning a desperate lovesickness that is diagnosed in the presence of the lady by his friend disguised as a doctor. The physician then takes her aside, explains the symptoms, and, like the doctor in *The Two Noble Kinsmen,* instructs her in the only course that can possibly save Fowler's life. By Shirley's day, the theatergram had become commonplace and could be used in this ironic way with full confidence in the audience to appreciate the play on motifs. Lovesickness had always intimated an element of trickery, in spite of its basis in physiological determinism. Here lovesickness is trivialized as part of the trickery itself—trickery, by the bye, that Shirley's heroine discovers and pays back to the perpetrator in a night trick of her own that exposes Fowler for a total cad.

During an age that produced the rise of the modern European theater, dramatists in Spain and England, though working indepen-dently from one another, found themselves, nevertheless, attracted to a common theatergram involving the lovesick hero, a clinical diagnosis, and a process of social manipulation whereby an object of sexual desire could be passed from father to son, or from friend to friend, without injury to honor. Lovesickness becomes not only the imperative that moves the action, insofar as erotic desire is absolute in its cravings and fatal if disappointed, but also the extenuating dimension of human nature that makes the audience tolerate extraordinary solutions. Both countries inherited the ingre-dients necessary for the dramatization of the sequence: the medical ideas made available through the received doctrines of Galenic medicine; and the romance narratives of Antiochus and Stratonice, whether directly from Plutarch and Appian, or indirectly through Boccaccio, Petrarch, and Bandello, together with the analogues and variants deriving from the medieval sources. But the aspect of this parallel that attracts most is that both theaters actually did seize upon this same nucleus of character types and exemplifying events, and that they created independent sets of variations on the classical dénouement that could seek new recombinant expression in both theatrical traditions through conflation with other compatible plot motifs. If one tries to look into the essence of that generic motif in order to psychoanalyze its appeal to an age, one arrives, perhaps, at the limits of critical speculation; or perhaps the question has already been answered. The story leads to reflection upon some of the most captivating themes of that intellectual era: the causes of the passions and tyrannical perturbations of the soul, the nature of the diseases of melancholy, the thresholds of sanity and insanity, the relationship between duty and honor, and the limits of personal sacrifice. Without calling these dramatists psychological writers, their plays were, nevertheless, one of the age's more penetrating means for examining what they at least took to be the ruling forces of the psyche—forces revealed on stage through a thematic relationship of action to human motivation. Given the common heritage of medical ideas and narrative models, it was perhaps inevitable that the search for theatrical novelty in both countries would lead the makers to the narrative model that began with the story of Antiochus and Stratonice and to the specific medical and characterological elements it contains. To be sure, the actual realizations in the two theaters belong to separate theater histories, yet the high incidence of parallelism involving theme, character, and narrative elements allows one at the same time to look upon these plays as belonging to a common tradition that forms a comprehensive theatrical essay on this generic medico-literary structure.

Notes

1. References are to Arnaldi de Villanova, *Opera medica omnia,* vol. 3, edited by Michael R. McVaugh (Barcelona: Edicions de la Universitat de Barcelona, 1985). My translations.

2. In the Latin West the tradition of coitus as a cure for *amor hereos* derives from Avicenna's *Liber canonis,* book 3, fen 1, tract. 5, chap. 32, sect. "De cura." Galen gives the same advice in *On the Affected Parts,* book 6, chap. 6 (Siegel 1976, 197). The recommendation is also found in Ficino's *Commentary on Plato's Symposium on Love* (Sears Jayne 1985, 168).

3. Two of the most important treatises in the Renaissance dealing with the diseases of erotic love are: Jacques Ferrand, *De la maladie d'amour ou mélancolie érotique* (Paris: Moreau, 1623), translated into English by Edmund Chilmead as *Erotomania* (Oxford: L. Lichfield, 1640), and André Du Laurens, "Second discours, au quel est traicté des maladies mélancholiques, et du moyen de les guarir" (Paris: Mettayer, 1613). This work was translated into English by Richard Surphlet as *A Discourse of the Preservation of the Sight, of Melancholike Diseases, of Rheumes, and of Old Age* (London: Felix Kingston for Ralph Lacson 1599).

4. For the concept of "theatergrams" see Clubb (1986, 15–33).

5. References are to António Ferreira, *La Comédie de Bristo,* translated and edited by Adrien Roig (Paris: Presses Universitaires de France, 1973). English translations are mine.

6. References are to Valerius Maximus, *Factorum,* book 5, chap. 7, edited by Carolus Kempt (Leipzig: Teubner, 1966).

7. References are to *Plutarch's Lives,* vol. 9, "Demetrius," translated by Bernadotte Perrin (Cambridge, Mass.: Harvard University Press, 1959).

8. For the English reader Bandello's story was novel 27 in *The Palace of Pleasure* (1575). For further information on the literary tradition concerning this story see the Introduction to Jacques Ferrand, *A Treatise on Love Melancholy,* 48–51, 161–62, 178–79, translated and edited by D. A. Beecher and Massimo Ciavolella, (Syracuse: Syracuse University Press, 1990).

9. References are to Fernando de Rojas, *Celestina or the Tragi-comedy of Calisto and Melibea,* translated by Phillis Hartnoll (London: J. M. Dent and Sons, 1959).

10. The *Trionfi* were also available to Camões in the Spanish translation of Antonio de Obregón, 1512.

11. The first play in English to treat the story by name was published in 1721 according to the *Companion to the Play-house,* 1:Btr (London: T. Becket etc., 1764).

12. References are to *Gesta Romanorum,* translated by Charles Swan (1876; reprint ed., New York: Dover, 1959).

13. References are to *The Two Noble Kinsmen,* edited by G. R. Proudfoot (London: Edward Arnold, 1970).

14. References are to *The Works of Francis Beaumont and John Fletcher,* edited by A. R. Waller, 10 vols. (1906; reprint ed., New York: Octagon Books, 1969), 4:108.

15. References are to *Philip Massinger,* edited by Arthur Symons, 2 vols. (London: Vizetelly, 1889), 2:347.

Works Cited

Bandello. 1890. *The Palace of Pleasure* (1575). Translated by William Painter. London: David Nutt.

Beaumont, Francis, and John Fletcher. 1969. *The Works.* Edited by A. R. Waller, 10 vols. 1906; reprint, New York: Octagon Books.

Clubb, Louise George. 1986. "Theatergrams." In *Comparative Critical Approaches to Renaissance Comedy,* edited by Donald A. Beecher and Massimo Ciavolella, 15–33. Ottawa: Dovehouse Editions.

Ferrand, Jacques. 1623. *De la maladie d'amour ou mélancolie érotique.* Paris: chez Denis Moreau.

———. 1640. *Erotomania.* Translated by Edmund Chilmead. Oxford: L. Lichfield.

———. 1990. *A Treatise on Love Melancholy.* Translated and edited by D. A. Beecher and Massimo Ciavolella. Syracuse: Syracuse University Press.

Ferreira, Antonio. 1973. *La comédie de Bristo.* Translated by Adrien Roig. Paris: Presses Universitaires de France.

Ficino. 1985. *Commentary on Plato's Symposium on Love.* Translated by Sears Jayne. Dallas: Spring Publications.

Galen. 1976. *On the Affected Parts.* Translated by Rudolph E. Siegel. Basel: S. Karger.

Gesta Romanorum. 1969. Translated by Charles Swan. 1876; reprint, New York: Dover.

Du Laurens. 1599. *A Discourse of the Preservation of the Sight, of Melancholike Diseases, of Rheumes, and of Old Age.* Translated by Richard Surphlet. London: Felix Kingston for Ralph Lacson.

———. 1613. "Second discours, au quel est traicté des maladies mélancholiques, et du moyen de les guarir." In *Toutes les Oeuvres,* translated by Théophile Gelée. Paris: P. Mettayer.

Kennedy, Ruth Lee. 1940. "The Theme of 'Stratonice' in the Drama of the Spanish Peninsula." *PMLA* 55:1010–33.

Massinger, Phillip. 1889. *Plays.* Edited by Arthur Symonds. 2 vols. London: Vizetelly.

Plutarch. 1959. *Lives.* Translated by Bernadotte Perrin. 11 vols. Cambridge, Mass.: Harvard University Press.

Rojas, Fernando de. 1959. *Celestina or the Tragi-comedy of Calisto and Melibea.* Translated by Phillis Hartnoll. London: J. M. Dent.

Shakespeare, William and John Fletcher. 1970. *The Two Noble Kinsmen.* Edited by G. R. Proudfoot. London: Edward Arnold.

Valerius Maximus. 1966. *Factorum.* Edited by Carolus Kempt. Leipzig: Teubner.

Villanova, Arnaldi de. 1985. *Opera medica omnia.* Vol. 3, *Tractatus de amore heroico.* Edited by Michael R. McVaugh. Barcelona: Edicions de la Universitat de Barcelona.

The Shadow of Antioch: Sexuality in *Pericles, Prince of Tyre*

Alexander Leggatt

When incest appears in Jacobean drama it is generally treated as a fundamental violation of nature, a criminal passion that horrifies even those who are in its grip. Arbaces in a *A King and No King* is driven temporarily mad when he believes he has conceived an incestuous desire for his sister; Ferdinand in *The Duchess of Malfi* will not admit his desire even to himself. Isabella in *Women Beware Women* will sleep with her uncle only when told he is not her uncle; when she learns the truth she murders the woman who deceived her. The love of brother and sister in *'Tis Pity She's a Whore* is made the vehicle for Giovanni's defiance of all conventional values, including religion; and Anabella finally recoils from what they have done. The treatment of incest in *Pericles* appears to fit this pattern. In the play's first scene Pericles comes to the city of Antioch to win the King's daughter by the romantic device of answering a riddle; and he discovers that the beautiful princess he wants to win is having an incestuous affair with her father. This represents a fundamental violation of both sexual and family ties, a violation that is put right later in the play by images of healthy courtship and sexual love, and of normal family relations. This is, in fact, one of the binding themes of this somewhat episodic play. To touch for a moment on the question of authorship: few believe *Pericles* to be entirely Shakespeare's; the writing is so inconsistent, not just in quality but in kind. There is, on the other hand, no general agreement about the identity of the other author, or authors, or about the nature of Shakespeare's involvement. To most critics the first two acts seem like hackwork, while in the last three they hear the voice of Shakespeare. Yet while no one can deny the power of the third-act storm sequence, there are passages of flat writing in the scenes that follow, and there are subtle and haunting passages earlier—including, I think, the opening scene in Antioch. The play does not seem to me fully coherent: there is some unassimilated political commentary, for example. But it explores sexual themes at least in a way that I find thoughtful, sensitive, and imaginative—in outline, if not always in execution. I would like to examine this aspect of the play, and for the sake of convenience I will call the author Shakespeare.

In most respects the treatment of the incest theme that begins the play is clear and straightforward. The violation involved in incest is so deep that it taints other areas of life. The riddle Pericles must answer shows a scrambling of relationships and a loss of identity, and we note that Antiochus's daughter has no name:

> I am no viper, yet I feed
> On mother's flesh which did me breed.
> I sought a husband, in which labour
> I found that kindness in a father.
> He's father, son, and husband mild;
> I mother, wife, and yet his child.
>
> (1.1.65–70)[1]

The image of cannibalism recurs later in the play, in the famine that draws the mothers of Tharsus to eat their own children (1.4.42–44). Gower, in his role as chorus, tells us that incest "Was with long use account'd no sin" (chorus 1, 30). As in Jonson's *Sejanus,* with the loss of moral values words lose their meanings. The fact that Antiochus has named his city after himself indicates a Tamburlainian arrogance, a refusal to accept the human community that controls individual wills. He orders Pericles' murder with the words, "It fits thee not to ask the reason why: / Because we bid it." (1.1.158–59). Recoiling from his discovery, Pericles uses an image of music turned to discord: "Hell only danceth at so harsh a chime" (1.1.86). All the values violated here are put right in later scenes. Against the arrogant tyranny of Antiochus, we hear the plain, frank speech between prince and counsellor in the relations of Pericles and Helicanus. In Pentapolis Pericles meets a good king, Simonides, with a fair daughter, Thaisa, whose beauty this time is not deceptive. In place of the riddle, Pericles proves himself in a tournament. Simonides, as Prospero will do more seriously later, briefly acts the role of the heavy father, as though to exorcise through comedy the memory of Antiochus. Point by point, the sequence in Pentapolis gives a benevolent form of the images that were violated at Antioch (Flower 1975, 33–34). So, later in the play, does Pericles' reunion with his lost daughter Marina, in a scene that depends on establishing true names and true identities: "Is it no more to be your daughter than / To say my mother's name was Thaisa?" (5.1.208–9).

Even the scrambling of relationships becomes a benevolent paradox (Barber 1969, 61) when Pericles addresses his daughter as "Thou that beget'st him that did thee beget" (5.1.195). The harsh chime, the discordant music of Antioch, is countered by true harmony in later scenes. Pericles entertains the court of Pentapolis with music, leading Simonides to compliment him: "Sir, you are music's master" (4.5.30). Marina, we are told, "Sings like one immortal" (chorus 5, 3), and on her reunion with her father Pericles hears what he thinks is the music of the spheres. (It is an interesting touch that, while Helicanus and Lysimachus do not hear it, Marina remains silent on the subject; such enigmatic silences at important moments will become a key device in *The Tempest*.)

So far all this is as we would expect. The incest of Antiochus and his daughter is, like the jealously of Leontes in *The Winter's Tale,* a threat that the rest of the play counters. Because of the play's episodic structure we do not feel the pressure of that problem throughout, as we do in much (though not all) of *The Winter's Tale;* but the echoes in language and situation are clear enough to show that the Antiochus episode is not just an arbitrary way to start the hero's adventures but an appropriate introduction to the play as a whole. Yet the development of the play's themes from this opening scene is not perhaps so straightforward as I have made it sound. There are some elusive undercurrents that, I think, broaden and complicate the play's vision. In what follows I will be dealing largely in hints and suggestions; and I think Shakespeare *wants* them to be hints and suggestions, no more. Some of the points to which I will call attention are actually stronger and more disturbing in other versions of the story—Gower's *Confessio Amantis,* Twine's *The Pattern of Painful Adventures,* and Wilkins's *The Painful Adventures of Pericles Prince of Tyre.* Shakespeare has toned them down. But he has not suppressed them altogether.

To begin with, there are suggestions that what Pericles experiences in Antioch is not just a quick, horrified glance at somebody else's sin, but an initial encounter with sexualty itself, including his own sexuality, an encounter that leaves him repelled and shaken. If this is so, then *Pericles* makes an appropriate transition from Shakespeare's dark comedies—which, as Kenneth Muir (1979, 103) has observed, are concerned with sex where his romantic comedies are concerned with love—into the final romances, with their broader concern with marriage and the ties of family. G. Wilson Knight (1965, 73–74) has suggested that the abstraction of the play's characterization makes it seem the life story of an Everyman figure. In that pattern, the scene in Antioch is the hero's sexual initiation, one that goes badly because his first encounter is with the dark side of sexuality. He greets Antiochus's daughter with an innocent celebration of her beauty:

> See where she comes apparell'd like the spring,
> Graces her subjects, and her thoughts the king
> Of every virtue gives renown to men!
> Her face the book of praises, where is read
> Nothing but curious pleasures.

> (1.1.13–17)

In that last reference to "curious pleasures" the springlike freshness of the opening is replaced by something a little more jaded and sophisticated. Though Antiochus compares his daughter to the apples of Hesperus, guarded by dragons—the dead knights who have preceded Pericles—Pericles' desire "To taste the fruit of yon celestial tree / Or die in the adventure" (1.1.22–23) suggests rather the apple of Eden. The threat of death that accompanies his wooing reminds us of the traditional linking of sex and death, a point to which I will return. In both respects Pericles is undergoing a loss of innocence: "Antiochus, I thank thee, who hath taught / My frail mortality to know itself" (1.1.42–43). He determines "to prepare / This body, like to them, to what I must" (1.1.44–45). As a man about to undergo a deadly ordeal, and as a prospective bridegroom, he is venturing his body, and the two ventures go together.

Wilson Knight's observation (1965, 38) that the hero's "plunge into sin and death is . . . associated with ravishing desire" may be stronger in tone than the writing of the scene will justify, but there are, I think, suggestions that Pericles is undergoing a kind of fall, not so much sinning himself as becoming aware of the existence of sin. He recoils from the discovery:

> Fair glass of light, I lov'd you, and could still,
> Were not this glorious casket stor'd with ill.
> But I must tell you, now my thoughts revolt;
> For he's no man on whom perfections wait
> That, knowing sin within, will touch the gate.
> You are a fair viol, and your sense the strings,
> Who, finger'd to make man his lawful music,
> Would draw heaven down and all the gods to hearken;
> But being play'd upon before your time,
> Hell only danceth at so harsh a chime.

> (1.1.77–86)

The sexual suggestion of the word "gate" will be unmistakable in the jealous ravings of Leontes; but it is clear enough here. Together with the reference to fingering it suggests not just Pericles' horror at incest but a queasy apprehension of, and recoil from, sexuality itself. In this light, the final punishment of Antiochus and his daughter is significant:

> A fire from heaven came and shrivell'd up
> Their bodies, even to loathing; for they so stunk,
> That all those eyes ador'd them ere their fall
> Scorn now their hand should give them burial.
>
> (2.4.9–12)

Like the putrefied core Hector finds inside the armor in *Troilus and Cressida,* this suggests a disgust with the body itself, a disgust echoed later in the brothel in Mytilene, whose employees "with continual action are even as good as rotten" (4.2.8–9).[2]

Pericles himself has not literally sinned. But in the allegorical mode the play occasionally touches, to encounter sin in another character is to entertain the possibility of sin in oneself. Some critics have seen Pericles' flight from Antiochus as a kind of penance (Thorne 1971, 47), though not everyone agrees, and at the literal level there is not much support for this reading. Helicanus offers it as a public explanation for the prince's flight: ". . . doubting lest he had err'd or sinn'd, / To show his sorrow he'd correct himself" (1.3.21–22), and this at least allows a shadow of the idea into the play. A stronger clue is Pericles' account of his own state on his return to Tyre: "Here pleasures court mine eyes and mine eyes shun them" (1.2.7). In retreating from Antiochus he may not be just saving his subjects from the tyrant but trying to retreat, in his own mind, from the dark knowledge Antiochus represents. When he comes to Pentapolis it is as though he is beginning his life over again; he is cast up on its shores as unaccommodated man, "bereft . . . of all his fortunes" (2.1.9). In this state he is allowed a fresh start, a new and healthier sexual initiation. It is significant that, while he comes to Antioch with no background that we know of, he begins his stay in Pentagolis by recovering his father's armor from the sea—the first reference in the play to his father. And he recovers his father in another way, in his recognition of Simonides: "Yon king's to me like to my father's picture" (2.2.37). In *As You Like It,* Rosalind recovers her father in the forest and then sets about her affair with Orlando. There is the same pattern here: courtship

begins from the base of a secure background in one's own family.
And it may be significant that the Pentapolis sequence ends with
the full recovery of Pericles' lost identity as Prince of Tyre.

And yet Pericles himself does not seem altogether secure. He is
wary of Simonides, in whom he sees a potential Antiochus: " 'Tis
the king's subtlety to have my life" (2.5.44). There is something a
little priggish in his denial of interest in Thaisa: he claims he "never
aim'd so high to love your daughter, / But bent all offices to honour
her," adding, "never did my actions yet commence / A deed might
gain her love or your displeasure" (2.5.47–48, 52–53). Is this proper
courtesy or needless caution? Simonides and Thaisa seem to take it
as the latter. The association of sex with eating, which takes a dark
form in the cannibalism of incest, is more cheerful in Thaisa's frank
desire for Pericles:

> By Juno, that is queen of marriage,
> All viands that I eat do seem unsavoury,
> Wishing him my meat.
>
> (2.3.30–32)

When he tries to play the gentleman, she will have none of it:

> PERICLES. Then as you are as virtuous as fair,
>   Resolve your angry father, if my tongue
>   Did e'er solicit, or my hand subscribe
>   To any syllable that made love to you.
> THAISA. Why, sir, say if you had, who takes offence
>   At what would make me glad?
>
> (2.5.66–71)

She herself had pretended reluctance when her father urged her to
talk to the strange knight, but this pretence did not last. Simonides'
eagerness for the match makes him sound like a cleaned-up Pandarus: "It pleaseth me so well, that I will see you wed; / And then,
with what haste you can, get you to bed" (2.5.91–92).[3] Pericles'
experience in Pentapolis is not just that of a hero who finds and
wins his bride; it is also that of a cautious young man whose girl
friend has to tell him it's all right to touch her and who makes the
even more astonishing discovery that her father approves.

Yet the sexual anxiety created in Antioch may not have been
completely disposed of. At the end of *Cymbeline,* another play in
which there is a certain recoil from the body, Imogen tries to
embrace Posthumus and, not knowing her, he flings her away,
earning the rebuke, "Why did you throw your wedded lady from

you?" The equivalent moment in *Pericles* comes when Marina approaches her father. Neither knows the other's identity. She is about to restore him to life, but his first greeting to her is a sub-human noise, "Hum, ha!" (5.1.83), to which editors generally add some such stage direction as "pushes her back," an addition justified by dialogue later in the scene. Her rebuke, "if you did know my parentage, / You would not do me violence" (5.1.99–100), suggests that the push is far from gentle. In Gower and Wilkins he strikes her in anger; in Twine, he kicks her in the face, drawing blood (Bullough 1966, 414; 466–67; 543). Shakespeare has toned down the violence, but it is still a startling and disturbing moment. While Lear at first shrinks away from the new life offered by Cordelia, Pericles lashes out at his daughter. In *The Winter's Tale* Shakespeare almost obliterates the problem of father-daughter incest that ends the source novel, Greene's *Pandosto*—almost, but not quite, for on first seeing her, before he knows her identity, Leontes finds his daughter Perdita rather too attractive (Melchiori 1960, 63–64). It may be that what surfaces when Pericles pushes Marina away is an old, instinctive fear that goes back to his encounter with Antiochus—who at one point, by the way, evidently flings down the riddle in a gesture that anticipates Pericles' flinging away Marina (1.1.57 SD; see Arden note). Seen in this light, Pericles' desire to leave Marina in Tharsus and his determination not to cut his hair till she is married may not be just arbitrary plot developments. They may suggest a desire to submit to an ordeal and a period of separation till his daughter is safely out of his reach. This recoil from the possibility of incest makes a direct link with the play's opening; but if, as I suggested, that opening expressed a fear of sexuality itself, then it is proper to notice that Marina is not the only woman Pericles flings away. Though the staging of the storm scene does not make this altogether clear, Pericles later says of Thaisa, "I threw her overboard with these very arms" (5.3.19). Even so Prospero will drown his book in the sea, getting rid of something that is potent, desirable, and dangerous. Thelma N. Greenfield (1967, 53) has rebuked Pericles for giving in too quickly to the sailors' demand, accusing him of lack of faith.[4] It may be that the problem runs deeper than that. And it may not just be arbitrary plotting when Thaisa herself declares:

>   since King Pericles,
> My wedded lord, I n'er shall see again,
> A vestal livery will I take me to,
> And never more have joy.
>
>   (3.4.7–10)

Like Pericles when he abandons Marina, she makes a decision that looks arbitrary but may suggest, by its very arbitrariness, an instinct to reject human involvement.

The relations of Pericles with Thaisa and with Marina are healthy, normal, and attractive. But they may be touched by shadows from Antioch—not just the crime of incest but the fear of an inherent corruption in all sexuality. The brothel scenes in Mytilene show the other side of the coin. Lysimachus is the converse of Pericles. The one comes to win a beautiful princess and finds an unnatural sinner; the other comes to do business in a brothel and finds a beautiful princess. And there is, I think, not much doubt that he *has* come to do business: the sly comedy of the Bawd's line, "Here come the Lord Lysimachus, disguis'd" (5.6.15–16), suggests that he is a regular customer whose disguise has long ceased to fool anybody (Flower 1975, 39). His manner is brisk and cynical: "How now! How a dozen of virginities?" and his first reaction to Marina is, "Faith, she would serve after a long voyage at sea" (5.6.19; 42). But as Pericles' innocent romanticism at Antioch may be touched by sensuality, so Lysimachus's cynicism has a nervous rattle; it is a little defensive, as though the man is half ashamed and keeping up his spirits. In his dialogue with Marina he is delicate to the point of being mealy-mouthed, and she challenges him to be honest and speak plainly:

LYSIMACHUS. Now, pretty one, how long have you been at this trade?
MARINA. What trade, sir?
LYSIMACHUS. Why, I cannot name't but I shall offend.
MARINA. I cannot be offended with my trade. Please you to name it.
(4.6.65–70)

Impressed by her virtue, he recoils from his own corruption to the point of claiming it never existed: "Had I brought hither a corrupted mind, / Thy speech had alter'd it" (4.6.103–4). It is a puzzling moment; and Wilkins's version of the scene, in which Lysimachus admits that he *was* corrupt and has now reformed, is much more logical. This version is adopted into the play in the new Oxford edition (10.127–36; Bullough 1966, 536). But the sheer illogic of the text as usually printed makes its own point: Lysimachus is trying to rewrite his life, and there may be more than just wishful thinking involved. When he declares, "I came with no ill intent; for to me / The very doors and windows savour vilely" (4.6.109–10), he may be telling part of the truth, in that he is now fully awake to feelings he was already aware of but never before acted on.

This is the man who will be Marina's husband. As in the Pentapolis sequence, the fixing of their relationship is accompanied by Marina's recovery of her parents. But the striking paradox is that Lysimachus finds a pure bride in a brothel, while the aggressively virginal Marina finds in a regular brothel customer her future husband. Love has pitched his mansion in the place of excrement. We may at first think that the brothel, like the court of Antioch, represents the dark side of sex, and so, up to a point, it does. (In performance the connections can be emphasized by the doubling of parts, as in the 1986 Stratford, Ontario, production in which Nicholas Pennell played both Antiochus and Boult.) But as there is unexpected corruption in Antioch, so there is unexpected innocence in the brothel. C. L. Barber (1969, 63) has called the brothel sequence a "comic exorcism of gross sexuality," and in fact the nature of its comedy is quite unexpected. We were prepared for a melodrama in which a helpless, innocent girl was threatened with a fate worse than death. In fact the helpless, innocent girl not only looks after herself quite nicely, thank you, but reduces her persecutors to laughable futility. Two of her customers stagger away, dazed and sheepish:

> 2. GENTLEMAN. . . . Come, I am for no more bawdy-houses. Shall's go
> hear the vestals sing?
> I. GENTLEMAN. I'll do anything now that is virtuous; but I am out of the
> road of rutting forever.
>
> (4.5.6–9)

Boult and the Bawd throw up their hands at her ultimate outrage:

> BOULT. Worse and worse, mistress; she has here spoken holy words to
> the Lord Lysimachus.
> BAWD. O abominable!
>
> (4.6.132–34)

The comedy turns in more than one direction. It is not just that Marina's tormentors are so helpless against her; that would suggest that the power of darkness they represent is so feeble it can be laughed off as not worth worrying about. There is also something self-mocking in the images of virtue triumphant, as though Marina's power is not quite real, not quite believable. And if some of the mockery touches chastity itself there may be a reason: as the Bawd complains of her new employee, "She's able to freeze the god Priapus, and undo a whole generation" (19. 13). Virginity is all very well but, as Benedick insists, the world must be peopled.

Marina's virginity and the brutal couplings of the brothel represent extremes, and each extreme is comic. The solution is the licensed sexuality of marriage. But sex itself remains an ambiguous force. Pericles wooing Thaisa was as reluctant to admit what he was doing as is Lysimachus when he comes to the brothel. In Wilkins's novel the storm in which Pericles' daughter is born and in which he loses his wife occurs not when he is going back to Tyre, but when he is going back to Antioch, to claim its kingship (Bullough 1966, 517–18). It is as though Antioch represents some dark fear at the heart of sexuality, and the storm that sunders the family is in some way connected with it. Perhaps in the story of Pericles Shakespeare is allegorizing the notion (which of course he would not have seen formulated) that, as our first sexual feelings are incestuous, so our sexuality thereafter is never free of the taint of incest. Perhaps. But once again I think the fear runs deeper than the fear of incest. Pericles is pursued from Antioch not just by the thought of a sexual taboo violated, but by a killer, the hired assassin Thaliard. As Pericles puts it, "Murder's as near to lust as flame to smoke" (1.1.139). Leonine, another hired killer, starts Marina on the path that leads her to the brothel. And in the brothel itself the danger persists: "The poor Transylvanian is dead, that lay with the little baggage. . . . She quickly poop'd him; she made him roast-meat for worms" (4.2.20–23). Antiochus, as we have seen, initiates Pericles not just into the dark mystery of sex but into the knowledge of death. His daughter comes "apparell'd like the spring" on to a stage decorated with severed heads:

> Before thee stands this fair Hesperides,
> With golden fruit, but dangerous to be touch'd;
> For death-like dragons here affright thee hard.
>
> (1.1.27–30)

The encounter in bed about which Simonides is so jocular leads to the pain of childbirth in a storm, where "The lady shrieks and well a-near / Does fall in travail with her fear" (chorus 3, 51–52). In bringing new life Thaisa apparently dies. Recalling his loss, Pericles shows how his imagination is haunted by the pain of childbirth: "I am great with woe / And shall deliver weeping" (5.1.105–6). In his reunion with Thaisa, Pericles welcomes his new life as a kind of death, telling the gods,

> You shall do well,
> That on the touching of her lips I may
> Melt and no more be seen. O come, be buried

A second time within these arms.

(5.3.41–45)

And Marina declares, "My heart / Leaps to be gone into my mother's bosom."

Whether feared or longed for, death is the constant companion of love. Shakespeare has already treated this theme in *Romeo and Juliet* and *Antony and Cleopatra*. One reason for the connection is that the procreative instinct is at once an answer to, and a reminder of, our mortality. And in the Christian tradition—until recently, at least—even wedded sexuality was never altogether free of a sense of sin: "Behold I was shapen in wickedness: and in sin hath my mother conceived me" (Psalm 51). In *The Tempest* Prospero celebrates the betrothal of Ferdinand and Miranda with vision of the ordered fertility that marriage represents. The vision is broken when Prospero remembers "that foul beast Caliban"—who, we recall, tried to rape Miranda, driven by an instinct to people the isle with Calibans. When Prospero subjects Ferdinand to an ordeal before he can win Miranda, he gives him Caliban's job of piling logs, as though his purpose is to test the Caliban in him.

From Caliban's attempt to rape Miranda to the vision of Ceres, *The Tempest* connects our sexuality to our bond with nature. And nature, in these last plays, is not just the "great creating nature" we hear of in *The Winter's Tale*. Even in that play, the force that produces daffodils that come before the swallow dares produces also a storm and a devouring bear. In *Pericles,* Cerimon evokes the benevolent and curative powers of nature in language that recalls Cordelia. He has studied

> the blest infusions
> That dwells in vegetives, in metals, stones;
> And can speak of the disturbances that
> Nature works, and of her cures.

(3.2.35–38)

But we notice that he also sees nature as ambiguous, like Friar Laurence, who can see poison and medicine in a single flower. Using fire and music, he brings Thaisa back to life. But he tells a servant who comes to him for help:

> Your master will be dead ere you return;
> There's nothing can be minister'd to nature
> That can recover him.

(3.2.7–9)

Nature can help us, but not forever; after a certain point she gives us up. Pericles, noting how Simonides resembles his dead father, may be said to have cheated time by finding a new father; but in the same speech he compares his father's glory with his own dejected state and concludes, "I see that Time's the king of men; / He's both their parent, and he is their grave" (2.3.45–46). Even a moment of recovery is touched by the thought of loss.

At several points the play refers to the arbitrary whims of Fortune, especially in the storm sequences: ". . . fortune, tir'd with doing bad, / Threw him ashore, to give him glad (chorus 2, 37–38); ". . . fortune's mood / Varies again" (chorus 3, 46–47). But this is a mechanical idea, mechanically stated. The puzzle of human life is conveyed more powerfully when Pericles addresses his seemingly dead queen. He evokes not Fortune but the mystery of birth and death in a natural world that is at once beautiful and terrifying, bound up with man yet finally indifferent to him:

> A terrible childbed hast thou had, my dear;
> No light, no fire: th'unfriendly elements
> Forgot thee utterly; nor have I time
> To give thee hallow'd to thy grave, but straight
> Must cast thee, scarcely coffin'd, in the ooze;
> Where, for a monument upon thy bones,
> And e'er-remaining lamps, the belching whale
> And humming water must o'erwhelm thy corpse,
> Lying with simple shells.
>
> (3.1.56–64)

Pericles speaks here of the natural world that surrounds us, whose elements we need for our comfort, even our survival; and he senses that this world ultimately goes its own way, indifferent to us. Not just indifferent, either, but overwhelmingly remote, capable of bearing down and destroying us without a moment's thought. But there is another, and perhaps greater mystery, in the power we carry in our own bodies. We need that power too, for our happiness and for the survival of our kind. But there is something in it that frightens us. And so we invent rules and codes to give ourselves the illusion that we control it. We moralize it, we separate it into right and wrong. But in the moralizing of sex in this play there is something shadowy and unreal: the guilt we sense but cannot literally justify in Pericles when he flees from Antioch, the purity Lysimachus claims in the brothel. Marina's chastity and the corruption of her employees seem equally artificial. The proper relations of husband and wife, father and daughter, are touched by thoughts of Antiochus and his daughter; and the play's final marriage begins in a brothel. It is as though all the play's characters are adrift on the same sea. The relations of Antiochus and his daughter are, from any civilized perspective, a horror that the rest of the play should counter and suppress. That is our first impression, it remains the dominant one, and I do not wish to dislodge it. But from another point of view, harder to analyze, harder to see clearly, and harder to accept, the play seems to suggest that power Pericles first meets in Antioch is the power that will haunt him all his life.

Notes

1. All references to *Pericles* are to the Arden edition by F.D. Hoeniger (London: Methuen, 1963).
2. Flower (1975, 39) connects the fire that consumes Antiochus and his daughter with the pox that is endemic to the brothel.
3. Stephen Dickey (1986, 559) calls Simonides' joking "a redirection of Antiochus' paternal lust into more proper channels: Simonides accepts rather than exploits his daughter's sexuality."
4. According to the Quarto (and most editors), Cerimon declares, "They were too rough / That threw her in the sea" (3.2.81–82). For "rough" Malone conjectured "rash" and his reading is adopted in the "reconstructed" Oxford text (1986, 12.77).

Works Cited

Barber, C. L. 1969. " 'Thou that beget'st him that did thee beget': Transformation in *Pericles* and *The Winter's Tale*." *Shakespeare Survey* 22:59–67.

Dickey, Stephen. 1986. "Language and Role in *Pericles*." *English Literary Renaissance* 16:559.

Flower, Annette C. 1975. "Disguise and Identity in Pericles, Prince of Tyre." *Shakespeare Quarterly* 26:30–41.

Greenfield, Thelma. 1967. "A Re-Examination of the Patient Pericles." *Shakespeare Studies* 3:51–61.

Knight, G. Wilson. 1965. *The Crown of Life*. London: Methuen.

Melchiori, Barbara. 1960. " 'Still Harping on My Daughter.' " *English Miscellany* II: 63–64.

Muir, Kenneth. 1979. *Shakespeare's Comic Sequence*. New York: Barnes and Noble.

Narrative and Dramatic Sources of Shakespeare. 1966. Edited by Geoffrey Bullough. London: Routledge and Kegan Paul.

Shakespeare, William. 1986. *The Complete Works*. Edited by Stanley Wells and Gary Taylor. Oxford: Clarendon Press.

Thorne, William B. 1971. "*Pericles* and the 'Incest-Fertility' Opposition." *Shakespeare Quarterly* 22:43–56.

The Incest Motif in Tirsian Drama: A Lacanian View

Henry W. Sullivan

For Francisco Ruiz Ramón

It is a widely accepted critical commonplace that Tirso de Molina was a daring dramatist: in his formal experiments, in his political satires, and especially in his portrayal of bizarre sexual behavior. I have touched elsewhere (Sullivan 1985a) on the issues of love, matrimony, and desire in the theater of Tirso de Molina, and consequently I wish to focus more narrowly in this study on the incest motif. This is a motif or theme where, one may say, the issues of love, matrimony, and desire intersect. As a problem in moral theology, it is notorious that the canon law on impediments to matrimony underwent intense scrutiny and reform in Southern Catholic Europe—and particularly Spain—during Tirso's lifetime (Sullivan 1976, 24–26). Tirso's special competence and insight around questions of the prohibited degrees of consanguinity derive in part, therefore, from his training as a Mercedarian friar, as well as from the practice or exercise of drama.

Though there are examples in the work of Lope de Vega and Calderón where the incest motif is exploited dramatically (and these will come readily to mind), Tirso is remarkable for the intensity and consistency with which, amid the portrayal of sundry sexual deviations, he pursued the dramatic implications of this central taboo. I would suggest, moreover, that Tirso did not toy with the incest motif merely for sensational effect (though this dimension cannot be denied), but rather that the deeper conflict in human society between desire and law (out of which the incest taboo arises) lies properly within the dramatist's realm of interest; indeed, it provides the very stuff of psychological conflict. In my view, the psychoanalytic insights of Jacques Lacan can make the character of this conflictual relationship more meaningful, as well as provide a historical clue to the genesis of comedy and tragedy as genres in both Spain and England.

Conventionally speaking, the tensions between sexual attraction and taboo within a single family are deemed matters suitable for psychoanalytic study. The interplay of sexual attraction and taboo between several families or groups of families—questions of endogamy and exogamy—fall within the purview of anthropology. But since the repression of psychosexual relations at the heart of family life furnishes the model and basic structure of all social ordering, the dramatist interested in commenting in general terms on social order can achieve his aims by dramatizing family conflicts in particular. It is in this double sense that Tirso pushed his wager with his Madrid public—in social satire and fundamental psychosexual questioning—further than any other playwright of the Golden Age.

Tirso's Interest in the Incest Motif

As a general prefatory observation, I can state that, where Tirso artfully hints at the possibility of incest but does not dramatize its consummation, his works are *comic* in tone and outcome. Where, on the other hand, the incestuous act is consummated—in the single, famous case of *La venganza de Tamar (Tamar's revenge)*— the play is tragic in tone and outcome. I have commented recently at considerable length on sibling symmetry and the incest taboo in Tirso's outstanding, though little-read comedy *Habladme en entrando (Speak to me on entering)* and do not intend to reproduce the entire argument here (Sullivan 1986). Suffice it to say that the equivocal sexual interest of the main action revolves around the suspicion of, or possibility of, incest between brother and sister (Don Diego and Doña Ana Hurtado de Mendoza) or between father and daughter (Don Luis and Doña Ana). The *ne plus ultra* of comic ambivalence is reached in the final prison scene, where the outraged son attempts to oblige Don Luis, unaware that this is his father, to marry his own daughter as honorable reparation for the apparent seduction of Ana. The father requests that Papal dispensations be sent from Rome to overcome an impediment: "Para que se case, es claro / una hija con su padre" ("So that a daughter can get married to her father, of course") (3.9.1252a).[1] The comedy then ends in revelation, reconciliation, and harmony.

The comedy *Averígüelo Vargas (Have Vargas check it out)* depicts a thirteen-year-old girl, Sancha, in love with her childhood playmate and older brother Ramiro, whom she pursues from

Momblanco, Portugal to Santarem disguised as a dwarf. They are really the children, born out of wedlock, of the deceased King Duarte of Portugal and an unknown noble lady and are unaware of their sibling relationship, though Sancha's jesting fictions come close to the truth. Sancha's obstinate pursuit of her brother ends in the consummation of her incestuous passion in the confusion of night, fortunately with the wrong man. Though the taboo is therefore avoided in this play too, the heroine was clearly prepared to violate it with the "right man" for her, Ramiro. In *El castigo del penséque (The punishment of what-I-meant-was)*, the *équivoque* is varied in yet other ways. Here Clavela is in love with Rodrigo, returned from abroad after long absence, in the mistaken belief that this is her brother Otón. In fact, Rodrigo only bears an uncanny resemblance to Otón. Nevertheless, Clavela expresses pining, lovelorn passion for her "brother," notably in two soliloquies from act 2, one of them a fine sonnet that shares many similarities with a sonnet on the incest theme in Tirso's tragedy *La venganza de Tamar*.[2] I may also mention *Amazonas en las Indias (Amazons in the Spanish Indies)*, where Gonzalo Pizarro contracts marriage with his carnal niece Francisca, the orphaned daughter of his dead brother Francisco Pizarro, in expectation of securing Papal dispensations from Rome (2.5.718a–b); and *La huerta de Juan Fernández (The orchard of Juan Fernández)*, where the possibilities of cross-cousin marriages are favorably considered, if not actually contracted, in the comic dénouement.

Claude Lévi-Strauss pointed out in his first masterpiece *The Elementary Structures of Kinship* (1969) that, however else societies and cultures might vary in tribal laws, customs, or taboos, one taboo was common to all of them: the prohibition of incest between mother and son (cf. Leach 1970). He argued further that the prohibition against a son's union with other close female relatives (such as a sister) led to the need for an exchange of women and gifts between men in order to avoid the incest taboo and that this exogamous marriage exchange provided the very basis of social structure in tribes or peoples.

Lacan, as is known, was deeply influenced by Lévi-Strauss's structural anthropology in the late 1940s and early 1950s. In his celebrated "Discours de Rome" of 1953, Lacan commented on this matter of marriage exchange, but added important new insights of his own. The organizing principles of societies was not the incest taboo *per se* (with the marriage exchange or kinship structures that arose from it), but the separating and boundary-setting function of what Lacan termed the law of the Name-of-the-Father. Recalling the Old Testament imprecation that confusion of generation (or bloodlines) was the desolation of the sinner and the abomination of the Word, Lacan argued that there are no *a priori* grounds in the Real of the body by which a brother can know his sister is a close blood relative (and hence taboo).[3] He can only know this by naming and, most importantly, by the siblings' mutual relationship to the Name-of-the-Father. In transcending Lévi-Strauss's static structures and mythic topologies through his insistence on "the Word" *(le Verbe)* and the "Name of," or word for, the Father, Lacan displayed his characteristic view of culture and the laws of the human psyche as language-based. Language for Lacan is the condition of imposing culture on nature.

But more fundamental even than language as negative injunction in the creation of human culture is this phenomenon of separation and psychic boundary setting. Lacan maintains that the human animal's prematuration and helplessness at birth require a protracted period of nurture at the hands of a caretaker, usually the biological mother. And yet said nurture is not simply a series of practical tasks such as feeding and cleaning, but the gradual formation in the neonate of a subject prior to speech, or *moi*—and this through the introjection of images and aural stimuli in the so-called premirror phase (zero to six months) and the mirror phase proper (six to eighteen months). At around eighteen months, the infant's strong bond of mirror identification or Oneness with the (m)Other—an illusion on the child's part that no actual boundaries exist between itself and the (m)Other—is ruptured by the perceived intervention of the father bidding for the mother's gaze. This divisive paternal action (which Lacan problematically and provocatively attributes to the phallic signifier or first pure signifier of difference) has a dual effect: 1) it breaks up the mother-infant dyad and causes the infant to perceive its separateness from its caretaker; and 2) to compensate for the sense of lack so created by separation, the child begins using language in order to fill the gap and to master the objects of its universe through naming. The passage from natural perception of objects to the cultural mastery of naming them at one remove is, of course, a process of alienation. This paternal imposition of divisive limits or boundaries on a small child's deluded sense of power is what Lacan means by castration, and this has nothing to do with bloody emasculation in Freud's literalist sense. He means the eclipse of the subject by the signifier. When societies invoke the imposition of restraints or limits on desirous behavior—all the way from infractions of etiquette to the death penalty—they are invoking the law of the Name-of-the-Father in the widest sense and imposing some form of castration.

From this brief account, it must be clear how remote Lacan's conception of the Oedipus complex is from Freud's. Not only does the process begin earlier (namely, at around eighteen months, not at five years); it presumes neither death wish toward the father nor desire by the son to commit incest with the mother nor, for that matter, any so-called "penis envy" on the part of a daughter. Lacan, indeed, pronounced the Oedipus complex to be Freud's own neurotic dream (Ragland-Sullivan 1985, 267). But, he maintained, the complex remained true in its structure, and this structure is what is retained by Lacan. The mother or Other of early care is, indeed, the neonate's first love object. The infant does, indeed, feel resentment and rage at the father's competing presence for the (m)Other's attention. A successful castration between eighteen months and five years (by which time a child has mastered the grammar of its mother tongue and gained a firm notion of its sexual identity) does, indeed, cause painful separation and loss—a sense of having been pitched forcibly from some Garden of Eden into a world of difference, compromise, negotiation, and the limits of law. In the unconscious, therefore, the nexus of desire-as-lack, loss, and what Lacan termed "primary narcissism" remains identified with the (m)Other; and a sense of authority, law, but also increased aggressiveness are unconsciously identified with the Father's Name.

The Dramatic Interest of Oedipal Relationships in Tirso

A straightforward, dictionary definition of "incest" is the following: "The crime of cohabitation or sexual commerce between persons related within the degrees wherein marriage is prohibited by law" (*Webster's New International*, 2d ed.). From a Lacanian perspective, however, such a definition is too narrow and one may say that the incest taboo is really the one law *par excellence*. In his *Seventh Seminar, The Ethics of Psychoanalysis*, Lacan (1986) observed that we disobey the Ten Commandments all the time. The only universally observed law that we do respect, however, is the incest taboo, and this is *not* one of the Ten Commandments. The taboo is the one law in the sense that it arises from the primordial prohibition of unlimited access to the (m)Other, in the Name-of-the-Father, and actually structures the emerging human subject as a speaking, representational being. Thus, the model of law as prohibition and the function of the Father's Name as a curb on the desire to which such prohibition has given rise together provide the framework of all future laws and prohibitions, as well as a receptivity in the subject to enter the world of compromise and law as a socially submissive being.

I have elsewhere (1985b) observed that, while Tirso and Calderón (for example) both dramatize the conflict between desire and law in their plays, desire in Tirso is frequently shown to triumph over law, whereas in Calderón law always ultimately triumphs over desire. This contrast is obviously one measure of the difference between the two men, and one can only speculate on the reasons for it. Nor do I mean to suggest by the frequent Tirsian triumph of desire over law that the Mercedarian urged the schizoid overthrow of taboos on desire in some strange anticipation of Deleuze and Guattari's *Anti-Oedipus* (1972). In his many *dama-busca-galán* or "girl seeks boy," disguise comedies, Tirso persistently depicts his trouserclad heroine obtaining the object of her desire, however improper or injurious to social observance her methods may have been. Inasmuch as authority figures condone and pardon the actions of these heroines, the protagonists' personal desire may be said to have triumphed over the prohibitions and limits of social convention. But I believe Tirso's readiness to return so regularly to this theme and thus to portray the utopian or dream world of wish-fulfillment is of a piece with his preparedness to toy with the incest taboo. The whole problematic of the oedipal structure lies far closer to the surface in Tirso than it does in the work of his contemporaries.

The basic axis of the desire/law relationship depends on a paradox. In the first place, desire-as-lack is created by the castrating activity of the paternal law or metaphor. On the other hand, without the existence of desire, there would be no need for law. In this sense, the two components are different aspects of the same thing and, from the vantagepoint of nature or the animal kingdom, arbitrary aspects at that. Now it is precisely this arbitrariness around the desire/law issue—the oedipal structure—that seems to fascinate Tirso, and he extends his questioning over the whole gamut of gender or sexual identity.

Am I saying, one might wonder, that Tirso de Molina was anticipatorily possessed of Lacanian insights? I am not, of course. When Freud was hailed as the discoverer of the unconscious mind, he replied modestly that, in fact, the unconscious had been discovered by artists and poets long before him. What he, Freud, had discovered was a scientific method by which the unconscious mind could be studied: psychoanalysis. Lacan, who perhaps somewhat less modestly considered himself Freud's true inheritor, also claimed that psychoanalysis was a science in the sense that it had a constant object of study: the unconscious. What I am saying is that Tirso de Molina was one of the great, perceptive poets to whom Freud referred and that he revealed his insights about the unconscous not in a scientific discourse, but in a dramatico-poetic discourse. His plays are his statements about the elusive moments of unconscious subjectivity and intersubjective dynamics.

I believe Tirso reveals great insight when he pushes the arbitrariness of the one law—the prohibition of incest by virtue of the Name-of-the-Father—toward the surface of his dramas. Contrary to Calderón, there is in Tirso a subversive pressure at work under the authority of the Father's Name. Marriage contracts arranged by fathers are rendered ineffectual by the contrary desires of their children. His powerful comedy *La república al revés (The republic upside down)* portrays the Byzantine Empire in absurd and lawless disarray by virtue of the young Emperor Constantino's revolt against his mother, the ex-Empress Irene, who is the signifier for the Father's Name despite her female sex. Don Juan Tenorio murders the father Don Gonzalo de Ulloa, who stands in the way of his access to the desired daughter, Doña Ana, and desecrates paternal dignity even in death by his famous mockery of the stone statue of Comendador Ulloa.

It has become a cliché of Tirso criticism to note that his male and female protagonists often seem to have acquired the stereotypical characteristics of the other sex. Thus his women are resolute, courageous, intelligent, and manipulatively cunning, whereas his men are passive, timid, fickle, and finally ineffectual. This inversion of masculine and feminine personality traits is sometimes aided by the convention of the heroine disguised as a man, but it goes deeper than a mere stage trick. The Lacanian view of sexual identity is that the masculine and feminine positions depend respectively on the subject's unconscious stance toward the phallic signifier: the repressed residue of the effects left by castration in the early years of oedipal formation. The commonest resolution for boys and young men is to identify themselves *with* phallic law and *away* from primordial loss, thus adopting the masculine position. The commonest resolution for girls and young women is to identify themselves *away* from difference and rather *with* sameness and the primordial loss associated with the (m)Other, thus adopting the feminine position.

This state of affairs, however, is merely the norm. Some biological males adopt the feminine position and some biological females adopt the masculine position. This is the topsy-turvy situation regularly dramatized by Tirso in, for example, *El vergonzoso en palacio (The shy man at court)* and *Don Gil de las calzas verdes (Sir Giles in green breeches)* and others. Few people, moreover, experience so clearcut an oedipal resolution as the norm (or even its inversion) as just described above. Men and women as individual subjects are infinite gradations along these axes, and oedipal questions (or "knots" in Lacan's terminology) often remain to plague the subject in the form of neurosis. Indeed, the hysteric's fundamental identity question, according to Lacan, is: "Am I a man or a woman?"

As an intuitive genius, then, Tirso may not "know" all this in the rigidly epistemological sense of the term "know," but he is able to write about it in a poetic discourse, and that is what is important. Furthermore, as a dramatist, he is aware of the effect on an audience of signifiers such as the incest motif or blurred gender identity. The effect is gripping. It is neither instructive nor entertaining *per se,* as the pragmatic motto in the title of Tirso's prose miscellany *Deleitar aprovechando (Delight with profit)* would suggest. An audience gripped is by definition "entertained" (*entretenu* or held), but also enlightened or instructed when its members attempt to bring their separate elements of cognition or understanding to the gripping emotional arousal of the performance. This double effect could appropriately be termed "the comic catharsis."[4]

So, Tirso, in his use of substitutions and displacements for incestuous material and the oedipal signifiers, knows he can grip an audience by pulling aside a self-protective veil at the safe remove of representation and, emotionally speaking, rattling the spectator's cage. This unconscious material is potentially the most powerful agency the playwright possesses to unite the conflicts and scenes of the stage with the unconscious conflicts and "other stage" (Freud's *anderer Schauplatz*) within each spectator. Herein, I submit, lies the dramatic interest of Oedipal relationships in Tirso.

The Growth of Comedy and Tragedy in Spain and England

I have promised some application of this line of reasoning to the question of the appearance of the comic and tragic genres in late-Renaissance Europe. The common *incipit* adopted for the popular national dramas of Spain and England, very properly in my view, is the year 1580. Whereas vernacular plays were composed earlier than this date in England and Spain, and even in France, it remains a fact that popular national dramas as such began in fixed theaters around 1580 in such centers as Madrid and London. The case of France is an interesting exception, and I believe the desire/law structures derived from the one law of the prohibition against incest can throw intriguing light on this overall situation.

I have maintained at some length that Tirsian comedy exerts a subversive pressure on the law of the Name-of-the-Father. One may go further and assert baldly that comedy is a dramatic genre that depicts the subversion of law. In practical terms, this law is usually incarnated in a tyrannical father, a guardian brother, a king or powerful man, who is ultimately bamboozled and outwitted in a comic intrigue. Tragedy, on the other hand, depicts the fate of victims of law's arbitrariness. In this way, both genres express unconscious attitudes toward the universal structures of desire and law.

Alone, or with Ellie Ragland-Sullivan, I have tried to formulate the nature of Spanish tragedy as a "Christian catharsis" in the works of Calderón, or as "ethical tragedy" in the works of Tirso (Ragland-Sullivan and Sullivan 1981; Ragland-Sullivan and Sullivan in press; Sullivan 1989). Suffice it to say for the purposes of the present argument that, in tragedy, the noble or outstanding hero is typically flawed in some way, as Aristotle stated centuries ago, but is in death punished far beyond his actual measure of wrongdoing. His punishment does not fit the crime. There is, therefore, an excess of punishment over wrongdoing exacted for the hero's flaw. But, by the same reasoning adduced above, each of us suffers an inner sacrifice of our desire to the demands of societal law as the price of living in our human community in sanity. This sacrifice of personal desire, according to Lacan, is what gives rise to feelings of guilt, even though we have not committed any particular crime. These guilt feelings may be said to accumulate as an excess of guilt over wrongdoing present in the spectator. What tragic catharsis does is to annihilate the spectator's excessive (and strictly unwarranted) guilt feelings by means of the excessive punishment of the hero. The collective mass of audience guilt is drained off as through a poetic "black hole" in the crisis and dénouement of the tragedy, and so purgation or ritual cleansing—as Aristotle claimed—is what catharsis or tragic effect is really about.

Clearly, however, for the comic and tragic genres to flourish, according to this theory, a definite fountainhead of law in the spectator community is indispensable. Without law, there can be no meaningful subversion of it, nor any perceptible idea of when law is just, arbitrary, or anything else. In Spain and England around 1580, Philip II and Elizabeth I had reigned as powerful monarchs for twenty-four and twenty-two years respectively. While their kingdoms were not entirely free of internal religious strife and dissension, these challenges rarely developed into a major political threat. Philip put down the Morisco Revolt of the Alpujarras from 1568 to 1570 after some hard campaigning; Elizabeth solved the Catholic threat posed by the person of Mary Stuart by having her beheaded in 1586 and willing England to her son James. The rebellion of the northern earls in 1569 and the Irish insurrections of Elizabeth's reign never seriously imperilled her status as monarch. In 1580, both rulers held their nations in a mood of devoted and unequivocal obedience.

In France, however, the situation could hardly have been more different. France was wracked from 1562 to 1598 by a series of seven internal and bloody religious wars. Henry III of France, for example, was virtually unable to assert royal authority during periods of his reign and was finally assassinated in 1589. The succession of civil disturbances, indeed, brought the French state close to disintegration and posed a threat to the crown not matched again until 1789. Inasmuch as no real sense of central law prevailed in France during the last third of the sixteenth century, it is hard to see—given our Lacanian genre theory—how any well-anchored vernacular French drama could have arisen at all. The experiments of Jodelle and Garnier do not constitute such a drama, in my opinion. It was only in the period of Cardinal Richelieu's authoritarian ascendancy as Louis XIII's first minister (1624–42) that a thriving French drama, with a strong generic distinction between comedy and tragedy, finally emerged. Corneille's *Le Cid,* the *terminus a quo* for French classical drama, triumphed in 1637 and, perhaps not incidentally, contains the murder of the heroine's father by the hero—an oedipal conflict if ever there was one—at the heart of the play's dilemma.

This is not to suggest that a state of war—either civil strife or international hostilities—suffices in itself to preclude a thriving national drama. In the period from 1648 to 1653, for example, there were two further civil wars, or Frondes, in France—a span of years during which Corneille was elaborating his mature tragedies along strict neoclassical lines (as they were then understood). But the first, so-called Fronde of the Parlement concerned grievances of both provincial and Parisian magistrates against Mazarin's attempts to dictate from the center in the interests of the state. Even rebel slogans of the time did not express disloyalty to the king himself, the callow Louis XIV. The second Fronde of the princes, led by Condé, was a pale reflection of the feudal reaction during the Wars of Religion and did not succeed in making common cause with the Parlement in any broad revolutionary threat to the crown. In the words of one historian: "Neither Fronde posed the grievous threat to the very basis of the state that had existed in the previous century. Mazarin was the chief object of enmity and that fact itself helps to explain the less serious nature of the threat. What was at issue was not the King's authority per se but the manner in which it had been exercised since Richelieu's time, in a less personal and therefore seemingly more arbitrary fashion" (*Encyclopaedia Britannica,* 15th ed., s.v. "France, History of," by J. H. Shennan).

Nor can the case of classical Greece be invoked to refute the Lacanian genre theory being advanced here. It is true that the ancient Greek drama achieved its highest perfection in the time of Pericles as an expression of Athenian cultural self-consciousness. The source of the tragic/comic distinction, moreover, is—*ex definitione*—this fifth-century B.C. popular theater. And warfare, whether against Persia in the early part of the century or, later on, against some wavering "ally" of the Athenian Empire or the Peloponnesian alliance, characterized the whole century. None of these wars, however, was revolutionary or subversive of the Athenian city-state itself. The long political and dramatic career of Sophocles (ca. 496–406 B.C.), indeed, illustrates the playwright's unassailable faith in the city and its ideals. Though Pericles had political opponents, the legitimacy by which he held power was manifest in his democratic re-election to the generalship each year. The spirit of law itself was never at stake in Periclean Athens, as it was in late sixteenth-century France. I repeat, therefore, that the genres of tragedy and comedy can only flourish as differential and unconscious attitudes toward law and the phallic signifier when these latter are firmly enshrined in the symbolic-order institutions of the host culture.

Conclusion

The preceding remarks do, I believe, help to articulate a little better the general impression that Tirsian comedy and tragedy leave behind. His comedies project a zany and topsy-turvy world of disintegrating boundaries and protean energy. Personality is elastic and the Name-of-the-Father fragile. It is a theater suffused in desire, almost lubricious. His tragedies are best termed "ethical" (one of Aristotle's four tragic categories) in the sense that the oedipally constituted structure of the human subject is essentially an ethical one.[5] While morals are often lightly put aside in Tirsian tragedy, ethics never are; and, as dramatist, Tirso is a severe judge of injuries to the ethical center of human life. His intuitive daring also explains his originality and unconventionality of dramatic design or craftsmanship. The same courageous capacity to question made him the only effective dramatic opponent to the Olivares régime, and, finally, this was the reason for the official suppression of 1625 that brought his brilliant career as playwright abruptly to an end.

Notes

1. All quotations from Tirso's works refer to *Obras dramáticas completas*, edited by Blanca de los Ríos, 3 vols. (Madrid: Aguilar, 1946–58).
2. Apart from the general thematic similarities of Clavela's and Amón's sonnets, there is an almost verbatim cross-reference in the closing lines of each. Clavela says: "La sangre hierve (me diréis) sin fuego. / Sí; pero amor de hermano no desvela / y cuando desvelara, no da celos" (2.2.691b) and Amón asks: "que, si la sangre, en fin, sin fuego hierve / ¿qué hará sangre que tiene tanto fuego?" (2.2.388b).
3. In the "Discours de Rome," Lacan wrote as follows: "The primordial Law is therefore that which in regulating marriage ties superimposes the kingdom of culture on that of nature abandoned to the law of copulation. The interdiction of incest is only its subjective pivot, revealed by the modern tendency to reduce to the mother and the sister the objects forbidden to the subject's choice, although full licence outside of these is not yet entirely open.

This law, therefore, is revealed clearly enough as identical to an order of Language. For without kinship nominations, no power is capable of instituting the order of preferences and taboos which bind and weave the yarn of lineage down through succeeding generations. And it is indeed the confusion of generations which, in the Bible as in all traditional laws, is accused as being the abomination of the *verbe* and the desolation of the sinner." Cf. Anthony Wilden (1968, 40).
4. The term "comic catharsis" is my own. For a discussion of the dual aspects of catharsis (arousal and cognition), see Adnan Abdulla (1985, 8).
5. I refer to the translation and edition of S. H. Butcher (1955), reproduced in Hazard Adams (1971, 48–66). In section 18, 2, Aristotle states: "There are four kinds of tragedy, the complex, depending entirely on reversal of the situation and recognition; the pathetic (where the motive is passion)—such as the tragedies on Ajax and Ixion; the ethical (where the motives are ethical)—such as the *Phthiotides* and the *Peleus*. The fourth kind is the simple" (p. 59). Regrettably, Aristotle never enlarges at all on his definition of "ethical tragedy" either in the *Poetics* or elsewhere, despite the obvious interest of such a category. But see Sullivan (1989).

Works Cited

Abdulla, Adnan K. 1985. *Catharsis in Literature*. Bloomington: Indiana University Press.

Butcher, S. H. 1955. *Aristotle's Theory of Poetry and Fine Art*. 4th ed. New York: Dover.

Critical Theory Since Plato. 1971. Edited by Adams Hazard. New York: Harcourt.

Deleuze, Gilles and Félix Guattari. 1972. *Capitalisme et Schizophrénie: L'Anti-oedipe*. Paris: Minuit.

Lacan, Jacques. 1986. *Le Séminaire*. Vol. 7, *L'Ethique de la Psychanalyse*. Texte établi par Jacques-Alain Miller. Paris: Seuil.

————. 1968. *The Language of the Self: The Function of Language in Psychoanalysis*. Translated by Anthony Wilden. Baltimore and London: The Johns Hopkins Press.

Leach, Edmund R. 1970. *Claude Lévi-Strauss*. New York: Fontana.

Lévi-Strauss, Claude. 1949. *Les structures élémentaires de la parenté*. Paris: Presses Universitaires de France.

————. 1969. *The Elementary Structures of Kinship*. Translated by J. H. Bell, J. R. von Sturmer and R. Nedham. Boston.

Ragland-Sullivan, 1985. *Jacques Lacan and the Philosophy of Psychoanalysis*. Urbana: University of Illinois.

Ragland-Sullivan, Ellie and Henry W. Sullivan. 1981. "*Las tres justicias en una* of Calderón and the Question of Christian Catharsis." In *Critical Perspectives on Calderón de la Barca*, edited by José A. Madrigal et al., 119–40. Lincoln, Nebraska: Society for Spanish and Spanish-American Studies.

————. "A Lacanian Theory of 'Christian' Catharsis." In *Psychoanalysis/Psychoanalysis as Critique*, edited by Richard Feldstein and Henry Sussman. Minneapolis: University of Minnesota Press, in press.

Shennan, J. H. "France, History of." In *Encyclopedia Britannica*. 15th ed.

Sullivan, Henry W. 1981. *Tirso de Molina and the Drama of the Counter Reformation*. 2nd ed. Amsterdam: Rodopi, 1976.

————a. 1985. "Love, Matrimony and Desire in the Theater of Tirso de Molina." *Bulletin of the Comediantes* 37, 1:83–99.

————b. 1985. "La razón de los altibajos en la reputación póstuma de Calderón." In *Hacia Calderón: Séptimo Coloquio Anglogermano*, edited by Hans Flasche, 204–11. Wiesbaden: Franz Steiner Verlag.

————. 1986. "Sibling Symmetry and the Incest Taboo in Tirso's *Habladme en entrando*." *Revista Canadiense de Estudios Hispánicos* 10, 2:261–78.

————. 1989. "Towards a Definition of Tirsian Tragedy". In *Texto y espectáculo: Selected Proceedings of the Symposium on Spanish Golden Age Theater*, edited by Barbara Mujica, 65–76. Lanham: University Presses of America.

Tirso de Molina (Gabriel Téllez). 1946–58. *Obras dramáticas completas*. 3 vols. Edited by Blanca de los Ríos Lampérez. Madrid: Aguilar.

Wilden, Anthony. 1968. *The Language of the Self: The Function of Language in Psychoanalysis*. Baltimore and London: The Johns Hopkins Press.

3
The Great Divide

Lisping and Wearing Strange Suits: English Characters on the Spanish Stage and Spanish Characters on the English Stage, 1580–1680

Don W. Cruickshank

In this essay my intention is to examine the theaters of Spain and England in the century from 1580 to 1680, in order to discover how Spaniards presented English people on the Spanish stage in this period and how English writers presented Spaniards on the English stage. My examination of the Spanish theater has been relatively comprehensive; in the English theater, where portrayal of Spaniards and of Spanish subject matter is common, I have examined only a selection of plays.

One of the factors that influence the perception one nation has of another is the state of diplomatic relations between the two. During the century in question, relations between England and Spain varied enormously. Under Ferdinand and Isabella, Spain's policy had been to seek allies against France. In England's case, this alliance involved a dynastic marriage when Katherine of Aragon married first Prince Arthur (1501) and then King Henry VIII (1509). Katherine was popular in England, and the early years of her marriage to Henry marked a high point of good relations between the two countries. Henry destroyed these good relations through his divorce and the schism of the English church.

Eight years after Henry's death, Philip II married his second cousin Mary Tudor. The marriage made relations even worse. Philip got on badly with foreigners, and this was remembered more than his efforts to curb the worst aspects of Mary's religious zeal. However, when Mary was succeeded by Elizabeth, Philip tried to maintain good relations and even offered to marry the new queen. The metaphorical honeymoon came to an end when Elizabeth sent aid to Huguenots in France (1562–63). Philip supported plots against

Elizabeth, who in turn connived at attacks on Spanish shipping and aided Philip's Dutch rebels. This led to a full-scale war that lasted until both Philip and Elizabeth were dead.

In 1604 James I, the new king of England, brought the war to an end and tried to foster better relations with Spain. He was ready to make concessions to English Catholics to promote the marriage between his son Charles and Philip IV's sister, but, when Charles and Buckingham returned empty-handed from the courtship in Madrid in 1623, they tried to persuade James to declare war in order to avenge the slight they had suffered. James resisted, but, when he died in 1625, Charles declared war and despatched an abortive attack to Cadiz. Hostilities eventually petered out and ended formally in 1630. From then on, increasing troubles at home kept Charles occupied. When he was executed in 1649, Spain dithered for nine years before agreeing to aid the royalist cause. As a result of this tepid assistance, Charles II did not hesitate, once he was restored in 1660, to recognize the existence of Portugal by marrying Catharine of Braganza. The last years of the period under examination are marked by England's role as a mediator: in 1668 between Spain and Portugal and between Spain and France; and again in 1678 between Spain and France.

One important point that should be made about this seesaw of relations is that English public opinion lagged behind government policy: Henry VIII's treatment of Katherine of Aragon was not popular with his subjects, and anti-Spanish feeling came only with Mary Tudor's marriage to Philip II. Once it had arrived, this feeling persisted long after James I's peace in 1604, to the extent that Charles I's negotiations with Spain in 1640 provoked riots in London. The situation improved with the Restoration, however, so that Samuel Pepys could write in 1661 that "we do naturally all love the Spanish and hate the French."[1]

As for Spanish public opinion, the two great bogeymen were Francis Drake in the sixteenth century and Oliver Cromwell in the seventeenth. Henry VIII and his daughter Elizabeth also had a bad name. However, I know of no Spanish play that features either Drake or Cromwell, and Henry and Elizabeth Tudor appear rarely. The fact is that Spanish dislike of the English seems never to have been as sweeping as English dislike of the Spaniards. The reasons are not entirely clear, but I shall return to this point later.

In Spain, the rise of the new drama under Lope de Vega coincides with a period of war between Spain and England. Lope (b. 1562) is the first of my Spanish dramatists. The others are Guillén de Castro (b. 1569), Mira de Amescua (b. 1574?), Luis Vélez de

Guevara (b. 1579), Tirso de Molina (b. ca. 1581), Juan Ruiz de Alarcón (b. ca. 1581), Rodrigo de Herrera (b. 1592), Alvaro Cubillo de Aragón (b. 1596?), Pedro Calderón (b. 1600), Juan Pérez de Montalbán (b. 1602), Francisco de Rojas Zorrilla (b. 1607), Juan de Matos Fragoso (b. 1608), Antonio Coello (b. 1611), Augustín Moreto (b. 1618) and Juan Bautista Diamante (b. 1625).[2] Of these fifteen dramatists, nine use English characters or settings: Lope de Vega, Guillén de Castro, Vélez de Guevara, Herrera, Calderón, Pérez de Montalbán, Matos Fragoso, Coello, and Diamante; the total number of plays involved is only twenty-seven. The surviving dramatic output of these fifteen dramatists is about eleven hundred plays, so that a total of twenty-seven is two-and-a-half per cent. English characters and settings are not common in the Spanish classical theater. Not surprisingly, the writer with the largest number of English characters and settings is Lope de Vega, with eleven plays—not surprisingly, because he wrote more plays than anyone else. Of these eleven plays, only four have English settings, and only one, *Los pleitos de Ingalaterra* (1598–1603), is set entirely in England; the others have one or more English characters but are set partly on the continent of Europe. According to Morley and Bruerton (1968), in chronological order, they are as shown in the accompanying table.

Title	Date	Publ.	Set	English Characters
El amor desatinado	1597	unpub?	?	1
La imperial de Otón	1598	1617	Germany	1
El gallardo catalán	1597–1603	1609	England, etc.	4
Los Ramírez de Arellano	1597–1603	1641	Spain	1
Los pleitos de Ingalaterra	1598–1603	1638	England	12
La condesa Matilde	1599–1603	1609	France	3
Los tres diamantes	1599–1603	1609	Italy, etc.	1
La corona merecida	1603	1620	Spain	1
Don Juan de Castro I	1604–8	1623	Spain, England	10
Don Juan de Castro II	1608?	1623	England, Spain	6
El animal de Hungría	1611–12	1617	Hungary	3

Several of these plays, such as *La imperial de Otón* and *Los Ramírez de Arellano,* have historical settings and even include historical events or characters. However, none of this history is ever central to any of the plays, which are all novelesque.[3] If one looks in Lope's plays for an interpretation of English history or for a portrayal of historical English figures, one would be disappointed. The dates of composition, which run from 1597 to 1612, cover a relatively short span of Lope's career and a period when Hispano-

English relations ranged from bad to quite good. One might expect the early plays in the list to portray the English as villains, rather as early James Bond books do with Russians. Not a bit of it: noble English men behave like gentlemen, noble English women like ladies, with never so much as a hint that any of them might be suspect in religious terms. English and Spanish noble families intermarry, and in *Don Juan de Castro II*, for example, when Rugero, a Spaniard, marries an English princess, he evidently takes on dual nationality, since he swears to King Edward "a fe de español inglés" that he will not return without the head of the king of Ireland. This was written in 1608, when relations between Spain and England were better, but the ruler of Ireland has a similar role in *Los pleitos de Ingalaterra*, which was written before the death of Elizabeth I. There is no trace, in any of these plays of Lope's, of Spanish government attitudes or policy, which for so long saw England as an enemy of the faith and Ireland as a potential ally. Even when there is a possible reference to conflict between Spain and England, it is made without rancour. Thus in *Los tres diamantes*, when Enrique, son of King Arthur of England, thinks the face of his disguised friend Lisardo is familiar, he asks

> ¿Tú, por dicha, a Ingalaterra
> con alguna armada has ido?
> (Biblioteca de Autores Españoles 234, 523a)

[Did you ever go to England with a fleet, by any chance?]

I take this to be Lope dropping a hint about his own supposed involvement with the Armada of 1588, although I happen to share Rudolph Schevill's view (1941, 65–78) view that Lope's involvement stopped short of actually sailing with the fleet.

There may be lost historical plays by Lope dealing with characters and events from English history in the way that he dealt with Francis Drake and Mary Stuart in some of his poems, such as his *Dragontea* (1598) and *La corona trágica* (1627), but none of the surviving plays shows the least animosity toward England or the English. The nearest Lope gets to poking fun at them is in *El gallardo catalán*, where a peasant, perhaps significantly called Belardo, puns feebly on *inglés* / *ingles* ("English / groins").

This attitude to England is not peculiar to Lope, however. Guillén de Castro's play *La humildad soberbia* (written about 1600) takes a historical setting with a historical hero, Rodrigo de Villandrando, and turns it into a novelesque entertainment.[4] King Edward of

England and his general in France, Talbot, appear briefly and without distinguishing features.

Vélez de Guevara added nothing to this "traditional" manner of presenting English characters on the Spanish stage. One of his plays, *Los agravios perdidos,* is set in England and Scotland; another, *El caballero del sol,* is set mainly in Italy, but has Febo, prince of England, as its hero; a third, *El rey naciendo mujer,* is set in France but also includes a Febo, prince of Wales, and his sister Flor de Lis. The name Febo and the title *El caballero del sol* derive from chivalresque romance, and Vélez's bibliographers, Spencer and Schevill, classify all three of these plays as novelesque. A fourth play, *Atila azote de Dios,* which gives a minor role to a king of England, is classified as historico-novelesque, but its details are not historical. All of these plays were printed in *suelta* editions. Only *El caballero del sol* has a firm composition date, 1617 (Spenser and Schevill 1937, 17–20).

The event that prompted a change in this fairy-tale view of England was apparently Charles Stuart's visit to Spain in the summer of 1623, although the change was not immediate. Plays were staged to entertain Charles, one of them probably being *Amor, honor y poder (Love, honor and power),* Calderón's first recorded play, which is set in the England of Edward III.[5] The subject is the king's alleged affair with the countess of Salisbury, but the play is not historical. The intention was no doubt to pay Charles a compliment, but the play presents typically Spanish characters concerned with typically Spanish themes: the contradictions between love and honor, honor and power, power and love. There is never any suggestion that anyone, from the king to the peasant Tosco, acts in an "English" manner. The model, as with one or two other early Calderón plays, is clearly Lope de Vega, and the source, in Bandello via Belleforest and Bovistan, is a typical Lope source.

The next Calderón play to concern us is *El sitio de Bredá (The siege of Breda),* possibly written in 1625, two years later (Whitaker 1978; Vosters 1981). Critics have noted that this play, like Velázquez's painting of the surrender of the city, portrays the defeated side in a sympathetic light. It presents an Englishman named Morgán as Justin of Nassau's deputy commander. This Colonel Morgan was a historical personage, who may have been Justin's stepson. He is portrayed as an intelligent and proud man who encourages and inspires the resistance of the besieged (1934–43). He is reluctant to surrender (943–47, 2203–4), but when the occasion arises, he can be charming and gallant to a lady (617–21, 632–34). He is no different from the Spanish officers in this respect.[6]

El sitio de Bredá sets out to glorify a Spanish victory and to show that Spanish troops were superior in fighting qualities and in magnanimity. It also shows, however, even after the fiasco of the Charles Stuart marriage and the resulting ill feeling, that a Spanish author could present on stage a hostile English officer who had the same noble qualities as his Spanish counterparts.

If *El sitio de Bredá* is as late as 1628, as has been suggested, then the first truly historical Spanish play to present English characters, and one which certainly derives from Charles Stuart's visit, is Rodrigo de Herrera's *La fe no ha menester armas (Faith needs no weapons)*. Herrera is an obscure figure with few surviving plays.[7] *La fe no ha menester armas* portrays Charles's 1623 visit and the English attack on Cadiz in October and November of 1625. The play is set entirely in Spain, but Charles, Buckingham, and Leicester appear. Philip IV rejects his sister's marriage with Charles on religious grounds, and Buckingham is portrayed as the villain. However, ordinary English soldiers are shown fraternizing with the *gracioso,* and, apart from Buckingham, the English are portrayed quite sympathetically. As a drama, unfortunately, the play is a poor thing. It must have been written after the English withdrawal in November 1625, but references to the *Cortes* of Monzón as being in the future imply that it was completed before they took place in March 1626. The earliest edition I know of is a *suelta* of the 1670s.

If a historical play is one which centers on and interprets a historical event or events, then the first historical play in Spanish to have an English setting is Calderón's *La cisma de Ingalaterra (The schism of England)*. In *La cisma,* Calderón shows how the moral failings of one man—Henry VIII—brought strife and misery to his country. It was once suggested that the play was written after the outbreak of the English Civil War and perhaps even after the execution of Charles I in 1649 (Parker 1958), so that Calderón's point was supported by historical events. However, there is reliable evidence that the play was performed as early as 1627 (Shergold and Varey 1961, 277).

The play is set in England, and most of the characters are English, although neither the setting nor the characters have any English characteristics, with one trivial exception, when the jester Pasquín makes a joke about the rain in London (577–79).[8] The characters are motivated by the same fears and desires as any group of Spaniards in a play set in Spain. What is significant is the fears and desires that Calderón attributes to the historical characters.

Henry is prudent, learned, and wise, but yet he is under Wolsey's spell. His love for Anne Boleyn, exploited by Wolsey, is his undoing. He knows the wrong he is doing to Catherine and to his kingdom (1723–71) and, when he discovers Anne's infidelity, he would gladly restore Katherine; but it is too late (2748–59). He would even reverse what he has done to the Church in England, but he cannot undo that either (2777–2801). He tries to salvage what he can by making Mary his heir, arguing that she will be able to do what he cannot (2802–32).

Wolsey is low-born but ambitious, willing to play one monarch against another to achieve his greatest desire, the papacy (213–52). He manipulates Henry skilfully (12–14, 129–32, 172–85, 1638–1716), but he is proud and arrogant toward those who cannot or will not further his ambitions (253–63, 647–72, 683–706). Having helped Anne to the crown, he is angry when she proves ungrateful, and threatens her; she engineers his downfall (2206–21, 2265–92). We see him recognise the wrong he has done to Katherine, but also see that he regrets his misjudgment rather than his wickedness (2410–2517).

As for Anne, she is the least sympathetic character: vain, haughty, ambitious, arrogant, and presumptuous, as well as a religious hypocrite (447–56). In the course of the play, we see her ambition lead her to abandon the man she loves to gain the crown; and she is revealed as envious, unfilial, and ungrateful (715–42, 2206–21, 2265–92).

This view of Anne, based on the understandably hostile portrayal of the Jesuit Rivadeneyra, is what one might expect from a Spanish dramatist. However, Calderón's view of Henry is much more sympathetic than Rivadeneyra's. Most unusual of all is his presentation of Mary Tudor. Mary's role is a minor one until the last scene, and the only trait seen in her up to then is devotion to her mother. In the last scene, however, she shows none of her mother's forbearance in her call for vengeance on Anne Boleyn (2769–76) or in her cry of triumph when she is presented with Ann's corpse (2862–65). Everyone with a smattering of historical knowledge is aware that the glories and triumphs she expects will be hollow ones (2866–69); and, when she pretends to swear to preserve the Church of England, Calderón reveals her mental reservation unambiguously (2983). The references to burning and to Mary's spark of resistance growing to a blaze are also quite clear (2966–67, 2976–79): Calderón sees Mary as a person whose intransigence will merely exacerbate the harm already done by Henry.

La cisma de Ingalaterra is obviously not an orthodox seventeenth-century Catholic view of English history from 1528 to 1534, but a portrayal of a ruler whose moral weakness is exploited by a corrupt and ambitious adviser and by a proud and ambitious woman. The good or upright characters (Katherine of Aragón, who is Spanish; Margaret Pole and Thomas Boleyn, who are English) are unable to prevent disaster, which, it is implied, will extend beyond the characters and the period encompassed by the play. The play takes liberties with historical fact to make its point: for example, Edward VI is suppressed, no doubt because he would have obscured Calderón's portrayal of Henry's repentance. The message is that, if the schism was not undone by Henry's repentance or by his daughter's misplaced zeal, it will not be undone by the uncompromising attitudes of writers like Rivadeneyra—or by those who threw away the opportunity to improve relations through royal marriage in 1623.[9]

Calderón is unique where English historical settings are concerned. His younger contemporary, Pérez de Montalbán, returned to the older Lope tradition and brought nothing new to the genre. He wrote one play, *Morir y disimular,* allegedly as early as 1619, set entirely in England; another, *El valiente más dichoso,* is set partly there and partly elsewhere.[10] Both are novelesque. A third, attributed play, *La desdicha venturosa y confusa Inglaterra,* while probably not authentic, is no different in this regard. As for Matos Fragoso, he has one play, *Callar siempre es lo mejor,* set in England, but it too is novelesque.

The writer who most challenges Calderón's uniqueness is Antonio Coello, with *El conde de Sex (The Count of Essex),* which was performed in 1633 and printed in 1638 (Rogers 1984, 198); it deals with the relationship between Robert Devereux, second earl of Essex, and Elizabeth Tudor. Apart from the Duke of Alençon, these are the only historical characters. Great liberties are taken with historical fact, and many of the events are novelesque, but the play is centered on a real event: the execution for treason of Robert Devereux, despite the queen's fondness for him.[11] What is interesting is that the play takes no sides: Essex and the Frenchman Alençon are presented as honorable and gallant gentlemen. Essex in particular is a victim of the conflicting demands of two passionate, jealous, and beautiful women, the queen and Blanca. The queen's dilemma is that her royal sense of duty and decorum conflict with her personal feelings. In the end, duty and decorum win, and the Protestant Elizabeth is seen to be more upright and principled than Blanca, a supporter of Mary Stuart.

A few months before he wrote *El conde de Sex,* Coello collaborated with Calderón on a controversial but well-received play on

Wallenstein and Gustavus Adolphus of Sweden. This play has been lost, but it is known to have presented the Protestant king flatteringly.[12] Between them, the two playwrights wrote four plays that depicted favorably the Protestant enemies of Spain, in particular Henry and Elizabeth Tudor. As Coello was only seventeen when Calderón's *La cisma* was performed, it seems likely that any influence was on Calderón's part.

I must mention another play here before I turn, more briefly, to English dramatists. The play is Diamante's *La reina María Estuarda (Queen Mary Stuart)*, which was performed in 1660. It deals with the execution of Mary Stuart in 1587, but the only historical characters are Mary and Elizabeth. In this regard *María Estuarda* is like *El conde de Sex,* but it is an inferior play: its dramatic tension is dissipated by the inopportune interruptions of the comic characters. *María Estuarda* is also different in that it points to the religious difference between Mary and Elizabeth. Many of the events are novelesque, but the presentation of Mary as martyr and Elizabeth as jealous of her is rooted in historical fact.[13]

What all these Spanish plays have in common is a lack of caricature of English people. One can find caricatures of Moors and Frenchmen and other foreigners who "speak funny" in Spanish drama, but not, it seems, English people. If English people are portrayed unfavorably, it is not because of their nationality. Spanish dramatists tended to portray the English as no different from themselves, and, when historical facts in the plot obliged them to refer to religious differences, they showed a considerable tolerance.[14]

They say that we only tolerate what we do not care about, and the fact is that few Spaniards knew or cared much about a small country on the fringe of northern Europe; they cared little, too, about its literature. England's attitude to Spain was quite different, and major—and even minor—works of Spanish literature were sources of inspiration for English dramatists for most of the sixteenth and seventeenth centuries.[15] Spanish plots, characters, references, and words are almost too numerous to count. I can only summarize.

English historical plays dealing with Spain, whether directly or allegorically, are not common, but they treat Spain unfavorably. For example, Dekker's *The Whore of Babylon,* and Heywood's *If You Know Not Me, You Know No Body,* Part 2, are set in England, but deal with the defeat of the Armada; and the lost plays *Pedro King of Spain* (or *The Tyrant*) and *The Spanish Duke of Lerma* (1641), while presumably set in Spain, are unlikely to have portrayed the protagonists favorably. The portrayal of individual Spaniards in plays dealing with English history is less subject to prejudice: one thinks of the saintly Katharine of Aragon in Shakespeare's *Henry VIII* or Blanch of Castile in *King John*. Even Heywood, in Part 1 of *If You Know Not Me*, was able to present Philip II acting as peacemaker between Mary and Elizabeth Tudor or putting to death a Spaniard who had treacherously killed an Englishman in a quarrel. This portrayal is not the less unusual for being historically accurate.

As in the Spanish theater, novelesque plays make up the largest group, but with a marked difference. Spanish novelesque plays about England and the English do not portray them with racial or cultural distinctions. English plays dealing with Spaniards tend strongly to present them as types: arrogant, proud, revengeful, or prone to duplicity and treachery. Examples are Kyd, *The Spanish Tragedy;* Middleton, *The Changeling* and *A Game at Chess;* Dekker, *Lust's Dominion;* Heywood, *The Fair Maid of the West*, Part 1, and *A Challenge for Beauty;* and Ford, *'Tis Pity She's a Whore,* in which Vasques rejoices that "a Spaniard outwent an Italian in revenge" (5.6). Even Beaumont and Fletcher, who are generally neutral in the portrayal of their many Spanish characters, are guilty of this stereotyping in *Love's Cure*. *A Game at Chess* is the most hostile of these plays. Staged in 1624, in the aftermath of the "Spanish marriage," it was extremely popular with London audiences. It gave offence to Spanish diplomats in London, and indeed to King James, who banned it and took proceedings against the author and the actors (Wilson and Turner 1949).

Of course, pride and arrogance, or obsession with status and revenge, are characteristics portrayed by Spanish writers in their own countrymen. Sometimes obsession is even caricatured and made ridiculous, as with Calderón's Don Mendo. It is clear, though, that some Spaniards are caricatured in English plays because they are Spaniards. Some of them speak oddly, and, while I know of no indications about dress, I am sure that some of them must have worn "strange suits." Those whose speech is odd include Don Adriano de Armado, the "fantastical Spaniard" in *Love's Labour's Lost;* Lazarillo de Tormes in Middleton's *Blurt, Master-Constable;* and the Spaniard in Dekker's *The Sun's Darling*. Those who merely behave oddly include Don Incubo de Hambre and Alphonso, the "choleric Don," in Beaumont and Fletcher's *Love's Pilgrimage;* Insultado in Dekker's *Old Fortunatus;* and Guzman, the "bragadoccio Spaniard" in Ford's *The Lady's Trial*. Perhaps it should also be noted that Barabas, Marlowe's Jew of Malta, speaks Spanish. There are other examples where the presentation of Spanish characters is quite positive, such as Dekker's *The Noble Spanish*

Soldier and Don Pedro in Beaumont and Fletcher's *The Knight of Malta*, but these are rare.

There is one more feature of English plays that may be mentioned: gratuitous abuse. I know of no instance where the English are gratuitously abused in a Spanish play, but examples of English abuse of Spaniards are frequent. Dekker and Webster spring to mind, with *Sir Thomas Wyatt:*

> . . . a Spaniard is a Camocho, a Callimanco, nay which is worse, a Dondego, and what is a Dondego? . . . a Dondego is a desperate Viliago, a very Castilian, God blesse vs. There came but one Dundego into England, and hee made all Paules stincke agen, what shall a whole army of Dondegoes doe my sweete Countrimen?
>
> (4.2.51–58)

and:

> . . . a Spaniard is cald so, because he's a Spaniard: his yard is but a span.
>
> (4.2.61–62)

One cannot say whether Dekker or Webster wrote these passages. It may be noted, though, that *Old Fortunatus,* which belongs to 1599 and is Dekker's only firmly dated play, also uses "Don Dego" as a term of abuse (2.2.267).[16]

England is part of an island, and Spain is part of a peninsula. The inhabitants of both countries have been accused of xenophobia, which may be a result of their geographical isolation. But English drama shows far more hostility toward Spaniards than Spanish drama does toward the English. This is understandable. The great age of Elizabethan drama was triggered off by the Spanish Armada, which promoted a new national consciousness in England; it is not surprising that plays hostile to Spaniards should have been written. However, I believe that the English plays show more hostility to foreigners in general: people who are caricatured or whose manner of speech is made fun of include Irish, Scots, and Welsh, as well as Italians, French, Dutch, and Spaniards. This sort of thing is rarer in Spanish drama. There are plenty of caricatures—the *comedia de figurón* is a genre of them—but they are Spaniards. And there are plenty of characters whose speech is meant to amuse, but most of them are Spanish rustics, whose language is quite stylized (although one of the most amusing, Beatriz in Calderón's *No hay burlas con el amor,* is a noblewoman).

Why should this be? Dramatic tradition may explain it in part.

But I suspect that one explanation for the lesser degree of antipathy shown by the Spaniards toward the English is to be found in misinformation, as often happens where prejudices are involved. When Philip II was planning his invasion of England, his informants assured him that up to two-thirds of the English were Catholics who would welcome his invasion for religious reasons. This was doubly false, but I think the misguided Spanish view survived, that most of the English were good Catholics, languishing under a heresy imposed on them by a tyrannical monarchy. I also think that an explanation is to be found in the rather different publics for whom the dramatists were writing. Madrid was a small capital city in terms of Spain's population during the Golden Age and contained a small number of foreigners. At the same time, although most of the dramatists lived there, even major acting companies had to go on tour, while plays were printed in a number of cities throughout the country. In England things were different. London contained a far greater proportion of the country's population. Provincial play-printing was nonexistent, and provincial theater hardly worth bothering about. London was the centre of the English theater in a way that was simply not true of Madrid.[17] And London was the home of the London mob. It has been said that "there was widespread resentment against foreigners in London, which throughout the sixteenth century made England, and especially its capital city, notorious in Europe for nationalist intolerance" (Ridley 1982, 78). One way to be a successful dramatist is to pander to the public's prejudices. I suspect that some of the English plays of this period are reflections of the demands of an indiscriminating and xenophobic public.[18]

At the same time, there is a more positive side to English drama's relations with Spain, especially during the periods from 1604 to 1623 and from 1630 onwards. In a passage from *The Alchemist* (1610), Ben Jonson alleged that:

> Your Spanish iennet is the best horse. Your Spanish
> Stoupe is the best garb. Your Spanish beard
> Is the best cut. Your Spanish ruffes are the best
> Weare. Your Spanish Pauin the best daunce.
> Your Spanish titillation in a gloue
> The best perfume. And as for your Spanish pike,
> And Spanish blade, let your poore Captaine speak.
>
> (4.4.9–15)

Moreover, apart from treating Spanish characters neutrally, Beaumont and Fletcher pay a great compliment to Spanish literature in their sources: *Rule a Wife and Have a Wife* combines Cervantes's *El casamiento engañoso* with Salas Barbadillo's *El sagaz Estacio* (Wilson 1948, 189–94), while *The Chances* is from Cervantes's *La señora Cornelia,* and *Love's Pilgrimage* from his *Las dos doncellas.* They also have debts to Lazarillo de Tormes, and no doubt others still unidentified. Finally, it should be remembered that even hostile works may often depend on Spanish sources. Thus William D'Avenant's "opera," *The Cruelty of the Spaniards in Peru* (1658), relies heavily on Las Casas. Staged during Cromwell's brief war against Spain, it was one of the last of its kind—that is, works inspired by conflict or fear of conflict, since the Peace of the Pyrenees in the following year showed conclusively that Spain had been overtaken by France as the major power in Europe. This is not the last piece of hispanophobia in English drama, however. Postclassical Spanish drama has sometimes portrayed English people extremely flatteringly. Flattering portrayal of Spanish people is rare on the English stage at any time. I am afraid that the Spanish waiter Manuel in the television series "Fawlty Towers" is typical of one of the two commonest ways of portraying Spaniards on the English stage: as sinister or as ridiculous. Perhaps one should take heart in the belief that the ridiculous is better than the sinister, but I doubt it. The English of the sixteenth and seventeenth centuries may not have liked the Spanish, but the educated among them respected both Spanish literature and the Spanish language. The same cannot be said today.[19]

Notes

1. *Diary,* 30 September 1661, edited by Robert Latham and William Matthews, 2:188 (London: Bell, 1970). A note suggests that the French were hated because they were many more French people in London and they competed for jobs with the natives.

2. To avoid having to read all the plays written by these dramatists, I have relied on the following: S. Griswold Morley and Richard W. Tyler, *Los nombres de personajes en las comedias de Lope de Vega,* 2 vols. (Valencia: Castalia, 1961); the *Obras* of Guillén de Castro, edited by E. Juliá Martínez, 3 vols. (Madrid: Revista de Archivas, 1925–27); E. Cotarelo y Mori, "Mira de Amescua y su teatro," *Boletín de la Real Academia Española* 17 (1930):467–505, 611–58; 18 (1931):7–90); F. E. Spencer and R. Schevill, *The Dramatic Works of Luis Vélez de Guevara: Their Plots, Sources and Bibliography,* University of California Publications in Modern Philology 19 (1937); the *Obras dramáticas completas* of Tirso, edited by Blanca de los Ríos, 3 vols. (Madrid: Aguilar, 1946–58); the *Obras completas* of Juan Ruíz de Alarcón, edited by Augustín Millares Carlo, 3 vols. (Mexico: Fondo de Cultura Económica, 1957–68); S. B. Whitaker, *The Dramatic Works of Alvaro Cubillo de Aragón* (Chapel Hill: University of North Carolina, 1975); Richard W. Tyler and Sergio D. Elizondo, *The Characters, Plots and Settings of Calderón's*

Comedias (Lincoln, Nebr: Society of Spanish and Spanish-American Studies, 1981); G. W. Bacon, "The Life and Dramatic Works of Juan Pérez de Montalbán," *Revue Hispanique* 26 (1912):1–474; E. Cotarelo y Mori, "Dramáticos españoles del siglo XVII: Don Antonio Coello y Ochoa," *Boletín de la Real Academia Española* 5 (1918):550–600; E. Cotarelo y Mori. "La bibliografía de Moreto," *Boletín de la Real Academia Española* 14 (1927):449–94; E. Cotarelo y Mori, "Don Juan Bautista Diamante y sus comedias," *Boletín de la Real Academia Española* 3 (1916):272–97, 454–97. I have not seen Margaret J. S. Chittenden, "Los nombres de personajes en las comedias de Tirso de Molina" (Ph.D. diss., University of Texas at Austin, 1964). In the case of Rojas Zorrilla and Matos Fragoso my investigations have been hampered by the lack of modern editions. I consulted the thirty plays of Rojas edited by Mesonero Romanos in Biblioteca de Autores Españoles 54, plus another eighteen in the Pennsylvania microfilm collection; for Matos I managed fifty-three titles from Biblioteca de Autores Españoles 47, Pennsylvania, and my own collection.

3. I have not seen the unpublished play *El amor desatinado,* but, as the only English character is King Roberto of England, it is clearly in the novelesque category, at least where English history is concerned.

4. For dates of plays by Castro, see Courtney Bruerton (1944, 124). His guess for this play is actually between 1595 and 1605.

5. Payment was made on 29 June 1623 for a performance of this play (Shergold and Varey 1961, 276).

6. References are to the edition published by Johanna R. Schrek (The Hague: University of Utrecht, 1957). There is some confusion about a captain Pablos Ballón, described in the cast list of the 1632 MS as "inglés"; but there is no support for this elsewhere in the MS or in printed editions.

7. There were at least two people of this name. This dramatist was apparently born in 1592 and died in 1657. (Pérez Pastor 1891–1907, 385–86; Kennedy 1937, 593–95).

8. References are to the edition published by Francisco Ruiz Ramón (Madrid: Castalia, 1981).

9. One more play should be mentioned here: *El mejor amigo el muerto,* by Belmonte, Rojas, and Calderón. It derives from Lope's *Don Juan de Castro I* and is wholly novelesque; it was published in 1657 and apparently played in 1636.

10. For dates of Pérez de Montalbán's plays, see J. H. Parker (1952). I must thank Professor V. F. Dixon for drawing my attention to *El socorro de Cádiz,* an unpublished *auto sacramental* by Pérez de Montalbán, which deals in allegorical fashion with the proposed royal marriage of 1623. Charles Stuart is El Error; the Infanta María, La Fe. The work may have been written after negotiations broke down, however; the surviving manuscript is dated 1626.

11. The historical Elizabeth liked to have dashing young men at her court, even when no longer young herself. *El conde de Sex* is set in 1588, when Essex was twenty-one and Elizabeth fifty-five, however.

12. A play entitled *El rey de Suecia,* which was probably this one, was performed on 1 February 1633; in March 1634 the Florentine ambassador described a play by Calderón and Coello about Wallenstein and the king, who had died at Lützen in November 1632 (Cruickshank and Page 1986, 79, n. 1232).

13. I have not investigated the source of Diamante's play, but it provided the starting point for *Lo que va de cetro a cetro, y crueldad de Inglaterra,* by José de Cañizares (1676–1750), which falls outside our period.

14. Although none of Cervantes's plays has an English setting, one should refer

here to his short story *La española inglesa,* which is set in England during the period from 1596 to 1613. Elizabeth is presented very favorably, although the hero and his family, as well as the heroine, are Roman Catholics. Interestingly enough, James Mabbe's translation (*The Spanish Ladie,* 1640) changes Londres to "Mundolin," suppresses all precise references to England, Scotland, and so forth, and makes his heroine and his hero's family merely Christians, implying that the "Northern Islanders" are not. Perhaps he feared that English public opinion would not accept the original story's good relations between Spanish and English people.

15. For major works, one need mention only *Calisto and Melebea,* "a new comodye . . . in maner of an enterlude," printed about 1530, and the lost comedy *Don Quixote* (1658). For minor works, one thinks of Samuel Tuke's *The Adventures of Five Hours,* from Coello's (?) *Los empeños de seis horas,* in comparison with which *Othello* seemed a "mean thing" (S. Pepys, *Diary,* 20 August 1666, 7:255).

16. I examined the work of fifteen English dramatists in the course of compiling this information: Kyd, Chapman, Marlowe, Shakespeare, Middleton, Dekker, Jonson, Heywood, Tourneur, Marston, Beaumont, Fletcher, Webster, Massinger, and Ford. The total number of surviving plays involved is fewer than 240, but approximately 37 of them, or 15 percent, have Spanish characters or settings. (One can only be approximate, since it is not always clear whether a "Prince of Arragon," for example, in a play set in Italy, is to be regarded as a Spaniard, or as a member of the Italian branch of the house of Aragon.)

17. "[Elizabethan drama] was essentially a creation of the capital" (Rowse 1972, 2:4). Of course drama was not confined to London; as Rowse goes on to point out, the schools and universities performed plays, and London companies toured the provinces; but what is called Elizabethan drama was written and first played in London.

18. "To be popular and successful, yet not to be at the mercy of the lowest part of the audience, was a task which none but Shakespeare accomplished" (Bradbrook 1951, 82).

19. When I prepared this paper, I had not seen John Loftis's recent book (1987). Professor Loftis examines some of the plays I have dealt with here, but, as his interest is specifically in history plays, we have covered somewhat different areas. He has a useful appendix on "English plays from the comedia" (235–62).

Works Cited

Bradbrook, M. C. 1951. *Shakespeare and Elizabethan Poetry.* London: Penguin.

Bruerton, Courtney. 1944. "The Chronology of the comedias of Guillén de Castro." *Hispanic Review* 12:124.

Calderón de la Barca. 1986. *No hay burlas con el amor / Love Is No Laughing Matter.* Edited and translated by Don Cruickshank and Sean Page. Warminster: Aris and Phillips.

Kennedy, Ruth Lee. 1937. "Los engaños y confusión de un papel. A Play by Rodrigo de Herrera y Ribera." *Modern Language Review* 32:593–95.

Loftis, John. 1987. *Renaissance Drama in England and Spain: Topical Allusion and History Plays.* Princeton: Princeton University Press.

Morley, S. G. and C. Bruerton. 1968. *The Chronology of Lope de Vega's Comedias.* New York: 1940. Translated and updated in *La cronología de las comedias de Lope de Vega.* Madrid: Gredos.

Parker, A. A. 1958. "Henry VIII in Shakespeare and Calderón: An Appreciation of *La cisma de Ingalaterra*". *Modern Language Review* 52:327–52.

Parker, J. H. 1952. "The Chronology of the Plays of Pérez de Montalbán." *PMLA* 67:186–210.

Pérez, Pastor, C. 1891–1907. *Bibliografía madrileña.* Madrid: Tipografía de los Huérfanos.

Ridley, Jasper. 1982. *The Statesmen and the Fanatic: Thomas Wolsey and Thomas More.* London: Constable.

Rogers, Dan. 1985. "*El médico de su honra* de Calderón y *El conde de Sex* de Coello." In *Hacia Calderón. Séptimo Coloquio Calderoniano,* edited by Hans Flasche, 175–82. Stuttgart: Franz Steiner, 1985.

———. 1984. "Los monólogos femeninos en *El conde de Sex* de Antonio Coello." In *Estudios dedicados a James Leslie Brooks,* edited by J. M. Ruiz Veintemilla, 175–90. Barcelona and Durham: Puvill.

Rowse, A. L. 1972. *The Elizabethan Renaissance.* Vol. 2, *The Cultural Achievement.* London: Macmillan.

Schevill, Rudloph. 1941. "Lope de Vega and the Year 1588." *Hispanic Review* 9:65–78.

Shergold, N. D. and J. E. Varey. 1961. "Some Early Calderón Dates." *Bulletin of Hispanic Studies* 38:274–86.

Vosters, S. A. 1981. "Again the First Performance of Calderón's *El sitio de Bredá,*" *Revista Canadiense de Estudios Hispánicos* 6:117–134.

Whitaker, Shirley B. 1978. "The First Performance of Calderón's *El sitio de Bredá.*" *Renaissance Quarterly* 31:515–31.

Wilson, E. M. 1948. "*Rule a Wife and Have a Wife* and *El sagaz Estacio.*" *Review of English Studies* 24:189–94.

Wilson, E. M. and Olga Turner. 1949. "The Spanish Protest against *A Game at Cheese.*" *Modern Language Review* 44:476–82.

The Advantages and Disadvantages of Secularity

Kenneth Muir

The main difference between the two Golden Ages of Elizabethan and Spanish drama is simply that in Spain the plays were written by Catholics for Catholics, whereas in England the drama was ostensibly secular, whatever the convictions of the individual dramatists.

As everyone knows, the earliest English drama was not merely religious but doctrinal: it was written by clerics to acquaint a largely illiterate audience with the basic story of the Fall and Redemption of man. The cycles all began with the Creation and nearly all ended with Doomsday. These mystery plays were succeeded by moralities, akin, except in quality, to what Shelley regarded as the incomparable religious allegories of Calderón[1]—a notable tribute from the author of *The Necessity of Atheism*.

Shakespeare knew, or knew of, some of the Mysteries, since he makes Hamlet refer to the ranting of Herod (3.2.14). He may well have witnessed some moralities, or even have read them; but by the time he began to write for the stage, after 1585, specifically religious subjects were largely avoided. It was possible to dramatize stories from the Old Testament, without running foul of the censorship, as Peele's *David and Bethsabe* and the play *A Looking-Glass for London and England* by Lodge and Greene about Jonah illustrate. But New Testament subjects were taboo. This was partly due to ecclesiastical censorship and to the government's determination to maintain the Elizabethan religious settlement. The actors, moreover, performed before people of diverse religious views and they did not wish to cause offence. It has to be remembered that many ordinary people born about 1530 would have been Catholics in 1545, that most of them would have been Protestants in 1550, Catholics in 1555, and Protestants again in 1560. Whatever their private views happened to be, they mostly conformed.

The dramatists were less inhibited by such restrictions than one might suppose. Marlowe, reputed to be an atheist, and certainly heretical, was able to criticize the hypocrisy of Christians in *Tamburlaine* and in *The Jew of Malta;* and if the ambiguities of his great morality play, *Doctor Faustus,* caused some uneasiness, he was brought before the Star Chamber on capital charges not on account of his plays but becuse of his blasphemous conversation. His great rival, Shakespeare, if we are to believe Professor Honigmann (1985), served as a tutor in a Catholic household, but it would be impossible to deduce from his plays where his sympathies lay. He cut out some of the crude antipapal propaganda from *The Troublesome Raigne of King John,* unless that two-part play succeeded Shakespeare's[2], but his motive may well have been aesthetic. In *Henry VIII* he sympathizes with Katherine of Aragon (as who would not?); but he did not, and could not, give an unfavorable portrait of Anne Boleyn, Elizabeth I's mother. He gives a sympathetic portrait of the Protestant martyr Cranmer, but an equally sympathetic portrait of the Catholic martyr Thomas More, in the scene he added to the banned play of the same name. Some of the ecclesiastics in his plays are on the side of the angels, but most are not. They are as timeserving as the bishops who flank Richard of Gloucester when he usurps the throne, as Machiavellian as the Archbishop in *Henry V,* as avaricious as Wolsey, as villainous as Cardinal Beauford; but in these four cases Shakespeare was following his sources. Nor can one draw any conclusion from his use of Harsnett's *Declaration of Egregious Popish Impostures,* for he also made some use of Harsnett's attack on Puritan exorcists.

Shakespeare is known to have been well acquainted with the Bible and with the Anglican prayer-book (Noble 1970). This is not surprising, as he had to attend church services week by week. His familiarity with the Bishops' Bible is therefore to be expected, and if, after 1600, his echoes are mostly from the Geneva version, this may be due to the fact that it was portable—no heavier than the new Oxford edition of Shakespeare's works. Even the fact that Berowne in *Love's Labour's Lost* (5.3.361) seems to be aware of the controversy about the translation of *agape* tells one nothing about Shakespeare's convictions. It will be recalled that Thomas Hardy, an avowed agnostic, wrote verse and prose that are steeped in biblical phraseology.

Only one of Shakespeare's plays has a scriptural title, *Measure for Measure;* and it seems to be concerned with the difficulty of reconciling the teaching of the Sermon on the Mount with practical problems of government; but to some critics it seems rather to be a satire on the belief that the world is providentially governed.

Shakespeare was writing for a secular stage for audiences which embraced a wide variety of religious belief; his plays were not designed to support or illustrate any particular doctrine; but this has not prevented critics from attempting to prove that he shared their own particular beliefs, whether Catholic, Anglican, agnostic, existentialist—even Freudian. It is a temptation difficult to resist, for we should all hate to think that the greatest of poets was less enlightened than ourselves.

There is no doubt, however, that, below the level of psychological realism, Shakespeare often implies a metaphysical conflict between good and evil. In *Macbeth,* for example, this conflict is continually stressed (Knights 1946). It is apparent in the contrast between the good supernatural, represented by Edward the Confessor, and the evil supernatural, represented by the Weird Sisters; in the contrast between the saintly Duncan and his successor; in the angels pleading trumpet-tongued against Duncan's murder; in Macbeth's confession that he has sold his soul to the common enemy of man; in Lady Macbeth's invocation of the powers of darkness to take possession of her.

The metaphysical dimension is apparent also in *Othello.* Most dramatists would credit Iago with jealousy or with his desire to get Cassio's place or with both these motives combined; but Shakespeare makes it clear by Iago's use of diabolic imagery and by his reference to "divinity of hell" (2.3.339) that, besides having such psychological motives, Iago is basically motivated by a hatred of goodness. Nevertheless, we get the impression that the ideological structure of each play is not imposed by the dramatist, but is evoked by the material Shakespeare was dramatizing (Bethell 1977). Northrop Frye (1986) expressed this epigramatically when he said that *Measure for Measure* ended in reconciliation and forgiveness, not because Shakespeare believed that such things were desirable, but because comedies had to end like that. Frye was warning his students against simplistic ideas on the nature and function of the drama. All the same, as Frye would doubtless admit, Shakespeare may well have believed in reconciliation and forgiveness; and he was writing for a nominally Christian audience, an audience of churchgoers, who were well aware that forgiveness was a duty.

It is worth mentioning that the tragicomedies of Beaumont and Fletcher, written at the same time as the so-called romances of Shakespeare's final period, and in the same genre, are escapist rather than ethically persuasive. Shakespeare, moreover, altered his material to ensure the triumph of forgiveness—Imogen's forgiveness of her husband, his forgiveness of Iachimo, Cymbeline's universal pardon, Hermione's forgiveness of Leontes. There could be no forgiveness for Pandosto, whose queen actually dies, especially when he falls in love with his own daughter. These plays are set in a pagan world, and even in *The Tempest* forgiveness is presented not as a Christian duty but as the rarer action, until Prospero, after the play, reminds the audience: "As you from crimes would pardoned be / Let your indulgence set me free." This means that the conduct Shakespeare seems to advocate does not depend on holy writ, but on the actions and motivations of his characters. Clifford Leech (1961, 18) declared that "the tragic picture is incompatible with the Christian faith. It is equally incompatible with any form of religious belief that assumes the existence of a personal and kindly God." The same view had been expressed by I. A. Richards (1928, 246): "Tragedy is only possible to a mind which is for the moment agnostic or Manichean. The least touch of any theology which has a compensating Heaven to offer the tragic hero is fatal." I do not think that this is true, but it is easy to see how two good critics could arrive at this conclusion. In all tragedies relatively good characters are destroyed, either through the actions of evil characters or through the malignity of fate—Ophelia, Desdemona, the Macduff family, Cordelia. Except in *Hamlet,* in which flights of angels are invoked to sing the hero to his rest, there is no promise that a future life will compensate for their sufferings on earth. One can understand why Rymer (1956), as insensitive a critic as Leech was sensitive, should recoil from the tragic loading of Othello's bed:

> What instruction can we make out of this Catastrophe? Or whither must our reflection lead us? Is not this to envenom and sour our spirits, to make us repine and grumble at Providence and the Government of the World? If this be our end, what boots it to be virtuous?

Even Dr. Johnson complained that Shakespeare seemed to write without any moral purpose. He was particularly disturbed by the gratuitous death of Cordelia, which could easily have been averted if the dying Edmund had spoken five minutes earlier.

King Lear is, indeed, a crucial case. Whereas the source play is set in the Christian era and ends with Lear's restoration, Shakespeare's play ends with the deaths of Cordelia and Lear. But he knew that the legendary Lear lived many years before the birth of Christ, and this alone might have made him reject a Christian setting. He also knew that the old dramatist had broken off in the middle of the story. All the chroniclers (despite Johnson's statement to the contrary) had described how, after Cordelia had succeeded to the throne, her nephews had rebelled against her and put her in prison, so that in despair she committed suicide. Such an ending would have outraged any audience, especially in the seventeenth century, when despair and suicide were regarded as sins.

By giving the play a pagan setting, Shakespeare was able to present conflicting views on the providential government of the world without directly impunging the Christian position. Albany's prayer for the safety of Lear and Cordelia is immediately followed, as critics as different as Bradley (1964, 326) and Empson (1951, 150) have emphasized, by the entrance of Lear with the body of Cordelia in his arms. But that pagan gods give a dusty answer to prayers does not necessarily imply that prayer to the Christian God is equally futile. There are many other places in the play where comments on the gods may cause disquiet. Gloucester, for example, after his blinding, speaks of them as sadistic monsters: "As flies to wanton boys are we to the gods: / They kill us for their sport" (4.1.37–38). Although this is often taken to be the keynote of the play, one may observe that Gloucester was blinded not by the gods, but by Cornwall and Regan; and that a few scenes later he addresses the gods as "ever gentle" (4.6.219). Lear in the storm, calls on the gods to find out their enemies (3.2.51), but later seems to imply that human beings can teach the gods a lesson by distributing wealth more fairly: "Expose thyself to feel what wretches feel / That thou mayst shake the superflux to them, / And show the heavens more just" (3.4.34–36). Edgar, who redeems his father from despair and forgives even his wicked brother yet reminds Edmund of the consequences of his father's adultery:

> The gods are just, and of our pleasant vices
> Make instruments to plague us:
> The dark and vicious place where thee he got
> Cost him his eyes.
>
> (5.3.170–72)

The final cost was more than Gloucester's eyes: it was Cordelia's life.

As several critics have pointed out, the characters in the play are partly defined by their attitude to the gods (Heilman 1963; Elton 1966). The villains are all atheists; Gloucester is superstitious; Albany has the somewhat naive belief that the gods intervene to punish wickedness, as when he hears of Cornwall's death: "This shows you are above, / You justicers, that these our nether crimes / So speedily can venge" (4.2.78–80).

Edgar and Cordelia seem to exhibit what one might call Christian virtues in a pre-Christian era. But to many critics today, living in an age of unbelief, Shakespeare seems to be saying—or the play seems to be saying—"Whether there are gods or not, whether there is a future life or not, it is in either case better to be Edgar than Edmund, better to be the victim, Cordelia, than her sisters." But here, as always, Shakespeare expresses the opinions of his characters without revealing his own, except through the dramatic logic, which teaches us, in Auden's words, "to unlearn hatred and to learn love." If, as I think, Shakespeare was more than a nominal Christian, he had to suspend his inner beliefs to be true to the pagan setting. This illustrates the remark I quoted from I. A. Richards about tragedy, that the writer of tragedy must be *for the moment* agnostic; and it may be that *King Lear* seems the greatest of the tragedies to the present age because it relies on no metaphysical certainties. It is true that Lear, recovering from his madness, takes Cordelia for a soul in bliss (4.7.48); but when at the end he looks vainly for signs of life in the hanged girl, not many readers regard his "Look there!" (5.3.310) as anything but delusion.

The same collection of essays by Clifford Leech (1961, 204) that contains his remarks on tragedy contains a brief account of Golden Age drama, relying on translations then available. It seems probable that his view that tragedy and Christianity were incompatible was influenced by his reading of Spanish drama. If the dramatist and his audience assume that the world is providentially governed, material that in Elizabethan hands would be treated tragically will in Spain be fitted with a happy ending. The good people and the repentant sinners are guaranteed salvation, and the unrepentant are punished in hell. It is true that in Shakespeare's "Christian" tragedies, the unshriven Claudius and even his tools, the unshriven Rosencrantz and Guildenstern, presumably are damned, though all three have their defenders. Othello believes he has damned himself by his murder of the innocent Desdemona, and Macbeth and his wife, who have deliberately chosen evil, are manifestly damned. But in each of these plays there is some ambiguity. Is the Ghost in *Hamlet* the devil in disguise, intent on damning the prince? Will Othello's repentance and his desire to be tortured for ever save what the play's first critic called the grieved Moor? Will he not be saved by the redemptive power of Desdemona's love? And even with Macbeth, the poet for the defence (which is always Shakespeare's attitude to his tragic heroes) can mitigate the verdict of the moralist.

It is instructive to compare two Elizabethan plays with *El Mági-*

co prodigioso (The prodigious magician). Cyprian in that play sells
his soul to the devil in order to seduce Justina (as Goethe's Faust
bargains with Mephistopheles to seduce Gretchen). But a greater
magician, God, substitutes a phantom of Justina, which is revealed
as a skeleton, who tells him "Such, Cyprian, are all the glories of
this world." Cyprian is converted to Christianity, shares Justina's
martyrdom, and so cancels his pact with the devil. What might have
been a tragedy is converted to a triumph. It is a great play; but one
is not surprised that Shelley, who translated some scenes so brilliantly, found the conclusion less interesting.

The Virgin Martyr, by Dekker and Massinger, has some slight
similarity to Calderón's play. Theophilus, a persecutor of Christians, egged on by an evil spirit, Harpax, is converted after Dorothea's martyrdom by a miracle in the shape of fruits from heaven
and is himself martyred. Both Dorothea and Theophilus are tortured on stage, and there is, perhaps, too much stress on Dorothea's
virginity. The use of the supernatural is awkward, and, although
Massinger wrote other plays on a religious theme, one has the
feeling that he was exploiting it for dramatic motives, rather than
using the drama to point a religious moral. Here the seriousness of
Calderón gives him a clear advantage.

Another play, Marlowe's *Doctor Faustus,* is about a learned
young man, like Cyprian, who signs away his soul for the sake of
knowledge and the power that knowledge brings. At the end of
twenty-four years Mephistophilis claims his side of the bargain.
Faustus tries vainly to repent and he is taken off to hell. Marlowe,
though a student of theology, was a heretic; but he shows that
Faustus acquires little knowledge from his bargain, that he indulges
in rather childish pleasures, that his supposed liaison with Helen of
Troy is actually with the devil in her shape, and that he cannot
repudiate the bargain when the twenty-four years have elapsed.
This is the inevitable tragic end of the story: even though Faustus
sees Christ's blood streaming in the firmament, the vision comes
too late. Although Faustus is initially attended by a Good Angel as
well as by an evil one, the powers of darkness make all the running.
If Calderón had written the play, the hero would have been allowed
to repent, even at the eleventh hour.

In some plays there is an uneasy mixture of religious belief and
melodramatic incident. In *La devoción de la cruz (Devotion to the
cross),* for example, the hero and heroine, who are in fact brother
and sister, are saved from incest by the crosses on their breasts.
Eusebio is allowed to retain consciousness after the death of his
body so that he can confess his sins and receive absolution. Julia,

too, has committed a number of murders, but she is apparently transported through the skies to the convent from which she has escaped. Calderón presumably regarded such incidents as symbolical rather than literally true, but the devotion to the cross is regarded by many modern readers as superstition. Alexander Parker (1949) assures us that Eusebio is saved not because of such superstitious reverence but because this reverence is the outward and visible sign of an inner moral and spiritual disposition. The cross is everywhere associated with mercy. The bandit is nearer than the ordinary man to sainthood. Professor Parker argues brilliantly, and I am sure he is right to contrast what he calls the "turbulent behaviour" of Eusebio and Julia with the cruel behavior of their father that causes it. The play has to be understood on two levels: the groundlings would accept it on the superficial level that Parker deplores. The more intelligent members of the audience would presumably understand the deeper significance.

I have written elsewhere (1985) of the plays by Shakespeare and Calderón on Henry VIII and tried to show that Alexander Parker undervalues Shakespeare's and overpraises Calderón's. In one respect alone Calderón seems to be nearer to the truth than Shakespeare. The latest biography of Anne Boleyn by Eric Ives (1986) is the first to lay stress on the genuineness of her Protestant views. Although Shakespeare's Wolsey calls her a Lutheran, this aspect is not brought out. Calderón's Anne interferes with Henry's defence of the faith, and the sole subject of Katherine's apologies is her warning against heresy. To my mind the weakness of Calderón's play is that his religious convictions prevent him from giving even-handed justice to his characters. Anne is depicted, at first, as an evil spirit, and then as a human being without a single good quality. The odd thing is that it would be quite possible to write a better tragedy by using accounts of Anne by Catholic writers. She was accused at her trial of committing adultery with half a dozen men and of committing incest with her brother.

The confessions were obtained by torture, and she was probably got rid of because of her failure to produce a male heir as well as for her religious views. In the reign of Henry VIII, as Sir Thomas Wyatt put the matter in a poem written at the time of the trial, "Wit helpeth not defence to earn, / Of Innocence to plead or prate" (Muir ed., 1961). Nevertheless, by accepting that the trial was not rigged, it would be possible to write a tragedy of an ambitious heretic who failed to produce a son and who realized that she would be superseded by the King's third bride.

I am not denying that Calderón was entitled to alter the facts of history (for example, by omitting the birth of Elizabeth) to suit his dramatic purposes and even his religious purposes. My uneasiness is that his revised version is less dramatic and less plausible than what really happened. Anne's love affair before her marriage and the King's discovery of it by eavesdropping are feeble compared with the revelation at the time of Anne's fall, whether the trial was fair or as improbable as the Moscow trials of the thirties. Moreover, the suggestion that Anne poisoned Katherine is gratuitous; Mary's ascending the throne over Anne's corpse is tasteless; and her implied promise, which she has no intention of keeping, not to restore the old faith, is something much worse—for its immorality apparently meets with the dramatist's approval. As Lucretius said: "Tantum religio potuit suadere malorum" (*De rerum natura* 1.101).

I turn now to the group of plays concerned with wife-murder, in which husbands murder their wives on the mere suspicion that they are unfaithful—*El médico de su honra (The surgeon of his own honor), A secreto agravio secreta venganza (Secret vengeance for secret insult)* and *El pintor de su deshonra (The painter of his own dishonor).*

As Edward M. Wilson (1980) pointed out, *Othello* has some affinities with the Calderonian plays concerned with honor: Brabantio's honor was tarnished by his daughter's elopement, Cassio's military honor by his drunken brawl, and Othello's marital honor by his wife's supposed unfaithfulness. One might add that Iago's suspicions about Emilia are not very different from those of the wife-murderers in Calderón's plays. The villain-hero of *El médico de su honra,* however, does not need a demidevil such as Iago to provide evidence against his wife. He finds her writing a letter to another man; she faints; and he immediately assumes that she has betrayed him. He never accuses her or gives her the opportunity of defending herself. He compels a surgeon to bleed her to death, thinking himself safe from discovery. The surgeon confesses to the King who refrains from punishing the husband, unless by insisting that he marries Leonor, a woman he does not love.

The crucifix over the bed while the murder was taking place doubtless reminded the audience of the contrast between the Christian code and the code of honor. Some of the audience would know that Don Gutierre would fall in battle. But what is disturbing to one brought up in the Shakespearian tradition is the restraint of his remorse. It can be defended only on the assumption that his grief is too profound to be expressed. Othello, by contrast, is stricken with remorse even before he knows that Desdemona is innocent. There is another vital difference. Whereas in Cinthio's tale the Moor and the Ancient together arrange for the murder to look like an accident, Othello commits the deed alone and does not attempt to evade responsibility. Calderón's murderous husbands think they can safeguard their honor only if their wives are murdered secretly. This is the theme of *A secreto agravio secreta venganza.* In it Don Lope murders Don Luis in what appears to be a boating accident and murders his wife, Leonor, by burning down the house. The murders are carefully planned. Don Lope twice avows that prudent vengeance demands patience, silence, and dissimulation. Leonor has married him by proxy when she hears that Luis, whom she loves, has been killed in battle. When, after her marriage, he reappears, her love revives, although her adultery is averted by her death. Professor Edward Wilson (1980, 110) declares that the "play has been interpreted as an allegory of prudence in a world obsessed by the code of honour." But I can see no sign that Don Lope's revenge is regarded as wrong. The King and Don Juan both approve of it; and Don Lope, planning revenge, asks heaven to be his guide. Yet it is a question of appearance rather than of reality. He is writing about the fallen world at odds with the religious dimension, and at moments some of the audience at least would be reminded of it.

In *El pintor de su deshonra,* the husband disapproves of the honor code but is nevertheless reluctantly forced to accept its dictates. It is the only one of the three plays that gives a sympathetic portrait of the wife. Like Leonor, Serafina marries Don Juan when she hears that Alvaro, the man she loves, is dead. Alvaro kidnaps her but is unable to persuade her to be unfaithful to her husband. At the end of the play the reluctant assassin confesses to the three men most involved—Serafina's father, Alvaro's father, who is his best friend, and the Prince. All three agree that the murder was justified, and they refuse to avenge it. Don Juan departs, knowing that his life would be haunted by horror of the dead. In a famous article A. A. Parker (1962, 233) demonstrated that the major characters were all responsible for the catastrophe—Don Luis's vanity, the Prince's secrecy, and his deception of Porcia, and so on. Professor Edward Wilson similarly says that the play "explores the common responsibility in the final dénouement of all those who take part in this tragedy" (1971, 112). But the moral is implicit rather than explicit, and Spanish audiences, used to veiled statements, would search for hidden meanings. For instance, they might debate the extent of Serafina's guilt. Did her dream, in which she was terrified of her husband's vengeance, and her appeal to Alvaro to protect her mean that "she had sinned in the unconscious mind" or was this a justifiable dread of her husband? In any case, I believe Wardropper (1950) was right to point out that "the secular play cannot by its nature, deal with the working of grace." The painter in the *auto sacramental* of the same title is Christ who shoots not his wife, La Naturaleza Humana (Human Nature) when she repents, but La Culpa (Sin) and Lucero. The contrast between the *comedia* and the *Auto* supports the view that in some of his plays Calderón kept his religious convictions in the background. Restricted by the beliefs of audience, Church, and State, Calderón was forced to be ambiguous in his secular plays, leaving it to the spectators to take sides.

I have been suggesting that the secularity of the Elizabethan stage, the conflicting religious views of the audience, and the disinterestedness of Shakespeare's mind all gave him considerable advantages. His conclusions are never questioned or in conflict with dogma, but the result of dramatic logic.

Shakespeare was able to enter into the minds of all his characters, so that they seem to speak for themselves. The man who agrees to murder Cordelia explains his consent with the words: "I cannot draw a cart or eat wild oats: / If it be man's work I'll do it." Here is an autobiography, a philosophy of life, and economic determinism in a line and a half. This extraordinary power by Shakespeare, described in Keats's words that he had as much delight in depicting Iago as Imogen, is a comparatively rare dramatic talent. Most dramatists take sides or are bored with the minor characters. The power is linked to what Keats called "negative capability," objectivity; and it is only possible in a secular drama.

It could be argued that Calderón had the advantage of a more homogeneous audience, though its faith was contaminated, one must suspect, by its adherence to the honor code. It has been seen that Calderón tried to get round the difficulty of writing Christian tragedy by keeping his religious views in the background or presenting the "hero" in an ambiguous light. When he does write directly religious plays containing miraculous elements, he appeals on two levels, where the simple would swallow a superstitious meaning and the intelligent—among whom one must class modern critics of Spanish drama—a more sophisticated and spiritual one.

I have said nothing about the allegorical dramas, which are the most satisfactory blend of poetry and religion. Despite the existence of the English morality plays, written by second-rate poets, the genre could not have been revived on the Jacobean stage. But it may be suggested that in some of his court masques, Jonson attempted to provide a kind of secular substitute. I am thinking particularly of *Pleasure Reconciled to Virtue*. Although Shakespeare avoided allegory, there are signs in *The Tempest* and *The Winter's Tale* of an allegorical subtext; and when one notices that *The Phoenix and the Turtle* is steeped in scholastic terminology, one could regret that we have no Shakespearian *autos*.

Notes

1. Cf. *Letters* 2:250: "I am bathing myself in the light and odour of the flowery and starry Autos," ed. Frederich Jones, Oxford University Press, 1964.

2. See the Arden edition of *King John,* edited by E. A. J. Honigmann. London: Methuen, 1954. Shakespeare quotations are taken from Peter Alexander's edition (London and Glasgow: Collins, 1951).

Works Cited

Bethell, S. L. 1977. "Shakespeare's Imagery: The Diabolic Images in *Othello*". In *Aspects of Othello,* edited by K. Muir and P. Edwards, 29–47. Cambridge: Cambridge University Press.

Bradley, A. C. 1964. *Shakespearean Tragedy.* London: Macmillan.

Calderón de la Barca, *Obras completas.* Edited by Angel Valbuena Briones. Madrid: Aguilar, 1973.

Elton, William. 1966. *King Lear and the Gods.* San Marion, Calif.: Huntingdon Library.

Empson, William. 1951. *The Structure of Complex Words.* Norfolk, Conn.: New Directions.

Frye, Northrop. 1986. *Northrop Frye on Shakespeare.* Edited by Robert Sander. New Haven: Yale University Press.

Heilman, R. B. 1963. *This Great Stage.* Seattle: University of Washington Press.

Honigmann, E. A. J. 1985. *Shakespeare: The Lost Years.* Manchester: Manchester University Press.

Ives, E. W. 1986. *Anne Boleyn.* Oxford: Basil Blackwell.

Knights, L. C. 1946. "How Many Children Had Lady Macbeth?" In *Explorations.* London: Chatto and Windus.

Leech, Clifford. 1961. *Shakespeare's Tragedies, and Other Studies in Seventeenth Century Drama.* London: Chatto and Windus.

Muir, K. 1985. *Shakespeare: Contrasts and Controversies.* Norman: University of Oklahoma Press.

Muir, K., ed. 1961. *Unpublished Poems of Wyatt and His Circle.* Liverpool: Liverpool University Press.

Noble, Richmond. 1970. *Shakespeare's Biblical Knowledge and Use of the Book of Common Prayer.* New York: Octagon Books.

Parker, A. A. 1949. "Santos y Bandoleros en el teatro del Siglo de Oro." *Arbor* 13:395–416.

―――. "Towards a Definition of Calderonian Tragedy," *Bulletin of Hispanic Studies* 39:222–37.

Richards, I. A. 1928. *Principles of Literary Criticism*. New York: Harcourt, Brace.

Rymer, Thomas. 1956. *A Short View of Tragedy (1693)*. In *Critical Works,* edited by Curt Arno Zimansky. New Haven: Yale University Press.

Wardropper, Bruce W. 1950. "The Unconscious Mind in Calderon's *El Pintor,*" *Hispanic Review* 18:285–301.

Wilson, Edward M. 1980. "A Hispanist Looks at Othello." In *Spanish and English Literature of the 16th and 17th Centuries*. Cambridge: Cambridge University Press.

———. 1971. *A Literary History of Spain: Golden Age*. London: Benn.

Calderón's View of the English Schism

Gregory Peter Andrachuk

On 30 January 1649, the decapitated body of Charles Stuart, king of England, was laid to rest beside that of Henry VIII in Saint George's Chapel, Windsor. This probably coincidental juxtaposition appears more significant when considered in the light of the theme and circumstances of composition of Calderón's *La cisma de Inglaterra (The schism of England)*. The final version of *La cisma* may, in fact, be the result of a perceived connection between Henry Tudor and Charles Stuart in the mind of Calderón.

The most important article yet published on Calderón's *La cisma de Inglaterra* is that by Alexander Parker (1948). In that article Professor Parker underlines the distortion of history found in Calderón's play and remarks, as others have, on the Spaniard's "extraordinarily compassionate" treatment of the English king. He suggests that this benevolent view of Henry is connected with what he calls "the purposes of his art" rather than with any "politico-religious thesis."[1] It is his view that Calderón intended the audience to view Henry as a symbol of tragic humanity stumbling under the weight of unbearable responsibilities. He hastens to add that, in saying this, he does not mean that it is Calderón as writer of the Autos Sacramentales who is interpreting history. He refers here to Calderón's depiction of man's progress toward salvation, which in the auto sacramental is achieved through the grace of the Holy Eucharist. Calderón's view of this struggle for perfection has been well described by Valbuena Prat (1967), Wardropper (1967), Arias (1980), and Ynduráin (1981). While I believe that Parker's article comes closest to Calderón's real reasons for writing this play and to the reasons for his deliberate twisting of historical facts, at the same time I find that I disagree with him in a fundamental way, for I intend to suggest that this play can be properly understood only if seen as the work of the same man who so forcefully expounded Catholic doctrine in the Autos Sacramentales.

I have argued elsewhere that the Auto Sacramental was distinctly and essentially anti-Protestant in nature (that is to say, not solely pro-Catholic) and that, furthermore, the genre evolved in accordance with the Roman Church's response to the threat of Protestantism (Andrachuk 1985). It is in the Auto of Calderón that theology and drama are most perfectly combined, and it is in his work that the doctrines of the Council of Trent are brought to bear with all their force on the theater of the age. Calderón shows in the autos a strong antipathy for Protestantism, balanced with a devotion to the Church of Rome and the absolute certainty that through its sacraments, particularly Penance and the Holy Eucharist, lies the path to Heaven. For Calderón, the danger presented to the Church by Protestantism is extreme, because the Protestant heretics are nothing less than agents of the Devil. In *La divina Filotea,* for example, the Devil says:

> el hereje es el que más
> me sirve en negar misterios.
>
> (sc. 7)

[The heretic is the one who serves me best, denying [sacred] mysteries.]

How, then, are we to reconcile this virile anti-Protestantism of the Counter Reformation with the gentleness with which Calderón deals with Henry VIII, who was, after all, the king who wrested the Church of England from allegiance to the bishop of Rome? I would suggest that the answer to this difficult question may lie in a "politico-religious" reading of the play itself and in a consideration of the events surrounding its composition. It is my belief that the question of religion is not incidental but essential in this work.

The *Cisma de Inglaterra* begins with a scene in which this matter is paramount. Henry has fallen asleep in the midst of writing his *Assertio septem sacramentorum,* a work in which he aggressively defends the Catholic system of seven sacraments against the Lutheran position that there are but two, Baptism and the Holy Eucharist. In recognition of the strategic importance of having the king of England take issue with Luther, the pope awards him the title of "fidei defensor," a title the English monarchs retain to this day. I believe that Calderón opens the play with this act of faith on the King's part because this orthodoxy and anti-Protestantism is central to his estimation of Henry. From the very beginning, the play centers on the issue of religion, rather than on that of Henry's lust. Even as Anne Boleyn enters Henry's dream, he praises her beauty in images that have a double interpretation:

Tente, sombra divina, imagen bella,
sol eclipsado, deslucida estrella.
Mira que al sol ofendes
cuando borrar tanto esplandor pretendes.
¿Por qué contra mi pecho airada vives?

$(1-5)^2$

[Wait, divine shade, lovely image, eclipsed sun, blackened star. Look
how you offend the sun as you try to erase such splendor. Why do you
oppose me so haughtily?]

In what seems to be a hyperbolic description of her beauty, he is
really referring to her heretical tendencies, and this passage is a
foreshadowing of the blame that attaches to her for the English
schism, for in Calderón's play it is Anne Boleyn and Cardinal
Wolsey who are primarily responsible, not Henry. In this passage,
one begins to glimpse Calderón's complex interweaving of theme
and imagery; the "sol" is the pope, and the "esplendor" is the
splendor of English Catholicism, typified in Henry's anti-Lutheran
treatise. And, from the beginning, Henry the orthodox is pictured
as set against the Protestant forces with their overweening pride;
thus: "¿Por qué contra mi pecho airada vives?" ("Why do you
oppose me so haughtily?"). He is mesmerised by her beauty; it is a
beauty that, like the Protestantism she represents, is at first attractive and luminous, but that ultimately, like the "sol eclipsado" or
the "estrella deslucida," is darkness. Henry is enchanted,[3] despite
Anne's answer that she is prepared to erase all that Henry writes.
Her comment has double meaning, for in marrying him not only
will she destroy everything he has to say about the sanctity of
matrimony in his treatise, but in a larger sense she will pervert and
undermine his defense of the Church of Rome. In the first seven
lines of the play the whole story is foretold, and the tragedy of
Henry's fatal flaw revealed, for his religious fervor is no match for
the strength of his physical passion. His own future difficulties, and
those of his realm, are assured by his attraction to the harlot of
Protestantism.

The scene immediately following, between Henry and Cardinal
Wolsey, is designed to reinforce the position of the king (as yet
untainted) as the defender of the faith, and to remind the audience
of the preeminent position of England within the Catholic fold and
of its obedience to the See of Rome. The king's speech is an
important one, for his characterisation of himself as a loyal son of
Rome forms a sort of leitmotif that appears again and again. For
Henry, England, as the "pillar of the Church militant" (31–32), is

ever faithful to the wishes of the pope. In this scene, Henry's orthodoxy, his submission to the See of Rome, the larger question of authority in the Church, his acceptance of the pope's right to grant dispensations, and his repugnance for the Protestant heresy, are all knit together:

> velo yo sobre los libros,
> escribiendo en la defensa
> de los siete sacramentos
> aquéste con que hoy intenta
> mi deseo confundir
> los errores y las sectas
> que Lutero ha derramado.
>
> (79–85)

[I pass the night with my books, writing in defense of the seven sacraments this book by which I mean to confound the errors and sects which Luther has spread about.]

The scene between Henry and Wolsey now develops into one in which the basic opposition of orthodoxy and heresy is brought to the fore. Wolsey brings letters from Pope Leo X and from Luther. As Ludwig Pfandl (1937) has explained, Henry performs a ceremonial gesture of acceptance, placing the letter of one above his head, while placing the other at his feet. But he, or Wolsey, has confused one letter for the other, and he accepts Luther while rejecting the Pope. Yet it must be emphasized that this was not his intention; for in taking the letters he clearly says:

> baje Lutero a mis pies,
> y León suba a mi cabeza.
>
> (159–60)

[Cast Luther at my feet, and let Leo rise to my head.]

Henry's intention is to remain firm in the Catholic faith. This is an important point, and one to which I shall return later. Despite his efforts to rationalize his error, he is shaken by this unintentional slip and takes it as an omen of misfortune. Indeed, as he was unable to control the placing of the letters, he will be unable to control the future course of events in his realm once he allows his passion to overcome his reason. By its use of imagery, this scene also reveals that the responsibility for the English schism lies with Cardinal Wolsey. While Henry has put Luther's letter above his head, that is, at the top of the pillar of the Church, ("yo la columna" [194] "I the pillar"), so Wolsey almost immediately afterwards states that he aims toward the top: "subiendo a la cumbre voy" (215) ("I am climbing to the summit"); he means towards the Papacy, but one is to understand that, having failed at that, he moves towards the Protestantism that Luther represents. It is Wolsey who allows Protestantism to take hold in England both by his scandalous behavior as a prelate of the Church of Rome and also by his fostering of the designs of Anne Boleyn, clearly stated to be a crypto-Lutheran: "en público la ves / católica . . . / en secreto, luterana," (454; 456) ("In public she acts the Catholic . . . in private, the Lutheran").

The audience can hardly fail to see the connection between the English schism and the rise of Anne Boleyn, for Calderón makes it clear that Wolsey has organized both as a means of revenge:

> Y aun contra el Papa me atrevo,
> por ser mi competidor,
> a introducir un error,
> el más prodigioso y nuevo.
> ¡Bolena! A buen tiempo viene:
> parece que la llamé.
>
> (1273–78)

[And I even dare to oppose the Pope because he is my rival, and to introduce heresy, the most novel and prodigious. Boleyn! Just in time! It seems that I called her forth.]

It is Wolsey who urges Henry to repudiate Katharine when he confesses his love for Anne Boleyn; it is Wolsey who convinces a weak king that his marriage to Katharine was no marriage at all, despite the dispensation of the pope; and it is Wolsey who advises Henry to go before his people to make his case. The address to the English people is preceded by a soliloquy of great psychological complexity and depth. Francisco Ruiz Ramón believes that it is in this passage—which reveals Henry's divided conscience—that the essential paradox of the work is to be found. I suggest that the passage is even more complex than he would allow, for it is not Henry's divided conscience that speaks, but his divided consciousness—his conscious mind and his subconscious mind. Both speak in the same passage; the conscious mind accepts Wolsey's arguments, utterly convinced that in divorcing Katharine he both remedies the error of having married his brother's wife and permits his marriage to Anne. But his subconscious mind knows that these arguments are false and that the pope did indeed have the power to grant Henry the dispensation. It is in this mode, that of the sub-conscious, that Calderón the Catholic apologist transmits his own message. The recourse to soliloquy on two levels permits the play-wright to give his audience an unerring Catholic viewpoint, while at the same time maintaining their sympathy for Henry.

The language of this passage, I believe, supports this interpreta-tion, and it is strange language indeed:

> Confieso que estoy loco y estoy ciego,
> pues la verdad que adoro es la que niego.
> Pues si un hombre el daño no alcanzara,
> aunque errara, parece que no errara;
> que en tan confusa guerra,
> sólo errara el que sabe cuándo yerra.

(1723–28)

[I confess that I am crazed and blind, for I deny the truth I adore. If man doesn't fall into the abyss, though he errs, it seems that he errs not. Only he who knows when he errs, errs.]

Henry is saying that, on the level of his conscious mind, he believes that what he does is right and that, furthermore, in difficult matters such as these, only he who knows himself to be wrong errs. He goes on to say that he knows that Wolsey has deceived him and that he has been satisfied by his arguments; here it is his subconscious mind that speaks, and in that subconscious speaks Calderón. Un-less one recognizes that Calderón is presenting two levels of mean-ing at once, it is impossible to understand the juxtaposition of "sólo errara el que sabe cuándo yerra," which is an obvious disculpation, and "Bien sé que me ha engañado Volseo" in the same speech. One cannot know that one has been duped and remain duped at the same time and on the same level of consciousness. Calderón uses the present perfect tense: "ha engañado"; it is a tense that indicates a continuing state of *engaño* or deception. Despite the awareness of his subconscious, his conscious mind has allowed itself to be con-vinced. If this scene were produced for the cinema, a director might have the conscious Henry frozen, while a shadowy Henry, the Henry of the subconscious, steps out to speak the paradoxical lines of the soliloquy.

Calderón has thus both transmitted the orthodox doctrinal state-ment his Spanish audience needs to hear, and at the same time justified in dramatic terms Henry's repudiation of Katharine. Thus Henry can begin his speech to the people by significantly protesting his orthodoxy and reminding them of his constant opposition to "that monster Luther" (1820). It is not to promote schism that he takes the action of repudiating Katharine; rather it is to quiet his conscience. As the speech continues, the audience is led to believe with Henry in his own essential orthodoxy, despite his struggle over the authority of the pope; but at the same time, they see that for Calderón the repudiation of Katharine and the schism of the English Church are inseparable, for, in denying her, Henry denies the power of the bishop of Rome to grant dispensations.

The two public speeches by Henry and by Katharine, the one following the other, are pivotal in the play, for, while ostensibly dealing with the dissolution of Henry's marriage to Katharine, they really speak of the struggle between Catholicism and Protestantism and of the danger that Henry courts:

> ya sabéis que, vigilante,
> a los errores me opongo
> con que nuestra fe perturba
> ese prodigio, ese monstruo
> de Lutero; y ya sabéis
> que . . .
> he sido quien ha evitado
> tantos errores y asombros,
> bien cierto es que no pretendo
> causar nuevos alborotos
> en la cristiandad; pues antes
> por excusar los estorbos
> a tantos heresiarcas
> . . . sólo
> asegurar mi conciencia
> pretendo.
>
> (1817–22; 1827–33; 1836–38)

[You know that I vigilantly oppose the errors with which that prodigy, that monster Luther disturbs our faith; and you know that [. . .] I have been the one who has deflected so many heresies and frights; In faith, I do not try to cause new disturbances in Christendom; rather I try to prevent the incursions of so many heresiarchs. I only try to calm my conscience.]

In the context of the theme of the play the irony could not be more pronounced. While protesting his defense of the Catholic faith, Henry severs his visible link with the rest of the Catholic world, which is obedience to the pope, and thus unwittingly promotes the very thing which he has striven to prevent.[4]

Katharine's response to Henry makes this very point. She sees that, in challenging the pope, Henry, who should be acting as the pilot of the allegorical ship of the Church, now attempts to be its captain by declaring himself Head of the Church in England. Only shipwreck can follow, in the form of schism, for the heretics, she says, infiltrate with pious demeanor but ultimately unmask themselves. Her warning of the insidious nature of heresy proves true at the beginning of act 3 when Anne Boleyn maneuvers Henry into exiling Princess Mary and when she claims that she will poison a letter to be sent to Katharine. It remains only for her to rid herself of Wolsey to think her reign secure.

As a true Calderonian protagonist, Henry now comes to repent of his errors. Having discovered Anne's unfaithfulness, he seeks to restore his world to innocence by calling Katharine back, but he is too late, for she is dead. He recognises the enormity of his mistake, but despite this *anagnorisis* he finds himself unable to repair the damage or to ease his conscience. The remedy for Henry, and for England, would be not only the recognition of his errors, but a willingness to make restitution. It is to this Tridentine ideal found in the Church's teaching on Penance that Calderón appeals when he has Henry face the consequences of his actions. What worries Henry most is not the misery he caused Katharine, but the breach made within the Church, symbolised in the confiscation of its goods in the dissolution of the monasteries. He is now in a dilemma, for, although he would like to make restitution, he cannot take this new-found wealth from his nobles. Henry is a man caught in a desperate web of circumstance, and his anguish is masterfully expressed by a playwright whose sympathy for his character is plain:

> dame favor, dame ayuda,
> pues ya quiero arrepentirme!
> Pero es muy tarde, no puedo.
> ¡Qué mal hice! ¡Qué mal hice!
>
> (2798–2801)

[Give me grace and help, for I want to repent! But it is too late. I cannot. What evil have I done! What evil have I done!]

It is this need to repent and his expressed desire to restore Katharine to her throne (2824–27) that removes Calderón's treatment of Henry from the merely historical, and from the expected and stereotypical anti-English attitude, to one of compassion for his weakened humanity. And it is in this desire for repentance that the figure of Henry in *La cisma de Inglaterra* approaches those of the Calderonian Auto Sacramental. In those post-Tridentine plays where man's redemption is directly dependent on his willingness to confess his errors and to reform his life, salvation comes only after fulfilment of the obligation to repent and make restitution. Henry does not obtain the cleansing grace of Penance because he is unable or unwilling to set aside the Macchiavellian rules of statecraft that govern his behavior (Bacigalupo 1976); thus his attempt at restoration by making Mary, as Princess of Wales, his legitimate successor is bound to fail. She, too, will take the path of expediency by feigning acceptance of the conditions of the oath of allegiance.[5] In all of this, Henry senses a tragedy greater than his own, that of an England separated from Rome. In the metaphor of the ship, the Church in England is sinking, for Henry has usurped the place of the Pope, the rightful captain:

> ¡Ayuda aquí, poderoso
> Señor, que el bajel va a pique!
> ¡En qué piélagos navega
> de confusiones Enrique![6]
>
> (2858–61)

[Succor here, great Lord, for the ship is sinking! In what a sea of confusion sails Henry!]

The final scene of the play is one that brings together the religious and the political themes. Henry, Defender of the Faith, and Mary, symbol of aggressive Tridentine Roman Catholicism, are seated upon the thrones; at their feet is the corpse of Anne Boleyn, the Protestant; it is a scene that is a fitting counterpoint to the one at the beginning of the play where Henry places the letter of Luther at his head and the letter of the pope at his feet. Henry has realised his errors, but he cannot now bow to the authority of Rome; he is forced to suffer the consequences of his blind passion. Mary, in refusing to agree to the new *status quo,* offers Henry the example of a faithful child of the Church willing even to renounce her claim to the throne if she is forced to deny the law of the Church. In a passage that I believe is indicative of Calderón's view of Henry, the king states that it is not the law of the Church that he denies, but only certain precepts of the Church that he must reject for political reasons. Henry is sure that this same political expediency will make Mary moderate her opinions, and in fact Mary ultimately accepts the homage of the people with secret reservations and with the warning that heretics will be burned at the stake. Thus the play ends, as it has begun, with a protest of loyalty to the faith. For

Calderón, this orthodoxy is more important than any historical consideration.

*   *   *

The source of Calderón's knowledge of Henry and the English schism is commonly believed to be Pedro de Ribadeneyra's *Historia Eclesiástica del Scisma del Reino de Inglaterra* of 1588 (Ruiz Ramón 1981, 55–58). Its viewpoint is one that Calderón, Spaniard, priest-to-be, and apologist of the Counter Reformation, could reasonably be expected to share. But, as has been seen, one does not find in Calderón the Henry that Ribadeneyra describes as vain, cruel, avaricious, and hypocritical as well as lustful. Calderón's Henry is a man who struggles with his appetites and his conscience, in the end coming to regret his treatment of Katharine as well as his conflict with Rome. Calderón's Henry, removed from the constraints of history, would be the Man of the Auto Sacramental, whose pangs of conscience would drive him to seek the cleansing of the Sacrament of Penance and finally the redemption offered in the Holy Eucharist.

What would cause Calderón to view Henry so sympathetically? It would, after all, have been a marvellous opportunity to rail against a schismatic whose defects of character were infamous. The reason, I believe, is linked to the religious, political, and social tensions of the early seventeenth century.

Various dates have been suggested for this play, ranging from the 1620s (Bacigalupo 1976; Vitse and Serralta 1983) to 1652 (Hilborn 1938), while Alexander Parker (1948) opined that it was written sometime during the Civil Wars in England. J. E. Varey and N. D. Shergold (1961) have found evidence that shows that, while the extant play was not published until 1684 (in the *Octava parte* published by Vera Tassis), payment for a play of the same name by Calderón was made on 31 March 1627, making it one of his earliest efforts.[7] My reading of the play reveals a mature handling of dramatic techniques, and I suggest that the extant play is not the play of 1627, but a reworking of it. I base this hypothesis on two points: first, the play of 1627 would have been written shortly after the failure of the marriage mission of Charles, Prince of Wales, in 1623. In that year Calderón wrote his *Amor, honor y poder (Love, honor, and power)*, in which the Prince is sympathetically portrayed, but by 1625 matters had changed, and the atmosphere was ripe for decidedly unsympathetic portrayals of the English. The generous treatment of Henry as English monarch does not jibe with the anti-English sentiments of the second half of the 1620s. Second, and perhaps more importantly, there is a small bit of textual evidence that links the content of the play with a much later period. Snubbed by Katharine, who sees through Wolsey's obsequious behavior, the Cardinal swears his revenge in words that project the historical aftermath of the Queen's fall into the reign of Charles I:

> padezca la Reina, pues.
> Ganarla de mano espero
> y será con civil guerra
> asombro de Inglaterra
> el hijo del carnicero.
>
> (702–6)

[Let the Queen suffer then. I plan to vanquish her and the butcher's son will be remembered as the wonder of England in Civil War.]

Calderón here is clearly referring to the Civil War between the Puritan forces and the Anglican Royalists in the mid-seventeenth century, for, despite dissatisfaction with Henry's reforms, nothing that could be called "civil guerra" took place before that time. Thus my reading of the play in the extant version supports Parker's dating. I believe that this play was written following the beheading of King Charles I. Parker (1948) himself remarks that, in Spain, Charles's fortunes were followed "with great sympathy, and the news of his execution was received with consternation and horror." This reaction would not be unnatural. After all, Charles had been in Madrid some twenty-five years earlier seeking a Spanish marriage, and he is said to have shown some interest in nurturing closer ties. By 1635 he was able to watch and presumably comprehend a Spanish play presented to him by a company of Spanish actors. In the context of this article, it would perhaps be useful to mention that the Anglican liturgy was translated into Spanish for the occasion of his visit to Spain.

But Charles Stuart was unpopular among certain factions of his own people, not only for his general unwillingness to compromise, but also for his Anglican High-Churchmanship and piety, for his appointment of the stern Anglo-Catholic Laud as archbishop of Canterbury, for his encouragement of traditional ritual practices, and for his Roman Catholic wife—all of which greatly offended the sensibilities of the Puritan party, who saw in him dangerously papistical tendencies.[8] The Spanish reaction to the English situation was one of dismay; the rise of Oliver Cromwell and his Puritan supporters greatly disturbed the Spanish, who saw this as an attack on both Church and State. They considered the challenge to a legitimate monarchy closely connected to the Established Church to be anathema. In Spain the cause of the Roman Church and the cause of the crown were one and the same, and the plays of the Counter-Reformation period are full of references to this fact. The *auto sacramental*, in particular, identifies the protection of the Church against Protestantism as the protection of the interests of the state.[9] Thus the situation in England, in which both Church and monarchy were being attacked at once, would have struck notes of vicarious alarm. I believe that it was this assault, combined with Charles's overtly Catholic (albeit Anglo-Catholic) behavior, that led to a sympathy for his position. At least one recent Spanish historian, Miguel Herrero García (1966, 481), associates the Puritan victory over the Anglican Royalist forces with the general assault of Protestantism on the Catholic Church:

> La última vez que en este siglo alarmó el pueblo inglés al catolicismo español fue cuando llegó Cromwell al poder con el título de Protector.

> [The English people last alarmed Spanish Catholicism in this century, when Cromwell came to power with the title of Protector.]

With the irony often displayed in political titles, Cromwell, the arch-Protestant and Lord Protector, succeeds Charles, High-Church Anglican and Defender of the Faith.

The subject matter for this play, whatever its form in 1627, now seemed eminently suitable for revision in the light of contemporary events in England and of Calderón's own growing interest in ecclesiastical matters. Calderón's analysis of the situation might well have been something like this: Charles was a properly anointed king and a known High-Churchman; he was known to have tolerated Roman Catholics while advancing the Catholic prelates of the Anglican Church to the disadvantage of the Protestant elements. The conflict with the Puritans resulted in his death, widely perceived as a martyrdom for the established faith. Thus Protestantism (in an extreme and highly aggressive form) had truly taken hold in England; Cromwell's official Church was now thoroughly reformed, with no apostolic episcopacy, no priesthood (García 1966, 458–85), and no ritual. All of this led Calderón to thoughts of England's earlier Reformation, begun in the reign of Henry Tudor. In the light of contemporary events in England, that Reformation must have seemed very mild indeed, and the faith of the English Church up to the death of Charles I would have seemed to Calderón to have remained essentially Catholic, as indeed the English Church has always claimed, particularly in contrast with the antisacerdotal religion of the Puritans. Thus Calderón looked on Henry as defender of the Catholic faith, and, while ignoring neither the forces of Protestantism that acted upon him nor his taking of the government of the Church, he chose to see Henry as a victim of his own naiveté and sexual urges. It is significant that in this play Henry is never seen to deviate from the orthodox doctrinal position, despite depriving the pope of his powers in England.

The title of his play is not *Enrique VIII*, but *La cisma de Inglaterra*, for it is the religious element of the "King's matter" that concerns Calderón. And if (given his hatred of Protestantism) one accepts that he is here principally concerned with religion, one might reasonably expect his title to be something like *La herejía de Inglaterra*. But it is not. Calderón's choice of title was, I believe, a deliberate sign of the context in which he wanted the play to be judged. The Covarrubias dictionary of 1611 (1987) gives the meaning of the word *cisma* as "division" and states:

> En la Yglesia Católica se dize aver avido cisma quando algunos se han apartado de la obediencia del romano pontífice y verdadero sucesor de San Pedro (425)

> [In the Catholic Church, schism is said to have occured when some have removed themselves from obedience to the Roman Pontiff, the true successor of Saint Peter.]

Similarly, the authoritative *Oxford Dictionary of the Christian Church* (1983, s.v. "schism") notes that schism is differentiated from heresy in that the separation involved is not "at basis doctrinal; whereas heresy is opposed to faith, schism is opposed to charity." Thus, from the Roman Catholic point of view, the breaking away of both the Anglican and Eastern Orthodox Churches was schismatical, while that of the Protestant Churches was heretical, for the Protestants rejected specific doctrines of the faith (Garbett 1950, 75). Henry, it must be remembered, is made to say: "One does not deny the law here" (2954). Calderón's sympathy for Henry is conditioned by Henry's *intention* to support and protect the faith; yet the play serves as a warning to those who would let themselves be governed by their emotions or duped by others. In Mary's words:

> . . . [renuncio]
> cuántas humanas promesas

me ofrezcan, si ha de costarme
negar la ley verdadera.

(2950–53)

. . . [I renounce] any human promise they may offer if the price is the
denial of the True Faith.]

Notes

1. An excellent exposition of Calderón's reaction to Protestantism is found in
Nicholas Shumway (1981). For an opposing viewpoint see Donald Dietz (1982).
2. All references are to *La cisma de Inglaterra*, edited by Francisco Ruiz
Ramón (Madrid: Castalia, 1981).
3. See J. Richards LeVan (1982, 188) for a definition of *encanto* in Calderón.
4. Henry required the clergy to promise to recognize him as "Supreme Head"
of the Church "as far as Christ's law allows."
5. Ana says: "Yo las recibo. *(aparte)* sin ellas" (2983).
6. Of Baptism and Penance, the Council Fathers said: "If anyone, confounding
the sacraments, saith that Baptism is itself the sacrament of Penance, as though
these two sacraments were not distinct, and that therefore Penance is not rightly
called a second plank after shipwreck; let him be anathema" (*The Canons and
Decrees of the Council of Trent* 1896).
7. *La cisma* was apparently printed before as a *suelta*, according to Vera Tassis.
Although Varey and Shergold (1961) cite Everett Hesse's belief that the 1684
version may be the same as the *princeps,* one has no assurance whatever that this
is the case. Indeed, as I show later, there are clear indications that it is not.
8. James P. Whitney (1940, 456), says that Laud "represented among Anglican
Catholics of England the movement for Reform which the Roman Church had
wrought for itself at Trent." Charles also favored Bishop John Cosin, a known
Anglo-Catholic, who had accompanied him to Spain in 1623 in quest of a marriage
pact.
9. Stanley G. Payne (1984, 48) says: "Clement VII, for example, might have
been able to head off the English schism had he not been under the coercion of
Spanish dynastic interests."

Works Cited

Andrachuk, Gregory Peter. 1985. "The *Auto sacramental* and the Reformation."
Journal of Hispanic Studies 10:7–38.

———. 1986. "El *Auto sacramental* y la herejía." *Edad de Oro* 5:21–33.

Arias, Ricardo. 1980. *The Spanish Sacramental Plays.* Boston: Twayne.

Bacigalupo, Mario. 1976. "Calderón's *La cisma de Inglaterra.*" *Symposium*
28:212–27, translated by J. Waterworth. London: Burns & Oates.

Calderón de la Barca. 1981. *La Cisma de Inglaterra.* Edited by Francisco Ruiz
Ramón. Madrid: Castalia.

The Canons and Decrees of the Council of Trent. 1896. Translated by J. Waterworth, London: Burns & Oates.

Covarrubias, Sebastián de. 1987. *Tesoro de la lengua castellana (1611).* Barcelona: Alta Fulla.

Dietz, Donald. 1982. "Liturgical and Allegorical Drama: The Uniqueness of Calderón's Auto Sacramental." In *Calderón de la Barca at the Tercentenary: Comparative Views,* edited by Wendell W. Aycock and Sydney P. Craven, 71–88. Lubbock: Texas Tech Press.

Garbett, Cyril. 1950. *The Church and State in England.* London: Hodder & Stoughton.

Herrero García, Miguel. 1966. *Ideas de los españoles del siglo XVII.* Madrid: Gredos.

Hilborn, Harry. 1938. *A Chronology of the Plays of D. Pedro Calderón de la Barca.* Toronto: University of Toronto Press.

LeVan, J. Richards. 1982. "Theme and Metaphor in the *Auto historial.*" In *Approaches to the Theater of Calderon,* edited by Michael D. McGaha, 187–98. Washington: University Press of America.

Oxford Dictionary of the Christian Church. 1983. Oxford: Oxford University Press.

Parker, A. A. 1948. "Henry VIII in Shakespeare and Calderon: An Appreciation of *La cisma de Inglaterra*" *Modern Language Review* 43:327–52.

Payne, Stanley G. 1984. *Spanish Catholicism: An Historical Overview.* Madison: University of Wisconsin Press.

Pfandl, Ludwig. 1937. "Ausdrucksformen des archaischen Denkens und des Unbewussten bei Calderón." *Gesammelte Aufsätze zur Kulturgeschichte Spaniens* (1937): 340–89.

Shumway, Nicholas. 1981. "Calderón and the Protestant Reformation: A View from the Autos Sacramentales." *Hispanic Review* 49:329–48.

Valbuena Prat, Angel. 1967. *Calderón de la Barca: Autos sacramentales.* Madrid: Espasa-Calpe.

Varey, J. E. and N. D. Shergold. 1961. "Some Early Calderón Dates." *Bulletin of Hispanic Studies* 38: 274–86.

Vitse, Marc and Frederic Serralta. 1983. "El teatro en el siglo XVII." In *Historia del teatro en España,* edited by J. M. Díez Borque, 1:473–687. Madrid: Taurus.

Wardropper, Bruce. 1967. *Introducción al teatro religioso del siglo de oro.* Salamanca: Anaya.

Whitney, James P. 1940. *History of the Reformation.* London: S.P.C.K.

Ynduráin, Domingo. 1981. *Calderón de la Barca: El gran teatro del mundo.* Madrid: Alhambra.

England's and Spain's Corpus Christi Theaters

Donald T. Dietz

In 1982, I called attention to the similarities of the Spanish sacramental theater and the early English medieval cycles (Dietz 1982b). In the first part of the present investigation, I will draw heavily upon the findings of my earlier study. In the second part, I go beyond these preliminary considerations to the nonparalleled or divergent aspects of the two dramatic histories under discussion. To discover the Great Divide between the parallels and divergences in the development of the Corpus Christi theaters of England and Spain, one must look to the Protestant Reform and its concomitant Counter Reformation. Finally, in order better to comprehend how the two national theaters went their separate ways with regard to the Corpus Christi dramas, I shall engage in a brief literary comparison of two post-Reformation plays, one from England, the other from Spain.

E. K. Chambers (1903), Karl Young (1933), Grace Frank (1954), and Richard B. Donovan (1958) all profess that the theater in Europe during the eleventh, twelfth, and thirteenth centuries originated with the Church's liturgy, especially with the two main ecclesiastical cycles of Christmas and Easter. Here, however, I focus upon a third liturgical season, the Feast of the Corpus Christi.

In 1264, fifty years after the official proclamation of the Dogma of Transubstantiation in 1215, Urban V issued his papal bull *Transiturus,* binding the Church to celebrate the doctrine of the Eucharist in some special way. Eventually, the Thursday after Trinity Sunday became the day given over to this commemoration and the Church required the consecrated host to be carried in public procession through the streets. Over the years, the Corpus Christi procession became increasingly elaborate and dramatic to the point where plays were written as an integral part of the ecclesiastical spectacle.

One might ask why Pope Urban incorporated the Feast of the

Corpus Christi into the Church's liturgy in the first place, when the Church had already set aside Maundy Thursday in Holy Week to be the day Christ instituted the Eucharist. In attempting to answer this question, scholars have found a clue to the nature and tone of the Corpus Christi plays themselves. V. A. Kolve (1966, 45) discovers Urban V's intention to associate the Eucharist in the papal bull with joy and gladness rather than sorrow and grief. As Kolve states, "Maundy Thursday is overcrowded with significant events," and the marvels of the Eucharist should be celebrated separately and divorced from the somberness of the Passion. This affirmation of jovial commemoration, firmly established in the papal bull that originated the Corpus Christi Feast, Kolve maintains, provided the early English dramatists with the desire to convey to their audiences God's presence in the world not only in the Eucharist but throughout history. The English writers sought a formula that would dramatize the Creator's involvement with his human creation from the beginning of time to the end, and this search ultimately resulted in the cycle form of the English Corpus Christi plays. Rather than one mystery play, the English medieval dramatic artist felt compelled to enact God's total involvement in human affairs as marked by his three advents into the world: his creation of man in the beginning, his redemption of man after the fall, and his judgment of man in the final coming. The English cycles may vary one from the other, insofar as the number and selection of biblical accounts to be dramatized are concerned, but all contain these dramatic movements in what Kolve distinguishes as the series's "proto-cycle," or core plays.

Ricardo Arias (1980, 16–20) also sees the papal bull's joyous spirit as significant in setting the tone for the Autos Sacramentales. He too points out that, at the Council of Vienna in 1311–12 where Pope John XXII ordered the Corpus Christi procession, the kings of England and Aragon were in attendance together with the king of France. Early documents attest that the Corpus Christi procession took on special prominence within Aragonese territorial boundaries in Gerona, Barcelona, and Valencia.

At this point it is important to reiterate and to stress the positive nature of the Feast of the Corpus Christi and the joyous and festive tone of both the English and Spanish plays, as noted by Kolve and Arias.

Kolve theorizes that the English dramatists wished to celebrate God's presence in the various moments in the history of mankind's salvation, and this impetus gave rise to the cyclical nature of England's miracle plays. But does one find a similar impulse among the dramatists in Spain?

In fact, there remains very little evidence, nor does one find any extensive scholarship to support the idea that Spain maintained any cyclical theater such as one finds in England. However, one does discover, for example in Leo Rouanet's collection of early *autos* (1977), many of the same biblical stories and events that make up the English cycles and that Kolve includes among his core plays. What is significant, moreover, is that the Autos Sacramentales, especially Calderón's, even though they consist of only one act, do depict, in one form or another, the entire history of man's salvation. It thus appears that the spirit of Christian joy and merriment infected the Spanish authors as it had their English counterparts and caused them, also, to search out a suitable dramatic formula in order to depict the theological significance of the Creator's continued presence within his creation.

One of the principal reasons why Hispanists have failed to see these parallels in the two Corpus Christi literatures can be attributed to the dominant influence of Alexander A. Parker's early work on the Auto Sacramental. In his now classic book *The Allegorical Drama of Calderón* (1943), Professor Parker indeed made an enormous contribution to the study of Spain's eucharistic drama, but he based some of his conclusions concerning the theme of the *autos* on a misunderstanding of Catholic theology. In his eagerness to explain why some of the sacramental plays had no immediately apparent connection to the Eucharist, and in his attempt to clarify some of the previously unsettled questions posed in the definitions of preceding scholars such as Eduardo González Pedroso (1952), Angel Valbuena Prat (1924), and others, Parker argues as follows: since the Sacrament, as he perceived it, is the central doctrine of Roman Catholicism, the underlying theme *(asunto)* of every *auto* is, therefore, the Eucharist, no matter what the plot *(argumento)* of the *auto* may be (Parker 1943, 59).

My previous study (1982b) treated Professor Parker's theories concerning the *auto*'s theme at great length, and it would be wrong to belabor the point here. However, it seems important at the present time to clarify, once again, the mistaken notion that the Eucharist is at the core of Catholic doctrine. Rather, at the heart of Catholic theology is God Himself, his true nature in the Trinity, and his manifestations to man in human history, the Incarnation, and Redemption.[1] Because it seems crucial to the present discussion, this study reaffirms what my earlier investigation indicated—that the major underlying theme which gives dramatic meaning to the Auto Sacramental, especially in its period of greatest development with Calderón, is God's presence with man on earth. There is no attempt here to refute the many who find the Eucharist to be major motive and concern in the *auto*. For, it must be remembered, the Eucharist remains the principal sacrament in the Church precisely because it affords God an opportunity of a real presence with man on this earth after the Redemption and before his coming again in final judgment. Whether or not man chooses to avail himself of the graces of the Eucharist by employing his free will in order to achieve salvation becomes still another very crucial theological concern for the *auto* dramatist, especially after the Reformation.

If one continues to maintain with Parker that the Eucharist is the principal dramatized theme of the Autos Sacramentales, then one will see little relationship between the Corpus Christi theaters of Spain and England other than the historical one. If, however, one shifts one's perception to the acceptance of the salvation history as the dynamic principle of the Spanish *auto sacramental,* then one can easily discover thematic and theological relationships in the origin and early development of the two Eucharistic theaters, especially before the Protestant Reformation.

Let me now turn to what happened to the Corpus Christi theaters after the Protestant Reformation in England and the Counter Reformation in Spain. In the first place, one must begin by dispelling an exaggerated notion concerning the development of Spain's theater during the sixteenth and seventeenth centuries. One has been led to believe that Spain was unique in Europe because her dramatists clung to the medieval theatrical traditions during the Renaissance in the dramatization of the sacramental plays, while the rest of Europe developed a national theater (Wardropper 1967, 117–29).

Although I readily admit that, comparatively speaking, the Corpus Christi drama flourished particularly in Spain, especially with Calderón's artistry, and continued long after Calderón's death, there is ample evidence that these liturgical dramas were performed in England and in other European countries beyond any date that one might have originally believed. For example, with regard to England, according to Sydney Clarke: "By far the most important and interesting of the four series or cycles of English miracle plays that have survived to the present day, are those that were performed in the streets of York, from the fourteenth to the sixteenth centuries, by the members of the craft and trade guilds, with the sanction, and under the active supervision, of the City Fathers" (Clarke 1964, 16). And speaking of the Chester plays Clarke writes: "The plays are twenty-five in number, and they were acted by the twenty-five trade companies of the city on the Monday, Tuesday and Wednesday in Whitsun week, from 1268 to 1577, and again in 1600" (34).

The point is that the demise of the medieval theatrical tradition of the religious drama after the Reformation was a gradual process for all of Europe that extended well into the seventeenth century. However, the Reformation and the Counter Reformation did profoundly influence the Corpus Christi theater in England and Spain, and the two countries found themselves on divergent paths. Let me now analyze these unparallels in the two theaters.

Harold C. Gardiner (1946, 95) states unequivocally that in England "the religious stage and its fate were intimately bound-up with the Reformation and the spirit it engendered." Referring specifically to the Corpus Christi plays, Craig (1955, 354) succinctly posits "that Reform was the chief enemy of the Mystery plays and it more than any other agency brought about their downfall." Craig cites political motives for suppressing the plays "because they were thought to be papistical in their influence" (355). During the reign of Elizabeth I many English cities such as Coventry, where the cycles were prominent, moved their major theatrical event from Corpus Christi to the more secular holidays in order to escape Reformation censure. Midsummer and Saint Peter's, which had already been established as days of public festivities in England before the Reformation, were newly designated times for dramatic presentations. Gradually, fresh plays were written to replace the Corpus Christi cycles, and even old pageant carts and scaffolds, which had been used in Corpus Christi plays, received minor modifications and were adapted to the newly performed secular plays (Nelson 1974, 151).

In the Iberian peninsula, of course, the Reformation caused quite a different reaction, with regard to the theater. Spain, the great champion of the faith, commissioned sacramental plays for the feast of the Corpus Christi and its processions, all of which became even more important as an expression of the confirmation of Catholicism. Most critics of Spanish drama have easily grasped the defensive posture of the sacramental plays seeing them as an *arma de combate* against Protestant heresies. Others have preferred to stress the utilitarian nature of the Auto Sacramental, which they have seen as a means for educating the populace in the sacred mysteries of their religion—a step made necessary by the revisionist spirit that had already manifested itself within the Spanish Church before the Reformation.[2]

Beyond the historical events and political repercussions precipitated by Martin Luther and Henry VIII, other more aesthetic reasons existed to explain the differences between the English and the Spanish religious theater after the Reformation. In England, during the days of the early Renaissance and even before the Reformation, the religious theater witnessed the appearance of the morality play. Unlike the medieval miracles and mystery plays of the liturgical cycles that depict stories from the Old and New Testament, the morality play allegorizes man's moral struggle with himself, with his circumstances and, with his environment. This allegorization of man's inner moral dilemma has its ancestry in Prudentius's *Psychomachia* and seemed to naturally take roots in the Renaissance spirit, in which man became the center of the universe.

David J. Leigh (1972, 260–78) offers another possible explanation for the appearance of the morality plays in England during the sixteenth and seventeenth centuries. Leigh argues that the Last-Judgment plays, which conclude all four of the English mystery cycles, contain distinctive features that separate them from all the other plays in the cycles. These "doomsday plays" are different in nature from the other plays because they treat not what happened in the Bible, but what might happen at the end of the world. In other words, according to Leigh, the eschatological subject, its symbolic techniques, its ambivalent time frame, all qualify the Last-Judgment play of the Corpus Christi cycle as the forerunner of England's morality play.

Before I undertake the last objective of this paper—a very brief analysis of two post-Reformation plays, one from England and another from Spain—let me direct special attention to an article by P. K. Ayers (1984) from the University of Toronto concerning two types of English morality plays. Professor Ayers distinguishes a fundamental difference between England's pre- and post-Reformation moralities. According to Ayers, in the pre-Reformation variety, allegorical Man, the main protagonist, initially appears weak and foolish and may even fall and sin, but, basically good by nature, he is therefore redeemable. In post-Reformation plays, which Ayers terms Protestant morality plays, written between 1550 and 1575, Man the protagonist appears fundamentally corrupt, for his "folly is not the result of a misapprehension of reality, it is the result of being who he is." According to Ayers, "this interpretation, characteristic of English Protestantism generally, stresses the innate sinfulness of man, the total corruption of his faculties, and his isolation from God." On the other hand, in the pre-Reformation morality, although weak and foolhardy, Man was always able to choose between good and evil. In order words, the pre-Reformation protagonist exercised his theological faculty of free will, while the post-Reformation protagonist embodied the theological teachings of Luther and, more especially, of Calvin, which posit that man is originally sinful and only a predetermined elect will be saved.

At this point in his reasoning, Ayers arrives at the major premise of his article. He maintains that, because the English post-Reformation morality tried to dramatize Protestant theology with its emphasis on the natural corruptibility of man and on predestination, the religious morality in England was destined to fail. The result of the post-Reformation moralities for Ayers remains clear: "Since the virtuous characters are defined by their virtue, and the vicious by their vice, there is and can be no conflict within a single character." As a result, "the protagonists are not rewarded or punished for what they do, but for what they are by nature." Conflict is the essence of drama. Thus, for Ayers, the theology of Protestantism runs contrary to the aesthetics of the theater. "Such drama, is meaningless in a context where men are saved or damned according to circumstances over which they have no control" (105). Ayers theorizes even further when he writes that "the importance of the Protestant moralities as religious drama suggests a wider significance in the context of Elizabethan dramatic history. . . . In themselves dramatic failures, they point to the precarious balance upon which Elizabethan drama rests; they suggest that later dramatists were able to write only by evading, consciously or unconsciously, the implications of religious orthodoxy."

In Spain, the scenario for the main protagonist of the morality plays and of the Auto Sacramental was quite different. Louise Fothergill-Payne (1977, 78–101), who has traced the development of the allegorical characters in the Spanish moralities and pre-Calderonian Autos, has established the degree to which Man, a *dramatis persona,* actually determines his own fate by taking an active dramatic role in the play. She contends that, as Spain's religious drama progressed during the sixteenth and seventeenth centuries, Man's role became more and more dominant until, finally, he was elevated to front and center stage.

After the Reformation, in the later Auto writers Valdivielso, Tirso, Lope, and especially Calderón, the religious theater of Spain, unlike that of England, continued to dramatize, even more strongly than before, man's right to choose freely, to act according to conscience, and to determine his own fate. In fact, as has been seen, the structural basis of the Calderonian Autos consists of Man's salvation history: after creation, Man falls of his own volition; after redemption, he must conscientiously repent; he must, then, want and merit salvation through the Church and the sacraments.

In other words, for the Spanish dramatist of the *auto sacramental* after the Reformation, there never really existed a question of theology versus theater, as there had, if one believes Ayers, for the English writer of the Protestant moralities. Catholicism comfortably embraces the following doctrinal concepts: that Man reflects the Creator's image (Essential Goodness); that, therefore, he is worthy of a second chance when he slips (Incarnation and Redemption); that only if Man makes good choices (Free Will) and uses the help (Church and Sacraments) available to him can he earn his final reward (Grace). Choice opens the door for inner conflict, which is precisely where the essence of drama resides.

Turning quickly to the last task projected for this study, let me now undertake a brief comparison of one of the Protestant moralities mentioned by Ayers, William Wager's *Enough Is As Good As a Feast,* to Pedro Calderón de la Barca's *El gran mercado del mundo (The great marketplace of the world).* I hope this rapid exercise in hermeneutics will serve to elucidate the two diverse paths of the Spanish and English Corpus Christi theatrical traditions after the Protestant schism from Rome. By contrasting Wager's and Calderón's strikingly similar works, my analysis will support Ayers's contentions as to why the English morality could not continue at full dramatic force while, at the same time, it will affirm the renewed vitality enjoyed by Spain's Corpus Christi theater, especially in the hands of its most capable playwright.

In Wager's play, two allegorical figures represent mankind: Worldly Man and Heavenly Man. The forces of Good are dramatized by Contentation, which symbolizes a peaceful state in which man contents himself with what he has rather than frolicking about the world in search of goods and pleasures. The allegorical figure Enough, which is found in the play's title, aids Contentation in enabling man to realize that the spirit of poverty and moderation brings peace. Covetousness leads the forces of evil. She, in turn, finds help in Precipitation, symbolic of rash judgment, and in Ignorance, Inconsideration, and Temerity. Although the very names of Wager's characters may intrigue audiences, they should take note of how the play's dramatic structure contains its ideological basis in the Protestant theology.

First, although two allegorical figures represent mankind, only Worldly Man functions dramatically in the play's action to any extent. Heavenly Man, who does take part in the play's opening scenes, remains conspicuously absent from the major movements and reappears but once more at the play's end.

Wager seems to assume that Heavenly Man will be saved almost by definition. Structurally, therefore, Worldly Man must carry the action of the play because he alone receives the attention of the evil figures. From the outset, there exists no doubt whatsoever that Wordly Man will not survive the onslaught of temptations thrown up to him by Covetousness and her cohorts. Indeed, when Worldly Man falls at last, Enough confirms to the audience that Man's downfall was inevitable because of his intrinsically evil nature. Nor could the audience ever have expected him to change: "It will not out of the flesh that is bred in bone verily. / The Worldly Man will needs be a worldly man still" (862–63).

Although Worldly Man walks side by side with Heavenly Man in what, for a moment, seems a conversion toward the good, the cards are stacked against him. By nature he cannot but succumb to the seductions of the evil forces that have singled him out.

Like Wager in his *Enough,* Calderón in his *El gran mercado del mundo* elects to dramatize the protagonist, Man, with dual personages, Mal Genio and Buen Genio. However, the entire structure of Calderón's play varies significantly from Wager's, in that both Mal Genio and Buen Genio enter into every facet of the drama on an equal footing. Both are created equally; both receive the same options and are allowed the same choices. After creation and before they go to the World's Marketplace, both Mal Genio and Buen Genio are assaulted by Culpa, Lascivia, and Gula, which represent the Devil's camp. It happens that Mal Genio selects Malicia as his instructor, and she helps him make choices, while Buen Genio relies on Inocencia for advice. On the way to the Marketplace, Buen Genio chooses the difficult mountain passes while Mal Genio prefers the more accessible flat lands. While at the World's Market, both discover the exact same merchandise—some worldly, some spiritual. Buen Genio purchases Penitencia and Fe, while Mal Genio pleases himself with Gula and Heresía. Just as Wager had in mind the promulgation of Protestant doctrine, there can be no doubt as to what Calderón intended. The allegorical Heresy clearly identifies herself as representing Calvin and Luther.

Even more than the scenes in the Marketplace, Calderón's opening scenes illustrate the extent to which he succeeded in fusing theology and drama—a fusion that defied Wager. Calderón's play begins with a conflict—the one inherent in the creation. Padre de Familias, who represents God the Father, has just finished making the world, complete with Man; and chaos immediately ensued. The two Man figures wield daggers as they struggle over which is to win the favor of the Princess, Gracia.

In *El gran mercado del mundo* the efficacy of grace is one of the principal doctrines of Calderón's dramatization. The allegorical figure of Gracia therefore provides a crucial key to an understanding of the play, especially in these initial scenes.[3] From the very beginning Gracia favors Buen Genio because, unlike his proud brother, he exemplifies humility. Padre de Familias, however, carefully admonishes Gracia that grace must be merited through good acts—an obvious refutation of the Protestant belief that faith alone suffices for salvation. When Gracia hints that she knows which one of the *genios* will act rightfully and win her hand, Padre de Familias again cautions that both must be given an equal opportunity and that neither she nor the audience will know until the play's very end which suitor will triumph—an obvious attack by Calderón on the heretical belief in predestination. In these scenes of admonition between Padre de Familias and Gracia, Calderón employs the technique of vertical conflict, in which allegorical figures of the same inclination, such as God and Grace, do not quite see eye to eye and argue, as it were, between themselves. This type of vertical conflict places Calderón technically a step above previous *auto* writers, who used exclusively the more conventional horizontal conflict, in which two opposing groups of allegorical characters, virtue and vice for example, square off against each other (Dietz 1982a).

Finally, one last note concerning this initial interaction of Gracia, Padre de Familias, Mal Genio, and Buen Genio. Just before the two man figures leave on their individual journeys to the Marketplace, Gracia responds to the Creator's admonition of equal treatment of the two Man figures, and she gives to each the gift of a rose, symbolic of the cross and God's love. Fittingly, it is Mal Genio who carelessly loses the rose on his journey. Thus he never takes advantage of Gracia's initial gift and, in effect, squanders it. Buen Genio, on the other hand, zealously guards his gift. He has it with him when he arrives at the Marketplace, and therefore it allows him to select more wisely from among the World's merchandise. In other words, Buen Genio uses grace to earn more grace—a fundamental truth of Catholic doctrine.

Thus, unlike the English playwright Wager, whose espousal of Protestant doctrine interfered with his ability to generate true dramatic conflict, Calderón, living in Catholic Spain, found theology and theater compatible. This historical and doctrinal compatibility, wedded to Calderón's artistic genius, resulted in a religious theater of the highest aesthetic quality.

I began this study by observing that, more than other European countries, Spain and England share a rich Corpus Christi literary tradition. Both nations possess the same historical and liturgical inspiration from Eucharistic festivity, and this motive led to a similar artistic impulse to dramatize in its entirety God's presence in human history. After the Reformation, however, both countries found themselves going separate ways. Spain, the great defender of the Roman faith, cemented her ties to the Eucharistic theatrical tradition that flourished in the sixteenth and seventeenth centuries. Meanwhile, England, the seat of northern Protestantism, enemy to the papacy, necessarily withdrew from her earlier commitment to the Corpus Christi tradition.

If history had not forced Spain and England down divergent pathways in their liturgical drama, theology and aesthetics alone would have hastened the demise of the Corpus Christi theater in the latter country and account for its flourishing in the former. Inherent in Protestantism lies the belief in man's inability to alter his destiny and to earn his salvation. Like the protagonists of Wager's play, men are predestined from the onset to decide nothing for themselves, and there remains no doubt in the believing audience what will become of each of them; thus, the Protestant morality finds itself devoid of any essential dramatic conflict. On the other hand, Roman Catholic doctrine places a heavy emphasis on free will and grace and allows for deliberation and decisive action on the part of the protagonist, as in Calderón's drama. Open confrontation with daily living provides dramatic tension. Choice implies personal responsibility; the protagonist's failure to act responsibly leaves the possibility open for dramatic tragedy—a topic whose investigation, however intriguing, I leave to another time.

Notes

1. In Douglas (1974, 985) one reads under "Trinity": "The central tenet of the Christian faith is that God is one, personal, and triune." See also Rahner and Vorgrimier (1965, 469) under "Trinity": "The name of the fundamental mystery of Christianity, that of one nature and the three Persons (Father, Son, and Holy Ghost) in God." In this latter dictionary, under "Trinitarian Theology," the doctrine of the Trinity is referred to as "the Supreme mystery in Christian Revelation" (468). Under "Trinidad Santísima" in the *Enciclopedia de referencia católica* (1970, 6: 1996), the Trinity is called "El misterio central de la religión cristiana."

2. Among those who argue that the Autos Sacramentales were an attack on Protestantism are Entwistle (1948, 223–38); Shumway (1981, 329–48); Andrachuk (1985, 7–38). Among those who debate the *armas de combate* theory and instead turn to the reform within the Roman Church itself are Crawford (1937, 148); Bataillon (1940, 193–212); Corrales Egea (1945, 83–86).

3. For the problems encountered by Calderón with the Grace figure and its development in terms of theology and drama see Dietz (1973), especially the discussion on *La viña del Señor* and *El día mayor de los días* (121–37, 110–17). Also helpful to understanding the importance of grace for man's salvation as expressed in the Calderonian *auto* is Falkel (1980, 39–48).

Works Cited

Andrachuk, Gregory Peter. 1985. "The *Auto Sacramental* and the Reformation." *Journal of Hispanic Philology* 10:7–38.

Arias, Ricardo. 1980. *The Spanish Sacramental Plays*. Boston: Twayne.

Ayers, P. K. 1984. "The Protestant Morality Play and Problems of Dramatic Structure." *Essays in Theater* 2:94–110.

Bataillon, Marcel. 1940. "Essai d'explication de l'auto sacramental." *Bulletin Hispanique* 42:193–212.

Calderón de la Barca, Pedro. 1952. *El gran mercado del mundo*. Vol. 3 of *Obras completas,* edited by Angel Valbuena Prat, 223–42. Madrid: Aguilar.

Chambers, Edmund Kerchever. 1903. *The Medieval Stage*. Oxford: Clarendon Press.

Clarke, Sidney M. 1964. *The Miracle Play in England*. New York: Haskell House.

Corrales Egea, J. 1945. "Relaciones entre el auto sacramental y la Contra-reforma." *Revista de ideas estéticas* 3:83–86.

Craig, Hardin. 1955. *English Religious Drama of the Middle Ages*. Oxford: Clarendon Press.

Crawford, J. P. Wickersham. 1937. *The Spanish Drama before Lope de Vega*. Philadelphia: University of Pennsylvania Press.

Dietz, Donald T. 1973. *The "Auto Sacramental" and the Parable in Spanish Golden Age Literature*. Chapel Hill: University of North Carolina Press.

———a. 1982. "Conflict in Calderón's *Autos Sacramentales*." In *Approaches to the Theater of Calderón,* edited by Michael McGaha, 175–86. Washington D.C.: University Press of America.

———b. 1982. "Liturgical and Allegorical Drama: The Uniqueness of Calderón's *Auto Sacramental*." In *Calderón de la Barca at the Tercentenary: Comparative Views,* edited by Wendell Aycock and Sydney Cravens, 71–88. Lubbock: Texas Tech Press.

Donovan, Richard B. 1958. *The Liturgical Drama in Medieval Spain*. Toronto: Pontifical Institute of Medieval Studies.

Douglas, J. D. 1974. *The New International Dictionary of the Christian Church*. Grand Rapids: Zondervan.

Enciclopedia de referencia católica. 1970. North Carolina: La Casa de la Biblia Católica.

Entwistle, Wiliam J. 1948. "La controversia en los autos de Calderón." *Nueva Revista de Filología Hispánica* 2:223–38.

Falkel, Robert W. 1980. "*El gran teatro del mundo* of Pedro Calderón de la Barca and the Centrality of Grace." *Bulletin of the Comediantes* 32:39–48.

Fothergill-Payne, Louise. 1977. *La alegoría en los autos y farsas anteriores a Calderón*. London: Tamesis.

Frank, Grace. 1954. *The Medieval French Drama*. Oxford: Clarendon Press.

Gardiner, Harold C. 1946. *Mysteries' End: An Investigation of the Last Days of the Medieval Religious Stage*. New Haven: Yale University Press.

Kolve, V. A. 1966. *The Play Called Corpus Christi*. Stanford: Stanford University Press.

Leigh, David J. 1972. "The Doomsday Mystery Play: An Eschatological Morality." In *Medieval English Drama: Essays Critical and Contextual*, edited by Jerome Taylor and Alan H. Nelson, 260–78. Chicago: The University of Chicago Press.

Los autos sacramentales desde su orígen hasta fines del siglo XVII. 1952. Edited by Eduardo Conzález Pedroso. Biblioteca de Autores Españoles 58. Madrid: Ediciones Atlas.

Marx, Milton. 1961. *The Enjoyment of Drama*. New York: Appleton-Century Crofts.

Morrow, Louis Laravoire. 1963. *My Catholic Faith*. Kenosha, Wis.: My Mission House.

Nelson, Alan H. 1974. *The Medieval English Stage*. Chicago: The University of Chicago Press.

Parker, Alexander A. 1935. "Notes on the Religious Drama in Medieval Spain and the Origin of the *Auto Sacramental*." *Modern Language Review* 30:170–82.

———. 1943. *The Allegorical Drama of Calderón*. Oxford: Dolphin.

Rahner, Karl and Herbert Vorgrimler. 1965. *Theological Dictionary*. New York: Herder and Herbert.

Rouanet, Leo. 1977. *Colección de autos, farsas, y coloquios del siglo XVI*. 4 vols. 1901; reprint, Hildesheim and New York: Georg Olms Verlag.

Shumway, Nicolas. 1981. "Calderón and the Protestant Reformation: A View From the *Autos Sacramentales*." *Hispanic Review* 49:329–48.

Valbuena Prat, Angel. 1924. "Los autos sacramentales de Calderón: Clasificación y análisis." *Revue Hispanique* 61:1–302.

Wager, William. 1967. *"The Longer Thou Livest" and "Enough Is As Good As A Feast"*. In *Regents Renaissance Drama Series*, edited by R. Mark Benbow, 81–146. Lincoln: University of Nebraska Press.

Wardropper, Bruce W. 1967. *Introducción al teatro religioso del siglo de oro: Evolución del auto sacramental antes de Calderón*. Salamanca: Ediciones Anaya, S.A.

Young, Karl. 1933. *The Drama of the Medieval Church*. 2 vols. Oxford: Clarendon Press.

Unparalleled Lives: Hagiographical Drama in Seventeenth-Century England and Spain

José M. Ruano de la Haza

Hagiographical plays were an extremeley popular form of theatrical entertainment in seventeenth-century Spain, with no real counterpart in seventeenth-century England.[1] The one exception was Thomas Dekker and Philip Massinger's *The Virgin Martyr,* which I shall be considering below.

All the great Spanish Golden-Age dramatists and a host of minor ones practised the genre.[2] Looking through the manuscript collection at the National Library in Madrid, one may be forgiven for thinking that every little village priest and seminarian in seventeenth-century Spain had a play in verse on the life of a saint in the bottom drawer of his writing desk, a suspicion shared by Agustín de Rojas (Ressot 1972, 154), who claimed that "al fin no quedó poeta / en Sevilla que no hiciese / de algún santo su comedia" ("in the end, there was no poet left in Seville who had not composed a play on the life of a saint").

In his *Catálogo,* La Barrera (1860) lists a little under 150 plays under San, Santo, and Santa, but this is probably only the tip of the iceberg, for La Barrera's list is far from complete and excluded from this number are those hagiographical dramas that do not bear the name of a saint in their title, such as *El esclavo del demonio (The Devil's Slave), El Purgatorio de San Patricio (Saint Patrick's purgatory),* and *El divino Africano (The divine African).* The number of hagiographical plays performed on Spanish stages between 1580 and 1680 must therefore have run into the hundreds. From this number I shall pay special attention in this paper to two representative ones: Mira de Amescua's *El esclavo del demonio* and Calderón's *El Purgatorio de San Patricio.*

Religious plays were performed in England during the seventeenth century (Campbell 1959, 225). Marlowe's *Doctor Faustus* and

Cyril Tourneur's *The Atheist's Tragedy* (1607) are religious plays in the proper sense of the term, as are those plays that, despite the Puritans' complaints that the word of God was being profaned by buffoonery, were based on biblical stories, such as a drama on Job by Greene (now lost), a dramatization of the story of the prophet Jonas included in Greene and Lodge's *A Looking-glass for London and England,* Peele's *David and Bethsabe,* and others that have not survived. But with the exception of *The Virgin Martyr,* already mentioned, no dramatizations of the lives of saints were performed on the English stage during the seventeenth century.

How shall one account for this discrepancy between English and Spanish dramatic taste during this period? Why were saints' plays not popular in England? H. C. Gardiner (1946) notes that the disappearance of cycle plays was the result of political anti-Catholicism.[3] But according to Walter Cohen (1985, 378), "religious differences between England and Spain cannot in any simple sense explain this generic divergence. Catholics opposed the public theater as much as Protestants, with Argensola particularly objecting to religious drama." For Cohen the real explanation lies in the fact that seventeenth-century English society had become, presumably unlike the Spanish, "relatively secular and modern" (379). In Spain, on the other hand, "the powerful church combined ideological hegemony with subordination to the interests of the monarchy. Under these conditions, Catholic dogma could function as an important vehicle for national self-definition" (ibid.). But, although this could provide an explanation of why religious drama was not discouraged in Spain, it cannot account for its popularity. Church and State politics, assuming that such a policy existed, cannot force people to flock to the theaters. The reasons for the popularity of these plays must be sought elsewhere, especially in the text of these plays.

Any *Flos Sanctorum*[4] would give a good idea of the nature of the plot of a typical hagiographical play. It is usually a tale of good versus evil that takes place in a world where, in the words of Francisco Ruiz Ramón (1967, 261), "lo profano y lo religioso, la 'naturalidad' y la sobrenaturalidad, la intrascendencia y la trascendencia, la superstición y la fe se superponen mediante una técnica teatral compleja y, a la vez, elemental" ("the profane and the religious, the 'natural' and supernatural, the transcendent and intranscendent, superstition and faith coexist by means of a complex and at the same time simple theatrical technique"). There were basically two types of stories, the first told the life of a saintly man, such as Saint Patrick in *El Purgatorio de San Patricio,* who is pitted against paganism or the forces of darkness; and the second related the life of an evil man or woman or of a pagan who repents or converts and, after incredible sufferings and penance, becomes a saint. Don Gil in *El esclavo del demonio* belongs to this second type. In the first type the figure of the saint is already accomplished perfection, beyond any doubts or earthly worries; in the second the action swings from evil to good, or from good to evil and back to good. In the first, the protagonist is usually a static figure, not very compelling dramatically; dramatic interest, therefore, has to be found in the saint's antagonist, the sinner or the pagan, or in the devil; in the second, the saint experiences some moral progress and can be dramatically interesting as a character in his own right. But in both types dramatic interest and conflict tend to gravitate toward the evil deeds of the evil character, or toward the evil deeds of the saint before his final conversion, and then toward the gruesome details of his penance and/or martyrdom. The miracles and good deeds of the saint are occasionally shown or described, but they usually take second place.

With their emphasis on torments, penance, sin, and death, the spectators of these plays find themselves in a world akin to the macabre and allegorical world of Hieronymus Bosch. The horrendous "discovery" of King Egerio's descent into hell, together with the long and detailed description of the torments suffered by the souls in Hell, in *El Purgatorio de San Patricio,* as well as the self-inflicted torments and humiliation of both Lisarda and Gil in *El esclavo del demonio,* are good examples of this Boschian world. In these plays Spanish dramatists were dealing, like Bosch, with the hidden fears of their Christian audiences, with the menacing world of the Christian Apocalypse. These plays are the stuff nightmares are made of. This notwithstanding, they also at times partake of some of the sentimentalism of the painters of the school of Murillo, especially in the description of the saints' good deeds and piety. The description, admittedly by the saint himself, of Patrick's parents and youth is an example of this mode.

But the element of horror is surely the most characteristic ingredient of the hagiographical plays. The genre lends itself to this type of treatment. And there is no doubt that this was part of its immense appeal, as can be seen by the fact that of the three long *relaciones* which Calderón wrote for *El Purgatorio de San Patricio—The life of Saint Patrick, The life of Ludovico Enio,* and the description of the latter's experiences in Saint Patrick's Purgatory— it was the last two, and in particular the second—the horrible list of crimes and atrocities committed by Egerio, which includes the rape of a nun—that were printed and reprinted most often in the seventeenth century as *pliegos sueltos* or broadsheets.

From the point of view of staging, all these characteristics contributed to the production of good visual drama. Staging, therefore, became one of the most attractive features of these plays for a seventeenth-century audience. They provided the stage manager with an opportunity to display all the theatrical tricks at his disposal. This inevitably led to abuses. And the worst among these plays tended to rely too heavily on stage machines and explosions, with angels and devils battling overhead. Both Calderón and Mira de Amescua use stage effects, but with a certain restraint. There is only one transportation scene in *El Purgatorio de San Patricio,* when an Angel descends on a cloud machine at the end of act 1 and carries Patrick off, while in *El esclavo del demonio* the only excesses of this sort are committed in act 3, where in a brief scene a figure of the Devil appears in a revolving *tramoya "disparando cohetes y arcabuces"* ("shooting rockets and harquebuses"), and immediately afterwards *"suenan trompetas, aparece una batalla arriba entre un Angel y el Demonio en sus tramoyas"* ("trumpets sound, the Angel and the Devil, each on his own stage machine, engage in battle overhead").[5]

The supernatural was not absent from the English seventeenth-century stage, to be sure. It was catered for, not by plays on the lives of saints, but by those with magicians and devils. According to Barbara H. Traister (1984, 33), "at least two dozen plays involving magicians, conjurors and enchanters are extant" dated in the period from 1570 to 1620. Special effects were used in Peele's *Old Wives Tale* (staged about 1590) where the magician Sacrapant strikes one character blind and another deaf, using spectacular visual effects such as "A voice and a flame of fire," "thunder and lightning," and "two furies" who are there to help the magician carry out his deeds. Some of the effects in *El esclavo del demonio* resemble those used in Barnable Barnes's anti-Catholic play, *The Devil's Charter,* which begins spectacularly with a dumb show in which Pope Alexander VI makes a pact with the devil in exchange for the triple crown of the papacy (Traister 1984, 58); and the transportation scene in *El Purgatorio de San Patricio* is paralleled in Greene's *Friar Bacon and Friar Bungay* when Bungay is carried off on the back of a devil.[6]

In many respects Dekker and Massinger's *The Virgin Martyr* shares many of the characteristics of a typical Spanish hagiographical play. Walter Cohen (1985, 375), for example, sees the plot of *The Virgin Martyr* as on a par with that of Calderón's *El mágico prodigioso (The prodigious magician)*: "In each the Virgin Martyr defeats the machinations of the devil, thereby leading a pagan man unwittingly in danger of damnation (Theophilus, Cipriano) to religious conversion, martyrdom and salvation." There is also the same emphasis on horror found in Spanish saints' plays. Theophilus kills his daughters on stage and then describes the torments of hell that he wishes upon them (3.2.115–24). Dorothea is beheaded on stage in 4.3.179. Theophilus soliloquizes on the torments he inflicted on Christians in Great Britain:

> A thousand wiues with brats sucking their brests,
> Had hot Irons pinch 'em off, and throwne to swine;
> And then their fleshy backparts hewed with hatchets,
> Were minc'd and bak'd in Pies to feede staru'd Christians.
>
> (5.1.20–23)[7]

And he continues in this vein for many more lines. A rack is actually brought on stage at 5.2.189, and Dioclesian describes in great detail the torments that await Theophilus before he is actually put to the torture on stage at 5.2.206.

In this play one also finds some of the supernatural effects that one has come to expect in a Spanish hagiographical drama. For example, "*Enter* Harpax *in a fearefull shape, fire flashing out of the study*" (5.1.123). And the play ends with "*Exit Angelo, the diuell sinks with lightning.*"

But the question remains: why was *The Virgin Martyr* the only hagiographical play in Elizabethan England? According to Walter Cohen (1985, 375) "Massinger's possible crypto-Catholicism may explain the work's anomalous position as the sole post-Reformation saint's play on the London stage." For her part, Louise Clubb (1964, 120) believes that "Massinger . . . must have realized that in England the central conflict of *The Virgin Martyr* would be apt for broad allegorical interpretation. . . . Only in a Protestant country could the representation of struggle between a saint and the state religion suggest to a Roman Catholic mind the actual conflict of religious right and wrong." But both Cohen and Clubb seem to forget that the play was coauthored by Thomas Dekker, whose *The Whore of Babylon* presents a diametrically opposite view of the Catholic Church. As Larry S. Champion (1985, 106) points out, if one is to accept *The Virgin Martyr* as a piece of Catholic propaganda one must assume "both an incredible lapse on the part of the English censors and a remarkable flexibility on the part of Dekker." Textual evidence seems to support Champion's view. For example,

Dorothea's attack on the image of worship (5.1.162–86) must have been seen by a contemporary audience as an attack on Catholic devotional practices. And when in the next scene a pagan priest enters "with the Image of Iupiter, Incense and Censors" (3.2.32), the audience could not but have been reminded once again of Catholic usage. The play, it seems to me, can be seen as defending Christianity against paganism, but not the Catholic Church against the Reformed English Church.

But the most important factor accounting for the very existence of *The Virgin Martyr* has to do not with the similarities it shares with Spanish plays but with the differences that separate them. And the most fundamental of these concerns its religious content. George Price (1969, 95–96) is right when, referring to *The Virgin Martyr,* he remarks that "the religiosity of the play has been detached from the specific doctrines and symbols of Christian faith which arouse imagination and feeling." For this critic, Dekker and Massinger "have lost touch with or have put aside theology." What one has in *The Virgin Martyr* is a play that is religious only on the surface. Its message is embodied in Theophilus' words to Angelo:

> Teach me what I must do, and do doe well,
> That my last act, the best may Paralell.
>
> (5.1.171–72)

It is a play, then, about the apotheosis of a saint, not about religion. The religious element in *The Virgin Martyr* takes the form of a simple and clear struggle between good and evil, represented on stage by Angelo and Harpax. There is in it no dramatic theology, no examination of a religious truth or theological principle. There is no challenge to the religious understanding of its audience. No new insight into religious truth is evinced by it. The spectators come out knowing as much as they did before they went in. Dorothea could just as well have been a Roman matron or a Greek priestess dying for her beliefs for all the difference the play makes to the religious sensibility of its audience.

What distinguishes a good Spanish hagiographical play, such as *El Purgatorio de San Patricio* or *El esclavo del demonio,* from *The Virgin Martyr* is precisely that its plot, the life of a saint, is in a sense a pretext to present on stage an exploration or poetic examination of some theological or religious principle.[8] Speaking of Lope's hagiographical dramas, Duncan Moir (Wilson and Moir 1971, 55) felt that many of them frequently contained subtle theology. These plays, then, are religious dramas in the sense that the real focus is not the saint or his antagonist but the divine or Christian background.

This background often contains a hidden meaning, a subtext, which the reader or spectator is supposed to discover by himself. According to B. W. Wardropper (1983, 191), "la verdad divina es el asunto de las comedias religiosas [de Calderón] . . . Pero supuesto que la verdad divina es también un misterio, se trata de un asunto destinado no ya a la interpretación pero sí a la dilucidación" ("Divine truth is the subject matter of Calderóns religious plays. But, since Divine truth is also a mystery, this subject matter has to be, not interpreted, but elucidated"). In elucidating the religious meaning of *El mágico prodigioso*, A. A. Parker (1968, 320) came up with the following conclusion: "The main idea is that of freedom"— namely that human beings are free to choose the higher (or spiritual) good instead of the lower (or sensual) one. The play associates freedom with *knowledge:* one is not free to resist passion unless one knows that there is a higher good. And knowledge is contrasted with ignorance: since knowledge means freedom, ignorance means the absence of freedom, or more properly the nonexercise of the will's freedom." For his part, Ziomek (1984, 79, 95) believes that *La fianza satisfecha (A Bond Honoured)* "expresses the irony in the relationship between Christian Providence and free will" and that Tirso's trilogy *La Santa Juana* (Saint Joan) "reflects a different stage of mysticism: (Saint Joan) the purgative, the illuminative and the unitive."

What are the religious meanings of *El Purgatorio de San Patricio* and of *El esclavo del demonio?* What religious truths do they explore?

Calderón's *El Purgatorio de San Patricio,* based on a short story by Juan Pérez de Montalbán, tells the uncomplicated story of Saint Patrick's conversion of the pagan Irish. In the opinion of some critics (Valbuena Briones 1974, 313; Dixon 1976, 154), the play's central theme is the evangelization of Ireland. From this perspective *El Purgatorio* can be considered a dramatic illustration of Saint Augustine's ideas on religious epistemology. Saint Augustine believed that there are two sources of religious knowledge: authority and reason, but only one way of acquiring full understanding of the mysteries of the Christian faith: divine illumination (Portalié 1975, 107–17). In accordance with these ideas, the first half of *El Purgatorio de San Patricio* is devoted to the presentation of Saint Patrick's credentials in order to establish his authority as a Christian witness. This takes two forms: a positive analogy between Saint Patrick's life and that of Christ, and a negative analogy between the actions and thoughts of Patrick on stage and those of the pagan characters and of Ludovico, a Christian in name but a pagan in deeds and attitudes.

The role of reason is next exemplified by the theological discussion that takes place, significantly, in the middle of the second act between the saint and King Egerio. The discussion centers on two aspects of the Christian faith: the immortality of the soul and the existence of reward and punishment in the next life—the two aspects most directly relevant to the pagan Irish.

Finally, the role of divine illumination is illustrated in a most subtle way in act 3 through the description Ludovico gives of his experiences in the cave of Purgatory of Saint Patrick. As I have argued elsewhere (1983), a comparison between Ludovico's experiences in the Purgatory as told in Montalbán's short story and in Calderón's play reveals subtle but significant differences. Calderón emphasizes the fact that once in the cave Ludovico saw "una luz, que no era luz" ("a light that was no light") with his eyes closed, that he then fell asleep, and that he thought ("me pareció") he fell into a deep well. In other words, unlike Montalbán, Calderón makes it quite clear that Ludovico did not actually visit the infernal regions in body and soul, as the legend seems to imply. This would have been in contravention of both natural and divine law, as attested by the fact that, according to the Bible, even Christ had to die before his descent to Hell. Calderón felt the need to provide a satisfactory and theologically sound explanation of the strange experience of the Purgatory, and he did so by implying that the "luz que no era luz" which Ludovico saw there was simply the "incorporeal light of a special kind" with which God bathes the soul at the moment of "divine illumination," while the "sombras" and "figuras," which, according to Saint Patrick, one sees in the cave, are the equivalent of the "kind of image" that, according to Saint Augustine, God produces in the soul at the moment of divine illumination. That this is indeed the case is made clear in the play by Ludovico himself when, on hearing a mysterious voice that advises him to go to the Purgatory, he exclaims:

> ¡Válgame el cielo! ¿Qué escucho?
> Acentos son sonorosos;
> iluminación parece
> del cielo, que misterioso
> da auxilios al pecador.

> (2437–41)[9]

[Heaven help me! What do I hear? It's a beautiful sound; it seems to be an illumination from heaven, which, in its mysterious ways, is trying to help a sinner.]

As is the case with divine illumination, Ludovico's vision in the Purgatory leads him, and through him his audience, to a deeper perception and understanding of the mysteries of the Christian faith. Accepted by the people of Ireland on the strength of Saint Patrick's authority and his use of reason, these truths' awesome reality can be fully comprehended only by the unearthly light of divine illumination that Ludovico sees in the Purgatory.

The solution to the mystery of what actually happens in the cave is not, however, explicitly stated in the play. It has to be discovered by the reader or spectator. Through the mouth of Saint Patrick, Calderón actually issues them a challenge to do precisely that. Referring to the Purgatory, he says that those who dare enter it

> Verán un amago breve
> de un prodigio dilatado,
> un milagro continuado,
> a cuya grandeza debe
> admiración quien se atreve
> a descifrar su secreto.
>
> (1953–58)

[They shall see a small sign of a great mystery, an everlasting miracle, whose awesomeness will confound him who dares to decipher its secret.]

The play dares one to solve the mystery of the cave so that one may arrive at one's own personal solution and through it come to an unquestioning acceptance of the poetico-theological conception of the Purgatory of Saint Patrick that it offers. One cannot imagine a more effective technique for imparting theological or poetic truths that, by definition, are not susceptible of demonstration in the cold light of pure reason. The poetic and theological truth of the dream the pilgrim experiences in the cave of Saint Patrick has to be felt intuitively in order to be believed and understood. It is a practical demonstration of the Augustinian formula, "credo ut intelligam."[10]

El Purgatorio de San Patricio may be seen, then, as presenting in an artistic and poetically coherent way the orthodox view of the Catholic Church regarding one of its dogmas: the existence of Hell, Purgatory, and Heaven. But not all Spanish hagiographical plays are orthodox in this way. Mira de Amescua's *El esclavo del de-*

monio may surprise audiences in the audacious way in which it dares them to examine the role of reason in helping man to attain salvation.

El esclavo del demonio belongs to the category of hagiographical plays called "de santos y bandoleros" ("saints and bandits") (Parker 1949). It tells the double story of Don Gil de Santarem and of Lisarda. Don Gil is a saintly man who succumbs to temptation on misunderstanding some words he overhears, words he thinks have divine provenance. Despairing of ever being forgiven by God, he becomes a bandit. Lisarda wants to marry the man who killed her brother, against her father's wishes. Faced with the stern opposition of her father, she decides to elope. When Don Gil takes the place of her lover, she despairs of ever being forgiven by her father and society and decides to run away with Don Gil in order to become a bandit like him. The play goes on to tell their extraordinary life of crime, climaxing in a scene in which Don Gil actually sells his soul to the Devil, thus becoming the Devil's slave. Eventually, however, both protagonists repent and, after terrible penance and hardship, are forgiven and attain salvation. It is a complex, extraordinarily compelling, and emotionally disturbing play, which has been interpreted as containing an important moral lesson: the need to yield to a superior power, be it a father in the case of Lisarda or God in the case of Don Gil (Rauchwarger 1976; Moore 1979a; Moore 1979b).

But, as I have argued elsewhere, this view of the play actually raises more questions than it answers.[11] For example, with his passion for revenge, his concern for his own authority, and his total disregard for the wishes of his daughter, Marcelo can hardly be seen as a just and reasonable parent. Can obedience to such a father be encouraged by the play? But perhaps the most problematic aspect of the theme of submission concerns obedience to God. Not because the Christian God may be presented in the play as unjust or irresponsible or as making excessive demands on his creatures, but because of the difficulties characters seem to encounter in understanding and forming a significant relationship with him.

In order to understand his relationship with God, Don Gil uses logic and reason. But an examination of the episodes in the play in which Don Gil attempts to use logic and reason in order to determine what his line of conduct should be shows that he invariably chooses the wrong path or reaches the wrong conclusion. The most obvious example of this occurs during the kledonomancy scene when Don Gil accepts the words his servant Domingo utters in his sleep as evidence that he is already damned. The unlikely dialogue that takes place between Don Gil and the sleeping Domingo serves to show that it is precisely Don Gil's intellectual efforts to make logical sense of the words he hears that leads to the misunderstanding. This misunderstanding has, however, deep psychological roots. Don Gil's unconscious desire to sin forces the misinterpretation. The structure of the play encourages the reader or spectator to conclude, not that Don Gil sins because, as he claims, he believes he is damned, but that he unconsciously wants to believe that he is damned so as to remove the only barrier separating him from the fulfillment of his repressed desire to sin. One outstanding feature of *El esclavo del demonio* is precisely the way in which characters use logic and reason to talk themselves into giving free rein to their basest instincts and passions. Mira has created a world where, instead of reason controlling passion, reason is misused in order to justify indulgence in passion. The play shows that logic, or the power of reasoning, can be a very dangerous weapon indeed. Logic is mostly responsible for the many tragic misunderstandings that occur in the play, as well as for Don Gil's sin and Lisarda's fall.

How, then, is one to find the path of righteousness and salvation? Paradoxically, the text of *El esclavo del demonio* persuades one that this path is best found by following one's instincts rather than one's reason. The best examples of how instinctive actions lead to conversion and eventual salvation are provided by the main protagonists, Lisarda and Don Gil. When the disguised Lisarda suddenly kneels in front of her father and asks him to forgive her in act 2, she is reacting out of pure instinct. Unlike her previous actions, this one is not preceded by any reasoning process. Yet, ironically, it is this action that sets her on the right path to salvation. It is the same with Don Gil, who will find salvation only by listening to his emotions rather than to his reason. His first impulsive act also occurs in act 2 when, struck by the beauty of Lisarda's sister, Leonor, he persuades Lisarda to spare her life. Whereas all of Don Gil's intellectual cogitation only led him to a belief in predestination and to a life of crime, his irrational feeling of love for Leonor will, paradoxically, lead to his eventual salvation. Transformed from intellectual into emotional beings, both Lisarda and Don Gil can then receive the gift of grace, which will make their salvation possible. It seems as if, in the world of this play, divine grace can only descend on characters who find themselves in a state of primitive innocence, in close contact with their feelings and emotions.

In his *Drama and the Dramatic,* S. Dawson (1970, 79) remarks that "literature is concerned with concepts in an entirely different way from philosophy. In literature the concern with concepts is primarily ironic, for irony is the mode of showing how the complexity of experience makes necessary a continual re-examination of our conceptual language, to check it, as it were, against the way things are, or may be." In other words, good literature has a tendency to subvert philosophy—or theology, for, with its insatiable curiosity to explore the dark side of our conceptual language, literature will inevitably manage to turn any established idea or belief upside down, just to see what the other side looks like. With its peculiar rhetoric, literature will attempt to persuade an audience, at least until the play is over or the last page of the book has been turned, to accept ideas that are not susceptible of demonstration in the cold light of reason, but that contain a certain ineffable poetic truth. The central poetic idea of *El esclavo del demonio* runs counter to the Thomistic reliance on reason as an aid in matters of faith and would probably have been rejected, not as heretical but simply as misguided, by theologians in seventeenth-century Spain. This is why Mira de Amescua decided that it was worth exploring in fiction. Calderón's explanation of Ludovico's experiences in the Purgatory of Saint Patrick probably lacks a theologically sound basis, and his demonstration of the phenomenon of divine illumination would probably have been dismissed by contemporary theologians, but the play persuades viewers to accept that, if it did not happen quite that way, here at least was a satisfyingly clear and poetically convincing account of the enigma of the Irish cave.

Both plays offer explanations of mysteries of the Christian faith that are poetically persuasive and intellectually challenging, even if at odds with more rigorous or orthodox interpretations. This is precisely what differentiates them from *The Virgin Martyr* and sets them a notch or two above the only English hagiographical play. It may also provide an explanation of why no more plays of this sort were written or produced in England during this period. If the English religious climate during the Elizabethan period actively discouraged the kind of religious speculation that we have seen in both *El esclavo del demonio* and *El Purgatorio de San Patricio*, it is no wonder that *The Virgin Martyr* is the only play of its kind. Compliance with religious orthodoxy tends to produce dull literature. In Spain, on the other hand, the genre was vibrantly alive because, *pace* the Inquisition, and provided one left certain inviolable "truths" alone, polemical discussion on religious matters remained a passionate activity.

Notes

1. Nor in France, since Boileau declared that "Une merveille absurde est pour moi sans appas" (*Art poétique,* 49). Very little has been written on these plays; see,

however, Romeu (1957); Aragonese Terni (1970), and Garassa (1960). The first dramatizations of the lives of saints in Spanish literature are probably those found in the fifteenth-century *misterios*. An important collection of 95 dramas written approximately between 1550 and 1575 and published by Leo Rouanet in 1901 already contains twelve plays dealing with the lives of saints. However, the plays generally considered as the forerunners of the seventeenth-century *comedias de santos* are Micael de Carvajal's *Tragedia llamada Josefina (A Tragedy Called Josephine)* (1535) and Bartolomé Palau's *Historia de la gloriosa Santa Orosia (History of the Glorious Saint Orosia)* (1550?).

2. Lope de Vega wrote a few *comedias de santos*, ranging from *El divino Africano*, dealing with the life of Saint Augustine and based on his *Confessions*, to the lives of Saint Genesius, patron saint of actors; Saint Isidro, patron saint of Madrid; Saint Diego de Alcalá; Saint Nicolás de Tolentino; and many others. Tirso composed some of them too: *Los lagos de San Vicente (The Lakes of Saint Vincent)*, the trilogy of *La Santa Juana 1, (Saint Joan 1)*, *Santo y sastre 2 (Saint and Tailor 2)* (on the life of Saint Homobono), and *El mayor desengaño (The Greatest Disenchantment)* (on Saint Bruno, founder of the Carthusian Order).

3. Quoted by Campbell (1959, 142, n. 1).

4. Two *Flos Sanctorum* available to them would have been those composed by Alonso de Villegas (published in 5 vols. between 1580 and 1603) and by Pedro de Rivadeneyra (published 1599).

5. All references to *El esclavo del demonio* are to the critical edition by James A. Castañeda (Madrid: Cátedra, 1980).

6. Line 807 of the version published by The Malone Society Reprints (Oxford University Press, 1926).

7. All quotations are from the critical edition by Fredson Bowers (Cambridge: Cambridge University Press, 1966).

8. Teresa Ferrer Valls (1986, 177) states, in reference to Gaspar de Aguilar's hagiographical play *La vida y muerte del santo Fray Luis Bertrán (Life and Death of Friar Luis Bertrón)*, that its author "sabía que lo que importaba era el impacto ideológico provocado en el espectador y no la fidelidad a cualquiera de las relaciones que sobre la vida de Bertrán se habían escrito" ("knew that what mattered was the ideological impact on the spectator, and not to remain faithful to any of the accounts of Saint Bertran's life that had been written"). Not all Spanish hagiographical plays were, however, religious in this sense. J. L. Sirera, (1986, 224), believes that in Gaspar de Aguilar's *El gran Patriarca don Juan de Ribera (The Great Patriarch, Don Juan de Ribera)* religion is of little consequence.

9. All quotations are from my critical edition of *El Purgatorio de San Patricio* (Liverpool: Liverpool University Press, 1988).

10. For a full analysis of this play see the Introduction to my critical edition of *El Purgatorio de San Patricio*.

11. See my introduction to *El esclavo del demonio. The Devil's Slave*, translated by Michael McGaha (Ottawa: Dovehouse, 1989).

Works Cited

Aragonese Terni, E. 1970. *Studi sulle "comedias de santos" de Lope de Vega*. Messina: D'Anna.

Barrera y Leirado, Cayetano Alberto de la. 1860. *Catálogo bibliográfico y biográfico del teatro antiguo español*. Madrid: Rivadeneyra.

Calderón de la Barca, Pedro. 1988. *El purgatorio de San Patricio.* Edited by J. M. Ruano de la Haza. Liverpool: Liverpool University Press.

Campbell, L. B. 1959. *Divine Poetry and Drama in Sixteenth-Century England.* Berkeley: University of California Press.

Champion, Larry S. 1985. *Thomas Dekker and the Traditions of English Drama.* New York: Peter Lang.

Clubb, Louise G. 1964. "*The Virgin Martyr* and the *Tragedia Sacra.*" *Renaissance Drama* 7:103–26.

Cohen, Walter. 1985. *Drama of a Nation.* Ithaca: Cornell University Press.

Dawson, S. 1970. *Drama and the Dramatic.* London: Methuen.

Dekker, Thomas. 1966. *The Dramatic Works of Thomas Dekker.* Edited by Fredson Bowers. Cambridge: Cambridge University Press.

Dixon, Victor F. 1976. "Saint Patrick of Ireland and the Dramatists of Golden Age Spain." *Hermathena* 121:142–58.

Ferrer Valls, Teresa. 1986. "Producción municipal, fiestas y comedia de santos: La canonización de San Luis Bertrán en Valencia". In *Teatro y prácticas escénicas. II: La Comedia,* edited by J. L. Canet Vallés, 156–86. London: Tamesis.

Garassa, D. L. 1960. *Santos en escena: estudio sobre el teatro hagiográfico de Lope de Vega.* Bahía Blanca: Universidad Nacional del Sur.

Gardiner, H. C. 1946. *Mysteries' End: An Investigation of the Last days of the Medieval Religious Stage.* New Haven: Yale University Press.

Mira de Amescua, Antonio. 1980. *El esclavo del demonio.* Edited by James A. Castañeda. Madrid: Cátedra.

———. 1989. *The Devil's Slave.* Translated by Michael D. McGaha. Introduction by J. M. Ruano de la Haza. Ottawa: Dovehouse.

Moore, Roger. 1979a. "Appearance (Evil) and Reality (Good) as Elements of Thematic Unity in Mira de Amescua's *El esclavo del demonio.*" *Perspectivas de la Comedia* 2:79–80.

———. b. "Leonor's Role in *El esclavo del demonio*". *Revista Canadiense de Estudios Hispánicos* 3:275–86.

Parker, A. A. 1968. "The Role of the *Graciosos* in *El mágico prodigioso.*" In *Litterae Hispanae et Lusitanae,* edited by Hans Flasche, 317–30. Munich: Max Hueber.

———. 1949. "Santos y bandoleros en el teatro español del Siglo de Oro." *Arbor* 13:395–416.

Portalié, Eugène. 1975. *A Guide to the Thought of Saint Augustine.* Translated by Ralph J. Bastian. Westport: Greenwood Press.

Price, George R. 1969. *Thomas Dekker.* New York: Twayne.

Rauchwarger, Judith. 1976. "Principal and Secondary Plots in *El esclavo del demonio.*" *Bulletin of the Comediantes* 28:49–52.

Rojas, Agustín de. 1972. *Viaje entretenido.* Edited by J. P. Ressot. Madrid: Castalia.

Romeu, J. 1957. *Teatre hagiogràfic.* Barcelona: Barcino.

Ruano de la Haza, J. M. 1983. "El sueño de *El Purgatorio de San Patricio.*" In *Actas del Congreso Internacional sobre Calderón y el teatro español del Siglo de Oro,* edited by Luciano García Lorenzo, 617–27. Madrid: C.S.I.C.

Ruiz Ramón, Francisco. 1967. *Historia del teatro español desde sus orígenes hasta 1900.* Madrid: Alianza.

Sirera, J. L. 1986. "Las 'comedias de santos' en los autores valencianos. Notas para su estudio." In *Teatro y prácticas escénicas. 2: La Comedia,* edited by J. L. Canet Vallés, 187–227. London: Tamesis.

Traister, Barbara H. 1984. *Heavenly Necromancers: The Magician in English Renaissance Drama.* Columbia: University of Missouri Press.

Valbuena Briones, A. 1974. "La extraña contrariedad en la armonía del mundo." In *Estudios literarios de hispanistas norteamericanos dedicados a Helmut Hatzfeld,* edited J. M. Solá-Solé et al., 309–21. Barcelona: Hispam.

Wardropper, B. W. 1983. "Las comedias religiosas de Calderón." In *Actas del Congreso Internacional sobre Calderón y el teatro español del Siglo de Oro,* edited by Luciano García Lorenzo, 185–98. Madrid: C.S.I.C.

Wilson, E. M. and Duncan Moir. 1971. *A Literary History of Spain. The Golden Age: Drama, 1492–1700.* London: Ernest Benn.

Ziomek, Henryk. 1984. *A History of Spanish Golden Age Drama.* Lexington: The University of Kentucky Press.

4
Unifying Myths

Metamorphosis as Challenge in the Theater of Calderón

Thomas Austin O'Connor

Introduction

In the fantastic world of fairies and spirits, strange and magical transformations of form do not rely on an overly credulous audience for acceptance, but on the creation of a verisimilar context for their presentation. When Bottom appears sporting the head of an ass in *A Midsummer Night's Dream,* his metamorphosis is totally congruent with that world ruled by Oberon, Titania, and Puck. Even in the more serious *The Tempest,* Ariel, "an airy spirit," is a believable denizen of the fantastic environment dominated by Prospero and peopled by the masquelike goddesses Iris, Ceres, and Juno. For some writers such a fantastic world becomes an abiding mode of expression, due perhaps not to personal preference, but to the conventions of the artistic forms in which they operate. The Jonsonian masque appears far removed from the satiric world of his drama. Once we realize that, in Stephen Orgel's words, "the transition from antimasque to masque is a metamorphosis" (Jonson 1970, 8) then one begins to understand the structural principles governing this artistic form. Contrary to drama's vicarious experience of what is performed on the stage, "Every masque," again according to Orgel, "concluded by merging spectator with masquer, in effect transforming the courtly audience into the idealized world of the poet's vision" (2). In Calderonian myth plays metamorphosis is not a structural function demanded by the form, but rather an outcome sanctioned by the traditional plot. Anyone who peruses Ovid's *Metamorphoses* recognizes very quickly that these myths, so brilliantly woven together by the poet, inspire reflection on selfhood and love in their various guises. When a metamorphosis occurs in Calderonian drama, we need to examine its organic function within the plot instead of looking for a rigidly systematic principle that triggers its appearance. What is a vital formula in Jonson becomes in Calderón a critical challenge to one's apprehension of dramatic experience.

In a recent study of Ovid and his influence, Leonard Barkan (1986) has observed that "metamorphosis is an outward sign that the ties that bind have been loosed. As such it proves that the moral freak is a physical freak. . . . metamorphosis is the destination for those who live by the passions" (66). Whereas for Jonson transformation represents a structural problem to be solved, for Ovid and Calderón it stands as a narrative outcome to be accounted for. Calderón discovered the dramatic potential of the metamorphic act just as Ovid realized its poetic potentiality. Both these artists have demonstrated, moreover, the enormous creative power contained in these narratives of metamorphosis. Barkan, in referring to the "darkest side of Ovid's poem," sheds light on the allure that such an artist as Calderón felt challenged to incorporate in his myth plays. Barkan speaks about "that realm where metamorphosis is fused with the perversions of love and family relations as well as with abominations that range from exogamy to cannibalism" (247). What separates the Ovidian and Calderonian uses of metamorphosis from the Shakespearean is the position they occupy in the respective narratives. The English dramatist is, in Barkan's words, "more interested in transformation as a cause than in transformation as an effect" (257). For this reason Bottom's metamorphosis occurs before the final curtain and furthers the plot line. Ovidian and Calderonian metamorphoses are tragic rather than comic and serve as stylized memorials to human suffering and destruction. The critical taxonomy I have established for Calderonian metamorphoses is an outgrowth of the analysis of their dramatic function, which, as I have stated, operates organically and not prescriptively within his works.

Metamorphosis as Outrage

In Calderón's *Fortunas de Andrómeda y Perseo (Fortunes of Andromeda and Perseus)* the metamorphosis of Medusa forms part of the background action to the play. Neptune's rape of Medusa in Minerva's temple led to the goddess's cruel vengeance on the victim. The beautiful golden hair that first attracted Neptune is converted by Minerva into curling snakes. The victim, however, becomes victimizer as Medusa avenges her unjust punishment on hapless wayfarers. This rape of the innocent Medusa symbolically conveys the emotional and psychological impact of rape on the woman herself. Twice victimized by the powerful gods, Medusa's transformation into a monster undercuts the notion of metamorphosis as punishment by revealing the arbitrary world of the gods. Where there is no justice, chance rules the world. Ovid reminded us: "non bene conveniunt nec in una sede morantur / maiestas et amor" (*Metamorphoses* 2. 846–47). Calderón's consistent position on rape as a transforming act is sanctioned by classical authority and alerts us to the fact that, as Barkan observed, "myths of magical change, again and again, will be stories celebrating the unfamiliar forms of the sexual impulse, with all their terror and allure" (13).

Metamorphosis as Escape

In two plays Calderón employs metamorphosis as escape from danger. *Celos, aun del aire, matan (Even jealousy of the air kills)* depicts the transformation of Aura into a nymph of the air. As Diana was about to punish this passionate girl who had profaned her temple, Venus intervened to save one of her own, but at a cost. Aura's incorporeal state makes clear the price paid for her rescue— the loss of personhood. Such a resolution becomes the motivating idea behind Calderón's *El laurel de Apolo (Apollo's laurel)*, where Daphne's rescue from the god's attempted rape stands ambiguously as both salvation and perdition. When Daphne is transformed into a laurel tree, we recognize once again the arbitrariness that governs the pagan world. There is neither justice nor law ruling over this world dominated by power and passion.

Metamorphosis as Punishment

In Ben Jonson's masque *The Golden Age Restored,* Pallas metamorphoses Iron Age and his evils, thereby demonstrating that, with this punitive transformation to stone, the way is now prepared for the return of Astraea and the Golden Age. In Calderón the punitive metamorphosis serves a more dramatic function by creating self-consciousness, because, according to Barkan, "it establishes a tension between identity and form, and through this tension the individual is compelled to look in the mirror" (46). In *La fiera, el rayo y la piedra (The beast, the thunderbolt, and the stone)*, Anaxarete consciously experiences her transformation to stone as she plans the murder of Iphis. The character is forced to confront the

unnatural direction of her life as she realizes that Venus is avenging
this mortal's hardheartedness, for "la que querer no sabe / más es
mármol que mujer" ("she who does not know how to love is more
marble than woman") (1635a).[1] The *gracioso* Lebrón's comment on
Anaxarete's metamorphosis is a distancing remark that undermines
transformation as reality but not as drama. Believing that the stone
statue should be placed over a fountain, he says:

> Mejor ponerla allí es;
> que no faltará otro bobo
> que la convierta en mujer.
>
> (1636a)

[It is better to place it over there, because we shall not lack another fool
eager to transform it back to woman.]

As the structural counterpart to Pygmalion's transforming and vivifying love, Anaxarete's punishment reveals to her and to us the
dehumanizing character of her barren and egocentric life. Her cold-
blooded plan to take Iphis's life becomes her destiny as hatred
drains away her human personality.

Metamorphosis as personal destiny takes an interesting turn in *El
golfo de las Sirenas (The sirens' gulf)*. First of all, both Scylla and
Charybdis are victims of masculine excesses, and their current
state as destroyers of men must be viewed in this context. Secondly,
the farcical concluding *mojiganga* suggests that metamorphosis is
not only a transformation of nature, but also a revelation of
character. The suicide of these two vengeful women ratifies the
destiny of their hate-dominated lives as they are transformed into
reefs, stone bariers to navigation, that will claim many a mariner's
life. While suicide is a self-directed and life-denying act, what is
important in this instance is the motivation of frustration behind it:
Scylla and Charybdis cannot satisfy their hatred of Ulysses and
thirst for his blood. Their punishment, curiously enough, is self-
inflicted, a situation Calderón used many years earlier to account
for Circe's retribution. Metamorphosis in *El golfo de las Sirenas* is a
negative image of those tragic deaths depicted by Ovid where
unending love defies annihilation. Scylla's and Charybdis's transformations stand as a memorial to death and hatred.

In *Apolo y Climene (Apollo and Clymene)* we find the clearest
and most straightforward presentation of metamorphosis as punishment. Clytie, Zephyrus, and Flora are transformed by Apollo into
sunflower, wind, and flower as a result of their calumny of Clymene.
This just retribution ironically contributes to the eventual realiza-

tion of Phaethon's fate. Thus, while one series of actions comes to a close, the plot is now prepared to advance, in a second part, along different and truly tragic lines. Calderón's penchant for unusual and surprising twists in his plots is also evident in *El laurel de Apolo,* previously examined as an example of metamorphosis as escape. From the perspective of the plot line of that play, Daphne's metamorphosis indeed serves as punishment, but, interestingly enough, as Cupid's punishment of Apollo's haughtiness. In this manner Cupid uses Daphne as a means of avenging an insult received from Apollo and his followers. Caught in a male power struggle, Daphne is dehumanized by two powerful and ruthless gods who surrender themselves to base passions.

Metamorphosis as Loss of Personhood

El laurel de Apolo reminds us that each metamorphosis signifies a loss, a loss of life, identity, and future. Besides the instrumental role Daphne plays in Cupid's revenge, her tragic transformation reveals a direction in her orientation toward life that is thematically reinforced by a premetamorphic hatred of all living things. Such varied interpretative possibilities for this play problematize our experience of the dramatic action, enriching thereby the work's significance and signifying operation. In such transformations there is no apotheosis, no triumph, no glory—only suffering and loss. At the conclusion to *El hijo del Sol, Faetón (Phaethon, son of the sun)* Clymene, Galatea, and the naiads are transformed into white poplars, symbols of their suffering and loss, as they witness Phaethon's fiery destruction. Since poplar trees distil amber, this substance now signifies the tears these distraught women are no longer capable of shedding—their suffering is too great. At the same time as Clymene's metamorphosis stands for her lament over her son's death, it represents a form of punishment for her prior transgression. Clymene is guilty of having fornicated with Apollo in Diana's temple, and her guilt, while it explains to some degree her punishment and death, only raises a more fundamental issue concerning a child's involvement in the guilt of his parents.[2] At the conclusion to the play, the *gracioso* Batillo emits one of those distancing remarks that refers at one and the same time to Phaethon's supposed presumption and to the metamorphoses of his mother, lover, and sisters. While presumption is indeed dangerous, Batillo states, so is metamorphosis. Since only fools believe in transformation, discreet people alone are capable of understanding the message of such a

play as *El hijo del Sol, Faetón*. And what is that message? The
answer lies not in the traditional allegorical explication of the plot,
but in its narrative significance that problematizes dramatic experience.

Eco y Narciso (Echo and Narcissus) is a tragic masterpiece that
typifies the full import of metamorphosis as loss. Leonard Barkan
has observed that "time and again, the metamorphic myths revolve
around the discovery of that newly isolated identity" (15). Narcissus's discovery of who he is leads to his death as well as to
Echo's. Once more the social context of tragedy, so evident in *El
hijo del Sol, Faetón*, distinguishes this play. One could argue, however, that the concluding metamorphoses of Narcissus into a flower
and Echo into a repetitious voice are apotheoses of the two characters, mitigating, therefore, their deaths. But all the characters remark that both heaven and earth are moved by the tragic deaths.
The *gracioso* Bato comments on the events recently transpired,
reminding audiences that only simpletons believe in fables. Transformation is change, but in the two metamorphoses that just occurred one is left only with memorials to the loss of two beautiful
young people. What should have been rites of passage to mature
adulthood and full sexuality—metamorphoses of a different kind—
are converted into funereal rites or stylized grief.

Metamorphosis as Apotheosis

Eco and Narciso raises a fundamental issue concerning the
nature of metamorphosis and whether change is positive, negative,
or possibly both. For Daphne, transformation was the result of her
desire to flee rape and accept death before dishonor. While the plot
is unambivalent in this regard, its interpretation, nevertheless, is
more ambiguous. There are only two plays in which metamorphoses are unambiguous and classifiable as apotheoses. In the
first, *Ni Amor se libra de amor (Not even Love is free from love)*,
Psyche becomes Cupid's wife and thus the goddess of love, but only
after many peripeties that are truly life-threatening. While the
apotheosis is a natural outcome of Cupid's dignifying love, what
prepares and foreshadows Psyche's transformation is Cupid's figurative transformation. His great love of this mortal converts him
from childish prankster into mature lover and husband. Barkan
considers apotheosis to be a typically Roman form of metamorphosis: "Like the final change of Vertumnus, apotheosis is a
metamorphosis that denies metamorphosis, producing a trans-

figured form of the individual that is and is not the human self" (82). In Psyche's case she obviously retains her personhood while at the same time she is elevated to the stature of godhead. Rather than loss, her transformation is gain. Likewise, Pygmalion's love of a stone statue in *La fiera, el rayo y la piedra,* while irrational and ludicrous, nonetheless symbolizes the ennobling and humanizing virtue in passionate love. Love is power, and Barkan states that in Pygmalion's case "the effect of that love is in turn a metamorphosis which justifies and purifies his love" (303, n. 52). Although love is only whole and vivifying when directed and oriented toward the other—a lesson Narcissus learnt too late—its other dimension involves the transformation realized within the lover himself— Cupid's great lesson. If Pygmalion appears to debase and dehumanize himself in loving some*thing* not human, we are foolish to hold such an opinion for it discounts love's transformational powers, exaggerated, of course, by the myth. What these two myths dramatize is the miraculous transformational power of mutual love, and for this reason they are apotheosic, celebrating life and goodness.

There are two plays whose final metamorphoses appear to be apotheoses. In each case there is tribute to love that defies death, but neither contains that wholeness and miraculous power found in apotheosic love. These transformations are significant critical challenges, principally due to the poetic manner in which they stylize human experience and response to loss. First of all, *La púrpura de la rosa (The rose's purple)* is an opera whose metamorphoses of Venus into a star and Adonis into a flower occur after the deaths of goddess and mortal. The play attempts to mitigate tragedy's horror ("El horror de la tragedia," 1783a) through metamorphic legerdemain. In spite of an apparent transcendence of death, there is an indelible trace of loss symbolized by the descent from goddess and man to star and flower. Venus's adulterous love of Adonis was doomed to failure right from the start, and Mars's jealous ire proves that his drive for vengeance is more powerful than the pair's flawed love. One is in the world of tragedy where guilt contaminates what in other circumstances would have been a good and wholesome relationship. The reason the metamorphoses cannot be called apotheoses is that the apparent glorification of the pair comes at the cost of the loss of their souls. Adonis's miraculous birth from the bitter myrrh tree, from a mother who seduced her own father, reveals metamorphosis as a prophetic sign for her son's life, tainting it with her own tragic experience. Myrrha's metamorphosis signals death, loss, and punishment with generational reach—a phenomenon on which the Bible and Saint Augustine comment extensively (Augustine 1948, 1:685). One problem this myth highlights concerns the deadly effect of passion on those who illicitly "love" one another. In the case of Venus and Adonis, passion cannot be transformed into love, and herein lies the cause of their tragedy, for their passion was deadly and fateful and neither dignifying, as in Psyche's case, nor life-giving, as in Pygmalion's Statue's. As erotic passion, their "love" is self-directed and thus ultimately, like that of Narcissus, barren and egocentric self-regard.[3]

The second example of apparent apotheosis occurs in *Celos, aun del aire, matan (Even jealousy of the air kills)*. In this opera the nymph Aura states that Venus and Jupiter order that the tragedy of Cephalus's and Procris's exquisite love be reformed without the horror of tragedy ("sin el horror de tragedia", 1813b), a phrase reminiscent of a similar statement in *La púrpura de la rosa*. I have already discussed Aura's metamorphosis as an example of escape. Procris's transformation into a star and Cephalus's into the wind Zephyrus are much more pathetic and problematic. The principal reason for this assertion is grounded in the *gracioso* Rustic's metamorphoses into various animals: a lion, bear, wolf, tiger, and greyhound. While the comic buffoon fears "demetamorphosis," his negative and burlesque experiences serve as a foil to the transformations of the noble characters. His ridiculous metamorphoses undercut the notion of transformation as apotheosis, an ennobling and dignifying act, by laying bare the fact that it represents a loss, a degradation, a descent in the great chain of being. One reason Rustic's various metamorphoses are so comic is because they are temporary; the others are permanent. In spite of the fact that the dramatist sought to mitigate the horror of tragedy, the loss of human life, and the pain of human suffering, tragedy's marks prove to be indelible. Where Diana is an avenging presence and where Aura seeks retribution for her own betrayal by Procris, love cannot triumph; only pathetic tribute may be paid to it. Although the dénouement stylizes audience response, memory cannot be erased nor cajoled into forgetting so much suffering.

Burlesque Metamorphosis

Rustic's comic experience in *Celos, aun del aire, matan* reminds one that only if metamorphosis were temporary could its negative effects be avoided. Whereas poetic will attempts to meet such an artistic challenge, the narrative impact of these stories proves to be more powerful and significant than the circumstances of their production. Myth has a way of ambushing those who come under its spell. The transformations of classical mythology are fanciful though false, but they do contain essential truths about human experience. While the *graciosos* distance audiences from belief, they also underscore the myths' truths. In *El laurel de Apolo* a different Rustic is transformed into a tree in order to spy on Daphne. His temporary transformation is a sign of his misfortune, not of his tragedy. The comic experiences he undergoes involve pain and suffering, and his consciousness of change is mitigated solely by the hope of eventual return to normalcy—something impossible for the noble characters. Once the self-consciousness that exploits the tension between identity and form reveals deformation, we possess the thread that leads us through and out of the metamorphic labyrinth. In *El mayor encanto, amor (Love the greatest enchantment)* Circe and Ulysses undergo subtler figurative transformations wrought by illicit passion. As comic foil to this process, Clarion metamorphoses from man to monkey—Circe's punishment for his insulting remarks about the witch. Although Clarion becomes an animal—a state similar to that to which passion has reduced Circe and Ulysses—his "demetamorphosis" serves a predictive function for Ulysses's eventual conversion. The *gracioso* accidentally escapes from his monkey form, but Ulysses's change must be a deliberately conscious act. Here metamorphosis is neither transcendence nor loss, but revelation of reality in a comic register. To further the tragic fate of Phaethon in *Apolo y Climene,* Satyr, who has been witness to Apollo's solicitous love of Clymene, appears at the conclusion of the plot transformed into his namesake, a satyr. Instead of informing the King of what has transpired, he frightens all away. The blind god of light cannot see how he has fallen into a trap set by the malevolent magician Python. Although Satyr's role is to provide comic relief, his metamorphosis stymies communication, thereby preventing revelation. The comic character has become what his life signifies, and, since Satyr was transformed by the magician, he too fails to prevent the continual development of the action in the second part. In this instance comedy has tragic resonances.

Figurative Transformations

Time and space do not permit a detailed examination of what could be labeled figurative transformations that occur in other myth plays, a phenomenon similar to the role of metamorphosis in *El mayor encanto, amor.* In *La estatua de Prometeo (Prometheus' statue)* there is a transformation of a stone statue to the woman Pandora, but the real transformation of the play involves Prometheus' attempt to remake Caucasian society in his image. His failure symbolizes his need for conversion and redemption, his need for Pandora, which eventually allows him to become whole and truly human. In *Los tres mayores prodigios (The three greatest prodigies)* Hercules is literally transformed into living fire, the symbol of his destructive jealousy and of his fear of public opinion. In *Fieras afemina amor (Love makes beasts effeminate)* that same hero is transformed by enervating passion into a passive, womanlike creature with the latest courtly coiffure. Achilles' pseudometamorphosis from woman to warrior takes place in *El monstruo de los jardines (The monster of the gardens),* a play about this youth's rite of passage to manhood and his assumption of the male system of values. The warped code of honor he fully and tragically adopts is dominated by the vengeance motive, and the consequence of its adoption is Achilles' forfeiture of life on the plains of Ilium.[4]

Conclusion

In the illusionistic theater the dramatist is obliged to create a sense of being present as the action unfolds. In the transition from presentational theater, like that of the Globe or a Spanish *corral,* to representational theater, like that staged in the courts of Europe, the dramatist confronted a changing set of conventions that taxed his artistry. With the use of perspective scenery, the proscenium arch, and stage machinery, the dramatic poet who wrote for the court theater had to intensify the oratorical aspects of his craft (Orgel 1975, 20). The plots he chose required great care so that theatrical spectacle would reinforce and heighten poetry rather than detract from it. One reason the myth play proved to be such a rich source of dramatic material is that myth and metamorphosis are sanctioned by classical authority and appeal to the imagination of poets. To stage an unbelievable plot in a realistic and verisimilar manner challenged the dramatist's creative genius and the stage designer's talent. By problematizing the concluding metamorphoses of so many plays, Calderón brought the light of reason to bear on the nature and meaning of metamorphosis, moving one's response away from spectacle, through language, and finally to thought. Metamorphoses appear to operate solely under the aegis of classical authority, but their real strength lies in a powerful appeal to the imagination. If one reaction was to tame and to minimize response through catechismal allegory, myth's own suggestive power could not be so easily controlled. The metamorphic myths challenge audiences continually to deal with them on their terms and not ours. Rather than producing certainty and assurance, oftentimes they create doubt and concern. These narratives indeed celebrate what Barkan denominates "the generative vitality of nature" (136), but they also demonstrate the enormous creative potential of metamorphic narrative to capture and hold fast our imaginations.

Notes

1. All quotations are from Pedro Calderón de la Barca, *Obras completas,* edited by A. Valbuena Briones (Madrid: Aguilar, 1969), cited by page and column. All translations are my own.
2. I have examined this issue in other studies, and it is a significant theme in Calderonian theater as evidenced by *La devoción de la Cruz* and *La vida es sueño.* See Thomas O'Connor (1988).
3. Barkan (1986) classifies Myrrha's metamorphosis as a punishment of passion.
4. There are two plays that take place in remote times and in which the gods play important though subsidiary roles. Since neither dramatizes a classical myth, I will not deal with either. Both *Amado y aborrecido (Loved and detested)* and *Fineza contra fineza (Regard opposed to regard)* are courtly plays that celebrate the transformational power of love, leading to true nobility of character and soul.

Works Cited

Augustine, Saint. 1948. *The Basic Writings of Saint Augustine.* Vol. 1. Edited by Whitney J. Oates. New York: Random House.

Barkan, Leonard. 1986. *The Gods Made Flesh: Metamorphosis and the Pursuit of Paganism.* New Haven: Yale University Press.

Calderón de la Barca, Pedro. 1969. *Obras completas.* Vol. 1. Edited by A. Valbuena Briones. Madrid: Aguilar.

Jonson, Ben. *Selected Masques.* 1970. Edited by Stephen Orgel. New Haven: Yale University Press.

O'Connor, Thomas Austin. 1988. *Myth and Mythology in the Theater of Pedro Calderón de la Barca.* San Antonio: Trinity University Press.

Orgel, Stephen. 1975. *The Illusion of Power: Political Theater in the English Renaissance.* Berkeley: University of California Press.

Ovid. 1977. *Metamorphoses.* Vol. 1. Translated by Frank Justus Miller. Cambridge: Harvard University Press.

"Bequeath to death your numbness, for from him / Dear life redeems you": Calderón, Shakespeare, and Romance

Susan L. Fischer

La vida es sueño (*Life Is a Dream*, 1635), *En la vida todo es verdad y todo mentira* (*Everything in Life is Truth and Illusion*, 1659), and *Hado y divisa de Leonido y Marfisa* ([*The*] *Fate and* [*Heraldic*] *Device of Leonido and Marfisa*, 1680) are three Calderonian plays that reveal a structural core of romance. Few critics, however, have noted the formal parallels between these plays and Shakespeare's four romances—*Pericles* (1608), *Cymbeline* (1609–10), *The Winter's Tale* (1611), and *The Tempest* (1611)—all of which center on the transcendence of tragedy and have plots that involve loss and (re)discovery, division and reconciliation, destruction and renewal.[1] There is a general movement toward the triumph of the principle of eros both in its narrower sense of sexual union and marriage and in its wider meaning of family solidarity and social harmony. Nevertheless, as Howard Felperin (1972, 54) has pointed out, Shakespeare's late works simultaneously temper the ideal or idyllic vision of romance with a strong antiromantic dimension of the real, thereby providing "a stern reprimand of romance (while remaining romance)" and testing to the breaking point not only the characters they contain but the mode they employ. Terry Eagleton (1986, 101) has made the same kind of observation with regard to Shakespeare's entire canon; what he says is especially applicable to the romances: "The complexity of Shakespeare's ideological dilemmas . . . arises from the fact that they do not take the form of 'simple'

This article owes its existence to the uninterrupted time and inspirational theatrical milieu I was able to enjoy at the Colorado Shakespeare Festival in Boulder; and to two performance texts of *The Winter's Tale:* the 1986 Stratford Shakespearean Festival of Canada production, directed by David William; and the 1986 Royal Shakespeare Company production at Stratford-upon-Avon, directed by Terry Hands. I am grateful to Bucknell University for providing a Faculty Development Grant that allowed me to take full advantage of those opportunities.

contradictions, in which each term is polar opposite of the other; on the contrary, in 'deconstructive' fashion, each term seems confusingly to inhere in its antagonist." At the center of this argument is Paul de Man's (1979, 17) (polemical) belief that literary texts are inherently self-deconstruction: ". . . a literary text simultaneously asserts and denies the authority of its own rhetorical mode."[2] In parallel fashion to Shakespeare's late works, *Hado y divisa de Leonido y Marfisa*, Calderón's last play and one that Bruce W. Wardropper (1982, 28) has called an "extravaganza of romantic adventure,"[3] at once illustrates the conventions of romance and, in Felperin's (1972) words with respect to *The Winter's Tale*, examines them "rigorously against the touchstone of brazen reality" (242). In the pages that follow, *Hado y divisa* will be explored not only for the way it fulfills the pattern of romance, but also for the degree to which it addresses the question formulated by Felperin vis-à-vis *The Winter's Tale*: "How do you manage to redeem all sorrow and repair all loss, as the romance form requires, while simultaneously bringing home the abiding sense of sorrow and loss, as they would certainly linger on in life?" (243).

According to Northrop Frye (1976, 53–54), the heroes and villains of romance exist primarily to symbolize a movement between two contrasting domains, one above the level of ordinary experience and the other below it (53). The first is an idyllic world associated with happiness, security, and peace; and the second is a demonic or night world of adventure that involves separation, loneliness, humiliation, and pain. "Reality" for romance is most readily associated with serenity, freedom, and the possession or recovery of identity, whereas "illusion" is mainly linked to anxiety, tyranny, and the absence of identity. Most romances begin with a departure from a state of identity and end with a return to it. Put another way, romance exhibits a cyclical movement of descent into a demonic world and an ascent to an idyllic world, often symbolized by marriage (54). Romance typically begins its series of adventures with some kind of "break in consciousnes," which often involves actual forgetfulness of the previous state, and may be internalized as a rupture in memory or externalized as a change in fortunes or social context (102). The themes and images of ascent are much the same as those of descent but in reverse, for they involve "escape, remembrance, or discovery of one's real identity, growing freedom, and the breaking of enchantment" (129).

Hado y divisa opens with a situation exemplifying Frye's so-called break in consciousness, which leads to the hero's symbolic descent to lower realms that are alternately subterranean and sub-

marine (1976, 148). This rupture is externalized as a disaster that
occurs when the disguised Leonido falls from his horse as he is
being pursued through the sylvan labyrinth of Trinacria (ancient
Sicily) because he has accidentally killed Queen Arminda's brother,
Lisidante, in a tournament.[4] Ironically, he had come to the court of
Trinacria in the hopes of ascending to the favor of Arminda by
challenging whoever had proclaimed Mitilene, an underworld
queen, the most beautiful woman in the world (2101a); and he is
forced at the outset to descend into a night world of confusion and
loss. A hunter turned hunted, he escapes from the dense, dark
forest out to sea and comes ashore on the island of Mitilene, with its
awesome cliffs and caverns and eddies crashing upon the rocks.
With his journey to Trinacria, then, Leonido has initiated a major
adventure or quest, which, according to Frye, has three main
stages: the perilous journey and the preliminary minor adventures;
the crucial struggle, usually some kind of battle in which either the
hero or his foe or both must die; and the recognition and exaltation
of the hero who has clearly proved himself even if he does not
survive the conflict (1968, 187).

The mystery surrounding the hero's identity is stressed from the
very beginning: before fleeing from Trinacria, Leonido searches for
his shield that bears the "divisa" or heraldic emblem which will
serve as a means of recognition, and he tells his faithful servant and
companion, Polidoro, that his identity must remain concealed: "que
me importa más que piensas / que no se sepa quién soy" (2099b)
("that no one discover who I am is more important to me than you
think"). But not even he is certain of his parentage. As the fear-
ridden servant Merlín reveals when captured in Trinacria, Leonido
is "un hijo expósito del hado" (2100b) ("a foundling abandoned to
his fate") whom the Duke of Tuscany has encountered in a cave as
an infant, richly clothed and wearing a medal whose inscription no
one could read. He grew up to be a warrior, having recently been
Landgrave in Tyre in Persia. As Leonido and Polidoro disembark
on the island of Mitilene, they are horrified and frightened by the
chaos they perceive, expressed in terms of confusion among the
natural elements:

> Y más al ver en sus primeras señas
> desnudos riscos de peladas peñas,
> sólo habitadas de funestos troncos
> que de quejarse al ábrego están roncos,
> cuyo susurro perezosas aves,
> graznando tristes y volando graves,

en entrambas esferas
alternan con los ecos de las fieras,
cuatro ruidos uniendo a sólo un ruido
el mar, el aire, el canto y el bramido.

(2103b)

[And more so on seeing among its first characteristics naked crags of rocks stripped bare, inhabited only by baneful treetrunks that are hoarse from complaining to the south wind, whose whisper slow-moving birds, squawking sadly and flying gravely, in both spheres alternate with the echoes of the wild beasts, four noises uniting in only one noise: the sea, the air, the song and the roar.]

At the same time, they feel awed by the strangely harmonious echoes they hear, whose overall effect is captured by a refrain that points to further marvels: "Dad paso a mis suspiros, / por si un prodigio vence otro prodigio" ("Make way for my sighs in case one marvel surpasses another") (2104b). Leonido expresses his wonderment by noting two sets of oppositions, one between the joyful music and the gloomy surroundings ("tan alegre / música en tan triste sitio"), and the other between the rugged underbrush and the pleasing path ("lo áspero de la maleza / con lo afable del camino" [2104b]). Frye (1965, 136) remarks that all the arts are used as regenerative symbols in romance, but music is the traditional one because it reflects the harmony of the soul. The hint of harmony within the chaotic world of Mitilene augurs the redemptive spirit of rebirth and renewal that follows a period of moral trial and adversity. Leonido's innate adventurous spirit makes him want to explore the island, but not before he hides his armor in the nearby cave and invents a false name and country of origin so as to conceal his true identity, so far as he knows it. According to Frye (1976, 105–106), shifts in identity can involve complete metamorphosis by association with something animal or vegetable, or they may stop at disguise or mere change of name.

The oracular cave that Leonido enters is inhabited by Marfisa, whose birth is also a mystery, having been brought up by the magician Argante. Clothed in animal skins and lamenting her captive state, she is captivated by the same musical sounds of shepherds that attracted Leonido; that she longs to imitate and hear them is perhaps a sign of their deep connection. Marfisa, as it turns out, is Leonido's twin sister who was carried off as an infant by a "monster" dressed in skins (2151b) and who possesses a companion medal to her brother's with a similar indecipherable inscription. Her subhuman imprisonment and isolation in a labyrinthine cave where the shapes of animals can confuse or torment is typical of the lower-world existence described by Frye (1976, 111). In fact, when she comes upon Leonido's discarded suit of armor, she mistakes it for a dismembered animal

> . . . que yace esparcido
> tan a pedazos, que a una
> parte el cuerpo dividido
> de su cabeza, y los brazos
> también del cuerpo distintos.
>
> (2105b)

[. . . that lies strewn cut into such pieces that on one side the body severed from its head, and the arms also distinct from the body.]

It is as though, in her own metamorphosed state as a "monstruo racional" (2106a), and denied her free will, she unconsciously responds to the symbolic transformation of a kindred soul.

Argante, a kind of white magician or Old Wise Man figure with timeless knowledge of life's processes, wants to protect Marfisa from a fatal amorous entanglement, for it was prophesied that, should she fall in love with a man or a man with her, one would kill the other (2116a). Having tried throughout to guard Marfisa against the bewitching temptation of harmonious mountain music (2106a), Argante is besieged by dire memories upon seeing the lion on Leonido's shield and the writing that matches that of the "lámina" ("metal plate") belonging to Marfisa. Astonished yet troubled, he laments his necessarily harsh treatment of his adoptive daughter, saying that there is "impiedad que es cariño, / . . . rigor que es agasajo / e injuria que es beneficio (2106b)" ("cruelty that is loving, severity that is kind, and pain that is beneficial"). Argante unwittingly has hit upon a central paradox that Felperin (1972, 62) calls the "bitter-sweetness of the romances as opposed to the sweetness of the comedies"; the characters in romance must follow a path that is, as Edgar says to Gloucester in *King Lear*, "horrible steep" in order to supersede tragedy and recover personal and social identity and spiritual integrity. The presence of Leonido's scutcheon and arms has also affected Marfisa strangely, and she speaks to Argante in open rebellion—perhaps a sign that she is about to embark on a journey that will culminate in rebirth and renewal:

> ya que ha influído
> tan nuevo espíritu en mí
> ese acero, que ha podido

> trocar el pavor en saña,
> mudar el temor en brío.
>
> (2107a)

[. . . since I have been filled with such a new spirit by that steel, that has succeeded in changing dread into fury, in transmuting fear into decision.]

Meanwhile, Leonido rustles through the labyrinthine brush, and Queen Mitilene and her fellow hunters apprehend him as a kind of "nuevo monstruo" in their midst (2107a–b). Such dehumanizing imagery serves to heighten his isolation and self-alienation, which become all the more apparent when he creates a false identity as the humble Lelio, a shipwrecked merchant from Alexandria (2107b). The storm at sea, though here a product of Leonido's meta-theatrical imaginings, symbolizes the "abyss of disorder" that lies below the ordinary physical world in romance and is associated with madness, illusion, darkness, destruction, and death itself (Frye 1965, 137). It is as though Leonido were unconsciously anticipating the portent of his own demise, which is made manifest to him when he overhears Mitilene's ambassador report that one Leonido of Tiro is the object of Arminda's revenge and, moreover, that he had come to Trinacria as a traitor seeking vengeance, despite appearances to the contrary (2109b). As Frye (1976, 115) points out, it is not uncommon for the hero of romance to experience further isolation and loneliness by being falsely accused of major crimes. Nevertheless, despite Arminda's apparent hatred of him, Leonido continues to love her passionately.

His emotional turmoil is intensified when he again comes upon Marfisa, for whom he feels another sort of inexplicable attraction:

> . . . un género tan nuevo
> de cierto amor, que no es
> amor ni deja de serlo.
>
> (2111b)

[. . . such a new kind of a certain love that at the same time it is and is not love.]

And she has a similar reaction to him:

> . . . también al mirarte siento
> no sé qué gozo en el alma,
> que sin entrar sin recelo,

te franqueara el corazón
sus más íntimos secretos.

(2111b)

[. . . as well on looking at thee I feel I know not what joy in my soul, for
without entering without mistrust, my heart would open wide to thee its
most intimate secrets.]

The special connection they feel represents a common motif in
romance (and comedy) of the separation of twins at birth and their
eventual rediscovery after much moral trial and testing. Leonido
and Marfisa have each embarked upon an individual quest, but their
journeys have become intertwined from the moment they meet. He
clearly wants to rescue her from incarceration, but she resists,
feeling the push-pull of fear and desire: "¿Quién pudiera defenderse
/ y no defenderse a un tiempo?" (2112a) ("If only it were possible to
protect oneself and give in at the same time"). Leonido does manage to carry her off, and his action prefigures Marfisa's heroic deed
later on when, believing her brother dead, she replaces him in a
duel in order to preserve his honor. Leonido's present act of heroism is aborted, however, when Argante invokes the supernatural
powers of the fury Megera to disturb the elements with "ter-
remotos" ("earthquakes") and "lluvias, rayos, relámpagos y true-
nos" ("rain, lightning, thunder"), and then to have a serpent whisk
Marfisa from her rescuer's grasp (2113a). But amid the tempestuous
chaos at the end of act 1 can be heard the musical harmony of the
spheres (2114a). Calderón, while stressing the opposition between
the destructive and the (re)creative, the tragic and the comic, is also
pointing ahead to the final reconciliation among warring factions
and the renewal of familial ties that are key elements of romance.

Act 2 opens as Leonido, seemingly less awed by all the "delirios,
/ penas, confusiones y ansias" (2114a), returns to the cave to search
out his armor as well as the identity of that creature in skins who
experiences fear like a real woman, yet disappears like a phantom
goddess—"si es verdad o fantasma / terror que como mujer / siente
y como deidad falta" (2114b). But he is amazed to find the terrifying
grotto wholly transformed into a marvelously decorated parlor with
gilded archways and studded pillars. He is equally astonished to see
Marfisa meatmorphosed from a "monstruo" into a "deidad," richly
garbed and attended against the backdrop of sweetly singing voices
(2116a). Although Argante is able to effect all these prodigies and
more, there are limits to his power, for he can divine Marfisa's
fortunes only so far, without really knowing how things will turn
out. Since it has been prophesied that her loving or being loved

would result in a death, Argante cautions his "daughter" against falling in love, while at the same time urging her to discover Leonido's intentions. There are flickers of incest as Marfisa wonders whether the "pasión" she feels toward her rescuer is the equivalent of love. Fear of incest is a common theme of the night world (Frye 1976, 137), but Marfisa manages to turn incipient pangs of love into genuine feelings of gratitude (2116b). She does in fact elicit a straightforward account of the stranger's origins and current circumstances: the obscurity of his parentage, the reasons for his flight from Trinacria by sea, his devotion to Arminda, and his need to find his armor so as to redress the rancor she feels toward him. That Leonido assumes no pretenses is significant, for, with each new name and identity created in the past, he became more and more isolated from his true self.

Marfisa, in a spirit of true friendship, regrets that she cannot procure the soldier's armor and offers him refuge instead, saying that "el tiempo / odios y cariños gasta" (2118a) ("time dissipates all feelings of hatred and love"). Thus time, which can be a perpetrator of disaster and death, can also be an agent of growth and natural development, of reunion and renewal. Marfisa's thoughts here recall those of the Chorus of Time in *The Winter's Tale,* which regard natural processes—death and life, destruction and recreation—as parts of one continuous whole: "I that please some, try all: both joy and terror / Of good and bad, that makes and unfolds error" (4.1.1–2).[5] Although Claderón stresses the positive influence of time, he simultaneously negates, in "deconstructive" fashion, its total omnipotence and autonomy by recalling the workings of the supernatural, of "Providence divine" (*Tempest,* 1.2.159). This is seen, for example, when Argante first conjures up and then dissolves before Leonido's eyes a splendiferous vision of Arminda in her palace in Trinacria as she embroils herself in two vendettas: one against her cousin Mitilene who, after Lisidante's death, has laid claim to the throne in the absence of a male heir; and the other against Leonido whom some suppose to be dead at sea and others believe to be concealing himself out of fear (2119ff.). In the same way that Prospero's "insubstantial pageant" must fade and "leave not a rack behind," so Argante's spectacle of "aparentes fantasmas" (2121b) must dissolve and be "melted . . . into thin air," especially when Leonido, in quixotic fashion, takes it to be "real" and tries to address Arminda directly so as to deny the accusations of cowardice (2121a). When the hero comes to see all the pomp disappear before his very eyes (2121b), the extradramatic audience is reminded of the illusory and dreamlike quality of life and, moreover, of the need for an imaginative equivalent of faith, faith in something superhuman—creative, unpredictable, and mysterious—in order for recreation and renewal to take place (Felperin 1972, 68–69). When Leonido inquires soon thereafter how best to escape from the labyrinth of conflicting responsibilities in which he is caught, Polidoro responds, "Dando tiempo al tiempo: que él / sabe ciertas sendas varias / que acá ignoramos" (2122a) ("By giving time to time: because it knows various sure paths of which we here are unaware"). But the fact that Polidoro stresses the regenerative powers of time alone means that the hero has received only a partial response to his query. Hence, Calderón's text in this instance can be said to be self-deconstructing, or "self-dismantling," for, as Miller (1976, 341) goes on to say, "its apparently solid ground is no rock but thin air."

The illusion created by Argante has served to clarify for Leonido the course of action he must follow. If, before, he wished to return to Arminda solely for love, now he must journey to Trinacria for reasons of honor as well: on the one hand, to defend Arminda because he feels responsible for her impending war with Mitilene, and on the other, to defend his own valor (2127a). Marfisa and Leonido exchange medals as part of their leavetaking, and each recognizes the heraldic device on the piece that he or she receives, exclaiming "Mas ¡qué miro! / Mas ¡qué veo! / Esta es la mía" (2122b) ("What is it I see? This is my very own!"). They hardly have time to express their astonishment at these remembrances before Marfisa, fearing Argante's approach, again pretends to scorn Leonido and runs off. Nevertheless, the discovery of what Frye (1976, 145) calls a "talisman of recognition," some token put beside an exposed infant that symbolizes the original identity, marks the beginning of the twins' journey out of the night world of confusion and darkness into a realm of waking consciousness, an ascent of which they are not as yet aware.

The rest of Calderón's play can be said to represent various stages in the cyclical movement upward toward the final recognition scene, despite continued evidence of division and conflict until the very end. When Leonido arrives at Trinacria in the midst of battle-cries from the armies of Arminda and Mitilene, he comes immediately upon his traitorous old servant Merlín, who at that moment is determining where he might best take refuge and so escape the wrath of his former master forever. Despite admonitions from the trustworthy Polidoro, Leonido raises his sword in vengeance against Merlín, for the latter had betrayed him to Arminda by revealing his name and place of origin. Ironically Leonido, disguised as an ordinary recruit, is almost captured for having drawn a weapon in the presence of Arminda's ensigns. It is Merlín who, in spite of being recognized as Leonido's servant, rescues his master by inventing the story of a gambling quarrel and swearing he will be that lowly soldier's "servant" forever (2128ff.). Tragicomic coincidence is pushed almost to its limits when master is made to swear gratitude to servant, especially before Prince Adolfo of Russia, who has been rivaling Prince Florante of Swabia in searching for Leonido so as to win Arminda's hand. If formerly Merlín's loquacity and fear had isolated him, now his prudent silence and bravery have reconciled him with Leonido. Merlín rises to the occasion in a way that his counterpart Clarín in *La vida es sueño* never does.

The symbolic embrace of reconciliation is dampened, however, by the appearance of even more chaos when the fury Megera incites a volcanic eruption. Paradoxically, a seeming "mensajera de daño" (2129b) ("harbinger of disaster") performs a beneficent deed by impeding a potentially tragic battle between two opposing forces, causing the one to escape to the mountains and the other to sea. When Arminda's quarters catch fire, the disguised Leonido rescues his beloved queen, thereby winning her eternal gratitude even though she is still ignorant of his true identity. Frye (1968, 203) states that the moment of epiphany in romance often occurs on a mountain top or an island and that the movement from a lower order of existence to a higher one may be heralded by a kind of sacrificial fire. If Act 1 ended with Leonido's aborted rescue of Marfisa from a tempest, act 2 closes with his successful deliverance of Arminda from flames, perhaps symbolizing the act of purification they must undergo before their union in marriage. The hero has acted generously and valiantly on two occasions, each time in an effort to assist women who, as it turns out, will play crucial roles in his process of self-discovery. His innate nobility stands in direct contrast to the egotism and jealousy of two rival suitors, Adolfo and Florante, who think only of their personal loss in not being the one to succor Arminda rather than of her good fortune at being saved (2130b). Leonido, however, perceives things to be getting worse and not better, for now all the elements seem to be working against him:

> El mar
> con sus tormentas me ofende.
> El Cáucaso con sus magias
> me aflige, con sus crueles

diluvios el aire, y ahora
el fuego con sus ardientes
iras.

(2130a)

[The sea with its storms offends me. The Caucasus with its spells afflicts
me, as does air with its cruel floods and now fire with its burning rages.]

But Leonido is like other romantic protagonists who, as Felperin
says (1972, 63), "are disabused of all romantic expectations and get
romance," in contrast to those tragic heroes who "persist in ex-
pecting romance and get tragedy."

In act 3, Calderón continues to establish a counterpoint between
the rhythms of external nature and of human life by focusing not on
tempest at sea and volcanic eruption on land (lower-world images of
winter, night, and death) but on an idyllic, vernal setting, symbolized by an exquisite garden (2131b) and the celebrations of
Carnival (2138a). The spirit of Venus, of love and redemption, is felt
in the lyrics of the musicians that are being sung to welcome to
Trinacria the old and wise Casimiro of Chipre (Cyprus), uncle to
both Arminda and Mitilene (and, as it turns out, true father of
Leonido and Marfisa). Casimiro's arrival is associated with "la paz"
(2131a), for he has come as arbiter to the warring factions and
considers it an "act of providence" that the volcanic eruption
suspended the battle before it could get under way (2132b). Casimiro is in some sense an agent of providence and serves a similar
reconciliatory function to that of the mythical deities and the magician (with his mysterious aura of divinity) in Shakespearean romance: Diana in *Pericles;* Jupiter in *Cymbeline:* Apollo's Oracle,
Time, and "great creating nature" in *The Winter's Tale;* and Prospero in *The Tempest.* It is not surprising, therefore, that Casimiro
will also act as "juez" and "padrino" (2140b) ("arbiter" and "spon-
sor") for the last hurdle Leonido and Marfisa must overcome before
the discovery of their true identity.

Metamorphosis, key to the cycle of romance and the essence of
theater itself, is pushed almost to its creative limits as the play
progresses toward the final recognition scene. Arminda, duly impressed by the chivalric comportment of that unknown youth who
had rescued her, urges him to serve her once again by challenging
one "fiero" Leonido in combat (2134a). She prides herself on
having devised a new plan whereby her brother's death will be
avenged without her appearing to be vindictive and savage in the
presence of Casimiro and Mitilene, and without committing herself

in marriage to the man who will perform the deed (as she had rashly promised earlier). Her goal is to force the enemy to present himself if he is alive and then to allow him to defend himself in a fair fight. That she is capable both of showing gratitude to her rescuer and of toning down her Amazon tendencies indicates a certain potential for growth that will make her worthy of the noble Leonido in the end. Also noteworthy is that, in his self-introduction to the Queen, Leonido tells as much of the truth as he can, describing himself simply as a German "hijo de la guerra" (warrior) who, having favored Arminda over Mitilene, came to fight on her behalf (2135a). Paradoxical though it may seem, Leonido actually moves forward in his quest for self-identity and self-knowledge as a result of this latest challenge. That the hero has been asked to serve not amid volcanic debris but in a setting of vernal splendor (2134b) is a positive sign. But the fact that he is at once challenger and the one challenged presents a seemingly insoluble dilemma that he voices to Polidoro:

> Que yo a mí me desafíe
> me manda: ¿cómo ha de ser
> llamarme y no responder? . . .
> ¿O cómo se ha de ajustar
> que sea yo el que he de esperar,
> y sea yo el que ha de venir?
>
> (2136b)

[She commands me to challenge myself: how is it possible for me to call myself and not answer? Or how is it possible for me to be both the one who waits and the one who is to come?]

Polidoro, the voice of reason and faithful counterpart to Camillo in *The Winter's Tale,* takes up the role of playwright and stage-manager in creating what is meant to be a comedy, but turns into a tragedy for him and into a romance for those who survive him. This inner play at once reduplicates and challenges Calderón's own dramatic structure.

Like many other authors of seventeenth-century comedy and romance, Polidoro crafts a plot that seems totally incredible, but only as incredible as the outcome he seeks to achieve: Leonido is to play the part of challenger, and Polidoro that of Leonido, who is known only by name and not by appearance; Polidoro will exercise his rights as the challenged "Leonido" and ask to fight on foot; the two will embrace, and "Leonido" will announce that he has fought merely to ensure that no one will be deemed more beautiful than

Arminda; the onlookers will then support "Leonido" and not allow
him to be attacked again (2137a). The climax of this inner play,
written for a particular actor in a particular setting, is a replication
of the catalytic event of Calderón's opening scene: Leonido's arrival
at Trinacria to challenge the man who had proclaimed another
woman more beautiful than Arminda (2101a). This repetition not
only underscores the movement of romance through the cycles of
nature and human life (Frye 1976, 150), but it also suggests that
truth is sometimes as strange as fiction. Ironically, Leonido-actor
questions the plausibility of the script, but Polidoro-author cleverly
tells him either to invent something more to his liking or to accept
what he has been given if he wishes to perform at all: "Señor, quien
se mira ahogar, / se ase de desnuda espada" (2137b) ("He who sees
himself suffocating [in a tight spot] had best avail himself of an
unsheathed sword"). Agreeing to do the role, Leonido assumes the
stage identity of a German gentleman who has fled his country after
a duel, and he goes before the proper authority at court to make his
acceptance official. His appearance elicits strong reactions from
potential on-stage audience members: Mitilene tries to recall where
she has seen him before; Adolfo and Florante are overcome by
jealousy, and each regrets not being the challenger and hence the
potential winner of Arminda's hand; Casimiro is dumbstruck—
"absorto y suspenso"—and duly impressed by the German gentleman's demeanor—"airoso, cuerdo, amable" ("graceful, prudent,
and affable"); and Leonido himself feels an inexplicable twinge of
joy as he hears Casimiro speak (2140a–b). Sensitive to the nature of
his audience, Polidoro perceives negative vibrations from Florante
and expresses concern over a potentially disastrous audience response to his projected comedy, but Leonido believes he is over-
reacting (2140a). Leonido thinks only of the costume and prop he
would like to have for the performance: his own armor and shield
that are still confined in Marfisa's cave on the island of Mitilene.

As Polidoro prepares to journey to Mitilene to obtain the desired
attire, Leonido unwittingly presages the structural evolution of his
companion's play from comedy to tragedy to romance, saying:

> Si esos
> maravillosos, extraños,
> raros y varios sucesos,
> ya en verdaderas historias,
> ya en fabulosos ejemplos
> el tiempo nos lo labrara,

¡qué ocioso estuviera el tiempo!

(2141a–b)

[If time were to make true histories or fabled examples of those marvelous, strange, rare and varied events, how idle time would then be!]

Meanwhile Florante, an unrequited and jealous actor who has not been cast as the lover he thinks he should be, disguises himself as a bandit, sails to the island, and kills Polidoro, thinking him to be the hunted Leonido (2144a). Through this irrational and selfish action, he hopes to curry the amorous favor of Arminda, but clearly he has confused the actor with the role, causing Mitilene to become "el teatro de [la] tragedia" (2145a). Marfisa, having heard by word of mouth (incarnated in the figure of "Fama") about the special performance of single combat to be held in Trinacria, decides to render homage to the apparently dead Leonido by secretly donning his armor and understudying his role. Mindful of the sad fate that prohibits her from loving or being loved, she responds selflessly and heroically to the demands of honor alone. But before she can make her début on the stage of the world, she must overcome one last obstacle: that of breaking out of her surrogate father's controlling power. This she accomplishes in part by breaking into his study, destroying his instruments, and procuring Leonido's armor, the donning of which reconnects her to her roots (2145b).

When Marfisa appears disguised as Leonido and challenges her opponent, the audience reaction is intense: Florante is dumfounded by the "rebirth" of Leonido, whom he left for dead; another rival, Adolfo, in contrast to Florante, distinguishes between the conflicting emotions of envy and respect he feels toward the "German" challenger, who is clearly in line for Arminda's hand; Casimiro is concerned lest fortune wrest from him that unknown gentleman who has affected him so; Merlín is also baffled by the advent of a "new" Leonido, because he was present when the other Leonido was supposedly killed (2148–49a). The final scene is a *tour de force* of disguise and revelation, for no one on stage, whether secondary actor or audience member, knows the true identity of *everyone* present. Leonido begins to act as directed, and, when he suspends the performance as planned, he is amazed to find himself playing opposite Marfisa rather than Polidoro; Marfisa is equally surprised to learn that Leonido is alive; and Casimiro is the most astonished of all when he deciphers the emblem on the medals produced by Leonido and Marfisa—which reads "Este hado y divisa / de quien soy te avisa" (2152a) ("This [fateful] device will advise you who I am")—and then acknowledges his long-lost children. Frye (1976, 145) says that the basis of the recognition scene is often "the restoring of the broken current of memory," and this is precisely the case with Casimiro, who learns of events surrounding the birth and infancy of his children only when he sees them fully grown.

Casimiro begins building to that climactic moment of recognition when he first lays eyes on Leonido. Retiring to Arminda's gardens, he ruminates on the paradoxical nature of time that, on the one hand, is a symbol of change in that it flies and allows sad old memories to die and, on the other, is an emblem of stasis for it expresses the continuity of generations and of life despite all that is done to disrupt and destroy those natural processes:

> Aunque suele la memoria
> morir a manos del tiempo,
> también suele revivir
> a vista de los objetos,
> mayormente cuando son
> para dolor sus acuerdos.
>
> (2146a)

[Although memory is wont to die at the hands of time, it is also wont to live again at the sight of things, and more so when their remembrance brings pain.]

Casimiro is moved by the passage of time to review the details of the forced abandonment of his beloved Matilde (secretly his wife). But only after Leonido and Marfisa suspend their contest does he learn that, when his wife died in childbirth, she left behind twins who were separated and lost in a shipwreck: the one being carried off by a lion and later rescued and raised by a duke; and the other being whisked away by a human monster clothed in animal skins who turns out to be Argante (2151). In the same way that Prospero "breaks his staff" and "drowns his book," thereby abjuring all forms of "rough magic" (5.1.50–57), so Argante repudiates the power of his (white) magic to manipulate Marfisa, who has done her *part* to assert her independence, first by destroying the instruments of his controlling art, and then by risking her life in noble defense of one who is actually a lost brother. But perhaps her greatest restorative action concerns not her surrogate father nor her brother, but her true father. In the same way that Pericles, Cymbeline, Leontes, and Prospero are all revitalized in humane terms by a daughter, so Casimiro ultimately comes to integrate his past, recreate his present, and redeem his future through the actions of Marfisa. Timeless continuity is assured by the multiple marriages at the end: Leonido to Arminda (who will retain Trinacria); Marfisa to Adolfo; and Matilda to Florante.

The atmosphere of rebirth and renewal is dampened, however, by the fact that Florante's crime remains unpunished, if not in a sense rewarded. Leonido's reaction to Polidoro's tragic death—"Perdí un verdadero amigo," (2151b) ("I have lost a true friend")—further qualifies or problematizes the final triumphs, thereby creating within the idyllic romance an antiromantic dimension that recognizes the claims of the real. Thus Calderón, in dramatizing the natural cycles of birth, death, and rebirth, reminds his audience of winter death even in the midst of vernal renewal. A similar juxtaposition is signaled in *The Winter's Tale* when, for example, the Old Shepherd says to his son—"Now bless thyself: thou met'st with things dying, I with things new-born" (3.3.111–12)—after the younger man has seen the mangling of Antigonus by a bear, and he himself has found the infant Perdita abandoned on the Bohemian coast.

In *Hado y divisa* and *The Winter's Tale,* the paradox of the romance form is most clearly seen in the final scenes, which in both cases represent a *tour de force* of metatheater. Perhaps this self-reflexivity becomes all the more meaningful in the case of *Hado y Divisa* if one considers the dramatic impact of the *loa* or prelude to the play, in which Calderón has the Spanish King Charles II and his French bride, María of Orléans, sit facing portraits of themselves as they witness the spectacle:

> En la frente del salón, ocupando el medio de la perspectiva, se hizo un tronco cubierto de un suntuoso dosel, debajo del cual había dos retratos de nuestros felicísimos monarcas, imitados tan al vivo, que como estaban frente de sus originales pareció ser un espejo en que trasladaban sus perfecciones, y el ansia que desea verlos en todas partes, quisiera hallar más repetidas sus copias. (*BAE* 14, 358)[6]

> [On the front wall of the hall, occupying the middle of the perspective, was a throne covered with a sumptuous canopy, beneath which were two portraits of our most happy monarchs, so lifelike that, as they were placed opposite their originals, they seemed to be a mirror into which their rare perfections were transferred; and because of our longing to see the monarchs everywhere, we would have liked to see the copies of them repeated more often.] (Wardropper 1982, 39)

Nevertheless, Calderón did not set up facing mirrors in the theater despite the spectators' clear desire for multiple reflections of their monarchs, perhaps because, as Wardropper posits, "if he had, with the privilege of perspective the only members of the audience who would have seen the sovereigns reproduced would have been the sovereigns themselves. . . . Only portraits permitted everyone in the hall to see the king and queen, present both as part of the audience and as part of the staging" (ibid.). The combined sociopolitical and esthetic significance of the portraits becomes apparent in that, in Wardropper's words:

> They confirm the need to demonstrate the idea of the transcendent, which exists beyond appearances, but which can only be expressed by the appearances themselves. . . . In the "appearances" of the royal portraits, one perceives, plainly, monarchy and empire; in them, less plainly, one also perceives, by means of correspondence, the isolation of the king in his own optical perspective—and even his social isolation. The king's gaze does not fall on the other spectators because it is fixed on his own portrait and on the accompanying dramatic prelude. The dramatic prelude presents, in a perspective that recedes with historical time, statues of seven kings who were Charles's ancestors. . . . But this historical retrospect, in perspective, does nothing to enlarge Charles's field of vision. The eyes of the last Spanish Hapsburg are symbolically fixed—fixated—on a glorious past and a narcissistic present. (ibid.)

Calderón, in repudiating the notion of multiple mirror reflections, focuses attention on the "appearances" of the royal portraits, with the result that the audience may yield themselves to the illusion and yet be critically aware of the distinction between reproduction and person, art and life. Thus, the prelude can be said to anticipate the play's grand finale, where the beneficient and destructive consequences of illusion are recognized, and the idea of transcendence is affirmed.

In *The Winter's Tale,* play-within-a-play techniques are most apparent from the outset: King Leontes is immediately the victim of a mad self-deception, becoming a surrogate dramatist and creating illusory roles for himself and for those around him. He imagines his wife to be engaged in false play—playacting—with his life-long friend Polixenes and himself to be the deceived husband, "so disgrac'd a part, whose issue / Will hiss me to my grave" (1.2.188–89). This invention is a travesty of the (outer) play's true action: it not only reveals the distorting effects of a jealous imagination, but it also exposes the perilously thin line that divides unreality from reality, artifice from truth, and the dangers of not properly distinguishing between the two. Moreover, by creating his own play on the world stage and for a time insisting upon its sole validity, Leontes denies the truth-divining art of higher powers such as the poet Apollo (3.2.140) or "great creating nature" (4.4.88). Nevertheless, upon learning of the death of the prince Mamillius, he suddenly realizes that he has been incapable of distinguishing truth from fiction, faithfulness from infidelity, and that he must beg pardon from Apollo for "my great profaneness 'gainst thine Oracle" (3.2.154). Once he learns of Hermione's death as well, he fully recognizes the tragic consequences of his playacting and vows a ritual of remorse, whereby tears shed at the chapel where his loved ones lie shall be his "recreation" (3.2.239–40). In his own mind the meaning of "recreation" is ironic, but what he does not know is that his unqualified penitence will result in the restoration or re-creation of his spirit. It is unlikely that this second interpretation will be stirred in the minds of the extradramatic audience at that point, but most theater spectators, along with Leontes, will perceive the distinction between creative and destructive art—art that mirrors or sounds out true nature and so enhances life, and art that distorts or destroys it.

Leontes' tragic immersion in a drama of his own making contrasts sharply with the comic—life-sustaining—authoring and playacting of others, such as the beneficent lord Camillo. Characterized throughout as "priest-like" (1.2.237), "clerk-like experienc'd" (1.2.392), "the medicine of our house" (4.4.588), Camillo becomes a spiritual helper to two kings, taking up the role of stage manager to repair the destructive behavior first of the jealous Leontes and then of the irascible Polixenes. He even imagines a scenario in Sicily (involving Florizel's reconciliation with his father Polixenes and his acceptance by a repentant Leontes) that becomes prophetically true. Felperin (1972) hits the mark when he says that "his kind of art is both moral and creative in a way which the earlier versions of art in the play are not" (239–40). Camillo's directorial skills pave the way for the revelations of act 5 that consist of a double recognition scene: the discovery of Perdita's parentage, followed by the awakening of the supposedly dead Hermione and the presenting of Perdita to her. The relationship between fiction and truth is further explored by the courtiers who recount the reunion of father and daughter, stressing its similarity to an old tale, but only to discount that similarity and establish the "reality" of what has occurred. In fact, what has happened is paradoxically "all the more miraculous in its effect than anything art in the usual sense could produce for being life itself" (Felperin 1972, 240), with the result that "ballad-makers cannot be able to express it" (5.2.24–25). Ultimately art is repudiated as life is affirmed.

The culminating moment of reconciliation occurs when the marble statue that Julio Romano had apparently carved of the dead Hermione turns into her living form. The mimetic realism that characterizes Romano's art is such that "had he himself eternity and could put breath into his work, [he] would beguile Nature of her custom, so perfectly he is her ape" (5.2.96–99). An imaginative dimension is added to this realism when Leontes' surprise and Lady Paulina's explanation focus on the aging effect introduced by the artist to suggest how old Hermione would have looked after the passage of sixteen years (5.3.25ff.). Romano's "excellence" (5.3.30), then, "consists in his ability to carve the passage of time into his work, to accommodate the realities of imperfection and flux even as he transcends them in marble" (Felperin 1972, 241). But at the same time the cold stone appears to reveal signs of "warm life" (5.3.35), and the spectators on stage begin to react to the statue as if it were alive: Perdita needs to be restrained from kissing its hand on the pretext that the colors are still wet; Paulina fears lest Leontes' fancy make him think it moves; and both kings think that it actually breathes, Leontes expressing his amazement as follows:

> Still methinks
> There is an air comes from her. What fine chisel
> Could ever yet cut breath?
>
> (5.3.77–79)

Both stage and theater audience gradually come to accept an art so natural that it seems capable of dissolving their rational distinctions between truth and imitation and of making them believe along with Leontes that "no settled sense of the world can match / The pleasure of that madness" (5.3.72–73). As it turns out, Julio Romano never sculpted a statue of the queen; the figure of Hermione is actually the result of the good Paulina's artifice. Playacting and disguise, then, can be as much an act of revelation as of concealment. But before the stage (and theater) audience can be disabused and feel Hermione's warm presence, "it is requir'd / [they] do awake [their] faith" (5.3.94–95)—faith, as Charles Frey (1980, 162) puts it, "in the powers of friendship, in the ordering harmony of love, in the redemptive continuity of generations, in the meaning and value of life itself." There follows a kind of spiritual incantation accompanied by music, and Paulina, a quasi agent of providence, addresses Hermione thus:

> 'Tis time; descend; be stone no more; approach;
> Strike all that look upon with marvel. Come!
> I'll fill your grave up: stir, nay, come away:
> Bequeath to death your numbness; for from him
> Dear life redeems you.
>
> (5.3.99–103)

The awakening of the "marble" statue is the ultimate reconciliation of art and nature, leading to the wonder of life restored, but also to a deeper perception of ordinary experience. Leontes' response— "If this be magic, let it be an art / Lawful as eating" (5.3.110–111)— suggests "an art as natural as the means by which life and health are sustained" (Felperin 1972, 242) and an acceptance of the marvelous as a part of the real in the same way that death is a part of life. That Shakespeare's plays exhibit a sense of theatricality that implies both the presence of an audience and that audience's awareness of the fact of stage performance is nothing new. Noteworthy in *The Winter's Tale,* however, is the treatment of the element of the marvelous that is characteristic of romance and seemingly antithetical to dramatic presentation: Shakespeare alludes frequently to the absurdity of what is happening, enabling the outer audience to believe and disbelieve simultaneously, to yield themselves to the theatrical experience with all its marvels and yet retain a skeptical sense that it is only "romance." In the end, Leontes and Hermione are "restored to life" when daughter Perdita is found, but neither son Mamillius nor Lord Antigonus are resurrected, although perhaps there is some compensation for their loss in the figures of Florizel, betrothed to Perdita, and of Camillo, who is to marry Antigonus's widow Paulina.

Felperin (1972, 62) says with regard to the endings of *The Winter's Tale* and of *The Tempest* that "restitution of loss is never perfect and complete, that rebirth is not the same as birth (no more than they are in life)," and the same would apply to *Hado y divisa de Leonido y Marfisa.* These three romances subsume tragedy in the process of transcending it. Both Shakespeare and Calderón subject the conventions of romance to the same sort of trial and testing that their characters undergo. In the end, they repudiate art in favor of life, while still recognizing art's mediating role in the apprehension of life's mysteries. Their late romantic works, then, are at once self-conscious and self-critical of the artifice they employ.

Notes

1. Two studies by William R. Blue (1981; 1982) recognize *Hado y divisa de Leonido y Marfisa* as romance and cite some parallels with Shakespeare's late works. From a Marxist perspective, Walter Cohen (1985) also recognizes a number of formal similarities between the three Calderonian plays and Shakespearean romance, concluding that "in each case, a dramatist at the end of an age found a way out of the persistent conflict of the present only in a utopian view of the future" (391).

2. Along similar lines, J. Hillis Miller (1976, 341) writes: "Deconstruction is not a dismantling of the structure of a text but a demonstration that it has already dismantled itself. Its apparently solid ground is no rock but thin air." For a judicious commentary on the usefulness and limitations of the deconstructionist method, see Christopher Norris (1982); and for a good discussion of the often unacknowledged dichotomy between critical theory and practice, see Elizabeth Freund (1987).

3. For Wardropper (1982), the play itself is not so interesting as the "uniquely complete description" of the staging of its first performance at the Coliseo in the palace of the Buen Retiro. Thought to be written by Calderón himself, this prose statement appears in Juan Eugenio Hartzenbusch's edition for the Biblioteca de Autores Españoles ([1850] 1945, 14:355–57). See also Sebastian Neumeister (1979, 83–91).

4. References to *Hado y divisa de Leonido y Marfisa* are given, by page and column, to Pedro Calderón de la Barca, *Obras completas*, vol. 2, edited by Angel Valbuena Briones (Madrid: Aguilar, 1960). Translations are mine.

5. References to *The Winter's Tale* are given by act, scene, and verse from the Arden edition of the works of William Shakespeare, edited by J. H. P. Pafford (London: Methuen, 1963). For an extensive topical survey of pertinent criticism of *The Winter's Tale,* see Sydney Homan (1986, 209–13). References to *The Tempest* are also given by act, scene, and verse from the Arden edition, edited by Frank Kermode (London: Methuen, 1954).

6. For fuller reference to the Biblioteca de Autores Españoles, see n. 3.

Works Cited

Blue, William R. 1981. "Romance Elements in Calderón's Last Plays." In *Studies in Honor of Everett W. Hesse,* edited by William C. McCrary and José A. Madrigal, 23–36. Lincoln, Nebr.: Society of Spanish and Spanish-American Studies.

———. 1982. "Calderón and Shakespeare: The Romances." In *Calderón de la Barca at the Tercentenary: Comparative Views,* edited by Wendell M. Aycock and Sydney P. Cravens, 89–102. Lubbock: Texas Tech Press.

Calderón de la Barca, Pedro. 1960. *Obras completas.* Vol. 2. Edited by Angel Valbuena Briones. Madrid: Aguilar.

Cohen, Walter. 1985. *Drama of a Nation: Public Theatre in Renaissance England and Spain*. Ithaca: Cornell University Press.

Eagleton, Terry. 1986. *William Shakespeare*. London: Basil Blackwell.

Felperin, Howard. 1972. *Shakespearean Romance*. Princeton: Princeton University Press.

Freund, Elizabeth. 1987. *The Return of the Reader: Reader Response Criticism*. London: Methuen.

Frey, Charles. 1980. *Shakespeare's Vast Romance: A Study of "The Winter's Tale"*. Columbia: University of Missouri Press.

Frye, Northrop. 1965. *A Natural Perspective: The Development of Shakespearean Comedy and Romance*. New York: Harcourt, Brace & World.

———. 1968. *Anatomy of Criticism*. New York: Atheneum.

———. 1976. *The Secular Scripture: A Study of the Structure of Romance*. Cambridge: Harvard University Press.

Homan, Sydney. 1986. *Shakespeare's Theater of Presence: Language, Spectacle, and the Audience*. Lewisburg: Bucknell University Press.

Man, Paul de. 1979. *Allegories of Reading: Figural Language in Rousseau, Nietzsche, Rilke and Proust*. New Haven: Yale University Press.

Miller, J. Hillis. 1976. "Stevens' Rock and Criticism as Cure, II." *The Georgia Review* 29:330–49.

Neumeister, Sebastian. 1979. "Los retratos de los reyes en la última comedia de Calderón (*Hado y divisa de Leonido y Marfisa,* Loa)." In *Hacia Calderón: cuarto coloquio anglogermano, Wolfenbüttel 1975,* edited by Hans Flasche, Herman Körner, and Hans Mattauch, 83–91. Berlin and New York: W. de Gruyter.

Norris, Christopher. 1982. *Deconstruction: Theory and Practice*. London: Methuen.

Shakespeare, William. 1963. *The Winter's Tale*. Edited by J. H. P. Pafford. London: Methuen.

———. 1954. *The Tempest*. Edited by Frank Kermode. London: Methuen.

Wardropper, Bruce W. 1982. "Calderón de la Barca and Late Seventeenth-Century Theater." *Record of the Art Museum Princeton University* 41, 2:35–41.

Astraea's Fall: Senecan Images in Shakespeare's *Titus Andronicus* and Calderón's *La vida es sueño*

Frederick A. de Armas

Ever since the German Romantics, led by August Wilhelm Schlegel, discovered Shakespeare and Calderón as examples of "writers of modern times who had produced great dramatic poetry untrammelled by the rules, and even in defiance of them,"[1] comparisons between these two playwrights have flourished. Calderón's *La vida es sueño (Life Is a Dream)* has been related to several of Shakespeare's plays including *As You Like It* and *The Taming of the Shrew.*[2] In his 1865 translation of the Spanish masterpiece, Edward FitzGerald transforms Calderón's title from *La vida es sueño* to *Such Stuff as Dreams are Made Of,* thus reflecting a much repeated link with *The Tempest* (de Armas 1986a). Kenneth Muir (1985, 107–26) explains: "Critics have often called attention to the resemblance between *La vida es sueño* and the speech of Prospero when he interrupts the nuptial masque."[3] It is not the purpose of this essay to take up these well-known relationships. Rather, I would like to bring together Calderón's masterpiece and one of Shakespeare's lesser known and less admired plays, one that on the surface has little connection with *La vida es sueño.* I am referring to *Titus Andronicus.*[4] These two dramatic texts can illuminate each other best, I would contend, in a triangular formation, by showing them to include elaborations of the myth of Astraea as derived, in part, from a scene in Seneca's most macabre tragedy, *Thyestes.*[5]

The fourth chorus in *Thyestes* constitutes my starting point. The Chorus learn that King Atreus has invited his brother Thyestes back to the city of Argos not to be reconciled but to be revenged. The King murders Thyestes' children and uses their flesh to prepare a macabre banquet. As the messenger explains Atreus's actions, "unnatural darkness" (157) settles over the land. The Chorus, at first, fear a new onslaught upon the heavens by the giants of old. Then, they tremble "lest all things fall shattered in fatal ruin and once more gods and men be o'erwhelmed by formless chaos" (159). The expression "once more" alerts us to the Stoic doctrine out of which this passage emerges: *metacosmesis,* the periodic destruction and renewal of the cosmos.[6] R. J. Tarrant (1985, 211) explains that the presentation of forthcoming chaos in *Thyestes* is carefully structured: "The celestial ruin proceeds in strict order. First, the sun, moon and planets, then the constellations of the zodiac, in sequence from Aries in early spring to Pisces in late winter, and finally to the cimcumpolar constellations." All are imagined to fall from the heavens "into one abyss" (159). In *Thyestes,* the sun, rather than following the zodiacal path, disappears, and these constellations abandon the heavens in their forward or seasonal order from Aries to Pisces. The images of their fall recall the two types of universal destruction proposed by Seneca: fire and flood. For example, the assertion, "Alcides' Lion, with burning heat inflamed, once more shall fall down from the sky" (161) is clearly indicative of *ekpyrosis.* However, it is water that dominates the expressions of destruction. Capricorn, as a goat, will break Aquarius's urn from which water flows. They, together with the Fish and the Wain or Bear (a circumpolar constellation that never sets) will plunge into the "all-engulfing waves"—possibly the primordial waters or chaos (161).

There is one more description that triggers associations of *metacosmesis.* Following the burning sign Leo, comes Virgo: ". . . the Virgin shall fall to the earth she once abandoned, and the Scales of justice with their weights shall fall" (161). In classical astral mythology the goddess Astraea is, together with Saturn, the most commonly mentioned immortal who lived on earth during the golden age. As the ages declined, she retreated from dealings with humanity and finally, through catasterism, was transformed into a zodiacal sign. Most classical authorities relate her to Virgo, but some also equate her with Libra, the scales, since the goddess was justice personified. The myth of Astraea's transformation into Virgo is found fully developed in the *Phaenomena* by Aratus (Callimachus 1955, 217). But here the cyclic conception is not made explicit since there is no return. Astraea or Virgo merely watches the decline of humankind. Seneca's version seems to present an ironic commentary on this catasterism. Although she had fled earth to escape the villany of the iron age, the chaotic end of that very age plunges her back to earth.

But there is a second context in which I must place Seneca's image, one that was particularly meaningful to Seneca as tutor of an emperor. The notion of Astraea's return, of her primordial importance in cyclic theories of the universe, is of Roman origin and is associated with imperial concerns. It appears in Virgil's famous *Fourth Eclogue* where we read: "Now is come the last age of the song of Cumae; the great line of the centuries begins anew. Now the Virgin returns, the reign of Saturn returns; now a new generation descends from heaven on high. Only do thou, pure Lucina, smile on the birth of a child, under whom the iron brood shall first cease, and a golden race spring up throughout the world! Thine own Apollo is now king!" (1934, 29) Here, Saturn and Virgo-Astraea are foreseen as returning to earth and bringing about a new golden age through the birth of a mysterious child.

The significance of this expanded myth as related to the Roman Empire is explained by Mircea Eliade (1954, 134). From the moment of its foundation, Rome was destined for destruction and regeneration. The city would last only a certain number of years, a "mystic" number that could be computed by utilizing the number twelve as revealed by Romulus's vision of twelve birds (1954, 134). In writing the *Fourth Eclogue* and the *Aeneid,* Virgil was well aware of the possible fate of Rome. Prophecies of the city's fall were at times related to the cosmogonic cycle of the Great Year (Macrobius 1952). To this fear of destruction, Virgil brings a vision of a return of the golden age without the need for previous destruction. In Anchises' prophecy in the *Aeneid* we learn that the age of Saturn will return under Augustus Caesar (1934, 561). The *pax romana* will be equated, from this moment on, with the distributive justice found in the first age and represented by this goddess, to whom Augustus will dedicate a temple of Justice (Germanicus 1975, x). Astraea has become the goddess of imperial Rome.

The just rule of Astraea stands in sharp contrast with the realities of the tyranny of Nero, under whose rule Seneca lived and perished. His vision of Astraea as revealed in *Thyestes* may well represent an answer to Virgil's imperialist and optimistic approach. In Seneca's play, Astraea's return becomes a fall into chaos. Interestingly this disaster is caused by mankind, and more specifically by a ruler who uses his powers for personal revenge. In a recent book, Denis and Elizabeth Henry (1985, 69) have examined the relationship between kings and cosmos in Seneca. They explain: "Because Kings—or Emperors—held a position in the social order which was analogous to that of the Sun in the cosmos, Seneca would say their acts of aggrandizement and cruelty must evoke analogous disruptions in the heavens, such as the darkening of the Sun in *Thyestes*." Atreus in the play takes on the nature of a fierce beast seeking to shed the blood of his own family to gain revenge. When the representative of a society is so debased, the world becomes topsy-turvy, and the heavens must respond with universal chaos beginning with the darkening of the Sun, the heavenly body that represents kingship.

But it is not one man alone who brings down the planetary gods and the starry firmament. Atreus, in spite of his unimaginable cruelty, is but one participant in an escalating familial rivalry based on revenge. He and his brother had already murdered their half-brother Chrysippus, and Thyestes had plotted to take Atreus's crown, having seduced his wife, Aerope. The two brothers resemble each other in their thirst for power and in their unscrupulous means to attain it and gain revenge. René Girard's study (1977) of violence and the sacred can shed light on this situation. He claims that, "as in Greek tragedy and primitive religion, it is not the differences but the loss of them that gives rise to violence and chaos" (51). Twins, for example, inspire a particular terror and are often put to death. He adds: "Even when the brothers are not twins, the difference between them is less than that between all other degrees of relations" (61). From Cain and Abel to Romulus and Remus, Girard points to the birth of fraternal violence. Atreus and Thyestes are no exception. Their lack of differences plunges them into an irrational battle where violence escalates. Once the desire for revenge is introduced, chaos can be the only result: "Vengeance professes to be an act of reprisal, and every reprisal calls for another reprisal. . . . Vengeance, then, is an interminable, infinitely repetitive process" (14). Sacrifice seeks to redirect such violence "toward victims that may be actual or figurative, animate or inanimate, but that are always incapable of propagating further violence" (18). In *Thyestes,* Atreus assassinates Thyestes' children in a sacrificial manner: "Nothing is lacking, neither incense, nor sacrificial wine, the knife, the salted meal to sprinkle on the victims" (149). But the act is an example of what Girard labels a sacrificial crisis, the failure to stop the rising tide of revenge by turning to the sacred. This failure arises when, instead of a *pharmakos,* the victims are chosen from among those related to the conflict. Omens ranging from dreaded comets to statues of deities that "in the temples weep" (149) clearly show that Atreus is intent on destroying the sacred order through his improper use of sacrifice. He is the harbinger of chaos. In *Thyestes* there is no resolution to the sacrificial crisis. Astraea, together with Libra, the scales of justice that promote order and differences, is consumed by chaos, just as a father consumes his own children, further erasing the notion of bounds, limits, differences. *Thyestes* depicts a world where rival brothers mirror each other in violence, where a human king behaves worse than the fiercest beast, where social order and consequently universal order are thoroughly subverted.

Titus Andronicus attempts to mirror the sacrificial crisis, the loss of order, and the threat of chaos that are symbolized by the fall of Astraea.[7] Indeed, the third scene of the fourth act emulates and comments upon the fourth chorus in *Thyestes*. "Terras Astraea reliquit" (4.3.4), recalls Titus from the *Metamorphoses*. It is most appropriate that at this point he cite Ovid since he had just learned the horrible truth about Lavinia through reference to the myth of Philomela and Tereus. Her attackers, in the same manner as Tereus, had removed her tongue so that she would not be able to publicize her outrage. Only by pointing to the *Metamorphoses* and turning to the appropriate page is the truth discovered. *Titus Andronicus* is truly a palimpsest where other texts can be read.[8] It is a work "patterned," as Titus notes, "by that the poet here describes" (4.1.58).

Maddened by the rape and mutilation of his daughter Lavinia, Titus orders a search for Astraea. He believes, having cited Ovid, that she no longer abides on earth. Perhaps, he claims, she can be found in the sea, or more likely in "Pluto's region" (4.3.13). Titus relates the iron age and the persent injustices to the "wicked" Emperor Saturninus and to "ungrateful Rome" (4.3.17). By associating the city and its emperor with Astraea, the play reveals yet another context, another level in the palimpsest—Virgil's *Aeneid* and the *Fourth Eclogue,* where the goddess assumes an imperial garb. A. C. Hamilton (1967), one of the few critics who have noted this connection, explains: "The tragic world becomes a diabolical mirror that reflects our world in inverted pastoral terms. For this reason the play parodies Virgil's fourth eclogue: in place of the age of gold that heralds a new birth of peace, with the earth pouring out her fruits and all beasts living in concord, it shows the age of Saturninus, where Tamora uses gold for revenge against the Andronici, and Rome becomes 'a wilderness of tigers' " (82–83). While Virgil had hailed Augustus's *pax romana* as a golden age, Shakespeare depicts a darker vision where Rome, years later, is destroyed not only by the Goths from without, but by tyranny, cruelty, and revenge from within, becoming a wilderness of tigers rather than a civilizing influence.

Alan Sommers (1960) claims that "the essential conflict of *Titus Andronicus* is the struggle between Rome, and all that this signifies in the European tradition to which we, and Shakespeare belong, and the barbarism of primitive, original nature" (276). But one cannot say that Roman and Goths represent civilization and barbarism, for, in order to regenerate Rome, the Goths unite with the great empire within the play. The truth is much more complex, as Ronald Broude (1970) has explained, since, next to the idea of Rome as the pinnacle of civilization, "there existed an image of the Goths as a people whose vitality and nobility were in marked contrast to the Romans' effeteness and decadence" (28). The play is not so much about the triumph of Romans or Goths but is an investigation into the violence that exists within civilization. Titus has had difficulty understanding the rising tide of violence and is maddened by the wilderness of tigers that Rome has become. In order to help Titus, Marcus suggests that his companions "feed his humour kindly" (4.3.29) by acting out the "fiction" of the search for Astraea. Such a suggestion is in keeping with medical theories of the epoch—it also forms the basis of a rather famous scene in a Spanish play of the period, *La estrella de Sevilla (The star of Seville)*, where the *gracioso* is able to save Sancho from total madness by following his humoral fantasies (Burke 1974; de Armas 1979). In both plays, such fantasies reveal a deeper truth about the situation that is being experienced. In *Titus Andronicus,* Publius reports that Astraea is not to be found in Pluto's realm, although the god of the infernal regions has revealed that she is "with Jove in heaven" (4.3.41). Publius's report triggers the central tableau in this scene as Titus orders his companions to shoot arrows at the heavens: "We will solicit heaven and more the gods / To send down Justice for to wreak our wrongs" (4.3.51–52). The six characters to stage will shoot arrows at six celestial deities, asking for the return of justice to the land. Four of these six gods and goddesses had already been invoked in the first scene of this act when Marcus had prayed for inspiration in discovering Lavinia's attackers. That prayer had ostensibly been answered. These four deities are: Apollo, Jove, Mercury, and Pallas. To these Titus adds two more, Mars and Saturn. As they are ready to shoot, Marcus countermands Titus's order and tells the others to shoot the arrows into the court so as to "afflict the Emperor in his pride" (4.3.63). Many seem to have followed this order, for Saturninus later discovers four arrows in his court. Two, however, are missing. A chart of the situation may help to clarify the significance of the deities.

ARCHER:	AIMED AT:	MARCUS' PRAYER:	ARROWS RECOVERED:
1. Marcus	Jove	yes	yes
2. Publius or Sempronius	Apollo	yes	yes
3. Publius or Sempronius	Mercury	yes	yes
4. Titus	Mars	NO	yes
5. Caius	Saturn	NO	NO
6. Lucius	Pallas	yes	NO

An audience versed in astrology, as Shakespeare's was (Allen 1941; Parr 1953; Shumaker 1972) must have noticed that five of the gods aimed at are planetary deities—Jove as Jupiter, Apollo as Sol, Mercury, Mars, and Saturn. Furthermore, the audience would have understood why Marcus did not include in his prayer the two planetary deities added by Titus: Mars and Saturn are the malefic two among the seven Ptolemaic planets. If Marcus wishes success in his endeavor, he should propitiate the benefic celestials, and this is what he does in invoking Jupiter, Sol, and Mercury—which form one of the positive triads.[9] Titus's addition of Mars, the planet he aims at, serves to reveal that his madness, his humoral imbalance, is due to an excess of choler. Mars rules this humor. Finally, he adds Saturn, perhaps recalling that the present Roman emperor was named Saturninus. His tyrannical rule stands in opposition to the benefic qualities of Saturn as ruler of the first golden age. For Saturn, it should be remembered, is a bipolar entity (Klibansky 1964; de Armas 1981). On the one hand, he is the most malefic of planets for the astrologers, presented iconographically as the devourer of his own children; and on the other, he is the planet of the highest wisdom, according to the Neoplatonists, and the ruler of the happiest first age of humankind. The arrow can serve to destroy the malefic aspects of the planet, as represented in the Emperor Saturninus, and to bring forth its benefic qualities through the prayer that accompanies the arrow, requesting the return of Astraea, a goddess who lived on earth with Saturn during the first age.

One deity remains still unaccounted for, Phallas. She is to be contacted by Lucius, Titus's grandson. Observing the trajectory of his arrow, Titus exclaims: "Good boy, in Virgo's lap; give it Pallas" (4.3. 65). Pallas, because of her virginity, was equated in ancient times with Virgo-Astraea. As such, she performs an important function in Marcus's prayer. She is a deity who will bring forth justice upon those involved in an innocent virgin's rape. Pallas is also the centerpiece of Titus's quest, for she is Astraea, the justice he seeks to bring back to earth. Marcus had ordered that the arrows be shot not toward the sky, but toward the Emperor's court. Saturninus finds four arrows. Significantly he does not find the two that are essential to Titus's quest—those aimed at Saturn and at Pallas-Virgo.[10]

The bringing down of celestial influences with arrows is not without its dangers. The heavens, in such a chaotic age, may falter and begin to fall. This is exactly what transpires, albeit in a parodic context. Titus complains that Publius has shot off one of Taurus's horns. Marcus replies with a humorous description, granting to Saturninus the Ram's horns, since his wife, Tamora, had just had a child by Aaron the moor (4.3.70–75). However, the fall of a constellation (or part of it) recalls the fourth chorus in *Thyestes*. In the Roman play, Taurus's horns are also the cause of celestial havoc: ". . . the Bull, who before him on bright horns bears the Hyades, shall draft the Twins down with him and the Crab's wide-curving claws" (1968, 161). Although the somber mood of the chorus contrasts with Marcus's wit, the situation in both plays is rather similar, since human beings create havoc in the heavens through their earthly actions. Instead of the return of Astraea, *Thyestes* portrays Virgo's and the zodiac's fall. In *Titus Andronicus*, parts of two constellations (Aries and Taurus) are also said to fall, albeit jokingly, and Virgo-Pallas receives an arrow, with ambivalent results. *Thyestes* refers to Sagittarius as "old Chiron" who "shall loose his shafts from the snapped bowstrings" (1968, 161) as he falls to earth. In *Titus Andronicus* Chiron is not mentioned as a zodiacal constellation. Instead, he is one of the ravishers of the virginal Lavinia. The shafts are no longer heavenly weapons, but are used by men. *Thyestes* and *Titus Andronicus* express the confluence of celestial, terrestrial, and even infernal planes to create an ambience and admixture akin to chaos. Both plays, as if commenting on Virgil's jubilant vision of the return of an imperial Astraea, have as a central figure a tyrant who triggers violence. Animal imagery is associated with both. Atreus as the "hungry tigress" (1968, 149), for example, may have triggered the description of Saturninus's Rome as a "wilderness of tigers" (3.1.54). Sacred and social ceremonies are crucial to the action in both works, but, rather than pointing to an end of the violence, they reveal a sacrificial crisis. Ironically, Titus is the initiator of violence in Shakespeare's play since he accedes to the sacrifice of Tamora's son, Alarbus, with a total disregard for kinship and degree. When Saturninus takes Tamora as his wife, the stage is set for her revenge. René Girard's (1980) comments on *Troilus and Cressida* are eminently applicable to *Titus Andronicus:* "Social and cultural differences disintegrate, and we are left with characters deprived of true identity or difference,

because they keep stupidly repeating the same violent deeds. . . .
The executioners of revenge are no different from their victims
since they, too, will become victims in their turn" (124). Perhaps,
when T.S. Eliot (1927) labeled *Titus Andronicus* as "one of the
stupidest . . . plays ever written" (xxvii), he was referring to the
action. For the spectator witnesses the proliferation of acts of
violence and the escalation of horror, culminating in a Thyestian
banquet that makes him wonder how the heroic label can remain
upon the perpetrators. Titus's final triumph is rather ambivalent.
Girard's words are again applicable to this early drama: "Shakespeare can always provide his audience with the victims it demands
while, on a more subtle plane, he ironically points to the injustice
and arbitrariness of this victimizing" (124).

In Virgil's *Fourth Eclogue,* a child was born who would lead
Rome into a new golden age. A. C. Hamilton (1967, 82–83) notes
that the only birth that takes place in *Titus Andronicus* is an-
nounced with bitter irony. We witness the birth of the illegitimate
child of Tamora, Queen of the Goths, and of her moorish lover, who
is one of the most compelling villains in Elizabethan drama (and
there are many). Not only has mimetic violence compromised
Titus's heroic role, but the very myth of Astraea seems to have been
undermined by the nature of the child's conception. Thus it appears
as if Shakespeare's play mirrors Seneca's pessimistic vision of
ensuing chaos. However, G. K. Hunter (1974), in his rejection of the
Senecan ambience of *Titus Andronicus,* asserts: "Even a play as
concerned to avoid explicit Christianity as Shakespeare's *Titus
Andronicus* suggests in the end that justice can return to the world
with comfort for the good as well as punishment for the wicked, and
decent behavior all around. . . . The play ends, not with the 'happy'
murderer enjoying his infernal reward . . . but with the brief madness of revenge atoned for in the true justice by an expiatory death"
(73, 77). For Hunter, order is restored at the end with the death of
the villains, together with Titus's suicide. In terms of the myth of
Astraea, such a conclusion can be supported if, instead of looking
to the illegitimate child, one looks at who shot the arrow that
reached Astraea. Paralleling the moorish child, one encounters
Lucius, the grandson of Titus. It is his father who leads the army of
Goths to Rome and thus helps to bring down the tyrannical rule of
Saturninus and who is proclaimed emperor at Titus's death. His
child has never participated in violence, except for his extraordinary feat in archery. As the legitimate heir, young Lucius can be
equated with Virgil's mysterious child who is to actualize the return
of Astraea. Titus's astral magic may have worked through the boy

Lucius, a name that carries magical connotations for the Renaissance, being the name of the protagonist of Apuleius's *Golden Ass.* In this supposedly hermetic text (Yates 1964, 10; de Armas 1983), Lucius is regenerated through the mysteries of Isis (Yates 1975, 32; Allen 1963, 462–3), the Egyptian goddess who, for some, was also representative of Astraea. If the name Lucius is derived from Shakespeare's favorite novel,[11] it is also one of Seneca's own names. Astraea may have returned at the conclusion of *Titus Andronicus,* but mimetic violence has come close to destroying the heroic nature of the characters and of the struggle. Saturninus as tyrant is akin to Saturn who, in his negative aspects, is the devourer of children. Through mimetic violence, Titus assumes this role, preparing a dinner where he serves to Tamora her own children. It is true that young Lucius, the child who called on Astraea, is untouched by violence, but the moorish child has not perished along with the father—so that conflict can be rekindled in future years. Celestial influences have aided in the restoration of justice, and Lucius may well be the mysterious child prophesied by Virgil. But Astraea's reign is as precarious in *Titus Andronicus* as it is absent in *Thyestes.*

By the time *La vida es sueño* came to be written, the myth of Astraea had become such a commonplace in the description of rulers and questions of empire that an even more subtle treatment of her return or fall might have been required to arouse interest in an audience. Rosaura assumes the name Astraea during the second act as a disguise at the court. Most critics agree that her role parallels that of Segismundo and that she also serves as his guide in his eventual transformation (Wilson 1965, Sloman 1965, Whitby 1965). Since Rosaura is an anagram for "auroras" (dawns), she could well symbolize the dawn of a new golden age. The name change is indicated in a somewhat frivolous palace scene as she attempts to recover a portrait held by Astolfo. This *capa y espada* scene allows the audience to contextualize this hint of astral mythology into a many-layered palimpsest. Astraea's association with Astolfo occurs in the *Orlando furioso,* where he listens to Andronica's prophecy of the return of Astraea—a new golden age that will dawn during the reign of Charles V. Astolfo also rides a hippogriff in Ariosto's poem, and it would be difficult for the audience to forget the very first line of *La vida es sueño:* "Hipogrifo violento" (*Diez Comedias* 1968, 13) ("Wild hippogriff" [Calderon 1961, 13]).[12] One is thus propelled back to the first scene of the Spanish play, when Rosaura-Astraea falls into Poland and falls from her horse-hippogriff. The fall from the horse, critics such as Valbuena Briones, Bandera, Maurin, and León have noted, is related since classical times to lack of control over one's passions. Rosaura's fall is thus a moral one: she has been dishonored by Astolfo. Visually, her fall from the horse or mythical creature is not so dramatic as her descent from the "monte eminente" (612) ("rough mountain," 14) to the dark depths where a prison dominates the landscape. This reveals another level in the palimpsest, for it is reminiscent of the fall of the constellations to earth as depicted in Seneca's *Thyestes.* In the Roman play, the Chorus sees in Astraea's fall not her triumphant return to establish a golden age, but the advent of chaos, as the heavens crumble, the sun disappears, and an unnatural darkness settles upon the land. Such is the situation also encountered at the begining of *La vida es sueño.* The hippogriff, a creature described in terms of the confusion of the four elements, represents the chaos created by lack of control over the sexual appetite, as Cilveti points out (1971, 163–72). As she falls, Rosaura is faced with "confuso laberinto / de estas desnudas peñas" (611) ("this labyrinth of naked rock," 13) rather than with a nature that provides man with bounteous gifts. Darkness, confusion, labyrinths, and prisons dominate the language, the scene, and the action.

The virginal goddess has fallen or returned as a dishonored and abandoned woman. In this sense, both Calderón and Shakespeare add one more dimension to Seneca's subversion of the joyous myth of Astraea as it appears in Virgil's *Fourth Eclogue.* In *Titus Andronicus,* the beautiful maiden Lavinia, Titus's beloved daughter, is raped and mutilated by Demetrius and his brother Chiron, the latter a name for a constellation that would be shot down by arrows reminiscent of those carried by this legendary centaur. Lavinia's plight is revealed to her family through an Ovidian legend that in turn triggers Titus's recollection of the Ovidian phrase, "terras Astraea reliquit" (4.3.4). Lavinia and Astraea are thus intimately interrelated. While the approaching chaos of the ever more violent and wicked iron age leads to the fall or return of Astraea in both Shakespeare and Calderón, the English playwright keeps goddess and "fallen" maiden, Astraea and Lavinia, as separate beings, while Calderón fuses the two. What more appropriate disguise for the virginal Astraea in "Kali Yuga" than that of a dishonored woman seeking redress? The recovery of Rosaura's honor will occur at the same time as the restoration of justice and order to the realm. Shakespeare's Lavinia, on the other hand, will perish at her father's hands in the name of honor.

The order restored at the end of *La vida es sueño* can come about only with Segismundo's transformation. He possesses, like Titus, a choleric and martial temperament that leads to violence and threatens the stability of the kingdom. Titus kills his Lavinia. Segismundo, on the other hand, has Rosaura as helper and guide. She alone can temper his choleric nature (1961, 18; 1968, 617). While the action of Shakespeare's play grips the audience through a runaway violence that is clearly self-reinforcing and escalates in its mimetic battle not only within its textual bounds but also in imitation of Seneca's macabre text, Calderón's *La vida es sueño* creates tension through the latent rather than the manifest. The instances of violence serve to reveal a staggering depth of feelings that will surface in the civil war of the third act to be quickly brought under control. The Spanish play is intent in providing resolution, in bringing about a new age as prophesied in Virgil's *Fourth Eclogue.* Shakespeare's text leads to a more ambiguous conclusion, but both include a mysterious Virgilian child. As with Rosaura-Astraea, Calderón simply and masterfully creates Segismundo.

The King of Poland, Basilio, had incarcerated his child because at his birth there were celestial and terrestrial portents that he deciphered as ominous and threatening. Among them is the sudden darkening of the sky (1961, 30; 1968, 629), which recalls the unnatural darkness that descends upon the earth in *Thyestes.* The description of the times in *La vida es sueño* is even reminiscent of the *ekpyrosis* narrated by Seneca in the *Naturales Quaestiones.* From these portents Basilio concludes that the child will grow up to be "el príncipe más cruel—y el monarca más impío" (629) ("The most cruel of all princes / The most wicked of all monarchs" 30), who would destroy the kingdom and depose him. In mythology, the tyrannical Saturn also believed that he would be deposed by his own child and therefore concocted a macabre dinner reminiscent of *Thyestes.* Basilio, as devourer, is revealed through his incarceration of Segismundo.[13] Rather than increasing violence, as in *Titus Andronicus,* the action here reduces it but opens signification to encompass the more violent mythological structures. It is the allusiveness of the test and not its explicitness that creates unease. Basilio reveals the secret birth at a moment when the problem of succession becomes critical. His justification for incarcerating his own son includes a reference to the "Séneca español" (1968, 632). As in *Titus Andronicus,* the Roman tragedian is inscribed into the text in order to subvert the surface meaning. Basilio's reference leads spectators to link him with the tyrannical figures in Seneca's life and art, while the Lucius in Shakespeare's play had led one to wonder if the child was a sure sign of a coming golden age or if Seneca's darker vision ruled the dénouement.

Segismundo is the counterpart both of Lucius and of Aaron's illegitimate child. Basilio sees him as a monster, an illegitimate child (de Armas, 1986c, 108–22) who will destroy the kingdom. Indeed, the prince compares himself with the giants of old who threatened the heavens ("porque fuera / contra vos gigante" 620), just as the Chorus in *Thyestes* wondered: "Are the conquered Giants again essaying war?" (157). As he wages war against his father in the third act, Segismundo once again takes up this comparison, but places it in a Roman context, reminding the audience of the fear of destruction that pervaded the Empire and that led Virgil to prophesy through Jupiter in the *Aeneid:* "For these I set neither bounds nor periods of empire; dominion without end have I bestowed" (1934, 1:261). Mircea Eliade (1954) explains that "it was not until after the publication of the *Aeneid* that Rome was called *urbs aeterna. . . .* Thus it was, that, liberated from the mythos of the twelve eagles and of the *ekpyrosis,* Rome could increase until, as Virgil foretells, it embraced even the regions 'beyond the paths of the sun and the year' " (135).

Segismundo evokes the fear of *ekpyrosis,* the dread of the end of the empire and of the universe, but, as the son of a malefic and tyrannical Saturn, he can also inspire hope. Jupiter, who later prophesied Rome's eternity, was the threatened child who, in defeating the father, established a new order in the heavens. At the end of the play, Segismundo defeats the father and does establish a new order reminiscent of heavenly peace and Roman hope. Its benefic nature is clarified when the prince forgives his father. All are reconciled except for the rebel soldier, who is imprisoned as a sign that civilization cannot allow mimetic violence to proliferate. He is an appropriate *pharmakos,* if one accepts Girard's theories,[14] since neither in kinship nor degree does he come close to the now reconciled factions. Furthermore, the principle of justice is not subverted since he is not an innocent victim, but a man guilty of treason (Heiple 1973).

Although modern criticism has foregrounded the soldier's fate, this is but a passing concern in the play. By sacrificing the rebel soldier, Segismundo may have deflected attention away from the essential and truly sacred sacrifice that brings about the final resolution. The central sacrifice around which the whole play is constructed is Segismundo's. In his father he had seen what Joseph Campbell (1972) refers to as "tyrant Holdfast—out for himself"

(15). In act two the prince had staged his mimetic desire. He became his father's rival since he wanted to be like his father in power and cruelty. Conquest of the self, Campbell explains, is equal to atonement with the father, since both are seen as reflections of the notion of egocentric self-aggrandizement. Not only does he forgive the father, but he also orders Astolfo to marry Rosaura, evincing the conquest of his passion. Segismundo is reborn (1961, 94; 1968, 696) in a new heroic mold where the externality of pride gives way to what Girard (1965, 300) calls a "victory over desire."[15] "Acudamos a lo eterno" (689) becomes Segismundo's motto as power and passion are transcended in a personal sacrifice that is so pleasing to the gods that Astraea-Rosaura is allowed to preside over the elevation of what had been a mysterious child to his proper Virgilian role.

To the prevalent Virgilian tradition of the return of Astraea and the advent of a mysterious child who would bring back a new golden age, and to the imperialist and optimistic notion of the eternal renewal of the Roman Empire, Seneca has brought a vision of violence and chaos. Living at a time when Augustus's rule and the *pax romana* had been replaced by tyrannical emperors whose sole purpose seemed to have been self-aggrandizement to the point of becoming gods, the Roman tragedian subverted in one easy stroke the grandiose return of the imperial Astraea by suggesting her fall. The power, revenge, and runaway violence that had been described by René Girard in terms of a sacrificial crisis led to the very disintegration of the heavens in *Thyestes,* to the advent of *ekpyrosis* and chaos in the midst of an iron age. A further degradation of the myth resulted from the macabre banquet, since it clearly paralleled Saturn's tyrannical rule depicted through his consumption of his own children. And Saturn, together with Astraea, was said to have lived on earth during the golden age.

The Renaissance was dazzled by the political, literary, and religious possibilities of Virgil's proclamations (Levin 1969, 112). Consequently, Seneca's darker vision, buried in a slight yet key allusion in *Thyestes,* remained forgotton, except that two of the greatest playwrights of that epoch saw its dramatic potential. Shakespeare's *Titus Andronicus* is an early play that experiments with Seneca's image of the fall in order to chart a runaway mimetic violence whence it is difficult to extract the heroic values. Here, the supposedly heroic Titus destroys the tyrant Saturninus at a Thyestian banquet that raises the question as to who is in reality the tyrannical Saturn. It may be that young Lucius has been able to contact Astraea in the arrow-shooting scene. He has called the goddess so that she may bring back to earth justice and chastity. Their absence is depicted in the rule of Saturninus and in the debasement of Lavinia. But if Lucius represents new hope and imperial *renovatio* through the unification of Goths and Romans, the moor's illegitimate child is proof that oppositions have not been wholly transcended.

While *Titus Andronicus* seeks to reach the end of violence by portraying its extremes, *La vida es sueño* strives for integration. Dramatic oppositions displayed in *Titus Andronicus* are internalized. Lucius and Aaron's son become the struggling Segismundo, either savior or destroyer. Lavinia and Virgo-Astraea are subsumed into one character, Rosaura. The darker side of each of these two Calderonian figures reflects Seneca's pessimistic portrayal, while their godlike and heroic natures point to a Virgilian resolution. The key to unification or integration is found in sacrifice. The Thyestian banquet, rejected by the gods, was replicated and magnified in Shakespeare's play. These blood sacrifices called upon chaos rather than upon the celestial pantheon promoted by the Roman civilization. Only Calderón's text is able properly to propitiate the gods through sacrifice, for *La vida es sueño* is built upon Segismundo's sacrifice of his own baser nature. By giving up lust and pride, he fulfills the promise of the mysterious child, thus replacing the "wilderness of tigers" with the harmony that forms the basis of the Virgilian *urbs aeterna*.

Notes

1. See Sullivan (1983, 176). Schlegel sums up his comparison of the two figures as follows: "What they have in common with each other is the spirit of romantic poetry, giving utterance to itself in a dramatic shape" (Schlegel 1846, 342).

2. "To say that life is a dream is to say that all the world is a stage, an assertion that Shakespeare reserved for the melancholy Jacques" (Maraniss 1978, 15). On *La vida es sueño*'s relationship to *The Taming of the Shrew* see, for example, Gerstinger 1973 and Duque 1983.

3. On this parallel see also Abel (1963). Schmidgall (1981, 93) discusses the temperance achieved by Prospero and Segismundo. See also Cope (1973, 259). Blue (1982) comments: "The power of art, of magic, of manipulation is something that must be mistrusted and finally abjured by Prospero and by Basilio in a play by Calderón," and Cascardi (1984, 16) states: "He [Basilio] is taken to be part Prospero of Shakespeare's *Tempest,* if less benevolent, part Hamlet, albeit not vengeful or mad. But more important, Basilio is a failed dramatist."

4. *Titus Andronicus* is one of Shakespeare's earliest compositions, "first performed in the years 1590–92 and . . . revised for the recorded performance of January 1594" (Waith 1984, 16). The supposed faults and horrors of this early play led many early critics to question Shakespearean authorship. J. M. Robertson (1924, 479–80), for example, states: "To the full extent to which aesthetic demon-

stration is possible, it is demonstrated by comparative evidence that most of the play is written by [George] Peele; and it is hardly less certain that much of the rest was written by Greene and Kyd, with some by Marlowe. . . . The case is thus proved against his authorship independently of the extremely strong presumption that the most coarsely repulsive play of the entire Elizabethan drama cannot have been the work of the greatest and most subtle of all dramatics of the age" (479–80).

5. All references to this play are to Seneca's *Tragedies,* vol. 2, translated by Frank Justus Miller, Loeb Classical Library (Cambridge: Harvard University Press, 1968). T. S. Eliot (1927, xxvii) once asserted that "there is nothing really Senecan at all" in *Titus Andronicus.* Perhaps this is a reaction to the term "Senecan," which had come to mean so many things, including the presentation of ghostly, bloody, and horrible excesses upon the stage. Indeed, Eliot defends Seneca against his Elizabethan imitators and claims that the many horrors of *Titus Andronicus* "Seneca himself would not have tolerated." J. D. Wilson (1948) in his edition of the English play describes it as "some broken-down cart, laden with bleeding corpses from an Elizabethan scaffold, and driven by an executioner from Bedlam" (xii). And yet, it is precisely the bloody feast that occupies the foreground of *Thyestes* which creates its major link with *Titus Andronicus,* where the grisly dinner is replicated at the end and, according to John W. Cunliffe (1965, 69), "even the gentle Lavinia helps to prepare the Thyestian banquet." My essay will show that Shakespeare's play is an attempt to understand the nature of the violence presented by Seneca. I would agree with Geoffrey Bullough's (1973, 196) recent assessment: "Il est fort probable qu'au début de sa carrière sa conception tragique dut beaucoup à Sénèque, dans les premières *Histoires* comme dans le traitement de l'histoire fictive de *Titus Andronicus.*" Unfortunately, Bullough (1966, 6:27) says very little of the arrow-shooting scene that concerns us most in this paper: "The confusion of the divine and zodiacal names in IV.3 may be a reminiscence of the derangement of the heavens foretold by the fourth Chorus in *Thyestes* after Atreus' crime."

6. A golden age would follow chaos, but this should not trigger excessive rejoicing for it would soon degenerate into another iron age: "But their innocence too will not last, except as long as they are new. Vice quickly creeps in. Virtue is difficult to find; it needs a director and guide. Vices can be learned even without a teacher" (Seneca 1971, 1:297).

7. All references are to *Titus Andronicus,* edited by Eugene M. Waith (Oxford: Clarendon Press, 1984).

8. On the notion of the palimpsests as applied to literary texts see, for example, Genette (1982) and the preface by Gayatri Chakravorti Spivak to Derrida (1974, lxxv–lxxvi).

9. "Along with the Mercury and Sol, he [Jupiter] is among the most human of planets, or so Ficino says in *The Planets.* In a letter to Lorenzo he adds Venus to the list and, by coupling Jupiter with Mercury, ends up with three planetary 'Graces' " (Moore 1982, 177). Although this is the basic formula for the three Graces in Ficino, the fact recorded in the above discussion that there are really four benefic planets causes an oscillation in Ficino's naming of the three. Sol, Jupiter, and Mercury is certainly a possible triad.

10. Among his finds is the arrow shot by Titus himself. This may be a clue that his madness is feigned and that he was aware of Marcus's directions to shoot the arrows into the Emperor's court. Given the importance of ceremonials in the play, this may be one more—where Titus, feigning madness, calls upon Saturn and Astraea to restore balance to a kingdom that seems to have become topsy-turvy since he approved the initial ceremony involving human sacrifice (Waith 1984).

11. "... but it is a fact that beginning with *Titus Andronicus,* all the plays in the canon which include Lucius, *Titus Andronicus, Julius Caesar, Timon of Athens, Antony and Cleopatra* and *Cymbeline,* whatever the other classical influences, have Apuleian material woven into their textures" (Tobin 1984, 19).

12. All page references to *La vida es sueño* are from *Diez Comedias del Siglo de oro,* edited by José Martel, Hyman Alpern and Leonard Mades, 611–97, (New York: Harper and Row, 1968). Translations are from Calderón, *Six Plays,* translated by Denis Florence MacCarthy with revision by Henry W. Wells (New York: Las Américas, 1961).

13. For a portrayal of Basilio as an icon of Saturn see de Armas, (1986b).

14. For an application of Girard to Calderón see Bandera (1975, 253–60).

15. "Great novels always spring from an obsession that has been transcended. The hero sees himself in the rival he loathes; he renounces the differences suggested by hatred. . . . This victory over desire is extremely painful."

Works Cited

Abel, Lionel. 1963. *Metatheater.* New York: Hill and Wang.

Allen, Don Cameron. 1941. *The Star-Crossed Renaissance.* Durham: Duke University Press.

Allen, Richard Hinkley. 1963. *Star Names: Their Lore and Meaning.* New York: Dover.

Bandera, Cesáreo. 1967. "El itinerario de Segismundo en *La vida es sueño.*" *Hispanic Review* 35:69–84.

———. 1975. *Mimesis conflictiva.* Madrid: Gredos.

Blue, William R. 1982. "Calderón and Shakespeare: The Romances." In *Calderón de la Barca at the Tercentenary: Comparative Views,* edited by Wendell Aycock and Sydney Craves, 89–102. Lubbock: Texas Tech Press.

Broude, Ronald. 1970. "Roman and Goth in *Titus Andronicus.*" *Shakespeare Studies* 6:27–34.

Bullough, Geoffrey. 1975. *Narrative and Dramatic Sources of Shakespeare.* 8 vols. New York: Columbia University Press.

———. 1973. "Sénèque et le jeune Shakespeare." In *Les tragédies de Sénèque et le théâtre de la Renaissance.* Paris: Centre National de la Recherche Scientifique.

Burke, James F. 1974. "*La Estrella de Sevilla* and the Tradition of Saturnine Melancholy." *Bulletin of Hispanic Studies* 51:137–56.

Calderón de la Barca, Pedro. 1961. *Six Plays.* Translated by Denis Florence MacCarthy with revision by Henry W. Wells. New York: Las Américas.

Callimachus. 1955. *Hymns and Epigrams.* Lycophron. Aratus. Loeb Classical Library. Translated by A. W. Mair and G. R. Mair. Cambridge: Harvard University Press.

Campbell, Joseph. 1972. *The Hero with a Thousand Faces.* 2d ed. Princeton: Princeton University Press.

Cascardi, Anthony J. 1984. *The Limits of Illusion: A Critical Study of Calderón.* Cambridge: Cambridge University Press.

Cilveti, Angel L. 1971. *El significado de "La vida es sueño."* Madrid: Albatross.

Cope, Jackson I. 1973. *The Theater and the Dream*. Baltimore: The Johns Hopkins University Press.

Cunliffe, John W. 1965. *The Influence of Seneca on Elizabethan Tragedy*. 1893; reprint, Hamden, Conn.: Archon.

de Armas, Frederick A. 1979. "The Apples of Colchis: Key to an Interpretation of *La estrella de Sevilla*." *Forum for Modern Language Studies* 15:1–13.

———. 1981. "The Saturn Factor: Examples of Astrological Imagery in Lope de Vega's Works." In *Studies in Honor of Everett W. Hesse*, edited by William C. McCrary and José A. Madrigal, 63–80. Lincoln, Nebr.: Society of Spanish and Spanish American Studies.

———. 1983. "Lope de Vega and the Hermetic Tradition: The Case of Dardanio in *La Arcadia*." *Revista Canadiense de Estudios Hispánicos* 7:345–62.

———a. 1986. "The Apocalyptic Vision of *La vida es sueño:* Calderón and Edward FitzGerald." *Comparative Literature Studies* 23:119–40.

———b. 1986. "*El planeta más impío:* Basilio's Role in *La vida es sueño.*" *Modern Language Review* 81:900–911.

———c. 1986. *The Return of Astraea: An Astral-Imperial Myth in Calderón*. Lexington: The University Press of Kentucky.

Derrida, Jacques. 1974. *Of Grammatology*. Translated by Gayatri Chakravorty Spivak. Baltimore: The John Hopkins University Press.

Diez Comedias del Siglo de oro. 1968. Edited by José Martel, Hyman Alpern, and Leonard Mades, New York: Harper and Row.

Duque, Pedro J. 1983. "Calderón-Shakespeare: algunas similitudes y diferencias." In *Calderón. Actas del Congreso Internacional sobre Calderón y el teatro español del Siglo de Oro*, edited by Luciano García Lorenzo, 3:1277–88. Madrid: Consejo Superior de Investigaciones Científicas.

Eliade, Mircea. 1954. *The Myth of the Eternal Return*. Translated by Willard R. Trask. Princeton: Princeton University Press.

Eliot, T. S. 1927. Introduction to *Seneca, His Tenne Tragedies Translated into English by Thomas Newton (1581)* by Seneca. New York: Alfred Knopf.

Genette, Gérard. 1982. *Palimpsestes*. Paris: Seuil.

Germanicus, 1975. *Les Phénomènes d'Aratos*. Edited and translated by André Le Boeuffle. Paris: Société d'édition "Les Belles Lettres."

Gerstinger, Henry. 1973. *Pedro Calderón de la Barca*. New York: Frederick Ungar.

Girard, René. 1965. *Deceit, Desire, and the Novel*. Translated by Yvonne Freccero. Baltimore: The John Hopkins University Press.

———. 1980. "Shakespeare's Theory of Mythology." In *Classical Mythology in Twentieth Century Thought and Literature*, edited by Wendell M. Aycock and Theodore M. Klein. Lubbock: Texas Tech University Press.

———. 1977. *Violence and the Sacred*. Translated by Patrick Gregory. Baltimore: The John Hopkins University Press.

Hamilton, A. C. 1967. *The Early Shakespeare*. San Marino: The Huntington Library.

Heiple, Daniel L. 1973. "The Tradition behind the Punishment of the Rebel Soldier in *La vida es sueño.*" *Bulletin of Hispanic Studies* 50:1–17.

Henry, Denis and Elizabeth Henry. 1985. *The Mask of Power*. Chicago: Bolchazy-Carducci.

Hunter, G. K. 1974. "Seneca and English Tragedy." In *Seneca,* edited by C. D. N. Costa, 166–204. London: Routledge and Keagan Paul.

Klibansky, Raymond, Erwin Panofsky and Fritz Saxl. 1964. *Saturn and Melancholy.* London: Thomas Nelson.

León, Pedro R. 1983. "El caballo desbocado, símbolo de la pasión desenfrenada en la obra de Calderón." *Romanische Forschungen* 95:23–35.

Levin, Harry. 1969. *The Myth of the Golden Age in the Renaissance.* Oxford: Oxford University Press.

Macrobius. 1952. *Commentary on the Dream of Scipio.* Edited and translated by William Harris Stahl. New York: Columbia University Press.

Maraniss, James. 1978. *On Calderón.* Columbia: University of Missoury Press.

Maurin, Margaret S. 1967. "The Monster, the Sepulcher and the Dark: Related Patterns of Imagery in *La vida es sueño.*" *Hispanic Review* 35:161–78.

Moore, Thomas. 1982. *The Planets Within.* Lewisburg: Bucknell University Press.

Muir, Kenneth. 1985. *Contrasts and Controversies.* Brighton: The Harvester Press.

Parr, Johnstone. 1953. *Tamburlaine's Malady.* University, Ala.: University of Alabama Press.

Robertson, J. M. 1924. *An Introduction to the Study of the Shakespeare Canon.* New York: E. P. Dutton.

Schlegel, Augustus William. 1846. *A Course of Lectures on Dramatic Art and Literature.* Translated by John Black. London: Henry G. Bohn.

Schmidgall, Gary. 1981. *Shakespeare and the Courtly Aesthetes.* Berkeley: University of California Press.

Seneca. 1971. *Naturales Quaestiones.* Loeb Classical Library. Translated by Thomas A. Corcoran. Cambridge: Harvard University Press.

———. 1968. *Tragedies.* Loeb Classical Library. Translated by Frank Justus Miller. Cambridge: Harvard University Press.

Shakespeare, William. 1984. *Titus Andronicus.* Edited by Eugene M. Waith. Oxford: Clarendon Press.

Shumaker, Wayne. 1972. *The Occult Sciences in the Renaissance.* Berkeley: University of California Press.

Sloman, A. E. 1965. "The Structure of Calderón's *La vida es sueño.*" In *Critical Essays on the Theater of Calderón,* edited by Bruce W. Wardropper, 90–100. New York: New York University Press.

Sommers, Alan. 1960. " 'Wilderness of Tigers': Structure and Symbolism in *Titus Andronicus.*" *Essays in Criticism* 10:275–89.

Sullivan, Henry W. 1983. *Calderón in the German Lands and the Low Countries: His Reception and Influence, 1654–1980.* Cambridge: Cambridge University Press.

Tarrant, R. J. 1985. Introduction to *Thyestes,* by Seneca. Atlanta: Scholar's Press.

Tobin, J. M. 1984. *Shakespeare's Favorite Novel.* Lanham, Md.: University Press of America.

Valbuena Briones, A. J. 1962. "El simbolismo en el teatro de Calderón: la caída del caballo." *Romanische Forschungen* 74:60–76.

Virgil. 1934. *Eclogues, Georgics, Aeneid 1–6.* The Loeb Classical Library. Translated by H. R. Fairclough. Cambridge: Harvard University Press.

Waith, Eugene M. 1984. "The Ceremonies of *Titus Andronicus.*" In *Mirror up to Shakespeare: Essays in Honour of G. R. Hibbard,* edited by J. C. Gray, 159–70. Toronto: Toronto University Press.

Whitby, William. 1965. "Rosaura's Role in the Structure of *La vida es sueño.*" In *Critical Essays on the Theater of Calderón,* edited by Bruce W. Wardropper, 101–13. New York: New York University Press.

Wilson, E. M. 1965. "On *La vida es sueño.*" In *Critical Essays on the Theater of Calderón,* edited by Bruce W. Wardropper, 63–89. New York: New York University Press.

Yates, Frances. 1975. *Astraea: The Imperial Theme in the Sixteenth Century.* London: Routledge and Kegan Paul.

———. 1964. *Giordano Bruno and the Hermetic Tradition.* Chicago: University of Chicago Press.

Contributors

GREGORY PETER ANDRACHUK is a professor at the University of Victoria. His scholarly interests include Medieval prose and poetry as well as the nature of the Auto Sacramental, and he has just completed an edition of the *Historia lastimera del príncipe Erato* (with Anthony Farrell).

JOHN J. ALLEN is from the University of Kentucky. Besides his edition of the *Quijote* (1977), his books on *Don Quijote, Hero or Fool,* I and II (1969 and 1979), and *The Reconstruction of a Spanish Golden Age Playhouse* (1983), Professor Allen is known for his involvement in the locating and reconstructing of early Spanish theaters.

FREDERICK A. DE ARMAS of Penn State University, is the author of a number of books including *The Invisible Mistress: Aspects of Feminism and Fantasy in the Golden Age* (1976) and *The Return of Astraea: an Astral Imperial Myth in Calderon* (1986). He has co-edited *Critical Perspectives on Calderon de la Barca* (1981) and contributed numerous articles to professional Journals.

DONALD A. BEECHER of Carleton University has translated and published Odet de Turnèbe's *Les Contens / Satisfaction All Around* and, with Massimo Ciavolella, Annibal Caro's *Gli Straccioni / The Scruffy Scoundrels* and Gian Lorenzo Bernini's untitled play *The Impresario,* as well as a critical edition and translation with Massimo Ciavolella of Jacques Ferrand's *Treatise on Erotic Melancholy* (1990). He is general editor of the Carleton Renaissance Plays in Translation Series and Dovehouse Editions, Ottawa.

DON W. CRUICKSHANK of the National University of Ireland has published editions, bibliographical and critical studies of Golden Age plays, notably Calderon's *Comedias* (with John Varey, 19 volumes, 1973), *Samuel Pepys's Spanish Plays* (with Edward Wilson, 1980), *El médico de su honra* (1981), and the bilingual *No hay burlas con el amor* / *Love is no laughing matter* (with Sean Page, 1986).

SHARON DAHLGREN VOROS of the Annapolis Naval Academy, works in the field of plot dynamics and performance codes. She is the author of *Petrarch and Garcilaso: A Linguistic Approach to Style* (1975) and numerous articles on the semiotic analysis of text.

DONALD T. DIETZ of Texas Technical University is the author of *The Auto Sacramental and the Parable in Spanish Golden Age Literature* (1973) and, as director of the Association for Spanish Classical Theater, has compiled an impressive collection of videotapes of Spanish plays in performance.

SUSAN L. FISCHER of Bucknell University has both edited and contributed to a volume of essays entitled *Comedias del siglo de Oro and Shakespeare* (1989). She has widely published in the field of Jungian approaches to the Comedia and comparative studies on Shakespeare and Golden Age playwrights.

TERESA J. KIRSCHNER is from Simon Fraser University. Besides her book on *El protagonista colectivo en 'Fuenteovejuna' de Lope de Vega* (1979) Professor Kirschner has published widely on Golden Age literature as well as modern authors.

ALEXANDER LEGGATT of the University of Toronto is the author of *Shakespeare's Comedy of Love* (1974), *Ben Jonson: His Vision and His Art* (1981), and *Shakespeare's Political Drama* (1988) as well as numerous articles on Elizabethan drama.

KENNETH MUIR, a professor emeritus of the University of Liverpool, has edited five of Shakespeare's plays, including the New Arden *King Lear* and *Macbeth* and, alone or in collaboration, numerous other Shakespearean works. He is the author of many books, including *Shakespeare's Tragic Sequence* (1972). His recent publications include the Penguin Masterstudies volumes on *King Lear* and *Antony and Cleopatra*. He has been the editor of *Shakespeare Survey* from 1965 to 1980 and has translated five of Racine's tragedies and seven of Calderon's Comedias in collaboration with Ann L. Mackenzie.

SEBASTIAN NEUMEISTER of Freie Universität, Berlin, has published books on Old Provençal Poetry and Modern French and German

Literature. He is the author of *Mythos und Repräsentation* (1978) and has coedited *Theatrum Mundi Hispanicum* (1986), *Res Publica Litteraria* (1987), *El mundo de Gracián* (1990) and the *Actas del IX Congreso de la AIH* (1989).

THOMAS AUSTIN O'CONNOR OF SUNY at Binghamton is the author of the much discussed article "Is the Spanish Comedia a metatheater?" (1975) and more recently of *Myth and Mythology in the Theater of Pedro Calderon de la Barca* (1988) as well as of numerous articles on the Spanish Comedia.

JOHN ORRELL of the University of Alberta is the author of *Fallen Empires: The Lost Theatres of Edmonton* (1981), *The Quest for Shakespeare's Globe* (1983), *The Theatres of Inigo Jones and John Webb* (1985), *The Human Stage: English Theatre Design, 1567–1640* (1988) and, with Andrew Gurr, *Rebuilding Shakespeare's Globe* (1989). He has contributed many articles to Journals on theater research.

CYNTHIA RODRIGUEZ-BADENDYCK of Baruch College, CUNY, is a comparatist who has translated Lope de Vega's *El mayordomo de la duquesa de Amalfi / The Duchess of Amalfi's Steward* (1985) as well as his *Castelvines y Monteses* (forthcoming). She is the founder of *Arrojes*, Association for the Promotion of Spanish Classical Theater in English Performance.

JOSÉ M. RUANO DE LA HAZA, University of Ottawa, works in the field of critical editions and the reconstruction of performance conditions. His main editions include Calderon's *Cada uno para si* (1982) and *El purgatorio de San Patricio* (1988). He has edited *El mundo del teatro español en su siglo de oro,* (1989) and is the co-editor of Ottawa Hispanic Series. He has contributed frequent articles on staging to a number of journals.

DAWN L. SMITH of Trent University has published a critical edition of Tirso de Molina's *La mujer que manda en casa* (1984) and coedited a volume on *The Perception of Women in the Comedia* (1990) besides articles on staging and reception aesthetics.

HENRY W. SULLIVAN, University of Missouri is author of *Juan del Encina* (1976), *Tirso de Molina and the Drama of the Counter Reformation* (1976, repr. 1981) and *Calderon in the German Lands and the Low Countries, 1654–1980* (1983). Professor Sullivan has also contributed substantial articles on the application of Lacan's philosophy to literature and is the editor of *The Freudian Field*.

JOHN E. VAREY, professor emeritus and former principal of Westfield College, University of London, has spent many years researching the documentation of the history of the Spanish stage. His most recent publications include *Fuentes para la historia del teatro en España* (with N. D. Shergold *et al.* 11 vols., 1971–90) and *The Comedias of Calderon* (a facsimile edition with textual and critical studies with D. W. Cruickshank, 19 vols, 1973). He is the author of numerous articles on staging and editor of Tamesis Books.

Index of Plays Cited